CW00569112

How to access your on-line resources

Kaplan Financial students will have a MyKaplan account and these extra resources will be available to you online. You do not need to register again, as this process was completed when you enrolled. If you are having problems accessing online materials, please ask your course administrator.

If you are not studying with Kaplan and did not purchase your book via a Kaplan website, to unlock your extra online resources please go to www.en-gage.co.uk (even if you have set up an account and registered books previously). You will then need to enter the ISBN number (on the title page and back cover) and the unique pass key number contained in the scratch panel below to gain access.

You will also be required to enter additional information during this process to set up or confirm your account details.

If you purchased through the Kaplan Publishing website you will automatically receive an e-mail invitation to register your details and gain access to your content. If you do not receive the e-mail or book content, please contact Kaplan Publishing.

Your code and information

This code can only be used once for the registration of one book online. This registration and your online content will expire when the final sittings for the examinations covered by this book have taken place. Please allow one hour from the time you submit your book details for us to process your request.

Please scratch the film to access your unique code.

Please be aware that this code is case-sensitive and you will need to include the dashes within the passcode, but not when entering the ISBN.

KAPLAN
PUBLISHING

CIMA

Subject P2

Advanced Management Accounting

Study Text

Published by: Kaplan Publishing UK

Unit 2 The Business Centre, Molly Millars Lane, Wokingham, Berkshire RG41 2QZ

Acknowledgements

We are grateful to the CIMA for permission to reproduce past examination questions. The answers to CIMA Exams have been prepared by Kaplan Publishing, except in the case of the CIMA November 2010 and subsequent CIMA Exam answers where the official CIMA answers have been reproduced.

Notice

The text in this material and any others made available by any Kaplan Group company does not amount to advice on a particular matter and should not be taken as such. No reliance should be placed on the content as the basis for any investment or other decision or in connection with any advice given to third parties. Please consult your appropriate professional adviser as necessary.

Kaplan Publishing Limited and all other Kaplan group companies expressly disclaim all liability to any person in respect of any losses or other claims, whether direct, indirect, incidental, consequential or otherwise arising in relation to the use of such materials.

Kaplan is not responsible for the content of external websites. The inclusion of a link to a third party website in this text should not be taken as an endorsement.

Kaplan Publishing's learning materials are designed to help students succeed in their examinations. In certain circumstances, CIMA can make post-exam adjustment to a student's mark or grade to reflect adverse circumstances which may have disadvantaged a student's ability to take an exam or demonstrate their normal level of attainment (see CIMA's Special Consideration policy). However, it should be noted that students will not be eligible for special consideration by CIMA if preparation for or performance in a CIMA exam is affected by any failure by their tuition provider to prepare them properly for the exam for any reason including, but not limited to, staff shortages, building work or a lack of facilities etc.

Similarly, CIMA will not accept applications for special consideration on any of the following grounds:

- failure by a tuition provider to cover the whole syllabus

- failure by the student to cover the whole syllabus, for instance as a result of joining a course part way through

- failure by the student to prepare adequately for the exam, or to use the correct pre-seen material

- errors in the Kaplan Official Study Text, including sample (practice) questions or any other Kaplan content or

- errors in any other study materials (from any other tuition provider or publisher).

British Library Cataloguing in Publication Data

A catalogue record for this book is available from the British Library.

ISBN: 978-1-78740-712-1

Printed and bound in Great Britain

Contents

Contents

Introduction

How to use the Materials

These official CIMA learning materials have been carefully designed to make your learning experience as easy as possible and to give you the best chances of success in your objective tests.

The product range contains a number of features to help you in the study process. They include:

- a detailed explanation of all syllabus areas

- extensive 'practical' materials

- generous question practice, together with full solutions.

This Study Text has been designed with the needs of home study and distance learning candidates in mind. Such students require very full coverage of the syllabus topics, and also the facility to undertake extensive question practice. However, the Study Text is also ideal for fully taught courses.

The main body of the text is divided into a number of chapters, each of which is organised on the following pattern:

- **Detailed learning outcomes.** These describe the knowledge expected after your studies of the chapter are complete. You should assimilate these before beginning detailed work on the chapter, so that you can appreciate where your studies are leading.

- **Step-by-step topic coverage.** This is the heart of each chapter, containing detailed explanatory text supported where appropriate by worked examples and exercises. You should work carefully through this section, ensuring that you understand the material being explained and can tackle the examples and exercises successfully. Remember that in many cases knowledge is cumulative: if you fail to digest earlier material thoroughly, you may struggle to understand later chapters.

- **Activities.** Some chapters are illustrated by more practical elements, such as comments and questions designed to stimulate discussion.

- **Question practice.** The text contains three styles of question:

    - Exam-style objective test questions (OTQs).

    - 'Integration' questions – these test your ability to understand topics within a wider context. This is particularly important with calculations where OTQs may focus on just one element but an integration question tackles the full calculation, just as you would be expected to do in the workplace.

- 'Case' style questions – these test your ability to analyse and discuss issues in greater depth, particularly focusing on scenarios that are less clear cut than in the objective tests, and thus provide excellent practice for developing the skills needed for success in the Management Level Case Study Examination.

- **Solutions.** Avoid the temptation merely to 'audit' the solutions provided. It is an illusion to think that this provides the same benefits as you would gain from a serious attempt of your own. However, if you are struggling to get started on a question you should read the introductory guidance provided at the beginning of the solution, where provided, and then make your own attempt before referring back to the full solution.

If you work conscientiously through this Official CIMA Study Text according to the guidelines above you will be giving yourself an excellent chance of success in your objective tests. Good luck with your studies!

Quality and accuracy are of the utmost importance to us so if you spot an error in any of our products, please send an email to mykaplanreporting@kaplan.com with full details, or follow the link to the feedback form in MyKaplan.

Our Quality Co-ordinator will work with our technical team to verify the error and take action to ensure it is corrected in future editions.

Icon explanations

Definition – These sections explain important areas of knowledge which must be understood and reproduced in an assessment environment.

Key point – Identifies topics which are key to success and are often examined.

Supplementary reading – These sections will help to provide a deeper understanding of core areas. The supplementary reading is **NOT** optional reading. It is vital to provide you with the breadth of knowledge you will need to address the wide range of topics within your syllabus that could feature in an assessment question. **Reference to this text is vital when self-studying.**

Test your understanding – Following key points and definitions are exercises which give the opportunity to assess the understanding of these core areas.

Illustration – To help develop an understanding of particular topics. The illustrative examples are useful in preparing for the Test your understanding exercises.

 Exclamation mark – This symbol signifies a topic which can be more difficult to understand. When reviewing these areas, care should be taken.

Study technique

Passing exams is partly a matter of intellectual ability, but however accomplished you are in that respect you can improve your chances significantly by the use of appropriate study and revision techniques. In this section we briefly outline some tips for effective study during the earlier stages of your approach to the objective tests. We also mention some techniques that you will find useful at the revision stage.

Planning

To begin with, formal planning is essential to get the best return from the time you spend studying. Estimate how much time in total you are going to need for each subject you are studying. Remember that you need to allow time for revision as well as for initial study of the material.

With your study material before you, decide which chapters you are going to study in each week, and which weeks you will devote to revision and final question practice.

Prepare a written schedule summarising the above and stick to it!

It is essential to know your syllabus. As your studies progress you will become more familiar with how long it takes to cover topics in sufficient depth. Your timetable may need to be adapted to allocate enough time for the whole syllabus.

Students are advised to refer to the examination blueprints (see page P.13 for further information) and the CIMA website, www.cimaglobal.com, to ensure they are up-to-date.

The amount of space allocated to a topic in the Study Text is not a very good guide as to how long it will take you. The syllabus weighting is the better guide as to how long you should spend on a syllabus topic.

Tips for effective studying

(1) Aim to find a quiet and undisturbed location for your study, and plan as far as possible to use the same period of time each day. Getting into a routine helps to avoid wasting time. Make sure that you have all the materials you need before you begin so as to minimise interruptions.

(2) Store all your materials in one place, so that you do not waste time searching for items every time you want to begin studying. If you have to pack everything away after each study period, keep your study materials in a box, or even a suitcase, which will not be disturbed until the next time.

(3) Limit distractions. To make the most effective use of your study periods you should be able to apply total concentration, so turn off all entertainment equipment, set your phones to message mode, and put up your 'do not disturb' sign.

(4) Your timetable will tell you which topic to study. However, before diving in and becoming engrossed in the finer points, make sure you have an overall picture of all the areas that need to be covered by the end of that session. After an hour, allow yourself a short break and move away from your Study Text. With experience, you will learn to assess the pace you need to work at. Each study session should focus on component learning outcomes – the basis for all questions.

(5) Work carefully through a chapter, making notes as you go. When you have covered a suitable amount of material, vary the pattern by attempting a practice question. When you have finished your attempt, make notes of any mistakes you made, or any areas that you failed to cover or covered more briefly. Be aware that all component learning outcomes will be tested in each examination.

(6) Make notes as you study, and discover the techniques that work best for you. Your notes may be in the form of lists, bullet points, diagrams, summaries, 'mind maps', or the written word, but remember that you will need to refer back to them at a later date, so they must be intelligible. If you are on a taught course, make sure you highlight any issues you would like to follow up with your lecturer.

(7) Organise your notes. Make sure that all your notes, calculations etc. can be effectively filed and easily retrieved later.

Progression

There are two elements of progression that we can measure: how quickly students move through individual topics within a subject; and how quickly they move from one course to the next. We know that there is an optimum for both, but it can vary from subject to subject and from student to student. However, using data and our experience of student performance over many years, we can make some generalisations.

A fixed period of study set out at the start of a course with key milestones is important. This can be within a subject, for example 'I will finish this topic by 30 June', or for overall achievement, such as 'I want to be qualified by the end of next year'.

Your qualification is cumulative, as earlier papers provide a foundation for your subsequent studies, so do not allow there to be too big a gap between one subject and another. For example, P2 *Advanced management accounting* builds on your knowledge of risks, costing and decision making from P1 *Management accounting* and lays the foundations for all strategic level papers.

We know that exams encourage techniques that lead to some degree of short term retention, the result being that you will simply forget much of what you have already learned unless it is refreshed (look up Ebbinghaus Forgetting Curve for more details on this). This makes it more difficult as you move from one subject to another: not only will you have to learn the new subject, you will also have to relearn all the underpinning knowledge as well. This is very inefficient and slows down your overall progression which makes it more likely you may not succeed at all.

Also, it is important to realise that the Management Case Study (MCS) tests knowledge of all subjects within the Management level. Please note that candidates will need to return to this material when studying MCS, as it forms a significant part of the MCS syllabus content.

In addition, delaying your studies slows your path to qualification which can have negative impacts on your career, postponing the opportunity to apply for higher level positions and therefore higher pay.

You can use the following diagram showing the whole structure of your qualification to help you keep track of your progress. Make sure you seek appropriate advice if you are unsure about your progression through the qualification.

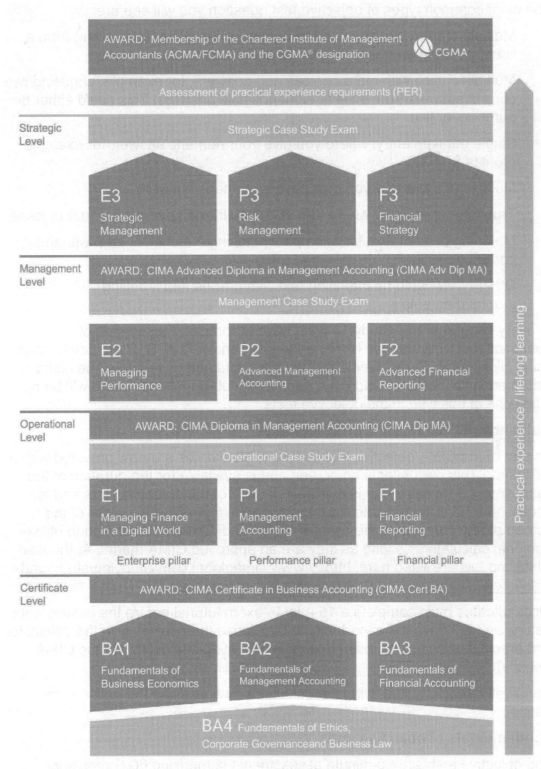

Reproduced with permission from CIMA

Objective test

Objective test questions require you to choose or provide a response to a question whose correct answer is predetermined.

The most common types of objective test question you will see are:

- Multiple choice, where you have to choose the correct answer(s) from a list of possible answers. This could either be numbers or text.

- Multiple choice with more choices and answers, for example, choosing two correct answers from a list of eight possible answers. This could either be numbers or text.

- Single numeric entry, where you give your numeric answer, for example, profit is $10,000.

- Multiple entry, where you give several numeric answers.

- True/false questions, where you state whether a statement is true or false.

- Matching pairs of text, for example, matching a technical term with the correct definition.

- Other types could be matching text with graphs and labelling graphs/diagrams.

In every chapter of this Study Text we have introduced these types of questions, but obviously we have had to label answers A, B, C etc. rather than using click boxes. For convenience, we have retained quite a few questions where an initial scenario leads to a number of sub-questions. There will be no questions of this type in the objective tests.

Guidance re CIMA on-screen calculator

As part of the CIMA objective test software, candidates are now provided with a calculator. This calculator is on-screen and is available for the duration of the assessment. The calculator is available in each of the objective tests and is accessed by clicking the calculator button in the top left hand corner of the screen at any time during the assessment. Candidates are permitted to utilise personal calculators as long as they are an approved CIMA model. Authorised CIMA models are listed here: https://www.cimaglobal.com/Studying/study-and-resources/.

All candidates must complete a 15-minute exam tutorial before the assessment begins and will have the opportunity to familiarise themselves with the calculator and practise using it. The exam tutorial is also available online via the CIMA website.

Candidates may practise using the calculator by accessing the online exam tutorial.

Fundamentals of objective tests

The objective tests are 90-minute assessments comprising 60 compulsory questions, with one or more parts. There will be no choice and all questions should be attempted. All elements of a question must be answered correctly for the question to be marked correctly. All questions are equally weighted.

CIMA syllabus 2019 – Structure of subjects and learning outcomes

Details regarding the content of the new CIMA syllabus can be located within the CIMA 2019 professional syllabus document.

Each subject within the syllabus is divided into a number of broad syllabus topics. The topics contain one or more lead learning outcomes, related component learning outcomes and indicative knowledge content.

A learning outcome has two main purposes:

(a)   To define the skill or ability that a well prepared candidate should be able to exhibit in the examination.

(b)   To demonstrate the approach likely to be taken in examination questions.

The learning outcomes are part of a hierarchy of learning objectives. The verbs used at the beginning of each learning outcome relate to a specific learning objective, e.g.

Calculate the break-even point, profit target, margin of safety and profit/volume ratio for a single product or service.

The verb '**calculate**' indicates a level three learning objective. The following tables list the verbs that appear in the syllabus learning outcomes and examination questions.

The examination blueprints and representative task statements

CIMA have also published examination blueprints giving learners clear expectations regarding what is expected of them.

The blueprint is structured as follows:

- Exam content sections (reflecting the syllabus document)

- Lead and component outcomes (reflecting the syllabus document)

- Representative task statements.

A representative task statement is a plain English description of what a CIMA finance professional should know and be able to do.

The content and skill level determine the language and verbs used in the representative task.

CIMA will test up to the level of the task statement in the objective tests (an objective test question on a particular topic could be set at a lower level than the task statement in the blueprint).

The format of the objective test blueprints follows that of the published syllabus for the 2019 CIMA Professional Qualification.

Weightings for content sections are also included in the individual subject blueprints.

CIMA VERB HIERARCHY

CIMA place great importance on the definition of verbs in structuring objective tests. It is therefore crucial that you understand the verbs in order to appreciate the depth and breadth of a topic and the level of skill required. The objective tests will focus on levels one, two and three of the CIMA hierarchy of verbs. However, they will also test levels four and five, especially at the management and strategic levels.

Skill level	Verbs used	Definition
Level 5 **Evaluation** How you are expected to use your learning to evaluate, make decisions or recommendations	Advise	Counsel, inform or notify
	Assess	Evaluate or estimate the nature, ability or quality of
	Evaluate	Appraise or assess the value of
	Recommend	Propose a course of action
	Review	Assess and evaluate in order, to change if necessary
Level 4 **Analysis** How you are expected to analyse the detail of what you have learned	Align	Arrange in an orderly way
	Analyse	Examine in detail the structure of
	Communicate	Share or exchange information
	Compare and contrast	Show the similarities and/or differences between
	Develop	Grow and expand a concept
	Discuss	Examine in detail by argument
	Examine	Inspect thoroughly
	Interpret	Translate into intelligible or familiar terms
	Monitor	Observe and check the progress of
	Prioritise	Place in order of priority or sequence for action
	Produce	Create or bring into existence
Level 3 **Application** How you are expected to apply your knowledge	Apply	Put to practical use
	Calculate	Ascertain or reckon mathematically
	Conduct	Organise and carry out
	Demonstrate	Prove with certainty or exhibit by practical means
	Prepare	Make or get ready for use
	Reconcile	Make or prove consistent/compatible

Skill level	Verbs used	Definition
Level 2 **Comprehension** What you are expected to understand	Describe	Communicate the key features of
	Distinguish	Highlight the differences between
	Explain	Make clear or intelligible/state the meaning or purpose of
	Identify	Recognise, establish or select after consideration
	Illustrate	Use an example to describe or explain something
Level 1 **Knowledge** What you are expected to know	List	Make a list of
	State	Express, fully or clearly, the details/facts of
	Define	Give the exact meaning of
	Outline	Give a summary of

Information concerning formulae and tables will be provided via the CIMA website, www.cimaglobal.com.

SYLLABUS GRIDS

P2: Advanced Management Accounting

Making medium-term decisions and managing costs and performance

Content weighting

Content area		Weighting
A	Managing the costs of creating value	20%
B	Capital investment decision-making	35%
C	Managing and controlling the performance of organisational units	30%
D	Risk and control	15%
		100%

P2A: Managing the costs of creating value

Cost management and transformation are priorities for organisations facing intense competition. This section examines how to use cost management, quality and process management, and value management to transform the cost structures and drivers to provide organisations with cost advantage.

Lead outcome	Component outcome	Indicative syllabus content	Chapter
1. Apply cost management and cost transformation methodology to manage costs and improve profitability.	Apply the following to manage costs and improve profitability: a. Activity based management (ABM) methodology b. Cost transformation techniques	• Engendering a cost-conscious culture • Logic of ABC as the foundation or managing costs • ABM to transform efficiency of repetitive overhead activities • ABM to analyse and improve customer profitability • ABM to analyse and improve channel performance	1
2. Compare and contrast quality management methodologies.	Compare and contrast: a. Just-in-time (JIT) b. Quality management c. Kaizen d. Process re-engineering	• Impact of JIT and quality management on efficiency, inventory and costs • Benefits of JIT and TQM • Kaizen, continuous improvement and cost of quality reporting • Elimination of non-value adding activities and the reduction of costs using process re-engineering	2
3. Apply value management techniques to manage costs and improve value creation.	Apply the following to manage costs and value creation: a. Target costing b. Value chain analysis c. Life cycle costing	• Determination of target costs from target prices • Components of the value chain • Profitability along the value chain • Life cycle costing and its implication for market strategies	3

P2B: Capital investment decision-making

Organisations have to allocate resources and key strategic initiatives to ensure that their strategies are properly implemented. Capital investment decision-making is the primary means by which such resources are allocated between competing needs. This section covers the criteria, process and techniques that are used to decide which projects to undertake. Of particular interest is the financial appraisal of digital transformation projects.

Lead outcome	Component outcome	Indicative syllabus content	Chapter
1. Apply the data required for decision-making.	Apply the following for decision-making: a. Relevant cash flows b. Non-financial information	• Incremental cash flows • Tax, inflation and other factors • Perpetuities • Qualitative issues • Sources and integrity of data • Role of business intelligence systems	4
2. Explain the steps and pertinent issues in the decision-making process.	Explain: a. Investment decision-making process b. Discounting c. Capital investments as real options	• Origination of proposals, creation of capital budgets, go/no go decisions • Time value of money • Comparing annuities • Profitability index for capital rationing • Decision to make follow-on investment, abandon or wait (capex as real options)	5,6
3. Apply investment appraisal techniques to evaluate different projects.	Apply the following to evaluate projects: a. Payback b. Accounting rate of return c. IRR d. NPV	• Process and calculation • Strengths and weaknesses • Appropriate usage • Use in prioritisation of mutually exclusive projects	5,6
4. Discuss pricing strategies.	Discuss: a. Pricing decisions b. Pricing strategies	• Pricing decisions for maximising profit in imperfect markets • Types of pricing strategies • Financial consequences of pricing strategies	7

P2C: Managing and controlling the performance of organisational units

The structure and strategies of organisations should align with each other to ensure effective strategy implementation. Responsibility centres are the organisational units that are allocated resources and charged with implementing organisational strategy. This section shows how to manage the performance of these organisational units to ensure that they achieve the strategic and other organisational objectives. Key concepts, techniques and issues are explored and examined.

Lead outcome	Component outcome	Topics to be covered	Chapter
1. Analyse the performance of responsibility centres and prepare reports.	a. Analyse performance of cost centres, revenue centres, profit centres, and investment centres. b. Prepare reports for decision-making.	• Objectives of each responsibility centre • Controllable and uncontrollable costs and revenue • Costs variability, attributable costs and revenue and identification of appropriate measures of performance • Use of data analytics in performance management of responsibility centres	8
2. Discuss various approaches to the performance and control of organisations.	a. Discuss budgets and performance evaluation. b. Discuss other approaches to performance evaluation.	• Key performance indicators (e.g., profitability, liquidity, asset turnover, return on investment and economic value) • Benchmarking (internal and external) • Non-financial performance indicators • Balanced scorecard	9
3. Explain the behavioural and transfer pricing issues related to the management of responsibility centres.	Explain: a. Behavioural issues b. Use and ethics of transfer pricing	• Internal competition • Internal trading • Transfer pricing for intermediate goods where markets exist and where no markets exist • Types of transfer prices and when to use them • Effect of transfer pricing on autonomy, and motivation of managers of responsibility centre • Effect of transfer pricing on responsibility centre and group profitability	10

P2D: Risk and control

Risk is inherent in the operations of all organisations. This section analyses risks and uncertainties that organisations face in the medium term. The risks are mainly operational in nature.

Lead outcome	Component outcome	Topics to be covered	Chapter
1. Analyse risk and uncertainty associated with medium-term decision-making.	Conduct a. Sensitivity analysis b. Analysis of risk	• Quantification of risk • Use of probabilistic models to interpret distribution of project outcomes • Stress-testing of projects • Decision trees • Decision-making under uncertainty	11, 12
2. Analyse types of risk in the medium term.	a. Analyse types of risk b. Manage risk	• Upside and downside risks • TARA framework – transfer, avoid, reduce, accept • Business risks • Use of information systems and data in managing risks	11,12

Activity-Based Costing and Activity-Based Management

Chapter learning objectives

Lead	Component
A1: Managing the costs of creating value	Apply cost management and cost transformation methodology to manage costs and improve profitability (a) Activity Based Management (ABM) methodology (b) Cost transformation techniques

1 Chapter summary

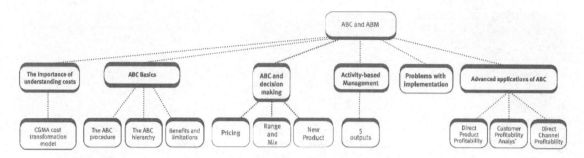

2 Knowledge brought forward

You will already have covered Activity-Based-Costing in previous CIMA papers. It is an important technique. In this chapter, we will explore ABC approaches such as Activity-Based Management, Direct Product Profitability, Direct Customer Profitability and Distribution Channel Profitability.

3 The importance of understanding costs

The understanding of costs is fundamental to your accounting studies.

In financial accounting all costs must be recorded so that profit can be calculated and the true and fair value of assets can be presented in the financial statements.

In management accounting an understanding of costs is required in order to carry out the three main functions of planning, control and decision making. If we understand and calculate costs, we can use this information in a number of ways such as:

- Determining the cost to manufacture a product or provide a service can be used to record costs in the financial statements as well as to inform decisions on our products or services.

- The cost per unit can be used to value inventory in the statement of financial position (balance sheet).

- Product and service costs can be used to determine the selling price we should charge for our products or services. For example, if the cost per unit is $0.30, the business may decide to price the product at $0.50 per unit in order to make the required profit of $0.20 per unit.

- Knowing the profit (or, as we will see in a later chapter, the contribution of a product) can help determine the products and services we should supply and in what quantity.

- The cost can also act as a benchmark for future performance. Differences from the expected (or standard) cost can be calculated (known as variances) and evaluated.

The CGMA Cost transformation model

The CGMA cost transformation model is designed to help businesses to achieve and maintain cost competitiveness:

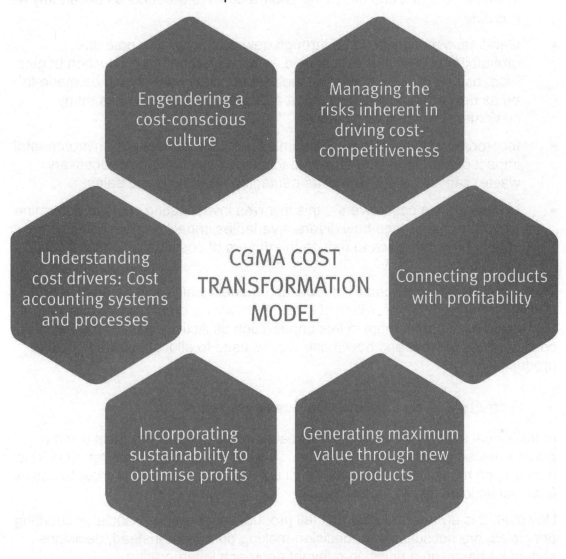

The model has 6 suggested changes for organisations that come together to achieve this objective. These changes are:

- Engendering a cost conscious culture – the organisation should aim to be a cost leader so that its costs are lower than rivals and set a competitive benchmark. Everyone in the organisation should be motivated and enabled to reduce costs in whatever way possible. Technology can play a key role in reducing costs.

- Managing the risks that come from a cost conscious culture – for example, reducing cost may result in reducing quality and customer satisfaction. The organisation should have a clear risk management process in place to identify, assess and manage such risks.

- Connecting products with profitability – it will be important that every product or service makes a positive contribution to overall organisational profits. This will involve understanding what drives costs for each individual product and allocating shared costs to products as accurately as possible.

- Generating maximum value through new products – the potential profitability of new products should be assessed before production begins. Also, as part of product design, the product or service should be made to be as flexible as possible so that it appeals or can adapt to as many customer segments as possible.

- Incorporating sustainability to optimise profits: Consider the environmental impact of products – negative impacts (such as creating unnecessary waste) can add costs as well as damaging reputation and sales.

- Understanding cost drivers – this involves investigating costs to determine why they change and how different variables impact on the cost. Plans should be put in place to reduce the drivers of costs as well as the costs themselves.

The model suggests a number of tools and models which can be used in order to achieve these changes. Many of these tools will be employed across your CIMA studies, some of them in this paper, such as Activity Based Costing which considers cost drivers and how these can be used to allocate shared costs to products.

4 Activity-Based Costing: Basics revisited

In traditional absorption costing, overheads are charged to products using a predetermined overhead recovery rate. This overhead absorption rate (OAR) is based upon the volume of activity. A full unit cost is computed in order to satisfy financial accounting requirements.

However, it is always stressed that full product costs, using financial accounting principles, are not suitable for decision-making purposes. Instead, decisions should be based on a decision-relevant approach incorporating relevant/incremental cash flows.

With this approach, decisions such as introducing new products and special pricing decisions should be based on a study of only those incremental revenues and expenses that will vary with respect to the particular decision.

This approach requires that special studies be undertaken when the need arises. However, studies have shown that the majority of companies base their decision making upon full product cost.

In the late 1980s Cooper and Kaplan developed a more refined approach for assigning overheads to products and computing product cost. This new approach is called activity based costing (ABC). It is claimed that ABC provides product-cost information that is useful for decision-making purposes.

Activity-Based Costing is **'an approach to the costing and monitoring of activities which involves tracing resource consumption and costing final outputs. Resources are assigned to activities, and activities to cost objects based on consumption estimates. The latter utilise cost drivers to attach activity costs to outputs'.**

CIMA Official Terminology

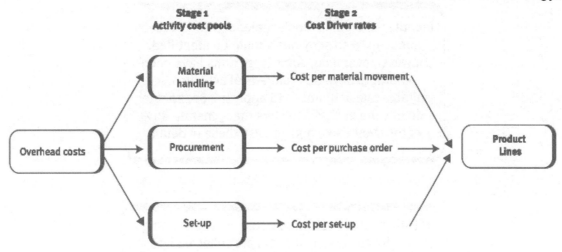

Traditional systems accurately measure volume-related resources that are consumed in proportion to the number of units produced of the individual products. Such resources include direct labour, materials, energy and machine-related costs.

However, many organisational resources exist for activities that are unrelated to physical volume. Non-volume related activities consist of support activities e.g.:

- materials handling
- material procurement
- set-ups
- production scheduling
- first-item inspection activities.

Traditional product-cost systems, which assume that products consume all activities in proportion to their production volumes, thus report distorted product costs.

5   The ABC procedure

Cooper and Kaplan stated that it was the support activities that were the cause of many overheads: material handling, quality inspection, setting up machinery, material acquisition, etc. Thus a simple three-step philosophy was developed:

- support activities cause cost
- the products consume these activities
- cost should, therefore, be charged on the basis of consumption of the activities.

ABC – Method

Identify the organisation's major activities. Ideally about 30 to 50 activities should be identified. However, over time, some large firms have been known to develop hundreds of activities. A suitable rule of thumb is to apply the 80/20 rule: identify the 20% of activities that generate 80% of the overheads, and analyse these in detail.

Estimate the costs associated with performing each activity – these costs are collected into **cost pools.**

Identify the factors that influence the cost pools. These are known as the **cost drivers**. For example, the number of set-ups will influence the cost of setting up machinery.

Calculate a cost driver rate, for example a rate per set-up, or a rate per material requisition, or a rate per inspection.

$$\text{Cost driver rate} = \frac{\text{Cost pool}}{\text{Level of cost drivers}}$$

Charge the overheads to the products by applying the cost driver rates to the activity usage of the products.

Example 1: Manufacturing Business

A manufacturing business makes a product in two models, model M1 and model M2. Details of the two products are as follows.

	Model M1	Model M2
Annual sales	8,000 units	8,000 units
Number of sales orders	60	250
Sales price per unit	$54	$73
Direct material cost per unit	$11	$21
Direct labour hours per unit	2.0 hours	2.5 hours
Direct labour rate per hour	$8	$8
Special parts per unit	2	8
Production batch size	2,000 units	100 units
Setups per batch	1	3

	$	Cost driver
Setup costs	97,600	Number of setups
Material handling costs	42,000	Number of batches
Special part handling costs	50,000	Number of special parts
Invoicing	31,000	Number of sales orders
Other overheads	108,000	Direct labour hours
Total overheads	328,600	

A customer has indicated an interest in placing an order for either model M1 or M2, and the sales manager wished to try to sell the higher-priced model M2.

Required:

(a) Calculate the profit per unit for each model, using ABC.

(b) Using the information above identify which product the sales manager should try to sell on the basis of the information provided by your ABC analysis.

Favourable conditions for ABC

The purpose of moving from a traditional costing system to an activity-based system should be based on the premise that the new information provided will lead to action that will increase the overall profitability of the business.

This is most likely to occur when the analysis provided under the ABC system differs significantly from that which was provided under the traditional system, which is most likely to occur under the following conditions:

- when production overheads are high relative to direct costs, particularly direct labour

- where there is great diversity in the product range

- where there is considerable diversity of overhead resource input to products

- when consumption of overhead resources is not driven primarily by volume.

6 The activity-based cost hierarchy: tiered contribution levels

Cooper and Kaplan (1991) propose a cost hierarchy framework based on four 'tiers'. Cooper and Kaplan assert that with activity-based costing, businesses will account for costs by classifying the source of the cost into one of four general groups: unit-based, batch-based, product-based and facility-based costs.

In other words, they maintain that costs are driven by, and are variable with respect to, activities that occur at four levels:

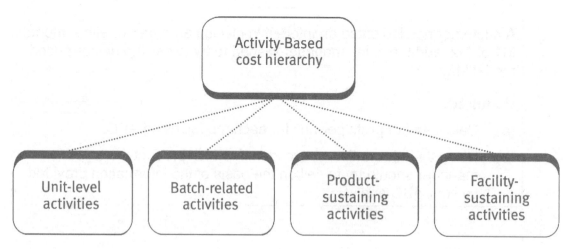

Unit-level activities are performed each time a unit of product is produced. Unit-level activities are consumed in direct proportion to the number of units produced. Expenses in this category include:

- direct labour
- direct materials
- energy costs
- machine maintenance.

Batch-related activities are performed each time a batch is produced. The cost of batch-related activities varies with the number of batches made, but is common (or fixed) for all the units within the batch.

For example, set-up resources are consumed when a machine is changed from one product to another. As more batches are produced, more set-up resources are consumed. It costs the same to set-up a machine for a run of 10 or 5,000 units.

Similarly, purchasing resources are consumed each time a purchasing order is processed, but the resources consumed are independent of the number of units included in the purchase order.

Product-sustaining activities are performed to support different products in the product line. They are performed to enable different products to be produced and sold, but the resources consumed are independent of how many units or batches are being produced.

Cooper and Kaplan (1991) identify engineering resources devoted to maintaining accurate bills of materials and routing each product as an example of product-sustaining activities. Product design costs and advertising costs of the specific product would also be counted as product-sustaining costs. The expenses of product-sustaining activities will tend to increase as the number of products manufactured increases.

Facility-sustaining activities. Some costs cannot be related to a particular product line, instead they are related to maintaining buildings and the facilities. Examples include:

- maintenance of the building
- plant security
- business rates.

Example 2: the activity-based cost hierarchy

A food-processing company operates an activity based costing (ABC) system. Determine whether the following would be classified as a facility- or product-sustaining activity (place a tick in the box corresponding to any that would apply)?

	Facility-sustaining	**Product-sustaining**
General staff administration		
Plant management		
Technical support for individual products and services		
Updating of product specification database		
Property management		

7 ABC: Benefits and limitations

Benefits

1. Provides more accurate product-line costings particularly where non-volume-related overheads are significant and a diverse product line is manufactured.

2. Is flexible enough to analyse costs by cost objects other than products such as processes, areas of managerial responsibility and customers.

3. Provides a reliable indication of long-run variable product cost which is particularly relevant to managerial decision making at a strategic level.

4. Provides meaningful financial (periodic cost driver rates) and nonfinancial (periodic cost driver volumes) measures which are relevant for cost management and performance assessment at an operational level.

5. Aids identification and understanding of cost behaviour and thus has the potential to improve cost estimation.

6. Provides a more logical, acceptable and comprehensible basis for costing work.

Limitations

1   Little evidence to date that ABC improves corporate profitability.

2   ABC information is historical and internally orientated and therefore lacks direct relevance for future strategic decisions.

3   Practical problems such as cost driver selection.

4   Its novelty is questionable. It may be viewed as simply a rigorous application of conventional costing procedures.

8   ABC and decision making

Activity-Based Costing has a role in longer-term decision-making.

ABC systems are primarily designed to furnish management with cost information relating to an organisation's products.

However, the production of this information is not an end in itself. Indeed it is the use to which such activity-based information is put that represents its real purpose, and its value should be assessed against this end-result.

An ABC system produces historical information relating to its products or service provision, which is of much assistance to management in analysing and explaining an organisation's profitability. However, many commentators including Robert Kaplan and Robin Cooper have viewed ABC as supporting major areas of strategic decision making with organisations, these being:

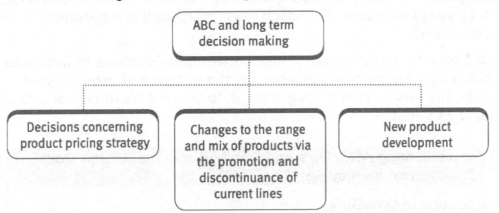

When ABC information is used in the above ways, then it will underpin policy decisions of senior management, and will therefore have a significant influence upon the longer term prosperity of an organisation.

Advocates of the use of ABC for strategic decision making maintain that its values lies in **greater accuracy attaching to product costing**, which in turn **increases the degree of reliability of cost information** used for the above purposes.

They further maintain that the use of ABC may give an indication for the **long-term variable cost of products**, which arguably is the most relevant cost information for use in decisions of the above type. Given the inherent uncertainty involved in strategic decision making, management may use ABC information in decision-modelling and sensitivity analysis to assist in the making of such decisions.

The end product of an ABC system is an estimate of the historical cost of each of an organisation's products. However, strategic decision making involves future time periods and thus it is future outlay costs that need to be taken into consideration, as opposed to historical costs.

Therefore, it is arguable that the results obtained from an ABC system should be aimed at assisting in the making of longer-term decisions. This is especially the case if ABC based product costs are viewed as estimates of longer term product costs as 'nothing is forever' and historical costs are susceptible to substantial change, since all factors of production become variable in the longer term.

Any cost information which has been produced based on past activities must be used with caution with regard to longer term decisions. Even so, ABC information may provide a sound starting point for the preparation of cost information to be used in strategic decision making. It has been argued that a significant advantage of ABC over conventional costing systems lies in its suitability for strategic decision making. Kaplan has argued that for decisions of a strategic nature, a long-term perspective is usual and maintains that an ABC system gives product cost information which matches this requirement particularly well.

This is evidenced by his assertion that **'conventional notions of fixed and variable costs are ignored because, for the purpose of product cost analysis, the time period is long enough to warrant treatment of virtually all costs as variable.'**

Implementing ABC: Do's and Don'ts (From the 'CGMA Cost Transformation model')

Actions to take/Do's

- Get buy-in from the rest of the business. ABC provides business managers, as well as the finance function, with the information needed to make value-based decisions.

- Use ABC for pricing and product prioritisation decisions.

- ABC should be implemented by management accountants as they are best placed to manage the process and to ensure benefits of its realisation.

Actions to avoid/Don'ts

- Do not get caught up in too much attention to detail and control. It can obscure the bigger picture or make the firm lose sight of strategic objectives in a quest for small savings.

- It is important not to fall into the trap of thinking ABC costs are relevant for all decisions. Not all costs will disappear if a product is discontinued, an example being building occupancy costs.

---

9 Activity-Based Management

One of the reasons for calculating costs is to enable organisations to manage and possibly transform their costs. Activity-Based Management (ABM) is a key technique that is used to achieve this objective, because of its link to ABC.

ABM is a **'System of management which uses activity-based cost information for a variety of purposes including cost reduction, cost modelling and customer profitability analysis.'**

CIMA Official Terminology

ABM is simply using the information derived from an ABC analysis for cost management. ABM seeks to classify each activity within a process as a value-added or non-value-added activity:

Non-value-added activities are unnecessary and represent waste. The aim should be to eliminate them. For example, time spent dealing with customer complaints is wasted time, but cannot be reduced until the customers have nothing to complain about!

ABM focuses on activities within a process, decision making and planning relative to those activities and the need for continuous improvement of all organisational activity. Management and staff must determine which activities are critical to success and decide how these are to be clearly defined across all functions.

Everyone must co-operate in defining:

- cost pools
- cost drivers
- key performance indicators.

They must be trained and empowered to act; all must be fairly treated and success recognised.

10 Outputs from the ABM Information System

Organisations that are designing and implementing ABM will find there are five basic information outputs:

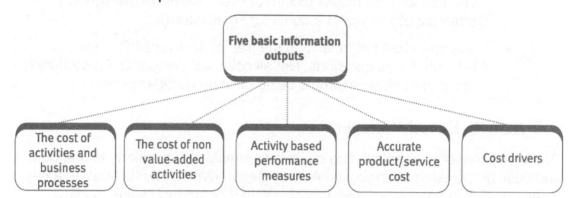

1   **The cost of activities and business processes**. Since activities form the very core of what a business does, the basic output of the ABM system must be to provide relevant cost information about what a business does. Instead of reporting what money is spent for and by whom, costs are assigned to activities.

2   **The cost of non value-added activities**. Identification of these wasteful activities is invaluable to management as it provides a crucial focal point for management.

3   **Activity based performance measures.** Knowing the total cost of an activity is insufficient to measure activity performance. Activity measures of quality, cycle time, productivity and customer service may also be required to judge performance. Measuring the performance of activities provides a scorecard to report how well improvement efforts are working and is an integral part of continuous improvement.

4   **Accurate product/service cost.** Products and services are provided to markets and customers through various distribution channels or contractual relationships. Because products and services consume resources at different rates and require different levels of support, costs must be accurately determined.

5   **Cost drivers.** The final output from the ABM system is cost driver information. With this information it is possible to understand and manage these activity levels.

- whether to continue with a particular activity

- how cost structures measure up to those of competitors

- how changes in activities and components affect the suppliers and value chain.

Clearly ABM and employee empowerment takes a critical step forward beyond ABC by recognising the contribution that people make as the key resource in any organisation's success.

- It nurtures good communication and team work.

- It develops quality decision making.

- It leads to quality control and continuous improvement.

ABM will not reduce costs, it will only help the manager understand costs better.

Strategic activity management recognises that individual activities are part of a wider process. Activities are grouped to form a total process or service.

For example, serving a particular customer involves a number of discrete activities that form the total service. Strategic activity management attempts to classify each activity within the whole as a value-added or non-value added activity. Non-value-added activities are unnecessary and should be eliminated.

Bellis-Jones (1992) noted that typically prior to the introduction of ABM, 35% of staff time was spent on diversionary (non-value-added) activities. After the introduction of ABM, total staff time declined and the percentage of time spent on diversionary activities fell to 20% of the reduced time.

Non-value-added activities are often caused by inadequacies within the existing processes and cannot be eliminated unless the inadequacy is addressed.

For example, dealing with customer complaints is a diversionary activity, but it cannot be eliminated unless the source of the complaints is eliminated. Another example is machine set-up time. Better product design so that fewer components or more standard components are used will reduce the set-up time between component runs. So management must concentrate on eliminating non-value-added activities.

But strategic activity management is more than just eliminating non-value added activities, important though this is.

By identifying the cost and value drivers for each activity, the firm can develop both the activities and the linkages between them, and so better differentiate the firm from its competitors. In addition, by understanding the factors which influence the costs of each activity, the firm can take action to minimize those costs in the medium term.

ABC information can be used in an ABM system to assist strategic decisions, such as:

1   Whether to continue with a particular activity.

2   The effect on cost structure of a change in strategy, e.g. from mass production to smaller production runs.

3   How changes in activities and components affect the suppliers and the value chain.

The value chain is simply a large activity map for the organisation and its position in the industry chain. It is covered in a later chapter of this Text.

11 Problems with implementing ABC/ABM

Research has focused on the problems of implementing the ABC system. Friedman and Lyne (1999) provide some clues as to why ABC has not been taken up with more enthusiasm from case study research they carried out. Some reasons they draw attention to are:

1   Where it was devised for a single project that was not taken up the system got dropped as well. As communication between business units in a large organisation is often not very good, the work was not developed further by other units.

2   Finance department opposed its implementation. Often finance staff appear less than dynamic and unable to perceive the needs of the production staff.

3   General ledger information too poor to provide reliable ABC information. The resulting figures would have been no better than traditional absorption methods.

Of course, if organisations do not have reliable ABC information then they also forgo the cost management advantages of an ABM system. Since ABC provides the basic building blocks of activities, without ABC there can be no ABM.

Illustration – ABC and ABM

Tool of the trade (extract)

Financial Management; London; Nov 2001; Stephanie Gourdie;

A company in New Zealand is one of the few to have implemented activity-based management successfully but it needed careful planning and a radical rethink of company culture.

Since professors Robert Cooper and Robert Kaplan codified and developed activity-based costing, many organisations have implemented it, but few are using it for cost management. The original emphasis of ABC was on developing more accurate product costs. It was based on the principle that resource-consuming activities caused costs, not volume of products, as assumed by traditional cost-allocation methods. Overhead costs were allocated and traced back to activities that consumed resources, such as purchasing, set-ups and material handling.

A cost driver was then selected for each activity centre. The choice of driver was based on two things: it had to measure the resources a product used for a particular set of activities; and it had to be linked to the changes of costs in the activity centre (cause-effect relationship).

Cost drivers can include the number of purchase orders, material movements or setup hours. The overhead rate for each activity was worked out by dividing the activity cost by the capacity of the cost driver. The costs of products were determined by multiplying the number of the cost driver of the activity used by the product, by the overhead rate for that activity, for all activities used by that product.

ABC systems could then be applied to cost management. This was labelled activity based management (ABM), defined by Don Hansen and Maryanne Mowen as "a system-wide, integrated approach that focuses management's attention on activities with the objective of improving customer value and the profit achieved by providing this value".

The progression to ABM involved a shift in focus from the original ABC system – producing information on activity-based product costs to producing information to improve management of processes. The idea is to analyse the activities that make up a company's processes and the cost drivers of those activities, then question why the activities are being carried out and how well they are being performed. ABM provides the activity information and the costs of inefficient activities, and quantifies the benefits of continuous improvements.

Companies can then improve operations by re-engineering (complete redesign of processes), redesigning plant layouts, using common parts, outsourcing or strengthening supplier and customer relationships and developing alternative product designs.

[...]

TIPS FOR ABM

- Get the support of senior management

- Recognise that ABM requires a major investment in time and resources

- Know what ABM can achieve and what information you want from the system

- Decide which model to use

- Choose the model approach that emphasises the operational understanding of all activities in the business

- Involve people in the field

- Transfer ownership of cost management from the accounts department to the departments and processes where costs are incurred

- Don't underestimate the need to manage the change process

- Link ABM to corporate objectives in the form of increased product profitability and added value for customers.

12   Direct Product Profitability (DPP)

As traditional absorption costing, which normally uses labour hours as a basis for absorption, is rarely suitable for service and retail organisations other methods had to be devised. One relatively new way of spreading overheads in retail organisations, which is used in the grocery trade in particular, is direct product profitability (DPP).

Direct Product Profitability is **'used primarily within the retail sector...DPP involves the attribution of both the purchase price and other indirect costs (for example distribution, warehousing and retailing) to each product line. Thus a net profit, as opposed to a gross profit, can be identified for each product. The cost attribution process utilises a variety of measures (for example warehousing space and transport time) to reflect the resource consumption of individual products'.**

CIMA Official Terminology

DPP started in the USA in the 1960s at General Electric, and was then taken up and used by Proctor and Gamble in the 1980s. In 1985 the Food Marketing Institute in the USA laid down a standard approach to the system and two years later DPP was taken up by the Institute of Grocery Distribution in the UK. The system described below was introduced in the late 1980s and has since undergone transformation as activity-based costing has developed.

Retail organisations traditionally deducted the bought-in cost of the good from the selling price to give a gross margin. The gross margin is a useless measure for controlling the costs of the organisation itself or making decisions about the profitability of the different products. This is because none of the costs generated by the retail organisation itself are included in its calculation. For example, it does not include the storage costs of the different goods and these costs vary considerably from one good to another. A method was needed which related the indirect costs to the goods according to the way the goods used or created these costs.

The table below shows the DPP for Product A. Directly-attributable costs have been grouped into three categories and are deducted from the gross margin to determine the product's DPP.

Direct product profit for Product A

	$	$
Selling price		1.50
Less: bought-in price		(0.80)
Gross margin		0.70
Less: Direct product costs:		
Warehouse costs	0.16	
Transport costs	0.18	
Store costs	0.22	
		(0.56)
Direct product profit		0.14

Warehouse and store costs will include items such as labour, space and insurance costs, while transport costs will include labour, fuel and vehicle maintenance costs. The usual way to spread these costs across the different goods sold is in relation to volume or area occupied, as most costs increase in direct proportion to the volume of the product or the space it occupies.

However, there are some exceptions to this; for example, insurance costs may be better spread on value or on a risk index. Risk is greater with refrigerated or perishable goods. Refrigeration costs must only be related to those products that need to be stored in the refrigerator. Handling costs can also be treated in a different manner as they tend to vary with the number of pallets handled rather than the volume of the good itself. The labour involved in shelf-stacking may also need to be spread on a different basis.

The benefits of DPP may be summarised as:

- Better cost analysis

- Better pricing decisions

- Better management of store and warehouse space

- The rationalisation of product ranges

- Better merchandising decisions.

 Example 3: DPP

A supermarket wholesaler sells over 40,000 product lines to retailers who visit the store. It has 45,000 m³ of general storage including 100 m³ of cold storage. General overheads are $90,000 and additional cold storage costs are $5,000. Two of the products sold are single frozen desserts (FD) and trays of 48 cans of soft drink (SD). Only frozen desserts are kept in cooled storage.

The wholesaler pays $0.4 for a FD, which is 0.03 m³ and sells for $4. The trays of SD are 0.3 m³ and are bought for $5 and sold for $30.

Calculated to two decimal places, the net profit per FD is:

$ [   ]

and per crate of SD is

$ [   ]

More On DPP

In recent years DPP has developed considerably in parallel with activity-based costing. DPP has become much more sophisticated and is now very similar to activity-based costing. One of the reasons for its development during the 1990s has been the development of EPOS and EFTPOS (electronic point of sale and electronic funds transfer point of sale) systems that have enabled access to the detailed data needed for direct product cost and profitability calculations.

Indirect costs may be analysed into basic cost categories as follows. These are very similar to those discussed later for activity-based costing.

- Overhead cost. This is incurred through an activity that is not directly linked to a particular product.

- Volume-related cost. Products incur this cost in relation to the space they occupy. This is the cost described previously and includes storage and transport costs.

- Product batch cost. This is often a time-based cost. If product items (i.e. a number of identical products which are handled together as a batch) are stacked on shelves, a labour time cost is incurred. If shipping documents have to be prepared for an order or batch, this again is a labour time cost.

- Inventory financing costs. This is the cost of tying up money in inventory and is the cost of the product multiplied by the company's cost of capital per day or per week.

- Each of the categories above will contain a number of individual activities, such as:

  1   Checking incoming goods

  2   Repacking or packing out for storing

  3   Inspecting products

  4   Refilling store shelf.

DPP software systems can be purchased to model costs. They require a number of key variables to analyse different situations. The variables are:

(a) **Buying and selling prices.** The retailer has the option to adjust the selling price. A price increase from a supplier can always be used to increase the gross margin, but the higher the selling price relative to other retailers the slower inventory movement is likely to be.

(b) **Rate of sale.** This is critical and needs to be as fast as possible in order to minimise space costs at the warehouse and the store, and to avoid loss of interest on money tied up in inventory.

(c) **Inventory-holding size.** The aim is to hold as little inventory as possible in keeping with JIT principles without running out of inventory.

(d) **Product size.** This is the cubic area that the product occupies and is important because space costs per item will be incurred according to size.

(e) **Pallet configuration.** The larger the number of cases on the pallet the cheaper handling costs per unit will be.

(f) **Ordering costs.** Obviously fewer orders will be cheaper but fewer orders will mean holding more inventory.

(g) **Distribution routes.** Are the goods transported direct to the store or is a central warehouse used? Transporting goods direct to the store is a high cost activity for the supplier and it is usually better to use a central warehouse, even for goods with a short shelf life.

13 Customer Profitability Analysis

In many organisations, it is just as important to cost customers as it is to cost products. Different customers or groups of customers differ in their profitability. This is a relatively new technique that ABC makes possible because it creates cost pools for activities. Customers use some activities but not all, and different groups of customers have different 'activity profiles'.

Customer Profitability Analysis is **'the analysis of revenue streams and service costs associated with specific customers or customer groups'.**

CIMA Official Terminology

Service organisations such as a bank or a hotel in particular need to cost customers. A bank's activities for a customer will include the following types of activities:

- Withdrawal of cash

- Unauthorised overdraft

- Request for a statement

- Stopping a cheque

- Returning a cheque because of insufficient funds.

Different customers or categories of customers will each use different amounts of these activities and so customer profitability profiles can be built up, and customers can be charged according to the cost to serve them.

Examples of CPA in a hotel

A hotel may have activities that are provided for specific types of customers, such as:

- well-laid-out gardens

- a swimming pool

- a bar.

Older guests may appreciate and use the garden, families the swimming pool and business guests the bar.

If the activities are charged to the relevant guests a correct cost per bed occupied can be calculated for this type of category. This will show the relative profitability and lead to strategies for encouraging the more profitable guests.

14 Customer profitability curve

Even a manufacturing organisation can benefit from costing its customers. Not all customers cost the same to serve even if they require the same products. Some customers may be located a long way from the factory and transport may cost more. Other customers may be disruptive and place rush orders that interrupt production scheduling and require immediate, special transport. Some customers need after sales service and help with technical matters, etc.

When an organisation analyses the profitability of its customers it is not unusual to find that a Pareto curve exists. That is 20 per cent of customers provide 80 per cent of the profit. This may be illustrated by a **customer profitability curve**. For example:

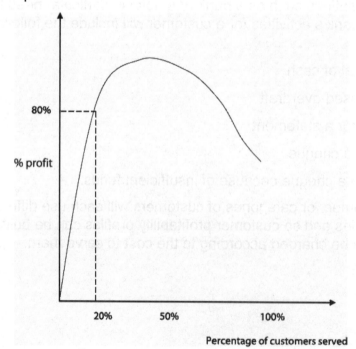

The diagram above shows that the last 80% of customers do not all generate profit. The last 50% actually reduce the total profit. There is no point in serving these customers as the situation stands but it may be foolish just to refuse to serve them. Instead it may be better to turn them into profitable customers if this is possible. A multifunctional team should be set up to find ways of making these customers profitable.

Usually it is the small volume/order customers who are unprofitable because of high production batch costs and order processing, etc. One organisation introduced a third party wholesaler into the supply chain and significantly reduced the cost of serving the small order customers. At the same time the organisation found that the product range and service to the small customers improved, and so the company saved costs and the customer received an improved service.

Illustration – CPA

XY provides accountancy services and has three different categories of client:

- limited companies

- self-employed individuals

- employed individuals requiring taxation advice.

XY currently charges its clients a fee by adding a 20% mark-up to total costs. Currently, the costs are attributed to each client based on the hours spent on preparing accounts and providing advice. XY is considering changing to an activity based costing system. The annual costs and the causes of these costs have been analysed as follows:

Accounts preparation and advice	$580,000
Requesting missing information	$30,000
Issuing fee payment reminders	$15,000
Holding client meetings	$60,000
Travelling to clients	$40,000

The following details relate to three of XY's clients and to XY as a whole:

	Client			XY
	A	B	C	
Hours spent on preparing accounts and providing advice	1,000	250	340	**18,000**
Requests for missing information	4	10	6	**250**
Payment reminders sent	2	8	10	**400**
Client meetings held	4	1	2	**250**
Miles travelled to clients	150	600	0	**10,000**

Required:

Prepare calculations to show the effect on fees charged to each of these three clients of changing to the new costing system.

Solution

Cost driver rates:

Accounts preparation and advice	$580,000/18,000 hours = $32.222 per hour
Requesting missing information	$30,000/250 times = $120 per request
Issuing fee payment reminders	$15,000/400 times = $37.50 per reminder
Holding client meetings	$60,000/250 meetings = $240 per meeting
Travelling to clients	$40,000/10,000 miles = $4 per mile

Client costs:

	Client		
	A	B	C
Accounts preparation and advice	$32,222	$8,055	$10,955
Requesting missing information	$480	$1,200	$720
Issuing fee payment reminders	$75	$300	$375
Holding client meetings	$960	$240	$480
Travelling to clients	$600	$2,400	$0
Total costs	$34,337	$12,195	$12,530
Total costs on original basis (*)	$40,280	$10,070	$13,695
Client fees – new basis (W1)	$41,204	$14,634	$15,036
Client fees – original basis	$48,336	$12,084	$16,434
Increase/(Decrease)	$(7,132)	$2,550	$(1,398)

(*) $725,000/18,000 hours = $40.28 per hour

(W1) **Client fees calculations, new basis**

Client A: Total costs $34,337 × (1 + 20% mark-up on costs) = $41,204

Client B: Total costs $12,195 × (1 + 20% mark-up on costs) = $14,634

Client C: Total costs $12,530 × (1 + 20% mark-up on costs) = $15,036

15 Distribution channel profitability

Distribution channels are in simple terms the means of transacting with customers. The channel is the point of purchase. It is not necessarily the point of communication, payment, delivery and after sales support. Companies may transact with their customers through direct channels e.g. sales teams, telephone, shops, Internet, or through indirect channels e.g. retailers, wholesalers, resellers, agents.

Regardless of whether a company's channels are direct or indirect, they should always consider the ultimate needs of the customer and therefore use the channels to ensure that those needs are satisfied. Customers will look for ease of access to the supplier, reciprocal communication, products and services which satisfy their needs, prompt delivery, after sales support to name but a few.

The channel a company selects is therefore a critical driver to business profitability. A company should not only aim to satisfy the needs of the customer but must also ensure that the products and services that they are providing are profitable. The method of channel distribution chosen can account for a significant proportion of total cost and choosing the wrong channel can result in significant losses for that particular product or service.

Example 4: Distribution channel profitability

Crale & Co manufactures replacement batteries for smartphones. The battery retails for $40 and costs $10 to make. Crale & Co currently sells 1 million batteries every year through its e-commerce website, and 1 million batteries a year via its network of retail distributors across the country.

Overheads incurred to recruit and retain website administrators amount to $800,000 yearly, and other employee costs amount to $310,000 for the e-commerce channel.

Via its retail distribution network, the company must also offer a $1.50 discount per unit to distributors; also, the administrative cost of processing retail orders amounts to $620,000.

Required:

(a) **Which of the two channels is more profitable for Crale & Co?**

Further analysis of Crale & Co's financial data reveals that:

- 2% of the batteries sold via the website go unpaid every year, due to payment fraud.

- Packaging and distribution costs linked to the website operation have been calculated at $0.80 per battery.

- Furthermore, 50% of the batteries ordered on the website qualify for free shipping due to web promotional vouchers. Batteries which qualify for this free shipping incur an additional cost of $1.20 per battery to process the vouchers and ship to customers (not including the $0.80 packaging and distribution costs mentioned above).

- The cost of shipping inventory in bulk to distributors is $1 per unit.

(b) **In light of this further analysis, which of the two channels is now more profitable?**

Key aspects that the company needs to consider in relation to their distribution channels include; access to the customer base, brand awareness, competitiveness, achieving sales and market targets, speed of payment, customer retention rates and most importantly of all profitability.

Distribution Channel Profitability and digital techniques

The world of retailing has changed dramatically in the past decade. The advent of the online channel and new additional digital channels such as mobile channels and social media have changed retail business models, the execution of the retail mix, and shopper behaviour.

Unilever

Customer and channel information in Unilever is gathered in standardised 'People Data Centres' (PDCs) to look at all their "people data". People data come from traditional 'Customer Relationship Management' (CRM) systems, 'social media harvesting' (a way to collect data from social media platforms unobtrusively and automatically), contact with customer service, any information from marketing initiatives or consumer research.

Unilever wanted to create one IT structure and one focal point for the business, so everyone knows where the data sits and how to make use of it. The 'People Data Centres' (PDCs) are actual physical spaces. The social listening aspect is heavily fuelled by Twitter data.

Employees (including cost accountants) can create their own specific queries and requirements to identify precise insights and ultimately control costs better.

Ben & Jerry's Ice Cream

It has been observed that about 80% of all Ben and Jerry's gets sold on a Saturday. Week after week, a constant sales spike is noted on Saturdays. However, it had also been observed that most of the conversations on social media happen on Thursdays and Fridays, not on Saturday. Now, for the ice cream category, this is rather intriguing, because ice-cream is typically a 'point of purchase' sale (the decision to purchase is made in the store, not before). That is the preconceived notion on which brands and advertising usually works. But Ben and Jerry's appears to be a little different. People actually think about their Ben and Jerry's purchase a couple of days ahead on a Thursday, which means consumers are open to digital influence on that day. Therefore, why run ads on a Monday or Tuesday, when probably 99% of impressions are wasted? But on Thursdays and Fridays, the value of impressions may go up 5% or 10%. That is a dramatic difference on the same level of advertising spend.

Source: 'Digital leadership', Cap Gemini Consulting

Costing channels

In companies, it is just as important to cost channels as it is to cost products and customers. Different channels will differ in profitability.

Activity based costing information makes this possible, because it creates cost pools for activities. Channels will use some activities but not all, and different channels will have different 'activity profiles'.

This makes channel profitability analysis possible, and allows companies to build up distribution channel 'profitability profiles'. So, it becomes possible to identify costly distribution channels for low margin products or services supplied through direct channels, which should be supplied through indirect channels instead. This is a typical example of cost transformation: switching channels would result in reduced channel distribution costs, and a better profitability profile for the product or service.

16   Practice Questions

Objective Test Question 1: ABC vs. traditional costing

Company A manufactures three smartphones. Company A currently operates a traditional absorption costing system, but has decided to use an activity based costing (ABC) system on a trial basis for its procurement operation. A time-based cost driver is used to charge the procurement costs to the smartphones under the ABC system. The following unit manufacturing costs have been determined using both traditional absorption costing and activity based costing:

	Traditional absorption	Activity Based Costing
Smartphone Type 1	$90	$108
Smartphone Type 2	$102	$104
Smartphone Type 3	$95	$85

Place each of the following statements in a grey cell, against the product to which it is most likely to relate:

Smartphone Type 1	
Smartphone Type 2	
Smartphone Type 3	

This smartphone uses a lot of parts and materials that are readily available. It does not require any special order: only one supplier is involved, who has been supplying Company A for years. All the components are readily available in the warehouse. Assembling the phone is very straightforward, and does not incur any specific costs.	This smartphone has relatively few components that are generally purchased in bulk. However, the camera components require a special order to a supplier overseas.	This smartphone uses a lot of parts and materials that are difficult to obtain, and so puts the buying department under pressure.

Objective Test Question 2: Activity Based Management

An engineering company is thinking about implementing activity-based management principles. Which of the following is a correct definition of activity-based management? Select the ONE definition that applies.

(i)   ABM is an approach to the costing and monitoring of activities which involves tracing resources consumption and costing final outputs. Resources are assigned to activities and activities to cost objects based on consumption estimates. The latter utilise cost drivers to attach activities costs to outputs.

(ii)   ABM involves the identification and evaluation of the activity drivers used to trace the cost of activities to cost objects. It may also involve selecting activity drivers with potential to contribute to the cost management function, with particular reference to cost reduction.

(iii)   ABM is a method of budgeting based on an activity framework and utilising cost driver data in the budget setting and variance feedback processes.

(iv)   ABM is a system of management which uses activity-based cost information for a variety of purposes including cost reduction, cost modelling and customer profitability analysis.

(v)   ABM is a grouping of all cost elements associated with an activity.

Objective Test Question 3: Direct Product Profitability

AB plc is a supermarket group which incurs the following costs:

(i)   The bought-in price of the good

(ii)   Inventory financing costs

(iii)   Shelf refilling costs

(iv)   Costs of repacking or 'pack out' prior to storage before sale.

AB plc's calculation of Direct Product Profitability would include:

A   All of the above costs

B   All of the above costs, except (ii)

C   All of the above costs, except (iv)

D   Costs (i) and (ii) only

E   Cost (i) only

Data Set Question: Walken Supermarkets

Walken Supermarkets sells over 30,000 product lines. It wishes to introduce Direct Product Profitability analysis and a team of management accountants have ascertained the following information relating to the following year:

Budgeted weekly overhead	$
Warehouse costs	75,000
Supermarket costs	40,000 per supermarket
Transportation costs	400 per delivery

The warehouse is expected to handle 10,000 cubic metres (m^3) of goods.

Each supermarket will handle 5,000 m^3 of goods each week.

Each transportation vehicle holds 40 m^3 of goods.

Three products sold by Walken are Kitchen Roll (KR), Tinned Spaghetti (TS) and Toothpaste (T):

	KR	TS	T
Retail price per item	$1.00	$0.60	$1.75
Bought-in price per item	$0.60	$0.30	$1.00
Number of items per case	10	25	40
Number of cases per m^3	20	30	20
Time in warehouse	1 week	2 weeks	3 weeks
Time in supermarket	2 weeks	4 weeks	2 weeks

Required:

Calculate the following figures, in $, to four decimal places:

The net profit per kitchen roll $ _____

The net profit per tin of spaghetti $ _____

The net profit per tube of toothpaste $ _____

Case Study Style question: Casamia

PRE-SEEN MATERIAL

Casamia plc purchases a range of good quality gift and household products from around the world; it then sells these products through 'mail order' or retail outlets. The company receives 'mail orders' by post, telephone and Internet. Retail outlets are either department stores or Casamia plc's own small shops. The company started to set up its own shops after a recession in the early 1990s and regards them as the flagship of its business; sales revenue has gradually built up over the last 10 years. There are now 50 department stores and 10 shops.

The company has made good profits over the last few years but recently trading has been difficult. As a consequence, the management team has decided that a fundamental reappraisal of the business is now necessary if the company is to continue trading.

Meanwhile, the budgeting process for the coming year is proceeding. Casamia uses an activity-based costing (ABC) system and estimated cost information for the coming year is available in the attached appendices.

Task: Report

You receive the following email from the Financial Controller:

> **From:** Clara Fuchs (Financial Controller)
> **Sent:** 03 June, 10.23 a.m.
> **To:** Senior Management Accountant
> **Subject:** Activity-Based Costing
>
> Thank you for your calculations on the expected profitability of the different types of sales outlets, for the coming year. I intend to submit these to the board. I would welcome some comments on the results of the figures you have prepared, particularly in the context of the re-appraisal of the business.
>
> Please also advise on how the information you have submitted may be revised or expanded to be of more assistance, and suggest what other information is needed to make a more informed judgement.

Appendix A: Calculation of net margin per type of outlet

	Department store	Own shop	Post	Mail order Telephone	Internet
Sales revenue	50,000	1,000,000	150.00	300.00	100.00
Gross margin[1] (50,000 + 1.30, etc.)	11,538	285,714	42.86	85.71	28.57
Less: Staffing etc.		300,000			
Telephone queries ($15 × 40, etc.)	600	5,250			
Sales visits ($250 × 2, etc.)	500	1,000			
Orders ($20 × 25, etc.)	500	3,000			
Packaging ($100 × 28, etc.)	2,800	15,000			
Delivery ($150 × 28, etc.)	4,200	22,500			
Order cost			5.00	6.00	3.00
Queries			4.00	4.00	1.00
Packing & delivery ($10 × 2, etc.)			20.00	20.00	10.00
Internet cost[2]					10.00
	8,600	346,750	29.00	30.00	24.00
Net margin	2,938	(61,036)	13.86	55.71	4.57
Net margin/sales	5.9%		9.2%	18.6%	4.6%
	4th	5th	2nd	1st	3rd

Appendix B: Calculation of total margin for each type of outlet

	Department stores $000	Own shops $000	Post $000	Mail order Telephone $000	Internet $000	Total $000
Total revenue	2,500	10,000	3,600	14,400	800	31,300
Total net margin	146.90	(610.36)	332.64	2,674.08	36.56	2,579.82

Appendix C: Gross margin calculation for 30% of purchase cost

$$100 = 0.3X + X$$
$$X = 76.92\%$$
$$0.3X = 23.076\%$$
$$\$50,000 \times 23.076\% = \$11.538$$

Appendix D: Mail order

Total number of mail orders = 80,000. So number of Internet orders = 80,000 × 10% = 8,000

Internet link cost per order = $80,000/8,000 orders = $10

Appendix E: Calculation of total revenues and net margins ($000)

		Total revenue		Total net margin
Department Stores 50 outlets	(× $50,000)	$2,500	(× 2,938)	146.9
Own shops 10 outlets	(× $1,000,000)	10,000	(× $61,036)	(610.36)
Mail order – post				
80,000 × 30% = 24,000 orders	(× $150)	3,600	(× $13.86)	332.64
Mail order – telephone				
80,000 × 60% = 48,000 orders	(× $300)	14,400	(× $55.71)	2,674.08
Mail order – Internet				
80,000 × 10% = 8,000 orders	(× $100)	800	(× $4.57)	$36.56

Answers to examples and objective test questions

Example 1: Manufacturing Business

Solution

(a)

Workings		M1	M2	Total
Number of batches		4	80	84
Number of setups		4	240	244
Special parts		16,000	64,000	80,000
Direct labour hours		16,000	20,000	36,000

Activity	Cost		M1	M2
	$		$	$
Setups	97,600	Cost per setup $400	1,600	96,000
Materials handling	42,000	Cost per batch $500	2,000	40,000
Special parts handling	50,000	Cost per part $0.625	10,000	40,000
Invoicing	31,000	Cost per order $100	6,000	25,000
Other overheads	108,000	Cost per hour $3	48,000	60,000
	328,600		67,600	261,000

	M1		M2	
	$	$	$	$
Sales		432,000		584,000
Direct materials	88,000		168,000	
Direct labour	128,000		160,000	
Overheads	67,600		261,000	
Total costs		283,600		589,000
Profit/(loss)		148,400		(5,000)
Profit/loss per unit		18.55		(0.625)

(b) The figures suggest that model M2 is less profitable than M1. The sales manager should try to persuade the customer to buy model M1. Note that the apparent loss on M2 does not necessarily mean that production should be ceased. To assess this management should consider the incremental relevant cash flows involved – e.g. is the product making positive contribution, how many overheads are avoidable? They could also consider ways to reduce the cost drivers for the product to reduce its share of the overheads and convert the product loss into a profit.

Example 2: the activity-based cost hierarchy

A food-processing company operates an activity based costing (ABC) system. Determine whether the following would be classified as a facility- or product-sustaining activity (place a tick in the box corresponding to any that would apply)?

	Facility-sustaining	Product-sustaining
General staff administration	✓	
Plant management	✓	
Technical support for individual products and services		✓
Updating of product specification database		✓
Property management	✓	

Example 3: DPP

The cold storage was included in the space of general storage, and therefore the frozen desserts should be allocated a share of the general costs as well as the cold storage costs.

General storage = $90,000/45,000 = $2 m^3

Cold storage = $5,000/100 = $50 m^3

Net profit of FD = $4 − $0.4 − 0.03 m^3 × ($50 + $2) = $2.04

Net profit of SD = $30 − $5 − (0.3 m^3 × $2) = $24.40

Example 4: Distribution channel profitability

(a) The website is without question the more profitable channel, offering an extra $1.01 in margin per battery.

	Website (e-commerce)	Retail distribution
Retail price	$40	$40
Direct costs	($10)	($10)
Contribution per unit	$30	$30
Unit sales	1,000,000	1,000,000
Total contribution	$30,000,000	$30,000,000
Website administration overheads	($800,000)	
Other employee overheads	($310,000)	
Cost of discounts to distributors $1.50 per battery		($1,500,000)
Admin cost of processing retail orders		($620,000)
Net profit	$28,890,000	$27,880,000
Net profit per unit	$28.89	$27.88

(b) When all channel-related costs are taken into account, the retail distribution channel becomes more profitable than the e-commerce channel. The management decisions that will be made as a result of this more thorough analysis will be far different.

	Website (e-commerce)	Retail distribution
Total net profit as in (a)	$28,890,000	$27,880,000
Bad debts (Payment fraud) (W1)	($800,000)	
Cost of free shipping (W2)	($600,000)	
Packaging and distribution costs	($800,000)	
Cost of shipping inventory in bulk (W3)		($1,000,000)
Net profit	$26,690,000	$26,880,000
Net profit per unit	$26.69	$26.88

Workings:

(W1) Payment fraud applies to 2% × 1,000,000 = 20,000 batteries

20,000 × $40 revenue per battery = total non-payment $800,000

(W2) Free shipping applies to 50% × 1,000,000 = 500,000 batteries

500,000 × $1.20 cost per battery = $600,000

(W3) Cost of shipping inventory in bulk applies to all batteries for retail

1,000,000 batteries × $1 per battery = $1,000,000 shipping cost.

Objective Test Question 1: ABC vs. traditional costing

Smartphone Type 1	This smartphone uses a lot of parts and materials that are difficult to obtain, and so puts the buying department under pressure.
Smartphone Type 2	This smartphone has relatively few components that are generally purchased in bulk. However, the camera components require a special order to a supplier overseas.
Smartphone Type 3	This smartphone uses a lot of parts and materials that are readily available. It does not require any special order: only one supplier is involved, who has been supplying Company A for years. All the components are readily available in the warehouse. Assembling the phone is very straightforward, and does not incur any specific costs.

Smartphone 1 has a higher cost under ABC, which suggests a more complex item using specific parts and materials.

Smartphone 2 has a marginally higher cost under ABC, which suggests the use of mostly readily available components.

Smartphone 3 has a lower cost under ABC, which suggests a standard product using few, if any, specific or complex components.

Objective Test Question 2: Activity Based Management

The answer is (iv): ABM uses the information provided by an ABC analysis to improve organisational profitability.

Option (i) defines ABC.

Option (ii) defines activity driver analysis.

Option (iii) defines activity based budgeting.

Option (v) defines an activity cost pool.

Objective Test Question 3: Direct Product Profitability

The answer is A: All of the costs described can be identified with specific goods and would be deducted from the selling price to determine the direct product profit.

Data Set Question: Walken Supermarkets

Warehouse cost $75,000 ÷ 10,000 = $7.50 per m³

Supermarket cost $40,000 ÷ 5,000 = $8.00 per m³

Transportation cost $400 ÷ 40 = $10 per m³

	KR $	TS $	T $
Retail price	1.00	0.60	1.75
Less bought-in price	(0.60)	(0.30)	(1.00)
Gross margin	0.40	0.30	0.75
Less overheads:			
Warehouse costs (see workings)	0.0375	0.02	0.0281
Supermarket costs (see workings)	0.08	0.0427	0.02
Transportation costs (see workings)	0.05	0.0133	0.0125
Net profit	**0.2325**	**0.2240**	**0.6894**

Workings:

Number of items per m³ $10 \times 20 = 200$ $25 \times 30 = 750$ $40 \times 20 = 800$

Warehouse charge:

Kitchen roll ($7.50 ÷ 200) × 1 week = 0.0375

Tinned spaghetti ($7.50 ÷ 750) × 2 weeks = 0.02

Toothpaste ($7.50 ÷ 800) × 3 weeks = 0.028125

Supermarket cost:

Kitchen roll ($8.00 ÷ 200) × 2 weeks = 0.08

Tinned spaghetti ($8.00 ÷ 750) × 4 weeks = 0.0427

Toothpaste ($8.00 ÷ 800) × 2 weeks = 0.02

Transportation costs:

Kitchen roll $10 per m³ (÷ 20 cases per m³) (÷ 10 items per case) = 0.05 per item

Tinned spaghetti $10 per m³ (÷ 30 cases per m³) (÷ 25 items per case) = 0.0133 per item

Toothpaste $10 per m³ (÷ 20 cases per m³)(÷ 40 items per case) =0.0125 per item

Case Study Style Question: Casamia

REPORT

To: Financial Controller

From: Management Accountant

Date: 03 June

Subject: Profitability of different types of sales outlets

The aim of this report is to determine the expected profitability of the different types of sales outlets for the coming year.

In summary, the calculations in the attached appendices show the following:

- Casamia's own shops will make a considerable 'loss'.

- The department store sales will not generate as good a profit as the 'mail order' side.

- The telephone mail order, that is 46% of the business, will generate 104% of the current total profit.

- The Internet business is not particularly profitable in the coming year, but it will presumably grow quite quickly. If this happens, the charge for maintaining the Internet, which is expressed by each order, will presumably decline as it is likely to be a semi-fixed cost.

1   **Usefulness of information**

The calculations show the profitability of the different types of outlet for the coming year only, which is of some use. For example, it shows that Casamia's own shops make a considerable loss and it would appear, on the surface, that the company would be better off without them, perhaps transferring the business to franchises within department stores. It also indicates that the emphasis of the business should be switched to the mail order side, as it is more profitable and, in particular, to the telephone section.

2   **The need for further information**

However, the latter shows how dangerous this kind of assumption can be because the telephone section may have peaked and, in future, growth in the Internet section may be at the expense of the telephone section. Therefore, decisions about future strategies cannot be made on predicted short-term costs and revenues. Any attempt to do so could prove disastrous. Growth in the market, competitors' moves, customers' needs and requirements must be the basis for any decisions.

The ABC costs could, however, be used to highlight areas for cost reduction and procedural changes which could assist longer-term profitability. ABC is a method for apportioning costs and it suffers from the same defects as every absorption method. In Casamia's case, the analysis does not look very detailed/accurate and so may be little better than a traditional absorption system.

The head office and warehousing costs need to be examined in detail to determine which type of outlet incurs what part of the cost, as these costs may be caused and used more by some types of outlets than others. If this is so, what would happen to cost if one type of outlet was abandoned and others increased in size?

3   **Other information needed to make a more informed judgement is likely to be:**

Customers' changing purchasing habits

Same customer purchases across outlet types, that is, do customers buy from shops and order by telephone.

Competitors' moves

New entrants into the market – especially in the Internet business .

Future economic conditions

Exchange rate movements – as some goods are imported.

Increase in disposable income

The image created by the different types of outlet, that is do their own shops create the brand or company name.

Past data to establish trends.

Then, specific information will need to be collected for the fundamental reappraisal of the business. For example, if the decision to close Casamia's own shops was being considered, a detailed study of the interrelationship between outlets should be carried out, as having the products on display in shops might be necessary in order to maintain the high level of telephone orders. For instance, potential customers may visit to see colours, quality, and so on.

Products on display are also a form of advertising for the company and this would be lost if the shops were closed.

The Modern Business Environment

Chapter learning objectives

Lead	Component
A2: Managing the costs of creating value	Compare and contrast quality management methodologies (a) Just-in-time (JIT) (b) Quality management (c) Kaizen (d) Process re-engineering

1 Chapter summary

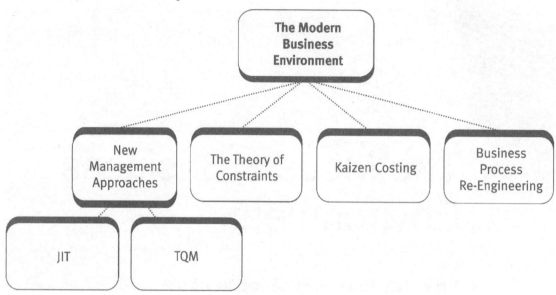

2 Introduction to the modern business environment

'To compete successfully in today's highly competitive global environment companies are making customer satisfaction an overriding priority, adopting new management approaches, changing their manufacturing systems and investing in new technologies. These changes are having a significant influence on management accounting systems.'

Colin Drury in 'Management and Cost Accounting'

The modern manufacturing environment is very different from the traditional production environment. It means that traditional costing methods are becoming less relevant.

In this chapter we explore how the modern production system has changed, and in the following chapters we examine how costing has adapted to this and created new ways to calculate a product's production cost.

3 Knowledge brought forward

You will already have covered some key concepts in Subject P1. We will build on this knowledge in P2 with more aspects of the modern business environment, but make sure you are comfortable with the assumed knowledge, that should have been brought forward as a base, in the following sections.

Characteristics of the modern business environment

Global environment

- Companies operate in a world economy.
- Customers and competitors come from all over the world.
- Products are made from components from around the world.
- Firms have to be world class to compete.
- International regulations.

Flexibility

- In a global environment, customers have far greater choice than ever before.
- There has been a huge increase in demand for new, cutting-edge innovative products.
- Customers are demanding ever-improving levels of service in cost, quality, reliability and delivery.
- Customers demand flexibility. Companies need to respond to this in order to survive.

As a consequence of this:

1 many companies now have very diverse product ranges, with a high level of tailor-made products and services

2 product life cycles have dramatically reduced, often from several years to just a few months.

The move away from standardised units of production towards individual customised units means that mass production techniques are redundant. Instead, it is of greatest importance to take an order from placement to completion in the shortest time possible. This means that production processes will be designed differently to accommodate flexibility of production rather than just throughput.

Employee empowerment

To ensure this flexibility, managers need to empower their employees to make decisions quickly, without reference to more senior managers. By empowering employees and giving them relevant information they will be able to respond faster to customers, increase process flexibility, reduce cycle times and improve morale.

Management accounting systems are moving from providing information to managers to monitor employees to providing information to employees to empower them to focus on continuous improvement.

World Class Manufacturing

The World Class Manufacturing approach to quality is quite different from the traditional approach because the primary emphasis is placed on the resolution of the problems that cause poor quality, rather than merely detecting it. These systems are more proactive and try to prevent problems from occurring in the first place rather than waiting for them to occur and then fixing them.

The system might be developed formally under Total Quality Management.

Just-In-Time

> CIMA's Official Terminology defines 'Just-in-Time' as a system whose objective is to produce or procure products or components as they are required by a customer or for use, rather than for inventory. A just-in-time system is a 'pull' system, which responds to demand, in contrast to a 'push' system, in which inventory acts as a buffer between the different elements of the system, such as purchasing, production and sales.'

JIT **production** is defined as:

A production system which is driven by demand for finished products whereby each component on a production line is produced only when needed for the next stage.

JIT **purchasing** as:

A purchasing system in which material purchases are contracted so that the receipt and usage of material, to the maximum extent possible, coincide.

These 'Official Terminology' definitions give JIT the appearance of being merely an alternative production management system, with similar characteristics and objectives to techniques such as MRP. However, JIT is better described as a philosophy, or approach to management, as it encompasses a commitment to continuous improvement and the pursuit of excellence in the design and operation of the production management system.

Toyota

Organisations in the West have traditionally used a 'push' production flow system. This system has the following stages:

1   Buy raw materials and put them into inventory.

2   Produce a production schedule based on sales forecasts.

3   Withdraw goods from inventory and make products according to the production schedule.

4   Put completed units into finished goods store.

5   Sell from finished goods store when customers request products.

Work in progress (WIP) is an unavoidable feature of such a system.

Toyota developed a different system known as JIT. This system is not a 'push' system but a 'pull' system. A product is not 'made' until the customer requests it, and components are not made until they are required by the next production stage. In a full JIT system virtually no inventory is held, that is no raw material inventory and no finished goods inventory is held, but there will be a small amount of WIP, say one-tenth of a day's production. The system works by the customer triggering the final stage of production, the assembly. As the product is assembled, components are used and this in turn triggers the component stage of production and a small amount of WIP is made ready for the next product. So the cycle goes on until the final trigger requests more raw material from the supplier.

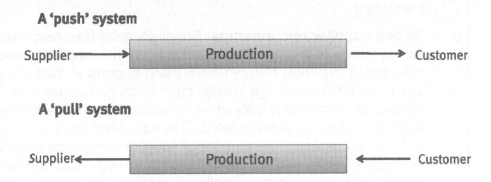

If a JIT system is to work satisfactorily, suppliers must deliver several times a day and so when the raw material arrives it may go straight into the factory and be used immediately. This means that the production lead time (i.e. the time from raw materials entering production to the finished goods emerging) should equal the processing time. In many Western organisations in the past it took several months to make a product from start to finish, despite the fact that if worked on continuously it could be made in, say, two days. The difference in time is largely due to WIP waiting to be used in the next process. It will be apparent that value is only added to the product during the actual processing stages. These have been estimated to represent as little as 10 per cent of the total manufacturing lead time in many companies, and thus up to 90 per cent of production time adds costs but no value.

JIT requires the following:

1   The **labour force must be versatile** so that they can perform any job within reason to keep production flowing as required. Workers in a JIT cell are trained to operate all the machines within it, and perform routine preventive maintenance on them.

2   Production processes must be **grouped by product line,** rather than by function in order to eliminate inventory movements between workstations and to speed flow.

3   A simple, **infallible information system**. Originally the Japanese used a system based on cards which were called Kanban. There would be a small container of components (WIP) between each workstation with a Kanban resting on top. When the container was taken for use by the following workstation the card would be taken off and left behind. This would act as a trigger for the previous workstation to produce another container of that component. Nowadays computer systems are likely to be used instead of cards but the basic simplicity of the system should not change.

4   A **'get it right first time'** approach and an aim of 'zero defects'. Defects cause breakdowns in the value chain: they stop the flow of production, create expensive rework and lead to late deliveries to customers.

5   **Strong supplier relationships**. Suppliers must take responsibility for the quality of their goods; the onus is on the supplier to inspect the parts or materials before delivery and guarantee their quality. The considerable savings in inspection costs go happily with the benefits of increased quality to achieve cost reduction – another facet of continuous improvement. This enhanced level of service is obtained by reducing the number of suppliers and increasing the business given to each of them. Longer-term commitments are entered into, assuring the supplier of continuity of demand, and enabling the supplier to plan to meet customers' production schedules. In essence the supplier becomes a key part of the value chain.

An important consequence of the 'pull' system, is that problems in any part of the system will immediately halt the production line, as earlier workstations will not receive the 'pull' signal and later stations will not have their own 'pull' signals answered. This has the powerful effect of concentrating all minds on finding a long-term solution to the problem. JIT exposes problems within a plant, and forces management to address problems and rectify them, rather than simply burying them by holding excess inventory.

The aims of JIT are to produce the required items, at the required quality and in the required quantities, at the precise time they are required.

4   TQM (Total Quality Management)

TQM is the general name given to programmes which seek to ensure that goods are produced and services supplied of the highest quality. Its origins lie primarily in Japanese organisations and it is argued that TQM has been a significant factor in Japanese global business success.

There are two basic principles of TQM:

1   **'Get it right, first time.'** TQM considers that the costs of prevention are less than the costs of correction. One of the main aims of TQM is to achieve zero rejects and 100% quality. One aspect of the Japanese management philosophy is a zero-defect target.

2   **Continuous improvement**. The second basic principle of TQM is dissatisfaction with the status quo. Realistically, a zero-defect goal may not be obtainable. It does however provide a target to ensure that a company should never be satisfied with its present level of rejects. The management and staff should believe that it is always possible to improve and to be able to get more right next time!

There are two approaches to Continuous Improvement: Kaizen Costing (in this chapter) and Target Costing (in the following chapter.)

The costs of quality

Quality costs are divided into compliance costs (or 'conformance costs') and costs of failure to comply ('non-conformance costs').

Conformance costs are further divided into prevention costs (incurred in preventing mistakes from happening) and appraisal costs (incurred in looking for mistakes before a product is manufactured).

Conformance costs

Prevention costs are the costs of ensuring that defects do not occur in the first place. For example:

1   Routine preventive repairs and maintenance to equipment.

2   Quality training for operatives to improve skills and efficiency. Training employees works, provided the employee also understand and accept the benefits of such training. Training can occur both inside and outside the workplace. Internal training may include the ideas of team working and quality discussion groups, which are known as quality circles.

3   Building of quality into the design and manufacturing processes. When a product is designed, its specification should consider factors that will minimise future rectification costs. Production methods should be as simple as possible and use the skills and resources existing within the sphere of knowledge of the organisation and its employees.

> 4   Determining whether quality factors have been correctly engineered into the design of products may only be apparent when costs are reported on a 'life cycle' basis. Effective performance management involves monitoring costs and results over the whole life cycle of a product. Just considering production costs over a one-month period (in the form of traditional standard costing and variance analysis) may be of marginal relevance.
>
> **Appraisal costs** are connected with measuring conformity with requirements and include:
>
> 1   Cost of incoming inspections (note that if suppliers adopt a total quality approach, the cost of incoming inspections can be eliminated)
>
> 2   Cost of set-up inspections
>
> 3   Cost of acquiring and operating the process control and measuring equipment.

Non-conformance costs are divided into 'internal failure' costs, that occur when the units produced fail to reach the set standard; and 'external failure' costs – These arise when the faulty product is not detected until after it reaches the customer.

Non-conformance costs

Internal failure costs include:

1   Costs of scrap

2   Reworking costs

3   Manufacturing and process engineering required to correct the failed process.

As we saw under JIT, it is the aim of total quality management (TQM) programmes to completely eliminate these internal failure costs by working towards a goal of zero defects. It is contended that, in many companies, the costs of internal failure are so great that a total quality programme can be financed entirely from the savings that are made from it – hence the expression *'quality is free'*.

There are several measurable costs of **external failure** to deliver a quality product:

1   Marketing costs associated with failed products and loss of customer goodwill

2   Manufacturing or process engineering costs relating to failed products

3   Compensation/replacement for units returned by customers

4   Repair costs

5   Travel costs to visit sites with faulty products

6   Liability claims.

Example 1: Costs of quality I

X Ltd is a manufacturing company. Its monthly quality costs are made up as follows:

	$
Cost of re-inspecting previously faulty finished goods after reworking them	5,700
Cost of scrap	12,000
Cost of calibrating and measuring testing equipment	8,500
Cost of inspecting incoming material	1,000
Cost of conducting supplier capability surveys	2,000

Which one of the following options identifies X's monthly prevention costs, appraisal costs and non-conformance costs?

	Prevention costs	Appraisal costs	Non-conformance costs
A	$10,500	$1,000	$5,700
B	$2,000	$1,000	$12,000
C	$2,000	$9,500	$17,700
D	$0	$21,500	$1,000

Example 2: Costs of quality II

Quality control costs can be categorised into internal and external failure costs, appraisal costs and prevention costs. In which of these four classifications would the following costs be included?

- The cost of a customer service team

- The cost of equipment maintenance

- The cost of operating test equipment.

	Customer service team	Equipment maintenance	Test equipment
A	Prevention costs	Appraisal costs	Internal failure costs
B	Prevention costs	Internal failure costs	Appraisal costs
C	External failure costs	Internal failure costs	Prevention costs
D	External failure costs	Prevention costs	Appraisal costs

It is generally accepted that an increased investment in prevention and appraisal is likely to result in a significant reduction in failure costs. As a result of the trade-off, there may be an optimum operating level in which the combined costs are at a minimum. In short, an investment in "prevention" inevitably results in a saving on total quality costs.

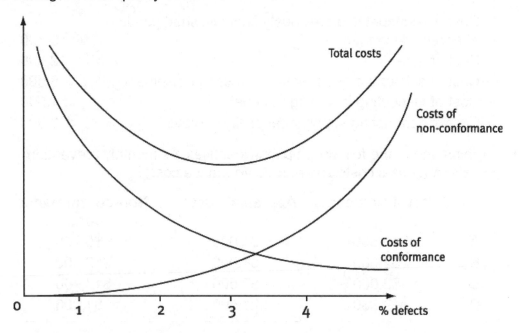

Recognising the importance of quality

1   Accept that the only thing that matters is the customer. The only way to stay in business is to relate everything to customer priorities.

2   Recognise the all-pervasive nature of the customer/supplier relationship. This includes internal customers. In a transfer environment, passing sub-standard material down to another division just to claim output is not satisfactory. Ultimately, the company must bear the cost of the defective product/service.

3   Move from relying on inspecting to a predefined level of quality, to actually preventing the cause of the defect in the first place.

4   Each operative or team of operatives must be personally responsible for defect-free production or service in their domain. This should not just be confined to production staff, it should be extended throughout the organisation. For example, sales, personnel, accounting and the after-sales departments should also ensure that their 'customers' are happy with their service.

5   In production there should be a move away from acceptable quality levels (AQL) to defect levels measured in parts per million.

6   Enforce zero defect programmes. These are an obsessive drive to get things right first time. Again this should be enforced throughout all departments.

7   Quality certification programmes such as BS5750/ISO9002 should be introduced. Although opinion is divided about these programmes, and they are often perceived to be a burden disproportionate to the benefits, the value of a third party audit of control and production procedures to ensure everything is properly controlled has both merit and, in the short term, an influence with customers.

8   The total cost of quality should be emphasised. Quality does generate savings. For example, better trained operators do not waste material nor do they abuse machines and equipment. Other savings can be achieved by reviewing suppliers, preventive machine maintenance and reduction of scrap and rework.

Commitment to quality

For TQM to bring about improved business efficiency and effectiveness it must be applied throughout the whole organisation. It begins at the top with the managing director, the most senior directors and managers who must demonstrate that they are totally committed to achieving the highest quality standards. The role of middle management is also crucial. They have to understand the importance of TQM and communicate this and their own commitment to quality to the people for whom they are responsible. It is essential that TQM is adopted by all parts of the organisation. Middle management must ensure that the efforts and achievements of their subordinates receive appropriate recognition, attention and reward. This helps secure everyone's full involvement – which is crucial to the successful introduction of TQM.

Quality chains

Throughout and beyond all organisations, whether they are manufacturing concerns, retail stores, universities or hotels, there is a series of quality chains. The ability to meet the customers' requirements is vital, not only between two separate organisations, but within the same organisation. These quality chains may be broken at any point by one person or by one piece of equipment not meeting the requirements of the customer, internal or external.

To achieve quality throughout an organisation, each person in the quality chain must be trained to ask themselves the following questions:

Customers

- Who are my internal customers?
- What are their true requirements?
- How do I find out what the requirements are?
- How can I meet those requirements?

Suppliers

- Who are my internal suppliers?
- What are my true requirements?
- How do I communicate my requirements?
- Do my suppliers have the capability to meet my requirements?

Each person in the organisation must also realise that they must respect their suppliers' needs and expectations if those suppliers are able to fully satisfy their requirements.

Successful implementation of TQM

An organisation should undertake to achieve each of the following to ensure TQM is successful:

- Total commitment throughout the organisation.
- Get close to their customers to fully understand their needs and expectations.
- Plan to do all jobs right first time.
- Agree expected performance standards with each employee and customer.
- Implement a company-wide improvement process.
- Continually measure performance levels achieved.
- Measure the cost of quality mismanagement and the level of firefighting.
- Demand continuous improvement in everything you and your employees do.
- Recognise achievements.
- Make quality a way of life.

Quality circles

A quality circle is a team of four to twelve people usually coming from the same area who voluntarily meet on a regular basis to identify, investigate, analyse and solve work-related problems. The team presents its solutions to management and is then involved in implementing and monitoring the effectiveness of the solutions. The voluntary approach and the process by which the team selects and solves its own problems are key features which give the quality circle a special character: a character which is very different to other problem-solving teams. The problems that circles tackle may not be restricted to quality of product or service topics, but may include anything associated with work or its environment. Items such as pay and conditions and other negotiated items are, however, normally excluded.

Management accounting reports

Management accounting systems can help organisations achieve their quality goals by providing a variety of reports and measures that motivate and evaluate managerial efforts to improve quality – including financial and non-financial measures.

Traditionally, the management accounting systems focused on output, not quality.

Examples:

- the strive to reduce the material price variance often led to the use of inferior quality material

- the costs of normal losses were absorbed by good output.

Non-financial measures include:

- Number of defects at inspection expressed as a percentage of the number of units completed.

- Number of reworked units expressed as a percentage of total sales value.

- Number of defective units delivered to customers as a percentage of total units delivered.

- Number of customer complaints.

- Number of defective units supplied by suppliers.

- Time taken to respond to customer requests.

5 Throughput accounting and the Theory of Constraints

The term throughput is defined by the following equation:

Throughput = Sales revenues less Direct material cost

The aim of throughput accounting is to maximise this measure of throughput. Goldratt and Cox advocate that managers should aim to increase throughput while simultaneously reducing inventory and operational expense.

This goal is achieved by determining what factors prevent the throughput being higher. This constraint is called a bottleneck. A bottleneck may be a machine whose capacity limits the output of the whole production process. The aim is to identify the bottlenecks and remove them or, if this is not possible, ensure that they are fully utilised at all times. Non-bottleneck resources should be scheduled and operated based on the constraints within the system, and should not be used to produce more than the bottlenecks can absorb.

Goldratt and Cox describe the process of identifying and taking steps to remove the constraints that restrict output as the **theory of constraints** (TOC).

The process involves five steps:

1   Identify the system's bottlenecks.

2   Decide how to exploit the bottlenecks.

3   Subordinate everything else to the decision in Step 2.

4   Elevate the system's bottlenecks.

5   If, in the previous steps, a bottleneck has been broken, go back to Step 1.

The bottleneck is the focus of management's attention. Decisions regarding the optimum mix of products must be undertaken. Step 3 requires that the optimum production of the bottleneck activity determines the production schedule of the non-bottleneck activities. There is no point in a non-bottleneck activity supplying more than the bottleneck activity can consume. This would result in increased work-in-progress (WIP) inventories with no increased sales volume. The TOC is a process of continuous improvement to clear the throughput chain of all the constraints. Thus, step 4 involves taking action to remove, or elevate, the constraint. This may involve replacing the bottleneck machine with a faster one, providing additional training for a slow worker or changing the design of the product to reduce the processing time required on the bottleneck activity. Once a bottleneck has been elevated it will generally be replaced by a new bottleneck elsewhere in the system. It then becomes necessary to return to Step 1.

Constraints on throughput

The idea of constraints is central to the throughput approach. Examples of constraints may include:

*   inadequately trained sales force

*   poor reputation for meeting delivery dates

*   poor physical distribution system

*   unreliability of material supplies, delivery and/or quality

*   inadequate production resources

*   inappropriate management accounting system.

Throughput accounting measures

Throughput = Sales revenues less Direct material cost

The only cost that is deemed to relate to volume of output is the direct material cost. All other costs (including labour costs) are deemed to be fixed. These fixed costs may be called total factory costs (TFC).

The role of the accountant in a throughput environment is to devise measures which will help production staff to achieve a greater volume of throughput. Attention should be drawn to the financial effects of bottlenecks. For example if a bottleneck resource fails to operate for one hour a whole hour's throughput is lost. Various performance measures have been devised to help measure throughput:

$$\text{Return per factory hour} = \frac{\text{Throughput per unit}}{\text{Product time on the bottleneck resource}}$$

$$\text{Cost per factory hour} = \frac{\text{Total factory costs}}{\text{Total time on the bottleneck resource}}$$

$$\text{Throughput accounting ratio} = \frac{\text{Return per factory hour}}{\text{Cost per factory hour}}$$

The accountant may advise management on how the TA ratio may be maximised.

Example 3: Throughput Accounting

X Limited manufactures a product that requires 1.5 hours of machining. Machine time is a bottleneck resource, due to the limited number of machines available. There are 10 machines available, and each machine can be used for up to 40 hours per week.

The product is sold for $85 per unit and the direct material cost per unit is $42.50. Total factory costs are $8,000 each week.

Calculate

(a) the return per factory hour

(b) the TPAR.

6 Kaizen costing

Continuous improvement, or 'Kaizen', is an integral part of the just-in-time management philosophy. 'Kaizen' is a Japanese term meaning to improve processes via small, incremental amounts rather than through large innovations. Kaizen costing is a planning method used during the manufacturing cycle that emphasises reducing variable costs of a period below the cost level in the base period. The target reduction rate is the ratio of the target reduction amount to the cost base.

- The organisation should always seek perfection. Perfection is never achieved, so there must always be some scope for improving on current methods and procedures. Improvements should be sought all the time.

- Improvements will be small and numerous rather than occasional and far-reaching.

- Cost reduction targets are set and applied on a more frequent basis than standard costs. Typically these targets are set on a monthly basis whereas standards within a traditional standard costing system are set annually or perhaps semi-annually. The table below (*adapted from Monden and Lee*) points out the differences between the two techniques:

Standard costing concepts	Kaizen costing concepts
Cost **Control** system.	Cost **Reduction** system.
Assume current manufacturing conditions.	Assume 'Continuous Improvement' in manufacturing.
Meet cost performance standards.	Achieve cost reduction targets.
Standard cost techniques	**Kaizen costing techniques**
Standards are set annually or semi-annually.	Cost reduction targets are set and applied monthly.
Cost variance analysis involving standard costs and actual costs.	Continuous Improvement (Kaizen) is implemented during the year to attain target profits or to reduce the gap between target profit and estimated profit.
Investigate and respond when standards are not met.	Cost variance analysis involving target Kaizen costs and actual costs reduction amounts.
	Investigate and respond when target Kaizen amounts are not attained.

Tool: Kaizen

Kaizen is a philosophy of customer-driven improvement. Its aim is to create a culture of continuous quality, cost and delivery (QCD) improvement across the value chain (*See 'value chain' later in this Text*).

Kaizen is based on three areas of improvement: housekeeping; waste elimination; and standardisation. In contrast to top-down approaches to driving improvements, like business process re-engineering, Kaizen democratises continuous improvement through the principle that the person performing the operation is most knowledgeable about it and, therefore, best qualified to improve it.

Everyone in the business is expected to be on the lookout for opportunities to eliminate waste in their workplaces and to implement them with their co-workers. Waste includes excessive effort ('muri') and excessive process ('mura') – for example defects, over-engineering and over-stocking.

A business' strategy should champion the values and behaviours expected of all employees in relation to Kaizen and provide guidance for employees on what is expected of them personally. Leaders across the business should cultivate participation in Kaizen activities and be seen themselves to engage in Kaizen activities. Individuals and teams should be rewarded for their contributions and results celebrated.

A Kaizen activity typically consists of the following steps:

- Standardise an operation or activity

- Measure the operation

- Compare measurements against requirements

- Innovate to meet requirements and increase productivity

- Standardise the new, improved operation

- Repeat on a continuous basis.

What benefits does Kaizen provide?

Kaizen's focus on housekeeping aims to enhance an employee's workplace ("gemba") by continuously improving cleanliness, ergonomics and safety, which in turn should improve morale and motivation.

It eliminates waste by minimising, for example, time wasted retrieving tools; fatigue; injury caused by poor workspace ergonomics; the number of human operations needed to perform a process.

Standardisation provides a standard against which operations can be compared. Deviations from standards highlight the need for remedial action (Kaizen) or to revise the standard. Standards are also key to knowledge management: they are a store of best practice, provide learning material for newcomers, and are the basis for performance management and performance improvement.

Implementing Kaizen? Questions to consider:

- Does strategy encourage buy-in from all employees and empower them to experiment in their workplace to improve operations?

- What motivating factors need to be implemented to encourage employees' participation in improvement activities on an ongoing basis?

- What training is needed to ensure all employees understand the company's approach to continuous improvement?

- What facilitation is needed to ensure improvement is ongoing, e.g. quality circles?

Actions to take: Do's

Ensure management is seen to be enacting Kaizen in its workspaces.

- Make Kaizen a strategy.
- Provide a budget for Kaizen activity.
- Measure the effectiveness of Kaizens.
- Celebrate small improvements.
- Align recognition and award frameworks to the business' Kaizen philosophy.
- Empower employees to implement Kaizens autonomously.
- Train all employees in the business' Kaizen philosophy.
- Compile baseline data to enable future comparison.

Actions to avoid: Don'ts

Don't try to exert management control over Kaizen activities.

- Avoid bureaucracy in Kaizen activities.
- Don't tie Kaizen to short term KPIs.

Example 4: Kaizen costing

Kaizen costing emphasises:

A   The need to bring about efficiency and effectiveness

B   Continuous improvement

C   A 'push' production flow system

D   The rapid elimination of all internal failure costs

Example 5: Kaizen costing II

The following statements have been made about Kaizen costing. Select ALL that apply:

- The focus is on eliminating waste, improving processes and systems and improving productivity.
- In Kaizen costing, employees are often viewed as the cause of problems.
- In Kaizen costing, costs are reduced by implementing continuous improvement.
- The aim of Kaizen costing is to achieve cost reduction targets.

7   Business Process Re-engineering

The continuous improvement philosophy contrasts sharply with the concept underlying business process re-engineering (BPR). BPR is concerned with making far-reaching one-off changes to improve operations or processes.

Michael Hammer & James Champy define BPR as 'the fundamental rethinking and radical redesign of business processes to achieve dramatic improvements in critical contemporary measures of performance such as cost, quality, service and speed.' In other words, BPR focuses on amending existing processes, streamlining processes that are already in place.

Five stages are normally recognised in any BPR project:

- Develop the business vision and process objectives. State which improvements are expected from processes based on some overall business vision of Total Quality Management.

- Identify the processes to be redesigned. Most firms tend to focus on the more important processes, although significant improvements may still be obtained by redesigning inefficient processes in any part of the organisation.

- Understand and measure the existing processes so that a baseline against which to measure improvement is set.

- Identify 'IT levers' that can be used to apply change.

- Design and build a prototype to show which changes are possible, and involve customers before implementing any revised system.

For example, consider a car manufacturing process. Cars are assembled by passing them along a conveyor belt, and adding parts to each one in a predetermined order, to arrive at the finished product. This process can be improved in terms of efficiency by making robots do some of the repetitive and less skilled operations. In this way, the process is being re-designed, to include and enhanced IT element to make it more efficient, and less prone to errors. In other words, BPR is being used to improve the existing process.

Business process re-engineering

A business process consists of a collection of activities that are linked together in a co-ordinated manner to achieve a specific objective. Business process re-engineering involves examining business processes and radically redesigning these processes to achieve cost reduction, improved quality and customer satisfaction. BPR is all about major changes to how business processes operate.

Material handling is an example of a business process and may consist of the following separate activities; material requisitioning, purchase requisitioning, processing purchase orders, inspecting materials, storing materials and paying suppliers. This process could be re-engineered by sending the material requisitions directly to an approved supplier and entering into an agreement which entails delivering high quality material in accordance with the production requirements. This change in business process could result in cost reduction by the elimination of; the administration involved in placing orders, the need for material inspection and storage. By re-engineering the material handling business process the company will reduce costs without compromising the quality of the products delivered to customers.

Example 6: BPR

Which of the following statements are TRUE regarding BPR? Select all that apply.

- BPR achieves incremental improvements in performance.

- BPR increases the organisation's ability to meet customers' needs.

- BPR uses technology to find innovative ways to do business.

- BPR increases organisational complexity as activities are decoupled.

- BPR can be used as a pretext for staff reductions and as a 'quick fix.

Value-added analysis

This BPR re-engineering pattern looks at the process (or sub-process) from a customer's perspective. A process or activity is said to add value if it increases the worth of a product or service to the customer (for example, adding a sun-roof to a car).To be classified as 'value-adding', an activity must meet three criteria:

1   the customer is willing to pay for the output

2   the activity physically changes the output in some way

3   the activity is performed correctly at the first attempt.

Value-adding activities are distinct from 'non-value-adding activities', such as:

- preparation and set-up

- control and inspection

- simply moving a product from one place to another without physically changing it

- activities that result from delays or failures of any kind.

Non value-adding activities are those that do not increase the worth of the product to the customer. Common examples are 'inspection time' and 'idle time' in manufacturing. It is usually not possible to eliminate these activities but it is often possible to minimise them.

Obviously, some of them (for example set-up activities) may be essential for the value-added activity to take place. These essential support activities are known as value-enabling activities, and cannot be eliminated altogether. However, they should be done simply and cost-effectively to allow resources to be focused as much as possible on the value-added activities.

Example 7: Value-adding and non-value adding activities

Indicate which of the following activities are value-adding, or non-value-adding, by dragging and dropping the tiles on the right ('Value adding activity' and 'Non-value adding activity' tiles) in the correct position:

Reporting	
Assembly	
Design engineering	
Transferring materials between two non-adjacent workstations	
Inspecting parts for quality defects	
Processing returned materials	
Project coordination	
Obtaining approvals	
Painting	

Value adding activity

Non-value adding activity

8   Supply chain management

Supply chain management is often explained with reference to Porter's value chain and value systems. A supply chain is the network of customers and suppliers that a business deals with.

Recent decades have seen an increasing rate of globalisation of the economy and thereby also of supply chains. The days when products were produced and consumed in the same geographical area are long past. In fact it is often the case that the different components of a product come from all over the globe. Such a trend causes longer and more complex supply chains and thus changes the requirements within supply chain management. This, in turn, affects the effectiveness of the IT systems employed within the supply chain. A longer supply chain often results in a lengthening of order-to-delivery lead times.

Supply chain management considers logistics but also relationships between members of the supply chain, identification of end-customer benefit and the organisational consequences of greater inter-firm integration to form 'network organisations'.

Supply chain management may be broken down into several areas:

Purchasing

It is important for a company to work closely with its suppliers. A true partnership will enable a better, faster and more reliable service. Purchasing costs can be reduced by more than 10% when information systems are linked. Day-to-day purchasing, progress chasing and stock control can all be eliminated.

Inventories

Efficient inventory control relies upon accurate customer records, well-managed customer information and effective inventory-control information systems. A close collaboration with suppliers and customers will enable inventory levels to be kept to a minimum. Working more closely with the supply chain partners will require mutual trust and investment in technology, but it will bring benefits to all concerned.

Customer ordering

From the customer's perspective the ordering process should be fast, flexible (meet individual customer needs) and efficient. A satisfied customer is more likely to return for repeat orders. Factors such as price, quality, availability from inventory etc. are important, but a fully automated fulfilment procedure also plays a key part in overall customer satisfaction. On-line ordering is becoming a prerequisite for many customers today.

Orders should be processed smoothly within the firm. Purchasing, inventory control, marketing and accounts should all be linked to the customer-ordering process.

Delivery and logistics

Delivering to the customer is often the culmination of all the business processes. Customers will expect fast, reliable, accurate and predictable delivery schedules. Tracking systems such as radio frequency identification (RFID) enable companies to trace the physical progress of the customer order. With RFID objects are tagged. During manufacturing and delivery the whereabouts of the order can then be traced electronically and remotely (items can be detected up to 100 feet away from the sensor). In the US many large companies such as Wallmart are already requiring their suppliers to use RFID.

Some companies use third party distributors. As technology becomes more complex and sophisticated outsourcing becomes more attractive. Some companies leave distribution to professional logistics companies.

Outsourcing

A significant trend in recent years has been for organisations and government bodies to concentrate on their core competencies. Outsourcing involves the buying in of components, sub-assemblies, finished products and services from outside suppliers rather than supplying them internally. It may be regarded as a management strategy by which an organisation delegates major non-core functions to specialised, efficient service providers.

Traditionally the insourcing/outsourcing decision was focused on a make-or-buy decision for manufacturing functions. However companies are now beginning to apply the decision analysis to nearly all functions and activities.

For example, the following functions are now coming under the outsourcing spotlight: sales; design and development, IT and distribution.

Advantages and disadvantages of insourcing

Advantages	Disadvantages
Higher degree of control over inputs	Requires high volumes
Increases visibility over the process	High investment
Economies of scale/scope to use integration	Dedicated equipment has limited flexibility
	Not a core competence

Advantages and disadvantages of outsourcing

Advantages	Disadvantages
Greater flexibility	Possibility of choosing wrong supplier
Lower investment risk	Loss of visibility and control over process
Improved cash flow	Possibility of increased lead times
Concentrates on core competence	
Enables more advanced technologies to be used without making investment	

9   Practice Questions

Objective Test Question 1: Just-in-time

The adoption of **JIT** normally requires which one of the following factors to increase?

A   Inventory levels

B   Work-in-progress levels

C   Batch sizes

D   Quality standards

Objective Test Question 2: Quality Costs

Match the cost to the correct cost category:

Costs

(a)   Reliability studies

(b)   Returned material processing and repair

(c)   Quality audits

(d)   Quality control investigations of failures

Cost categories

•   Prevention costs

•   Appraisal costs

•   Internal failure costs

•   External failure costs

Objective Test Question 3: TQM

Use the words and phrases in the table provided below to complete the following paragraphs:

quality	output	production problems
Total Quality Management (TQM)	customer goodwill	quality
delays	buffer inventory	

In a company operating on JIT principles, the absence of inventories deprives production of a safety net or '_____'. This exposes the business to production problems or _____and, ultimately, to lost sales and damaged _____.

In this context, the adoption of a _____ philosophy is key. In this,

_____ is a feature rooted in the production process and every individual is responsible for the quality of his/her _____.

This will encourage good quality at all times and therefore minimise _____that would otherwise occur due to poor _____.

Objective Test Question 4: BPR II

Which of the following statements are TRUE regarding BPR? Select all that apply.

- BPR is often used as the pretext for staff reductions.

- BPR is a long term approach to gaining a competitive advantage.

- BPR overlooks the impact on human resources.

- BPR increases organisational complexity.

- BPR focuses too much on improving existing business rather than developing new and better lines of business.

Data Set Question: Throughput accounting

The following data relates to three products manufactured by BJS Ltd:

	Product X	Product Y	Product Z
Selling price per unit	$12	$16	$14
Direct material cost per unit	$3	$10	$7
Maximum demand (units)	15,000	40,000	20,000
Time required on the bottleneck (hours per unit)	3	1.5	7

The firm has 80,000 bottleneck hours available each period, and total factory costs amount to $100,000 in the period.

Task: Calculate the following:

The TPAR (throughput accounting ratio) for Product X

The TPAR (throughput accounting ratio) for Product Y

The TPAR (throughput accounting ratio) for Product Z

The maximum profit achievable by BJS, in $ (this involves a calculation of the optimum product mix)

Case Study Style Question – X Ltd

X Ltd manufactures and distributes three types of car (the C1, C2 and C3). Each type of car has its own production line.

The company is worried by extremely difficult market conditions, and forecasts losses for the forthcoming year.

It has been suggested by an external consultant, JIT ExtC Ltd, that a JIT system should be introduced to address these worries. Their communication reads as follows:

> *We have lots of experience in introducing Just-In-Time (JIT) measures in businesses similar to X Ltd.*
>
> *It is our view that many of X Ltd competitors have already introduced this type of JIT measures. We are certain that in order to remain competitive and achieve concrete cost savings, X Ltd should implement JIT measures as a matter of urgency.*
>
> *We estimate that the introduction of the JIT system would have the following impact on costs (fixed and variable):*
>
> *Direct labour   Increase by 20%*
>
> *Set-ups   Decrease by 30%*
>
> *Materials handling Decrease by 30%*
>
> *Inspection   Decrease by 30%*
>
> *Machining   Decrease by 15%*
>
> *Distribution and warehousing   Eliminated*

You receive the following email from the Chief Financial Officer (CFO):

> **From:** Charles Fern Oxley (CFO)
> **Sent:** 04 June, 10.11 a.m.
> **To:**   Senior Management Accountant
> **Subject:** JIT
>
> I have attached the executive summary of a report prepared by some external consultants on how we might benefit from switching to JIT.
>
> Please draft me a report that I can submit to the board on the conditions that are necessary for the successful implementation of a JIT manufacturing system.

Answers to examples and objective test questions

Example 1: Costs of quality I

The correct answer is C.

Re-inspecting previously faulty goods incurs **internal failure costs**, occurring prior to delivery of the product to the customer. These are non-conformance costs. Likewise, scrap costs are internal failure costs of non-conformance.

Costs of calibrating testing equipment are associated with measuring products/services to assure conformance to quality standards. These are appraisal costs. Likewise, costs of inspecting incoming material will be classified as appraisal costs.

The costs of conducting supplier capability surveys are prevention costs, incurred to prevent poor quality in products or services.

Example 2: Costs of quality II

The correct answer is D.

A customer service team deals with customer queries and complaints from outside the organisation, typically after goods have been delivered to the customer. The costs of this team arise from quality failures and are preventable. They are external failure costs. Maintenance is intended to prevent machine breakdowns and so to prevent quality failures, and they are therefore prevention costs. Test equipment is used for inspection/appraisal.

Example 3: Throughput Accounting

Return per factory hour = ($85 – $42.50)/1.5 hours = $28.33

Cost per factory hour = $8,000/(10 × 40 hours) = $20

TPAR = $28.33/$20 = 1.4165

Example 4: Kaizen costing

The answer is B, Continuous Improvement.

Kaizen Costing is one of two approaches of Continuous Improvement; (target costing being the other).

Kaizen is the Japanese term for making improvements to a process through small incremental amounts, rather than through large innovations. Kaizen costing is applied during the manufacturing stage of the product's life cycle. This focuses on achieving cost reductions through the increased efficiency of the production process. Improvement is the aim and responsibility of every worker in every activity, at all times.

Through continual efforts significant reductions in cost can be achieved over time. In order to encourage continual cost reductions an annual (or monthly) Kaizen cost goal is established. Actual results are then compared with the Kaizen goal and then the current actual cost becomes the base line for setting the new Kaizen goal the following year.

Example 5: Kaizen costing II

- Kaizen focuses on eliminating waste, improving processes and systems and improving productivity. **TRUE**

- In Kaizen costing, employees are often viewed as the cause of problems. **FALSE**: one characteristic of Kaizen is that it involves all employees and all areas of the business.

- In Kaizen costing, costs are reduced by implementing continuous improvement. **TRUE**

- The aim of Kaizen costing is to achieve cost reduction targets. **TRUE**

Example 6: BPR

- BPR achieves incremental improvements in performance. **FALSE**

- BPR increases the organisation's ability to meet customers' needs. **TRUE**

- BPR uses technology to find innovative ways to do business. **TRUE**

- BPR increases organisational complexity as activities are decoupled. **FALSE**

- BPR can be used as a pretext for staff reductions and as a 'quick fix. **TRUE**

Example 7: Value-adding and non-value adding activities

Indicate which of the following activities are value-adding, or non-value-adding, by dragging and dropping the tiles on the right ('Value adding activity' and 'Non-value adding activity' tiles) in the correct position:

Reporting	Non-value adding activity
Assembly	Value adding activity
Design engineering	Value adding activity
Transferring materials between two non-adjacent workstations	Non-value adding activity
Inspecting parts for quality defects	Non-value adding activity
Processing returned materials	Non-value adding activity
Project coordination	Non-value adding activity
Obtaining approvals	Non-value adding activity
Painting	Value adding activity

Value adding activity

Non-value adding activity

Objective Test Question 1: Just-in-Time

Answer D. An increase in quality standards is one of the key factors that allows the other items listed to be reduced.

Objective Test Question 2: Quality Costs

(a)   Prevention costs

(b)   External failure costs

(c)   Appraisal costs

(d)   Internal failure costs

Objective Test Question 3: TQM

In a company operating on JIT principles, the absence of inventories deprives production of a safety net or **'buffer inventory'**. This exposes the business to production problems or **delays** and, ultimately, to lost sales and damaged **customer goodwill**.

In this context, the adoption of a **TQM (Total Quality Management)** philosophy is key. In this, **quality** is a feature rooted in the production process and every individual is responsible for the quality of his/her **output**.

This will encourage good quality at all times and therefore minimise **production problems** that would otherwise occur due to poor **quality**.

Objective Test Question 4: BPR II

- BPR is often used as the pretext for staff reductions. **TRUE**

- BPR is a long term approach to gaining a competitive advantage. **FALSE**

- BPR overlooks the impact on human resources. **TRUE**

- BPR increases organisational complexity. **FALSE**

- BPR focuses too much on improving existing business rather than developing new and better lines of business. **TRUE**

Data Set Question: Throughput accounting

The TPAR (throughput accounting ratio) for Product X	**2.4**
The TPAR (throughput accounting ratio) for Product Y	**3.2**
The TPAR (throughput accounting ratio) for Product Z	**0.80**
The maximum profit achievable by BJS, in $ (this involves a calculation of the optimum product mix)	**200,000**

Cost per factory hour = $100,000/80,000 = $1.25

	Product X	Product Y	Product Z
Selling price per unit	$12	$16	$14
Direct material cost per unit	($3)	($10)	($7)
	—	—	—
Throughput p.u.	$9	$6	$7
Time required on the bottleneck	3	1.5	7
Return per factory hour	**$3**	**$4**	**$1**
T. A. ratio	$3/$1.25	$4/$1.25	$1/$1.25
	= 2.4 : 1	= 3.2 : 1	= 0.80
	2nd	1st	3rd

Ranking

Product	Number of units	Hours per unit	Total hours	Throughput per hour	Total throughput
Y	40,000	1.5	60,000	$4	$240,000
X	6,666	3.0	20,000	$3	$59,994
			80,000		$299,994
Less total factory costs					($100,000)
Total profit					**$199,994**

Case Study Style Question – X Ltd

To: Charles Fern Oxley, X Ltd

From: Management Accountant

Date: 04 June

Subject: Successful implementation of JIT

Introduction

The following report explains some of the conditions that are necessary for the successful implementation of a JIT manufacturing system within X Ltd. These conditions include:

Supplier relationships

JIT systems require a huge reduction in inventory levels. In order to facilitate this, inventory order sizes must be small. Hence suppliers must be capable of AND willing to deliver small quantities on a regular basis. X Ltd will need to have a good relationship with its accredited suppliers.

JIT systems aim to eliminate raw material inventories. In order to do this, suppliers must be capable of achieving all aspects of quality – delivering the correct quantity to the correct location at the correct time. Ideally suppliers should also deliver defect-free items.

Quality issues

For JIT to be effective achieving the highest possible levels of quality is essential. Production scheduling becomes demand-based and in order to meet customers' requirements quality problems need to be eliminated. It is often necessary to implement a quality programme such as Total Quality Management. The aim is to prevent the problems in the first place.

Quality should be considered from several angles:

From suppliers – as mentioned above.

In machinery – equipment should be well-maintained to avoid breakdown and the manufacture of sub-standard output.

In staff – all staff should be appropriately trained and skilled to carry out the task required of them.

Education and training

JIT will only be successful if our employees are willing to make it so. All levels of staff throughout the organisation should be appropriately trained and educated as to the objectives of the new system and the benefits that it will bring to X Ltd.

Work scheduling

Cellular manufacturing or group technology brings great benefits for JIT companies. This is where whole products are made within each manufacturing cell. X Ltd appears to have this system already as each car has its own production line.

Information systems

The new management systems that will be put in place will require new information systems. There will be major changes in the communication line with suppliers and the work scheduling system may need redeveloping in order to cope with the new pull-system.

Financing

Appropriate funds must be available to finance the development and implementation of JIT. Without sufficient funding JIT will fail.

Conclusion

In order to move forward with the JIT proposal we should investigate which of the conditions can be met.

Should you require any further advice, then please do not hesitate to contact me.

AN Accountant

Management Accountant

X Ltd

E: mact@xltd.co.uk

3

Costing Techniques

Chapter learning objectives

Lead	Component
A3: Managing the costs of creating value	Apply value management techniques to manage costs and improve value creation
	(a) Target costing
	(b) Value chain analysis
	(c) Life Cycle costing

1 Chapter summary

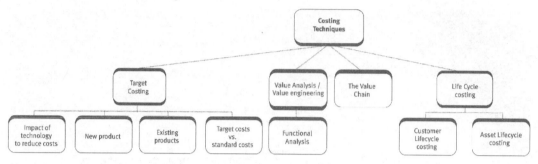

2 Knowledge brought forward

You will already have covered some of these concepts in P1. We will build on this knowledge in P2 with more aspects of some key costing techniques, but make sure you are comfortable with the assumed knowledge, that should have been brought forward as a base, in the following sections.

3 Background

Because traditional overhead absorption was designed for production companies, it dealt with production costs only and, as a consequence, it is less suitable for service or retail organisations. Also, because inventory had to be valued at full production cost only in the published accounts, other costs such as R&D, administration, and marketing have not been related to products.

When traditional absorption costing evolved last century, overheads were only a small part, say, 10 per cent of the cost of production for the average company. Direct labour costs were much higher, say, 50 per cent of the cost of the product. This meant that the absorption method spread 10 per cent of costs on the basis of 50 per cent of costs. Because overheads were such a small part of total costs any inaccuracies in the absorption process were small and insignificant and did not distort product costs.

A few organisations may have this cost structure today, and in such cases traditional absorption costing is perfectly adequate. Most companies, however, now have those percentages reversed and it creates a considerable degree of inaccuracy if 50 per cent of the costs are spread on the behaviour of 10 per cent of the costs. Yet it is vital that an organisation's costing system spreads overheads accurately.

Traditional absorption costing was not designed to make decisions of a short-term nature, and can never be used for this purpose. Marginal costing (variable costing) should be used when short-term decisions on matters such as product/service profitability are required. But if long-term decisions need to be made, an absorption costing system is needed. The system must be accurate and for all the reasons outlined above, total absorption costing is unlikely to produce the required accuracy; alternative costing techniques are needed.

4 Target costing

Target costing is driven by external market factors. Marketing managers first estimate the performance characteristics and market price requirements in order to achieve a desired market share for a proposed product. A standard profit margin is then subtracted from the projected selling price to arrive at the target cost for the product. The product development team must then, through its product and process design decisions, attempt to reach the product's target cost.

One of the definitions of target costing reads as follows:

> Target costing is a pro-active cost control system. The target cost is calculated by deducting the target profit from a pre-determined selling price based on customers' views. Functional Analysis, value analysis and value engineering are used to change production methods and/or reduce expected costs so the target is met.

The target profit requirement should be driven by strategic profit planning rather than a standard mark-up. In Japan this is done after consideration of the medium-term profit plans which reflect management and business strategies over that period. Once it is set, the target profit is not just an expectation; it is a commitment agreed by all the people who have any part in achieving it. Therefore the procedures used to derive the target profit must be scientific, rational and agreed by all staff responsible for achieving it; otherwise no-one will accept responsibility for achieving it.

This procedure is just the opposite of that followed by many companies today in which the product is designed with little regard either to the manufacturing process or to its long-run manufacturing cost. With this traditional procedure of first designing the product and then giving the design to process engineers and costs analysts, the product cost is developed by applying standard cost factors to the materials and processes specified for the design. Frequently, this cost may be well above that which can be sustained by market prices and the product is either aborted or, if marketed, fails to achieve desired profitability levels.

Using target cost in the concept and design stages

With the target-cost approach, the new product team, consisting of product designers, purchasing specialists, and manufacturing and process people, works together to jointly determine product and process characteristics that permit the target cost to be achieved. The target cost approach is especially powerful to apply at the design stage, since decisions made at this stage have leverage to affect long-run costs.

The great majority of manufacturing costs become locked in early in the life cycle of the product. Once the product is released into production, it becomes much harder to achieve significant cost reductions. Most of the costs become committed or locked in much earlier than the time at which the major cash expenditures are made.

The target-costing approach is a vital total cost control tool because research has shown that up to 90 per cent of costs are 'built in' at the product's design stage. Below are some examples of costs that become locked in place at the design stage:

- The design specification of the product including extra features

- The number of components incorporated in the product

- Design of components

   These should be designed for reliability in use and ease of manufacture. Wherever possible standard parts should be used because they are proven to be reliable and will help reduce inventory and handling costs. Where new components are required it is important that their manufacturing process is considered before the component is finally designed so that they can be manufactured as cheaply as possible consistent with quality and functionality.

- Type of packaging required

   This includes product packaging and packing per case and per pallet. The aim is to protect the product and to minimise handling costs by not breaking pallets or cases during distribution.

- The number of spare parts that need to be carried

   This ties in with the number of components used. Parts must sometimes be held for up to 15 years or so. They may be made while the product is still in production and stored for years, which is costly. The alternative is to disrupt current production to make a small batch of a past component, which is very costly.

Target costing is an iterative process that cannot be de-coupled from design. The pre-production stages can be categorised in a variety of different ways; in the detailed discussion below five different stages are used and the different activities are now listed.

1 **Planning**

   This includes fixing the product concept and the primary specifications for performance and design. A very brief product concept might be a small, town car for two people with a large amount of easily-accessible luggage space and low fuel consumption – aimed at those in their mid-twenties and so style is important. (In reality the concept would be much fuller.) Value engineering and analysis (VE) could be used to identify new and innovative, yet cost-effective, product features that would be valued by customers and meet their requirements.

   Once the concept has been developed a planned sales volume and selling price, which depend on each other, will be set, as well as the required profit discussed earlier. From this the necessary target cost (or allowable cost as it is often known) can be ascertained.

   Target cost = Planned selling price – Required profit

Example 1: Target Costing

A company requires a return of 12% in the coming year on its investment of $1,000,000 in product J. The selling price of product J is set at $52.00 for each unit, and sales for the coming year are expected to reach 5,000 units. What is the target cost for each unit for the coming year?

A $24

B $28

C $44

D $50

2   **Concept design**

The basic product is designed. The target cost is now divided into smaller parts reflecting the manufacturing process - see diagram below. First an allowance for development costs and manufacturing equipment costs are deducted from the total. The remainder is then split up into unit costs that will cover manufacturing and distribution, etc. The manufacturing target cost per unit is assigned to the functional areas of the new product. For example, a functional area for a ballpoint pen might be the flow of ink to the tip and a functional area for a car might be the steering mechanism.

The breakdown of target cost

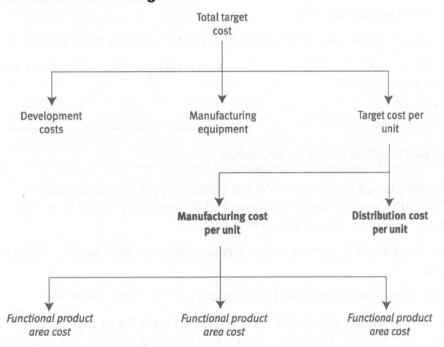

3   **Basic design**

The components are designed in detail so that they do not exceed the functional target costs. Value engineering is used to get the costs down to the target. If one function cannot meet its target, the targets for the others must be reduced or the product redesigned.

4   **Detailed design**

The detailed specifications and cost estimates are set down from the basic design stage.

5   **Manufacturing preparation**

The manufacturing process, including new machines, is designed in keeping with the target cost. Standards for the materials and labour hours that should be used are set. These values are presented to the staff in the factory immediately after they are set so that approval can be given.

The purchasing department negotiates prices for bought-in components.

Example 2: Target Costing and the cost gap

The predicted selling price for a product has been set at $56 per unit. The desired mark-up on cost is 25% and the material cost for the product is estimated to be $16 before allowing for additional materials to allow for shrinkage of 20% (for every 10 kg of material going in, only 8 kg comes out).

Labour is the only other cost, and 2 labour hours are needed.

What is the most the business can pay per hour if a cost gap is to be avoided?

$_____

Target costing for existing products

Cost control is not forgotten once the product goes into production. Manufacturing performance is measured to see if the target is being achieved. The reasons for doing this are:

1   to see who is responsible for any cost excess and to offer them help; and

2   to judge whether the cost-planning activities were effective.

If after three months the target cost is missed by a large margin an improvement team is organised which will conduct a thorough value analysis (VA) and will stay in existence for about six months.

Although the Japanese use standard costing to some extent they do not consider it to be suitable for ongoing cost control. They see standard costing as part of budget accounting where the same value is maintained throughout the budget period, whereas they use target costing to control production cost and as a consequence revise it monthly. Monden (1989) expressed the limitations of standard costing this way:

'Since standard costing systems have constraints from a financial perspective, they are inappropriate measures for management. A typical constraint is the infrequency in which quantity standards, such as processing time per production unit or material requirements, are revised.

Normally these standards are maintained at the same level throughout the year.'

Target costing, therefore, continues to be used to control costs throughout the product's life. After the initial start-up stage target costs will be set through budgets, which in Japan tend to be set every six months rather than yearly. This type of target costing is a different technique in the eyes of the Japanese and they call this Genka Kaizen. It is widely used in Japan; about 80 per cent of assembly environments use it. If a manager cannot meet the target cost for a function, a committee will be set up to help achieve it. All costs including both variable and fixed overheads are expected to reduce on a regular basis, usually monthly.

Target costing is widely used among industries in different countries. Mercedes, Toyota, Nissan, and Daihatsu in the car industry, Matsushita, Panasonic and Sharp in the electronics industry, and Apple, Compaq and Toshiba in the personal computer market all use target pricing and target costing.

 Example 3: Reducing the cost gap

Which of the following would be a legitimate strategy to reduce a cost gap for a product that existed in a competitive industry with demanding shareholders?

A Increasing the selling price

B Reducing the expectation gap by reducing the selling price

C Reducing the desired margin on the product

D Mechanising production in order to reduce average production cost

The impact of technology to reduce costs

> **Technology eliminating costs as a barrier to entry: The CGMA Cost Transformation Model**
>
> Technology is eliminating cost as a barrier to entry. Fixed costs of production are now becoming less costly. For example:
>
> - Computer aided design (CAD) software has become a commodity, with some basic versions free to download.
>
> - 3D printing is making the printing of components that previously needed costly machining processes.
>
> - Digital technology has made it technically possible produce a film at a fraction of the fixed cost that used to be needed.
>
> **Uber**
>
> In some disruptive business models variable costs are significantly reducing. An example of this is transport company Uber. After setting up a web based platform (its primary fixed cost) all that remains to grow its business is for operators (individuals or fleet operators) to sign up to the Uber platform at very low marginal cost to Uber.
>
> With rapid and ongoing improvements in communications and logistics competitors can be anywhere. Increasingly, producers are having to change the way they do business to maintain competitiveness. The supply chains of the largest businesses have become global to take advantage of lower cost centres and the ready availability of high calibre people globally. Components of business models retained as core competencies have to be continuously improved to generate value on a sustainable basis.
>
> **Tata**
>
> "After 2008, we were feeling the effects of an economic climate where a strong pound was making imports cheaper than locally produced goods and impacting our sales volumes. The steel industry is fixed cost intensive and reducing our variable costs would not have a significant enough impact. Our challenge was to find a way to re-structure our fixed costs base and differentiate our sales."
>
> Claire Osmundsen-Little, ACMA, CGMA, Finance Controller, Packaging,
>
> Tata Steel Europe

In summary:

Standard costing	Target costing
A **Push** system: a standard cost per unit (onto which a mark-up is added) is the basis for calculating the selling price.	A **Pull** system that requires understanding of market demand and competition, so that the price required to achieve a target market share or sales level can be set.
An **Internal** tool in mass production environments that do not emphasise continual improvement.	Driven by **External** market prices and may not be attainable in the short term.
A **Cost control** technique.	A **Cost reduction** activity.
A **Reactive** technique – the selling price of a new product will be determined by estimating its standard cost and adding the required profit margin to the cost.	A **Proactive** technique that starts before the design of the product is formalised. Once this target price has been determined, a required long-term profit margin is agreed. It is only once the target cost has been agreed that the design team can begin their work. Our products must be designed with a pre-determined cost ceiling.

 Target costs and standard costs

There are some similarities between target costs and standard costs but the significance of a target cost lies in the process of how it is developed. They both provide unit cost targets but here the similarity ends and significant differences include:

- The focus upon what a product should cost in the long term. In constructing the target cost of a new item consideration should first be given to the price at which the product should be sold in order to attract the desired market share. Once this selling price has been determined the required profit margin needs to be deducted in order to arrive at the target cost. A standard cost would tend to be based on attainable standards of efficiency whereas a target cost may incorporate a cost gap which can only be achieved over a longer term.

- A market orientated approach. The use of standard costs which have been derived from target costs ensures that external factors that are related to the marketplace are taken into account. A standard cost is usually based on production cost information only.

- Focus on continual improvement. The target cost may incorporate a series of cost targets which are continuously reduced until the target is achieved. A standard is normally set at the outset of production and may not be reviewed on a regular basis.

- Team approach. Target costing requires that all departments working on the product should be involved in the target costing exercise and should contribute to the target cost being achieved. This includes research and development, marketing and sales as well as production. This contrasts with standard costs which are normally production costs only.

- A target cost will be set before major development costs are incurred. This allows cost reductions to be designed into the product or a decision to be made to abandon the product if the required cost target cannot be achieved. In contrast, standards are set when production commences, by which time 70% to 80% of costs may already be committed.

Kaizen costing and Target costing

Kaizen is the Japanese term for making improvements to a process through small incremental amounts, rather than through large innovations.

Target costing is aimed at reducing the costs incurred because of the way the product is designed, and occurs at the very start of the process.

Kaizen costing is applied during the manufacturing stage of the products life cycle. Kaizen costing therefore focuses on achieving cost reductions through the increased efficiency of the production process. Improvement is the aim and responsibility of every worker in every activity, at all times. Through continual efforts significant reductions in cost can be achieved over time. In order to encourage continual cost reductions an annual (or monthly) Kaizen cost goal is established.

Actual results are then compared with the Kaizen goal and then the current actual cost becomes the base line for setting the new Kaizen goal the following year. It should be noted however that as the products are already at the production stage the cost savings under Kaizen costing are smaller than target costing. Because cost reductions under target costing are achieved at the design stage where 80–90% of the product costs are locked in, more significant savings can be made.

5 Value analysis/Value engineering

Value analysis (value engineering) helps to design products that meet customer needs at a lower cost, while assuming the required standard of quality and reliability.

Value analysis relates to existing products. **Value engineering** relates to products that have not yet been produced.

CIMA's Official Terminology definitions read as follows:

> Value analysis is 'the systematic interdisciplinary examination of factors affecting the cost of a product or service, in order to devise means of achieving the specified purpose most economically at the required standard of quality and reliability'.

> Value engineering is 'the (re)design of an activity, product or service so that value to the customer is enhanced while costs are reduced or at least increased by less than the resulting price increase).

Value analysis/engineering focuses on activities that add value to the product/service **as perceived to the customer**. It examines business activities, and questions why they are being undertaken, and what contribution they make to customer satisfaction:

- What do customers want?

- What do customers regard as significant in the buying function: function, appearance, longevity or disposal value?

The purpose of value analysis is to identify any unnecessary cost elements within the components of goods and services. It is more comprehensive than simple cost reduction, because it examines the purposes or functions of the product and is concerned with establishing the means whereby these are achieved. Any cost data that do not add value to the product or service should be eliminated.

Types of value

Cost value: this is the cost incurred by the firm producing the product.

Exchange value: the amount of money that consumers are willing to exchange to obtain ownership of the product, i.e. its price.

Use value: this is related entirely to function, i.e. the ability of a product to perform its specific intended purpose. A basic small car provides personal transport at a competitive price and is reasonably economic to run.

Esteem value: this relates to the status or regard associated with ownership. Products with high esteem value will often be associated with premium or even price-skimming prices.

Value is a function of both use and esteem. Value analysis aims to maintain the esteem value in a product, but at a reduced cost value. The result of value analysis is to achieve an improved value/cost relationship.

Method of value analysis

- Determine the function of the product and each component that is used within the product.

- Determine the existing costs associated with individual components.

- Develop alternative solutions to the needs met by the components. This may involve design changes, manufacturing method, materials used, etc.

- When analysing a components a questioning attitude should be adopted. Some of these points may be considered:

  - How does this component contribute to the value of the product?

  - How much does it cost?

  - Are all its features and specifications absolutely necessary?

  - Is there another similar part that may be used?

  - Can an alternative part be used?

  - Will an alternative design perform the same function?

- Evaluate the alternatives and their anticipated effect.

- Implement the recommendations.

A key aspect of this is to understand which features of the product are essential to customer perceived quality, and which are not. This process is known as 'value analysis'. Attention should be focused more on reducing the costs of features perceived by the customer not to add value. So, value analysis will often lead to the reduction of components used in a product, the use of alternative, cheaper components and the standardisation of parts across several product lines. (Value-adding activities and non-value adding activities were discussed in the previous chapter.)

6 Functional analysis

Functional analysis is defined in CIMA's Official Terminology as an analysis of the relationships between product functions, their perceived value to the customer and their cost of provision.

Functional analysis uses the functions of a product as the cost object and is used either in initial designs or in the review of existing products. It can be extended to services, overhead expenses, and organisation structure and even to the overall strategy of the company.

The central theme of functional analysis is, like value analysis, customer focus. An important aspect when gathering information is to identify the functions of the product that customers' value and identify alternative ways of achieving these functions.

So, for example, a newsletter sent out by an accounting company may have the functions of advertising services, keeping clients up to date with new developments, providing details of social events and networking opportunities. There may be many ways of achieving these functions, e.g. by sending out letters, by sending emails or by posting information on a website. Analysis will be carried out to find out which alternative achieves the required function at the least cost.

Once an alternative has been chosen, it must be implemented. Then, performance is measured to assess the degree to which the objective has been achieved. Lessons may be learned to help in future functional analyses.

Functional analysis

In functional analysis, the company will first break down the product into its many functions. For example, a mobile phone may offer an MP3 player, a voice-recording feature, a camera and an internet browser in addition to the ability to make and receive calls and texts.

Research is also carried out to identify the importance the customer attaches to each feature. This information may be obtained from a mixture of past purchasing patterns and customer interviews and questionnaires. Research will also be carried out into the amount the customer would be willing to pay for the final product – this can be used to find the overall target cost for the product by deducting an appropriate profit margin.

The company will then calculate the target cost of providing each of these functions. This is calculated as a percentage of the overall target cost based on the relative importance of each feature to the customer.

The next step will be to compare the expected cost to provide each function with the target cost. If the expected cost of the function exceeds the target (i.e. has a value ratio of less than one) then the function should be either modified, re-evaluated and an alternative found, or eliminated.

7 The value chain

The value chain is a linked set of value-creating activities starting from basic raw material sources or component suppliers through to the ultimate end-use product or service delivered to the customer. Co-ordinating the individual parts of the value chain together creates conditions to improve customer satisfaction, particularly in terms of cost efficiency, quality and delivery. A firm which performs the value chain activities more efficiently, and at a lower cost, than its competitors will gain competitive advantage.

The value chain was designed by Professor Michael Porter of the Harvard Business School (1985).

Porter's value chain

It is necessary to understand how value chain activities are performed and how they interact with each other. The activities are not just a collection of independent activities but a system of interdependent activities in which the performance of one activity affects the performance of other activities.

The activities which comprise the value chain are as follows:

Primary activities

These are the activities which involve the physical movement of raw materials and finished products, production of goods and services, marketing sales and subsequent services to outputs of a business unit.

1   Inbound logistics – which entail receiving, storing, materials handling, warehousing, inventory control, vehicle scheduling, returns to suppliers.

2   Operations – which entail transferring inputs into final product form (e.g. machining, packaging, assembly, equipment maintenance, testing, printing and facility operations).

3   Outbound logistics – which entail distributing the finished product (e.g. finished goods warehousing, material handling, operation of delivery vehicles, order processing and scheduling).

4   Marketing and sales – which entail inducing and facilitating buyers to purchase the product (e.g. advertising, activities of sales personnel, preparation of quotations, channel selection, channel relations, pricing of goods and services).

5   Service – which entails maintaining or enhancing the value of the product after the sale has taken place (installation, commissioning, repair, training, parts supply and product adjustment).

Support activities

Support activities are those activities that provide support to the primary activities, and also to each other.

1   Procurement – which entails purchasing of raw materials, consumable items and capital items.

2   Technology development – which entails the use of know-how, procedures to be applied and the technological inputs required in every activity which forms part of the value chain.

3   Human resource management – which entails the selection, retention and promotion of staff, the appraisal of staff and performance-rewards linkage, management development and employee relations.

4   Firm infrastructure – which entails general management, accounting and finance, quality management and planning activities.

Each activity within the value chain provides inputs, which after processing constitute added value to the output, which the customer ultimately receives in the form of a product or service or as the aggregate of values at the end of the value chain.

Each primary and support activity has the potential to contribute to the competitive advantage of the business unit by enabling it to produce, market and deliver products or services which meet or surpass the value expectations of purchasers in comparison with those resulting from other value chains.

Focusing on each of the nine activities enables management to see how each creates value that may be understood as the difference between cost and revenue.

According to Porter, an organisation can develop sustainable competitive advantage by following one of two strategies:

1   **Low-cost strategy**. Essentially this is a strategy of cost leadership, which involves achieving a lower cost than competitors via, for example, economies of scale and tight cost control.

2   **Differentiation strategy.** This involves creating something that customers perceive as being unique via brand loyalty, superior customer service, product design and features.

Shank and Govindarajan (1993) advocate that a company should evaluate its value chain relative to the value chains of its competitors or the industry. They suggest the following methodology:

1   Identify the industry's value chain and then assign costs, revenues and assets to the value activities. These activities are the building blocks with which firms in the industry created a product that buyers find valuable.

2   Diagnose the cost drivers regulating each value activity.

3   Develop sustainable cost advantage, either through controlling cost drivers better than competitors or by reconfiguring the chain value. By systematically analysing costs, revenues and assets in each activity, a firm can achieve low cost. This is achieved by comparing the firm's value chain with the value chains of a few major competitors, and identifying actions needed to manage the firm's value chain better than competitors manage their value chains.

Example 4: The Value chain

Which of the following is not considered a primary activity in the value chain developed by Michael Porter? Select ALL that apply:

- Sales

- Operations

- Outbound logistics

- Procurement

- Inbound logistics

- Human resources management

- Firm infrastructure management

- Technology development

8 Life-cycle costing

Life-cycle costing is the accumulation of costs for activities that occur over the entire life cycle of a product, from inception to abandonment.

Products and services, like human beings, have a life cycle. This is represented by the generic curve shown below:

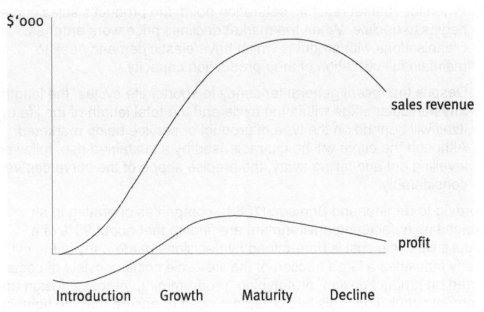

The length of the life cycle varies considerably from a year or so, for some children's toys, to hundreds of years, as in the case of binoculars, for example.

The product life cycle is divided into four basic stages as shown in the figure above; each stage has different aims and expectations.

The four stages in the life cycle are described below:

(i) **Introductory phase**

Demand will be low when a product is first launched onto the market, and heavy advertising expenditure will usually be required to bring it to consumers' attention. The aim is to establish the product in the market, which means achieving a certain critical mass within a certain period of time. The critical mass is the sales volume that must be achieved in order to make the product viable in the medium term.

(ii) **Growth**

Once the hurdle of the introductory stage has been successfully negotiated, the product enters the growth stage, where demand shows a steady and often rapid increase. The cost per unit falls because of economies of scale with the greater level of production. The aim at this stage is to establish a large market share and to perhaps become the market leader.

(iii) **Maturity**

The increase in demand slows down in this stage, as the product reaches the mass market. The sales curve flattens out and eventually begins to fall.

(iv) **Decline**

When the market reaches saturation point, the product's sales curve begins to decline. When the market declines price wars erupt as organisations with products which have elastic demand seek to maintain full utilisation of their production capacity.

Despite the recent general tendency to shorter life cycles, the length of any particular stage within the cycle and the total length of the life cycle itself will depend on the type of product or service being marketed. Although the curve will be characterised by a sustained rise, followed by levelling out and falling away, the precise shape of the curve can vary considerably.

According to Berliner and Brimson (1988), companies operating in an advanced manufacturing environment are finding that about 90% of a product's life-cycle cost is determined by decisions made early in the cycle. In many industries a large fraction of the life-cycle costs consists of costs incurred on product design, prototyping, programming, process design and equipment acquisition. This has created a need to ensure that the tightest controls are at the design stage, because most costs are committed or 'locked-in' at this point in time. Management accounting systems should therefore be developed that aid the planning and control of product life-cycle costs and monitor spending and commitments at the early stages of a product's life-cycle.

Product life-cycle costing

There are a number of factors that need to be managed in order to maximise a product's return over its life cycle. These are:

* design costs out of the product

* minimise the time to market

* maximise the length of the life cycle itself.

These factors will be considered in turn.

Design costs out of the product

It was stated earlier that between 80% and 90% of a product's costs were often incurred at the design and development stages of its life. That is decisions made then committed the organisation to incurring the costs at a later date, because the design of the product determines the number of components, the production method, etc. It is absolutely vital therefore that design teams do not work in isolation, but as part of a cross-functional team in order to minimise costs over the whole life cycle.

Minimise the time to market

In a world where competitors watch each other keenly to see what new products will be launched, it is vital to get any new product into the marketplace as quickly as possible. The competitors will monitor each other closely so that they can launch rival products as soon as possible in order to maintain profitability. It is vital, therefore, for the first organisation to launch its product as quickly as possible after the concept has been developed, so that it has as long as possible to establish the product in the market and to make a profit before competition increases. Often it is not so much costs that reduce profits as time wasted.

Maximise the length of the life cycle itself

Generally the longer the life cycle the greater the profit that will be generated, assuming that production ceases once the product goes into decline and becomes unprofitable. One way to maximise the life cycle is to get the product to market as quickly as possible because this should maximise the time in which the product generates a profit. Another way of extending a product's life is to find other uses, or markets, for the product. Other product uses may not be obvious when the product is still in its planning stage and need to be planned and managed later on. On the other hand, it may be possible to plan for a staggered entry into different markets at the planning stage.

Many organisations stagger the launch of their products in different world markets in order to reduce costs, increase revenue and prolong the overall life of the product. A current example is the way in which new films are released in the USA months before the UK launch. This is done to build up the enthusiasm for the film and to increase revenues overall. Other companies may not have the funds to launch worldwide at the same moment and may be forced to stagger it.

Skimming the market is another way to prolong life and to maximise the revenue over the product's life. This will be discussed in the pricing chapter.

Example 5: Life cycle costing

The following statements have been made about the benefits of lifecycle costing. Select ALL that apply:

- Its use may assist management in allocating resources to non-production activities.

- A company is in a strong position if all its products are at the same phase of the life cycle.

- Planning and design costs are not included when calculating the life cycle costs of a product.

- Lower costs can be achieved earlier by designing out costs.

Example 6: Company B

Company B is about to begin developing a new product for launch in its existing market. They have forecast sales of 20,000 units and the marketing department suggest a selling price of $43/unit. The company seeks to make a mark-up of 40% product cost. It is estimated that the lifetime costs of the product will be as follows:

1 Design and development costs $43,000

2 Manufacturing costs $15/unit

3 Plant decommissioning costs $30,000

The company estimates that if it were to spend an additional $15,000 on design, manufacturing costs/unit could be reduced.

What is the life cycle cost?

A $18.65

B $22

C $22.87

D $24

Customer life cycle costing

Not all investment decisions involve large initial capital outflows or the purchase of physical assets. The decision to serve and retain customers can also be a capital budgeting decision even though the initial outlay may be small. For example a credit card company or an insurance company will have to choose which customers they take on and then register them on the company's records. The company incurs initial costs due to the paperwork, checking creditworthiness, opening policies, etc. for new customers. It takes some time before these initial costs are recouped. Research has also shown that the longer a customer stays with the company the more profitable that customer becomes to the company.

Thus it becomes important to retain customers, whether by good service, discounts, other benefits, etc. A customer's 'life' can be discounted and decisions made as to the value of, say, a 'five-year-old' customer. Eventually a point arises where profit no longer continues to grow; this plateau is reached between about five years and 20 years depending on the nature of the business. Therefore by studying the increased revenue and decreased costs generated by an 'old' customer, management can find strategies to meet their needs better and to retain them.

Many manufacturing companies only supply a small number of customers, say between six and ten, and so they can cost customers relatively easily. Other companies such as banks and supermarkets have many customers and cannot easily analyse every single customer. In this case similar customers are grouped together to form category types and these can then be analysed in terms of profitability.

For example, the UK banks analyse customers in terms of fruits, such as oranges, lemons, plums, etc. Customers tend to move from one category to another as they age and as their financial habits change. Customers with large mortgages, for example, are more valuable to the bank than customers who do not have a large income and do not borrow money. Banks are not keen on keeping the latter type of customer.

The life cycle cost budget

The application of life cycle costing requires the establishment of a life cycle cost budget for a given product which in turn necessitates identification of costs with particular products. Actual costs incurred in respect of the product are then monitored against life cycle budget costs.

A company is in a weak position if all its products are at the same phase of the life cycle. If they are all in the growth phase there are problems ahead; if they are all in one of the other phases there are immediate difficulties.

Companies try to overcome this problem by introducing new products that are growing as the old products are declining and by having products with life cycles of different lengths.

In applying life cycle costing a supplier will recognise that the life of the product commences prior to its introduction to the marketplace. Indeed up to 90% of costs result from decisions made prior to its 'launch' concerning issues such as functions, materials, components and manufacturing methods to be adopted.

Life cycle costs may be classified as follows:

* development costs

* design costs

* manufacturing costs

* marketing costs, and

* distribution costs.

A pattern of costs will emerge over the life cycle of the product. Invariably the absolute level of costs will rise and this trend should 'track' the pattern of sales of the product. The supplier will always be monitoring relevant costs and revenues in an attempt to ensure that the rise in resultant sales revenues is greater than the rise in the attributable costs of the product.

Moreover, the supplier will expect reductions to occur in the unit cost of a product as a consequence of economies of scale and learning and experience curves. In order to maximise the profits earned by a product over its life cycle management need to give consideration to minimising the time required to get the product to the marketplace. This may enable an organisation to 'steal a march' on its competitors who will invariably attempt to launch a rival product at the earliest available opportunity. Hence 'time to market' assumes critical significance since it affords an organisation that is first to the marketplace with an opportunity to make profits prior to arrival of competitor products.

Once the product has reached the marketplace management attention should be focused upon maximising the length of the product's life cycle. In this regard 'time to market' is also critical since by definition the earlier a product reaches the marketplace the longer will be its resultant life cycle.

Management should always be searching for other potential uses of the product and/or finding alternative markets for the product. Whilst it may be difficult to envisage other potential uses for product at the planning stage it may be possible for an organisation to draw up a plan which involves the staggered entry of the product into geographically separate markets with the resultant effect of increasing the overall life cycle of the product. A major benefit of this staggered approach which is often adopted by global players lies in the fact that the income streams from one market may be used to fund the launch of the product into another market.

The application of life cycle costing requires management to consider whether the anticipated cost savings that were expected to be achieved via the application of cost reduction techniques, both prior to and following the product's introduction, have actually been achieved. Its use may also assist management in allocating resources to non-production activities. For example, a product which is in the mature stage may require less marketing support than a product which is in the growth stage.

Asset lifecycle costing (The CGMA Cost Management Model)

For the user of an asset, the initial purchase price may only be part of the ownership cost. Other costs of operating the asset over its life may even dwarf the initial purchase price. These could include: maintenance; repair; downtime; energy consumption; consumables consumption; and environmental costs – such as emissions treatment, or compliant or safe material storage or disposal.

The management accountant should ensure they are aware of all the costs associated with safe and compliant acquisition, operation, asset disposal and associated processes – and incorporate these factors into the buying decision-making. Since ownership costs can vary between rival products at different stages of asset lives, the total ownership costs should be compared on a discounted cash flow basis.

Actions to take/Do's

Involve people from all relevant functions in product development decision making.

- Encourage a whole-life product profitability mindset among multidisciplinary teams.

- Take the customer perspective – minimise the total cost of ownership, not just the acquisition cost.

- Consider the consumption and transformation of natural capital in creating products and managing product portfolios – not just the financial costs.

- Think about the societal impact of product development and management, and asset acquisition, operation and disposal.

Actions to avoid/Don'ts

Avoid rushing development to be fast to market – 80% of costs are locked in at the design phase.

- Avoid treating natural capital as costless.

9   Practice Questions

Objective Test Question 1: Target costing

The selling price of product Z is set at $250 for each unit and sales for the coming year are expected to be 500 units.

If the company requires a return of 15% in the coming year on its investment of $250,000 in product Z, the target cost for each unit for the coming year is:

A $145

B $155

C $165

D $175

E $185

Objective Test Question 2: Value analysis

Casabee was established in 2010 and manufactures a range of kitchen utensils, which it makes from material purchased from a number of suppliers. The recently appointed Managing Director has expressed increasing concern about the trends in falling sales volumes, rising costs and hence declining profits over the last two years.

There is general agreement amongst the managers of Casabee that these trends are the result of the increased intense competition that has emerged over the last two years. Casabee continues to have a reputation for high quality, but this quality is now being matched by the competition.

The competitors are taking Casabee's share of the market by selling equivalent products at lower prices. It is thought that in order to offer such low prices, the production costs of the competitors must be lower than Casabee's. Its MD is now proposing the following to improve sales volumes, costs sand profits:

(i)   We must enter a Value Analysis exercise. Value Analysis is a cost reduction and problem solving technique that analyses an existing product, in order to identify and reduce or eliminate any costs which do not contribute to value or performance.

(ii)   We must enter a Value Analysis exercise. Value Analysis focuses on the value to the customer of each function of the product, and consequently allocates resources to those functions from which the customer gains the most value.

(iii) We also must enter a Functional Cost Analysis exercise. Functional cost analysis is a method that can be applied to examine the component costs of a product or service, in relation to the value as perceived by the customer. Functional cost analysis can be applied to new products, and breaks the product down into its component parts. For example, a kitchen utensil may have the function to be dishwasher- and microwave-safe, and therefore require less manual cleaning.

(iv) Both value analysis and functional cost analysis have potential to help Casabee, but Value Analysis is likely to be a more useful technique, because kitchen utensils are products that are sold more on the basis of their use value, rather than their esteem value.

Which of the foregoing arguments are valid?

A   (i), (iii) and (iv)

B   (i), (ii), (iii) and (iv)

C   (i) and (iii)

D   (ii) and (iv)

Objective Test Question 3: Life cycle costing

A company has carried out extensive product research and, as a result, has just launched a new innovative product unlike anything else that is currently available on the market. The company has launched this product using a market skimming pricing policy, i.e. charging very high prices initially.

The market in which it operates is highly competitive and historically success has been achieved by being the first to market with new products. Only a small number of companies have survived in the market, and those that remain are constantly aiming to develop new products either by improving those already in the market, or by extensive product research.

Select ALL that apply:

- In the introduction stage, the product is unique and therefore the company can charge a high price.

- In the introduction stage, competitors will buy the product to carry out reverse engineering and see how the product works, so that they can develop their own similar, but different product.

- In the introduction phase, the company will seek to avoid this competition by maintaining its selling price at the end of the introduction stage.

- In the growth stage, the company will adopt a lower selling price to continue to attract new purchasers of the product.

- In the growth stage, if the product cannot be differentiated in other ways, the company may need further reductions in selling price to maintain growth.

- The growth stage is the ideal time to offer short term one-off offers or discounts for multiple purchases.

- In the maturity stage, the selling price of the product becomes unstable and the product is not financially viable anymore.

- In the decline stage, the product may continue to be sold, provided its margin is positive.

- If the product's margin is not positive in the decline phase, the product may be bundled with other products or sold for less than its unit cost in order to clear the company's inventory of what has become an obsolete product.

Data Set Question: Target costing and cost gap

Company S is a specialist car manufacturer and intends to produce a new, limited edition 'Compact Executive' car in 2016. The car will be called the S2016. The production will be limited to 1,000 units of the S2016 car.

Company S is considering using a target costing approach and has conducted market research to determine the features that consumers require in a car of that type. Based on this market research and knowledge of competitors products, Company S has decided to price the S2016 at $19,950. Company S requires an operating profit margin of 25% of the selling price of the car. Company S uses activity-based costing principles to assign overhead costs to units of production, and details for the forthcoming year are as follows:

Forecast direct costs for a S2016 car: Labour $5,000, Material $9,500.

Forecast annual overhead costs: Production line costs $4,630,000 (see note 1) and transportation costs $1,800,000 (see note 2).

Note 1: The production line that would be used for S2016 has a capacity of 60,000 machine hours per year. The production line time required for one S2016 is 6 machine hours per car. This production line will also be used to make other cars and will be working at full capacity.

Note 2: Some models of cars are delivered to showrooms using car transporters. 40% of the transportation costs are related to the distance travelled.

The car transporters are forecast to make a total of 640 deliveries in the year, and carry 10 cars each time. The car transporter will always carry its maximum capacity of 10 cars.

The total annual distance travelled by car transporters is expected to be 225,000 kms. 50,000 kms of this is for the delivery of the S2016 only. All 1,000 S2016 cars that will be produced will be delivered in the year using the car transporters.

Task: Calculate the following:

The production line cost per S2016 car

The transportation cost per S2016 car

The total overhead cost per S2016 car

The full product cost for a S2016 car (forecast)

The target cost of a S2016 car

The current cost gap for a S2016 car

Case Study Style Question – Jord Homes

Formed in 1966, Jord Homes (Jord) quickly gained a reputation for the construction of high-quality, prefabricated timber-framed houses in its home country of Corvola. Under the leadership of the founder, Karl Larsson, this reputation continued to grow with Jord successfully completing over 30 houses by 1970. The success continued and resulted in the need to build a factory in 1980, where the manufacturing facilities, showroom and head office are all still currently based.

Some shareholders have suggested it is time to grow the business in other directions.

You receive an email from the finance director:

To: Finance Manager
From: Carla Holm
Date: Today
Subject: Budget housing project

Hi,
As you know, we are looking at expanding into the budget housing market. Our aim will be to provide high quality prefabricated housing at a price affordable enough to become market leader in this market.

This obviously comes with some significant changes to the way that we currently operate in the high end market.
I'd like our project team to consider the use of target costing and value analysis to help determine the scope of what we may be able to build to fit with our project aim.

Could you put some notes together covering the principles behind target costing, why it would be useful for this project and how we could apply it?

Thanks,
Carla

Prepare a response to Carla's email.

Answers to examples and objective test questions

Example 1: Target Costing

The correct answer is B.

Sales revenue = 5,000 units @$52.00	$260,000
Return on investment required = $1,000,000 × 12%	$120,000
Total cost allowed	$140,000
Target cost per unit = $140,000/5,000	$28

Example 2: Target Costing and the cost gap

The maximum rate per hour is $12.40

	$
Selling price	56.00
Profit (56 × 25/125)	11.20
Target cost	44.80
Material cost (16 × 10/8)	20.00
Labour – 2 hours	24.80
Labour rate per hour = 24.80/2	$12.40

Example 3: Reducing the cost gap

D

Answer A is not correct: increasing the selling price is not possible, the industry is competitive so product will not sell effectively at higher prices.

Answer B ('Reduce the expectation gap by reducing the selling price') is not target costing.

Answer C ('Reducing the desired margin on the product') is not possible either: shareholders are demanding, and would expect a good return.

Example 4: The Value Chain

- Procurement is not a primary activity and neither are human resource management, firm infrastructure management or technology development.

Example 5: Life cycle costing

- Its use may assist management in allocating resources to non-production activities. **TRUE** (lifecycle costing may assist management in allocating resources to non-production activities. For example, a product which is in the mature stage may require less marketing support than a product which is in the growth stage.)

- A company is in a strong position if all its products are at the same phase of the life cycle. **FALSE** (A company is in a weak position if all its products are at the same phase of the life cycle. Companies try to overcome this problem by introducing new products that are growing, as the old products are declining and by having products with life cycle of different lengths.

- Planning and design costs are not included when calculating the life cycle costs of a product. **FALSE**

- Lower costs can be achieved earlier by designing out costs. **TRUE**

Example 6: Company B

Answer: A

The original life cycle cost per unit = ($43,000 + (20,000 × $15) + $30,000)/20,000 = $18.65

Objective Test Question 1: Target costing

Answer: D

	$
Sales revenue 500 units @ $250	125,000
Return on invst. required 15% × 250,000	37,500
Total cost allowed	87,500
Target cost per unit	175

Objective Test Question 2: Value analysis

A

(ii) defines Functional Cost Analysis.

Objective Test Question 3: Life cycle costing

- In the introduction stage, the product is unique and therefore the company can charge a high price. **TRUE**

- In the introduction stage, competitors will buy the product to carry out reverse engineering and see how the product works, so that they can develop their own similar, but different product. **TRUE**

- In the introduction phase, the company will seek to avoid this competition by maintaining its selling price at the end of the introduction stage. **FALSE**: the company will seek to avoid this competition by lowering it selling price towards the end of the introduction stage, to deter competitors from entering the market and also to make its product more affordable to the wider market.

- In the growth stage, the company will adopt a lower selling price to continue to attract new purchasers of the product. **TRUE**

- In the growth stage, if the product cannot be differentiated in other ways, the company may need further reductions in selling price to maintain growth. **TRUE**

- The growth stage is the ideal time to offer short term one-off offers or discounts for multiple purchases. **FALSE**: the maturity stage is the ideal time for this.

- In the maturity stage, the selling price of the product becomes unstable and the product is not financially viable anymore. **FALSE**

- In the decline stage, the product may continue to be sold, provided its margin is positive. **TRUE**

- If the product's margin is not positive in the decline phase, the product may be bundled with other products or sold for less than its unit cost in order to clear the company's inventory of what has become an obsolete product. **TRUE**

Data Set Question: Target costing and cost gap

The production line cost per S2016 car	$463
The transportation cost per S2016 car	$328.75
The total overhead cost per S2016 car	$791.75
The full product cost for a S2016 car (forecast)	$15,291.75
The target cost of a S2016 car	$14,962.50
The current cost gap for a S2016 car	$329.50

Workings:

$4,630,000/60,000 annual production line machine hours = $77.17 per machine hour, $77.17 × 6 machine hours for a S2016 = $463

Transportation cost

60% delivery related = $1,080,000

40% distance travelled related = $720,000

$1,080,000/640 deliveries = $1,687.50 per delivery

$1,687.5/10 cars = $168.75 per car

$720,000/225,000km = $3.20 per km travelled

$3.20 × 50,000km = $160,000

$160,000/1,000 cars = $160 per car

Target selling price $19,950

Profit margin 25% Target cost $14,962.50

Forecast cost $15,291.75

Cost gap $329.25

Case Study Style Question – Jord Homes

To: Carla Holm, Financial Director

From: Management Accountant

Date: 21 November 2014

Subject: Target Costing – Briefing note

Target costing principles

Target costing is a proactive cost control method that can be used to ensure that a product should be feasible in terms of revenues, costs and profits in the market it is aimed at.

The principles behind its use are that the company would initially decide on the level of specification of the product it wishes to launch into the market.

It would then determine a market-based price for the product.

Based on the desired margin for the product it will then calculate a target cost – the maximum affordable cost given the price and margin required.

This target cost is then compared to the expected cost of producing the product. If the target cost is equal to or higher than the expected cost, the product is feasible.

If the target cost is lower than the expected cost, the company would not be able to produce the product and gain the margin that it desires. In this case, the difference is known as a cost gap and the company should aim to use cost reduction techniques, such as value analysis, to see if the expected cost can be reduced below the target cost and production can be made feasible.

Target costing usefulness

Target costing would also allow us to determine anticipated prices and margins for the project, as well as to bring our focus onto the exact specification of house that we wish to bring to the market.

It would be particularly useful for this project as it is almost inevitable that our current production processes, which are tailored to produce very high specification houses, would lead to product costs that are not low enough to fit into a budget production model.

Use of target costing would give us a figure to work towards in terms of reducing the anticipated build costs to a level that makes the project feasible, forcing us to think about adaptations to our procurement and production processes to make this happen.

Target costing application to project

To start the target costing process off, we should initially determine a level of specification for the budget houses that would put us into the appropriate market segment. This may mean looking at the specifications offered by other suppliers of budget housing and tweaking them to place us at the high end of that specification to fit with our project aim.

Having done this, we can look at existing suppliers to see what prices they are able to charge for such houses. We need to ensure that we set a price that is comparable to other players in the market, that is at the top end to reflect the high quality level we seek to offer, but that doesn't price us out of the budget market completely.

We then need to determine the margin that we would like to earn on this type of housing. This will be a decision for the board, who should realise that it is unlikely that we would be able to make the same margins in this market as with our premium offerings. The determination of the margin required will be one of the key factors in whether production of budget housing can be made feasible or not. Deducting the margin from the sales price will produce the target cost.

The anticipated build costs should then be determined. We need to bear in mind the market that we are aiming at and aim to use cheaper, lower quality materials and as much automation as possible, perhaps by making the design less bespoke, in order to keep the costs down to a minimum.

When the comparison is made between anticipated cost and target cost, we will know if there is a cost gap or not. If there is, we should look for other ways to reduce costs. If the cost gap cannot be closed, we should consider reducing the target margin.

AN Accountant

Management Accountant X Ltd

Data required for decision-making

Chapter learning objective

Lead	Component
B1: Capital investment decision making	Apply the data required for decision making (a) Relevant cash flows (b) Non-financial information

1 Chapter summary

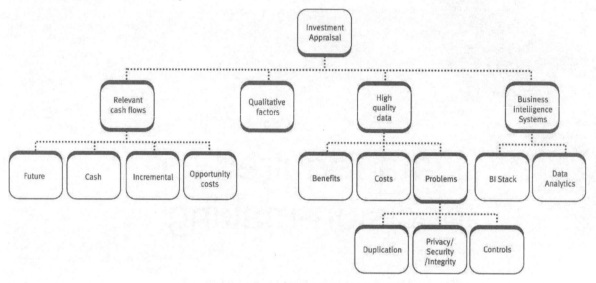

Capital investment decisions normally represent the most important decisions that an organisation makes, since they commit a substantial proportion of a firm's resources to actions that are likely to be irreversible. Many different investment projects exist including the replacement of assets, cost-reduction schemes, new product/service developments, product/service expansions, etc.

Each of these decisions is based on relevant costing principles. Therefore, a recap of relevant costing will be useful.

The quality of decisions depends on the quality and type of data available to decision makers. In a digital world, data needed by medium-term decision makers would come from data lakes, through to data warehouses and business intelligence systems.

2 Relevant cash flows

Investment decisions, like all other decisions, should be analysed in terms of the cash flows that can be directly attributable to them.

Relevant costs are those which will be affected by the decision being taken. All relevant costs should be considered in management decision-making.

A relevant cash flow is a 'future, incremental cash flow'.

- **Future**

    Only future cash flows that occur as a result of the decision should be considered, e.g. any future costs or revenue.

    Sunk costs (i.e. costs that have already been incurred in the past) are not relevant to the decision, and should therefore be ignored – we cannot change the past.

- **Incremental**

  Only extra cash flows that occur as a result of the decision should be considered, e.g. extra costs or revenues.

  Fixed costs should be ignored unless there is an incremental fixed cost as a result of the decision.

  Committed costs (i.e. costs that are unavoidable in the future) are not affected by the decision and should therefore be ignored.

  Opportunity costs should be included when we are aware of the next best alternative use of a resource.

- **Cash flows**

  Only cash items are relevant to the decision. For example, depreciation is never relevant, since it is not a cash flow.

Example 1: Butte Ltd

As part of a new product development, Butte Ltd has employed a building consultant to perform an initial survey. This initial survey has cost $40,000. But there will be an ongoing need for her services if the company decides to proceed with the project. This work will be charged at a fixed rate of $20,000 per annum.

What relevant cost should be included for the building consultants services in the first year when considering whether the project should proceed?

A $0

B $20,000

C $40,000

D $60,000

Example 2: Relevant costs

Identify which of the following costs are relevant to the decisions specified:

(a) The salary to be paid to a market researcher who will oversee the development of a new product. This is a new post to be created especially for the new product but the $12,000 salary will be a fixed cost.

Is this cost relevant to the decision to proceed with the development of the product?

> (b) The $2,500 additional monthly running costs of a new machine to be purchased to manufacture an established product. Since the new machine will save on labour time, the fixed overhead to be absorbed by the product will reduce by $100 per month.
>
> Are these costs relevant to the decision to purchase the new machine?
>
> (c) Office cleaning expenses of $125 for next month. The office is cleaned by contractors and the contract can be cancelled by giving one month's notice.
>
> Is this cost relevant to a decision to close the office?
>
> (d) Expenses of $75 paid to the marketing manager. This was to reimburse the manager for the cost of travelling to meet a client with whom the company is currently negotiating a major contract.
>
> Is this cost relevant to the decision to continue negotiations?

3 Opportunity costs

Opportunity costs are relevant, and should be included in investment decisions.

An opportunity cost is a special type of relevant cost. An opportunity cost can be defined as 'the value of the benefit sacrificed when one course of action is chosen in preference to an alternative. The opportunity cost is represented by the foregone potential benefit from the best rejected course of action' (CIMA Official Terminology).

With opportunity costs, we are concerned with identifying the value of any benefit forgone as the result of choosing one course of action in preference to another.

Examples of opportunity costs

The best way to demonstrate opportunity costs is to consider some examples.

(a) A company has some obsolete material in stock that it is considering to use for a special contract. If the material is not used on the contract it can either be sold back to the supplier for $2 per tonne or it can be used on another contract in place of a different material that would usually cost $2.20 per tonne.

The opportunity cost of using the material on the special contract is $2.20 per tonne. This is the value of the next best alternative use for the material, or the benefit forgone by not using it for the other contract.

(b) Chris is deciding whether or not to take a skiing holiday this year. The travel agent is quoting an all-inclusive holiday cost of $675 for a week. Chris will lose the chance to earn $200 for a part-time job during the week that the holiday would be taken.

The relevant cost of taking the holiday is $875. This is made up of the out-of-pocket cost of $675, plus the $200 opportunity cost, that is the part-time wages forgone.

Notional costs and opportunity costs

Notional costs and opportunity costs are often similar. This is particularly noticeable in the case of notional rent. The notional rent could be the rental that the company is forgoing by occupying the premises itself. This could be treated as an opportunity cost. However, it is only a true opportunity cost if the company can actually identify a forgone opportunity to rent the premises. If nobody is willing to pay the rent, then it is not an opportunity cost.

If an examination question on relevant costs includes information about notional costs, read the question carefully and state your assumptions concerning the relevance of the notional cost.

4 Avoidable, differential and incremental costs

There are two other types of relevant cost that you will need to know about: avoidable costs and differential/incremental costs.

Avoidable costs

CIMA defines avoidable costs as 'the specific costs of an activity or sector of a business which would be avoided if that activity or sector did not exist'.

For example, if a company is considering shutting down a department, then the avoidable costs are those that would be saved as a result of the shutdown. Such costs might include the labour costs of those employed in the department and the rental cost of the space occupied by the department. The latter is an example of an attributable or specific fixed cost. Costs such as apportioned head office costs that would not be saved as a result of the shutdown are unavoidable costs. They are not relevant to the decision.

Differential/incremental costs

CIMA defines a differential/incremental cost as 'the difference in total cost between alternatives. This is calculated to assist decision making'.

For example, if the relevant cost of contract X is $5,700 and the relevant cost of contract Y is $6,200, we would say that the differential or incremental cost is $500, that is the extra cost of contract Y is $500.

Non-relevant costs

If a cost will remain unaltered regardless of the decision being taken, then it is called a non-relevant cost or irrelevant cost.

Costs that are not usually relevant in management decisions include the following:

(a) Sunk or past costs. This is a 'cost that has been irreversibly incurred or committed and cannot therefore be considered relevant to a decision. Sunk costs may also be termed irrecoverable costs' (CIMA Official Terminology). An example of a sunk cost is expenditure that has been incurred in developing a new product. The money cannot be recovered even if a decision is taken to abandon further development of the new product. The cost is therefore not relevant to future decisions concerning the product.

(b) Absorbed fixed overheads that will not increase or decrease as a result of the decision being taken. The amount of overhead to be absorbed by a particular cost unit might alter because of the decision; however, this is a result of the company's cost accounting procedures for overheads. If the actual amount of overhead incurred by the company will not alter, then the overhead is not a relevant cost.

(c) Expenditure that will be incurred in the future, but as a result of decisions taken in the past that cannot now be changed. These are known as committed costs. They can sometimes cause confusion because they are future costs. However, a committed cost will be incurred regardless of the decision being taken and therefore it is not relevant. An example of this type of cost could be expenditure on special packaging for a new product, where the packaging has been ordered and delivered but not yet paid for. The company is obliged to pay for the packaging even if they decide not to proceed with the product; therefore it is not a relevant cost.

(d) Historical cost depreciation. Depreciation is an accounting adjustment but does not result in any future cash flows. They are merely the book entries that are designed to spread the original cost of an asset over its useful life.

(e) Notional costs such as notional rent and notional interest. These are only relevant if they represent an identified lost opportunity to use the premises or the finance for some alternative purpose. In these circumstances, the notional costs would be opportunity costs.

Conclusion

It is essential to look to the future when deciding which costs are relevant to a decision. Costs that have already been incurred, or that will not be altered in the future as a result of the decision being taken, are not relevant costs.

5 Incremental revenues

Just as incremental costs are the differences in cost between alternatives, incremental revenues are the differences in revenues between the alternatives. Matching the incremental costs against the incremental revenue will produce a figure for the incremental gain or loss between the alternatives.

Cash flows to include

The cash flows that should be included are those which are specifically incurred as a result of the acceptance or non-acceptance of the project. In some cases, these may be opportunity costs.

When deciding what figure should be included in any decision making situation, it sometimes helps to tabulate for a particular element of cost.

Cash flow if project   –   Cash flow if project   =   Relevant cash flow
accepted   rejected

Example 3: Calaveras Ltd

Activity 1

A mining operation uses skilled labour costing $4 per hour, which generates a contribution, after deducting these labour costs, of $3 per hour.

A new project is now being considered that requires 5,000 hours of skilled labour. There is a shortage of the required labour. Any used on the new project must be transferred from normal working. Calculate the relevant cost of using the skilled labour on the project. Calculate the contribution cash flow that is lost if the labour is transferred from normal working.

Activity 2

Suppose the facts about labour are as above, but there is a surplus of skilled labour already employed (and paid) by the business which is sufficient to cope with the new project. The presently idle men are being paid full wages.

Calculate the contribution cash flow that is lost if the labour is transferred to the project from doing nothing.

6   Qualitative factors

In reality, investment decisions are also influenced by many qualitative factors that must also be borne in mind in the investment appraisal exercise.

Illustration – qualitative factors

Consider the typical example of the proposed purchase of a new machine in a manufacturing plant. The machine offers both quantitative and qualitative costs and benefits, as below.

Quantitative costs include:

* the purchase price of the machine

* installation and training costs.

Quantitative benefits include:

* lower direct labour costs

* lower scrap costs and items requiring rework

* lower stock costs.

> **Qualitative costs include:**
>
> - increased noise level
>
> - lower morale if existing staff have to be made redundant.
>
> **Qualitative benefits include:**
>
> - reduction in product development time
>
> - improved product quality and service
>
> - increase in manufacturing flexibility.

Because the qualitative factors are difficult to state in numerical terms, they are conventionally ignored in the investment appraisal exercise. Such an approach is flawed: qualitative factors that could additionally be brought into the decision need to be pointed out.

7 Sources of management information

Data are facts or figures in a raw, unprocessed format. **Data** consists of numbers, letters, symbols, raw facts, events and transactions, which have been recorded but not yet processed into a form that is suitable for making decisions.

To become useful to a decision maker, data must be transformed into **information**.

Information is data that has been processed in such a way that it has a meaning to the person who receives it. This person may then use this information to improve the quality of decision-making.

Types of information

Internal information	External information
Examples include: - accounting records - personnel and payroll information - timesheets - production information.	Examples include: - competitor information, e.g. prices and product ranges - customer information, e.g. with regards to their needs - supplier information, e.g. prices, quality, delivery terms.

Internal sources

Internal sources of information may be taken from a variety of areas such as the sales ledger (e.g. volume of sales), payroll system (e.g. number of employees) or the fixed asset system (e.g. depreciation method and rate).

Examples of internal data:

Source	Information
Sales ledger system	Number and value of invoices
	Volume of sales
	Value of sales, analysed by customer
	Value of sales, analysed by product
Purchase ledger system	Number and value of invoices
	Value of purchases, analysed by supplier
Payroll system	Number of employees
	Hours worked
	Output achieved
	Wages earned
	Tax deducted
Fixed asset system	Date of purchase
	Initial cost
	Location
	Depreciation method and rate
	Service history
	Production capacity
Production	Machine breakdown times
	Number of rejected units
Sales and marketing	Types of customer
	Market research results

External sources

In addition to internal information sources, there is much information to be obtained from external sources such as suppliers (e.g. product prices), customers (e.g. price sensitivity) and the government (e.g. inflation rate).

External source	Information
Suppliers	Product prices
	Product specifications
Newspapers, journals	Share price
	Information on competitors
	Technological developments
	National and market surveys

Government	Industry statistics
	Taxation policy
	Inflation rates
	Demographic statistics
	Forecasts for economic growth
Customers	Product requirements
	Price sensitivity
Employees	Wage demands
	Working conditions
Banks	Information on potential customers
	Information on national markets
Business enquiry agents	Information on competitors
	Information on customers
Internet	Almost everything via databases (public and private), discussion groups and mailing lists

The internal and external information may be used in **planning** and **controlling** activities. For example:

- Newspapers, the Internet and business enquiry agents (such as Dun and Bradstreet) may be used to obtain external competitor information for benchmarking purposes.

- Internal sales volumes may be obtained for variance analysis purposes.

Example 4: Externally generated information

What are the limitations of using externally generated information?

8 Collecting, analysing and presenting high quality data

The quality of management information expected by business users is expanding both in terms of the range of data to be considered, and the level of analysis required. There is an increased demand for information at all levels.

From strategic issues to routine tasks, executives, managers, information workers and staff all expect more information and clearer insights to support decision making. Financial information alone does not suffice. Management information must relate financial to non-financial data and not just report past performance, but also monitor the current operations and help to predict the future.

Benefits

One key challenge is to extract knowledge from information. Organisations turn to technology for help and rely on IT to improve the quality of decision making by getting them the right information at the right time. IT is now regarded as a source of competitive advantage, rather than simply as a driver of cost-efficiency.

Collecting, analysing and presenting high quality data presents the following benefits to the business:

- **Collaborative working**

  Whether managing a remote workforce, running a globalised R&D project or working with customers to design a solution, the organisation will be more dependent on the flow of data between different locations inside and outside the boundaries of the organisations. 'The better we are connected to our customers and suppliers, the better off we will all be,' says Terry Assink, CIO at Kimberly-Clark Corp, a health-and-hygiene company.

- **Customer insight**

  Identifying changes in customer behaviour is often cited as the most significant challenge to product and service innovation faced by organisations. A greater understanding of customers' business or personal needs is similarly essential to the personalisation of products and services. Inventory management will be more responsive, too – many businesses expect demand, not supply, to drive the production of goods and services in the future. Companies employ data analytics to address these challenges, and the quality of feeder data is key.

- **Risk management**

  Businesses must prepare all manner of emergency plans, such as data backup and recovery.

- **Governance**

  Shareholders, managers and board members demand more transparency than ever. Significant due diligence processes are regularly established. The quality of corporate governance is increasingly a source of differentiation in its own right, with a noted correlation between brand value and good governance.

Costs

The collection, analysis and presentation of high quality data often brings the following costs to the business:

- **Software licenses costs** – the cost of initially acquiring and deploying the software

- **Software maintenance costs** – annual charges

- **IT training costs** – the cost of training IT personnel to manage and maintain the software and infrastructure
- **User training costs** – the cost of training users to use the software
- **Integration costs** – the cost of making multiple products work together
- **Redundant infrastructure costs** – the cost of managing and maintaining multiple data stores, metadata repositories and other components.

9 Problems associated with collecting, analysing and presenting high quality data

Duplication

Systems such as Enterprise Resource Planning (ERP) systems have done much to improve processes and rationalise operational data, but information still gets duplicated and copied on to multiple systems, making it difficult to ensure consistency and security. Finance, sales and operations reports rarely agree. Even when the data comes from the same ERP source, the reports may not reconcile because of the extraction process.

Privacy, integrity and security concerns

IS are exposed to privacy and security issues. Risks can be listed as follows:

Potential threat	Solution
Natural disasters – e.g. fire, flood.	<ul><li>Fire procedures – fire alarms, extinguishers, fire doors, staff training and insurance cover.</li><li>Location, e.g. not in a basement area liable to flooding.</li><li>Physical environment – e.g. air conditioning, dust controls.</li><li>Back up procedures – data should be backed up on a regular basis to allow recovery.</li></ul>
Malfunction – of computer hardware or software.	<ul><li>Network design – to cope with periods of high volumes.</li><li>Back up procedures (as above).</li></ul>

Viruses – a small program that once introduced into the system spreads extensively. Can affect the whole computer system.	• Anti-virus software – should be run and updated regularly to prevent corruption of the system by viruses. • Formal security policy and procedures, e.g. employees should only download files or open attachments from reputed sources. • Regular audits to check for unauthorised software.
Hackers – deliberate access to systems by unauthorised persons.	• Firewall software – should provide protection from unauthorised access to the system from the Internet. • Passwords and user names – limit unauthorised access to the system. • Formal security policy and procedures, e.g. organisations that allow employees to use personal devices at work should ensure that there is a policy for device usage and that technology is used to prevent hackers. • User awareness training of the risks should be available. • Data encryption – data is scrambled prior to transmission and is recovered in a readable format once transmission is complete.
Electronic eavesdropping – e.g. users accessing private information not intended for them.	• Data encryption – As above, data is scrambled prior to transmission and is recovered in a readable format once transmission is complete. • Passwords and user names (as above).
Human errors – unintentional errors from using computers and networks.	• Training – adequate staff training and operating procedures.
Human resource risk – e.g. repetitive strain injury (RSI), headaches and eye strain from computer screens, tripping over loose wires.	• Ergonomic design of workstations should reduce problems such as RSI. • Anti-glare screens reduce eye strain. • Cables should be in ducts.

Illustration 1 – Virus infection in the NHS

In 2017, the NHS (National Health Service) faced a week of chaos after hackers demanding a ransom infiltrated the health service's computer system.

Operations and appointments were cancelled and ambulances diverted as up to 40 hospital trusts became infected by a ransomware (malicious software) attack demanding payments to regain access to vital medical records.

The attack was part of the biggest ransomware attack in history with 57,000 infections in 99 countries being observed.

Controls

There are two forms of IT/IS controls that exist to safeguard the privacy and security of data as well as ensuring complete and accurate processing of data:

General controls – ensure that the organisation has overall control over its information systems, e.g.:

- Personnel controls – includes segregation of duties, policy on usage, hierarchy of access.

- Access controls – such as passwords and time lock-outs.

- Computer equipment controls – to protect equipment from destruction, damage or theft.

- Business continuity planning – a risk assessment to decide which systems are critical to the business continuing its activities.

Application or program controls – performed automatically by the system and include:

- Completeness checks to ensure all data is processed.

- Validity checks to ensure only valid data is input/processed.

- Identification and authorisation checks to ensure users are identified and authorised.

- Problem management facilities to ensure problems are recorded/managed on a timely basis.

Example 5: Integrity and security

Data integrity and security is a particular issue in a database. For data to have integrity, it must be accurate, consistent and free from accidental corruption.

Required:

What controls are required in a database to ensure that data integrity and security are maintained?

In recent years, specialist software houses have developed performance management applications to address the shortcomings of the accounting modules offered by the major ERP vendors. These are better than ERP systems for performing activities such as consolidation, budgets and reforecasts.

Some can also deliver insightful management information directly to managers' desks. They can be used by business users to view scorecards or dashboards, generate their own reports, drill down for more information or conduct analysis. They are a form of business intelligence (BI) application.

10 Business intelligence systems

The term business intelligence ('BI') is often used to describe the technical architecture of systems that extract, assemble, store and access data to provide reports and analysis.

'Business Intelligence' is also used to describe the reporting and analysis applications or performance management tools associated with that architecture.

Illustration 2 – Walmart

It is widely reported that Walmart (Asda) tracks data on over 60% of adults in the US. Data gathered includes online and instore purchasing pattern, Twitter interactions and trends, weather reports and major events. This data, according to the company, ensures a highly personalised customer experience.

But business intelligence is not just about hardware and software. It is about a company wide recognition that a company's data is an important strategic asset that can yield valuable management information and implement change so that this information is used **to improve decision making**.

Business Intelligence ('BI') systems provide management accountants with a wider range of information in more accessible formats. In addition to reporting and monitoring, BI systems can provide more forward-looking analysis based on a combination of both financial and non-financial information.

Business intelligence is about improving decision making. It involves developing processes and systems that collect, transform, cleanse and consolidate organisation wide and external data, usually in an accessible store (a data warehouse), for presentation on users' desks as reports, analysis or displayed on screens as dashboards or scorecards. The term BI is sometimes used to describe this structure or 'stack' of software systems and applications.

The typical BI 'stack' (or architecture) can be represented as having a series of layers:

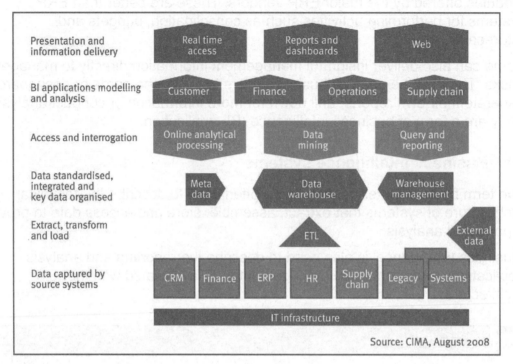

The base of the 'stack' above is usually shown as source data systems from where data is extracted, translated and loaded by extract, transform and load (ETL) software into a data warehouse. Above this is an application layer (or BI layer) and on top of this the presentation or delivery layer which can include executive dashboards, scorecards and other tools that make it easier for managers to find and understand the information and proactively use it in decision making.

BI is broader than technology. It is about using the information available to a business to improve decision making. With technology, the right information can be accessed, analysed and presented at the right time to the right people in the right format. But it must then be used by them to inform evidence based decision making. This requires leadership and cultural change.

11   Data analytics and data mining

'Data analytics' is the complex analysis, data mining and predictive modelling enabled by BI applications which can access both financial and non-financial data from the business's data warehouse and external sources.

In other words, 'data analytics' is the process of collecting, organising and analysing large sets of data to generate trends and other information to aid decision making.

Amazon, Capital One, Marriott and UPS are identified as companies that compete on analytics. These leading companies already have the right focus, culture and people, in addition to the right technology and software in place.

Data mining

'Data mining' is the process of sorting through data to identify **patterns** and **relationships** within a data set between different items, usually with the use of statistical **algorithms:** For example, data mining could help identify a customer's buying trends in order to send focused marketing data to each customer.

Business intelligence considers structured data from relational databases and brings to light patterns and trends that could guide business decisions. But its scope is now expanding to include unstructured data.

Structured data: Data that is contained within a field in a data record or file (e.g. databases, data warehouses and spreadsheets). In a data warehouse for example, everything is archived and ordered in a defined way – the products are inside containers, the containers on shelves, the shelves are in rows, and so on. This is the way that data is stored in a traditional data warehouse.

Unstructured data: Data that is not easily contained within structured data fields, such as pictures, videos, webpages, PDF files, emails or blogs. Often, unstructured data is stored in 'data lakes'. A data lake contains data in its rawest form – fresh from capture, and unadulterated by processing or analysis.

In a data lake, data is just poured in, in an unstructured way. A molecule of water in the lake is equal to any other molecule and can be moved to any part of the lake, where it will feel equally at home.

This means that data in a lake has a great deal of agility, in that it can be configured or reconfigured as necessary, depending on the job the users of data/information want to do with it. Data stored without structure can be more quickly shaped into whatever form it is needed.

Illustration 3 – What is a data lake?

In his 2015 article published on the World Economic Forum website, Bernard Marr explains the concept of data lakes. Link here to the full article: https://www.weforum.org/agenda/2015/02/what-is-a-data-lake/

12 Business Intelligence and new business opportunities

BI can be used for new reports and analysis which should lead to increased profitability through improved operating performance and better strategic focus on profitable products and segments. For example:

- Sales people who are better informed about a customer's situation and preferences, product holdings, cost to serve and profit margins should be able to achieve more profitable sales.

- Greater transparency enhances performance. Internal benchmarking between individuals and divisions which are measured on a consistent basis can help to identify best practice and raise standards.

- Negotiators can be better informed about the economics of current or comparable arrangements when agreeing contracts with suppliers or customers. Potentially uneconomic arrangements can be identified promptly and renegotiated at the earliest opportunity.

- Advertising and promotional spend can be better focused on initiatives with a higher probability of success based on better analysis of the evidence about the performance of past campaigns.

- Some data may have value outside the business. For example, supermarkets sell EPoS data to their suppliers. In turn, analysis from a financial perspective of data from EPoS (Electronic Point of Sale) and CRM systems can yield valuable insight.

13   Business intelligence and reducing costs

Activity based costing solutions are of growing interest as companies look to understand cost allocation at a granular level to be able to reduce costs and improve process efficiencies.

BI tools can be used to produce management information that is already produced in-house. With the benefit of BI, it should be possible to provide this information on a more up-to-date basis, in a more user-friendly format with greater accuracy.

There should be quantifiable savings in the production of this information and in the re-working of figures.

- BI tools are user-friendly. Users will be empowered to conduct ad hoc analysis which would previously have required support from the IT function.

- These savings will include efficiency gains, often expressed as numbers of full time equivalent (FTE) employees. To realise these as actual cost savings, for example through redundancies, can be difficult but the capacity released can be deployed to provide more valuable support to the business.

- The BI tools may, to some extent, replace a disparate array of tools already being used. This should yield benefits in terms of savings in software licensing and training costs.

- Virtualisation (bundling applications on a smaller number of servers) can save costs as fewer servers will be required.

- The ability to comply with reporting and regulatory requirements is a form of licence to trade. Without a BI solution, these requirements can only be met with ad hoc analysis. There should be a potential saving here too.

- Changing reporting standards will require greater transparency about business performance and prospects. Narrative reporting requires commentary on financial and non-financial indicators.

- Compliance with regulations can require disclosure of data that may not be readily accessible without a BI solution.

14 Intangible benefits of BI

Some benefits of BI may be intangible. These too can be of value and considered as part of the business case if they will be used by the business to generate value:

- The use of planning tools and the ability to identify trends early should allow a company to forecast more accurately. More prompt closing of period end accounts gives an impression of good systems. Over time, these can reduce investors' perception of the level of risk and increase shareholder value.

Performance management – BI planning tools

Enterprise performance management (EPM), corporate performance management (CPM), enterprise information systems (EIS), decision support systems (DSS) and management information systems (MIS) are all terms used to describe BI tools which measure key business metrics and present this information as feedback to decision makers and managers of operations or processes.

Too much business planning can be focused on budgets and financial metrics. These are often measures of outcomes in the short run rather than indicators of performance towards achieving strategic intent. Non-financial metrics may better describe progress towards achievement of a sustainable competitive advantage for the long run.

The financial and non-financial metrics and the click-throughs for further analysis most readily available through a packaged application may not be the right ones to present. Tracking the wrong metrics or using the wrong metrics in recognition or reward mechanisms can lead to perverse outcomes.

The metrics presented and the analysis allowed should enable management to investigate properly and take prompt action to improve business performance. Determining what the right metrics to track are and the right lines of enquiry is a challenge which management accountants can help organisations address.

- Greater clarity about which products, segments and customers are most profitable and those which are uneconomic can be used to improve the retention of valuable relationships. These can be defended from competitors and business developers can focus attention on winning more relationships with similar potential. The profitability of less economic products or customer relationships might be improved through using lower cost channels, cross-selling or more appropriate pricing.

- Emerging trends can be spotted earlier and improved or new products and segments developed. The challenge is to make these benefits clear so as to win buy-in from business managers and their commitment to make use of the benefits which the IT investment will enable to deliver value.

Answers to examples and objective test questions

Example 1: Butte Ltd

The correct answer is B

The initial $40,000 fee will be deemed to be a sunk cost – it has already been committed and won't be affected by any decision to proceed from this point.

The $20,000 is a future cost. Despite the fact that it is called a fixed cost it will only be incurred if the project proceeds. It is therefore an extra or incremental cost of the project and should be included in any future decision making.

Example 2: Relevant costs

(a)   The salary is a relevant cost of $12,000. Do not be fooled by the mention of the fact that it is a fixed cost, it is a cost that is relevant to the decision to proceed with the future development of the new product. This is an example of a directly attributable fixed cost. A directly attributable fixed cost may also be called a product-specific fixed cost.

(b)   The $2,500 additional running costs are relevant to the decision to purchase the new machine. The saving in overhead absorption is not relevant since we are not told that the total overhead expenditure will be altered. The saving in labour cost would be relevant but we shall assume that this has been accounted for in determining the additional monthly running costs.

(c)   This is not a relevant cost for next month since it will be incurred even if the contract is cancelled today. If a decision is being made to close the office, this cost cannot be included as a saving to be made next month. However, it will be saved in the months after that so it will become a relevant cost saving from month 2 onwards.

(d)   This is not a relevant cost of the decision to continue with the contract. The $75 is sunk and cannot be recovered even if the company does not proceed with the negotiations.

Example 3: Calaveras Ltd

Activity 1

	$
Contribution per hour lost from normal working	3
Add back: labour cost per hour that is not saved	4
	7

The contract should be charged with 5,000 × $7 = $35,000

Activity 2

Nothing. The relevant cost is zero.

Example 4: Externally generated information

- External information may not be accurate.
- External information may be out of date.
- The company publishing the data may not be reputable.
- External information may not meet the exact needs of the business.
- It may be difficult to gather external information, e.g. from customers or competitors.

Example 5: Integrity and security

- Control of access to workstations.
- User identification required for access by individual passwords.
- Users only see the icons for the functions where they have access rights.
- Restrictions on access to certain aspects of the database, e.g. using passwords.
- Users only to have access to those aspects that they need to do their job.
- Restrictions on use of functions or programs, e.g. writing off debts as bad debts.
- Transaction logs maintained automatically for checking and for back-up purposes.

The investment decision-making process

Chapter learning objectives

Lead	Component
B2: Capital investment decision making	Explain the steps and pertinent issues in the decision-making process (a) Investment decision-making process (b) Discounting (c) Real options
B3: Investment appraisal techniques	(c) IRR (d) NPV

1 Chapter summary

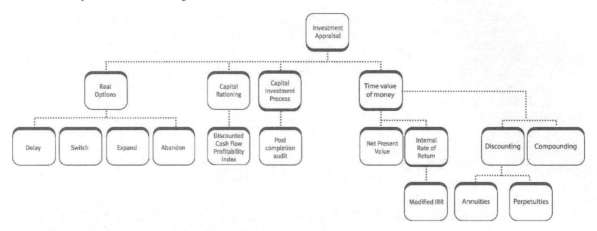

This chapter will focus on the steps that are typically incurred for simple as well as complex capital investment decisions.

One characteristic of all capital expenditure projects is that the cash flows arise over the long term (a period usually greater than 12 months). Under this situation, it becomes necessary to carefully consider the time value of money.

The concept of the time value of money translates into compounding and discounting techniques, and the use of discount factors to reflect the cost of capital, or shareholders' required return, in investment appraisal.

Capital rationing, a key decision making approach, then applies when investment funds are limited and not all profitable projects can be undertaken.

Flexibility can also be added to investment appraisal with the use of real options theory. Conventional investment appraisal techniques typically undervalue flexibility in projects with high uncertainty, and real option theory attempts to classify and value flexibility in general by taking the ideas of financial options pricing, and developing them.

2 The capital investment process

A decision making model for capital expenditure decisions is shown below:

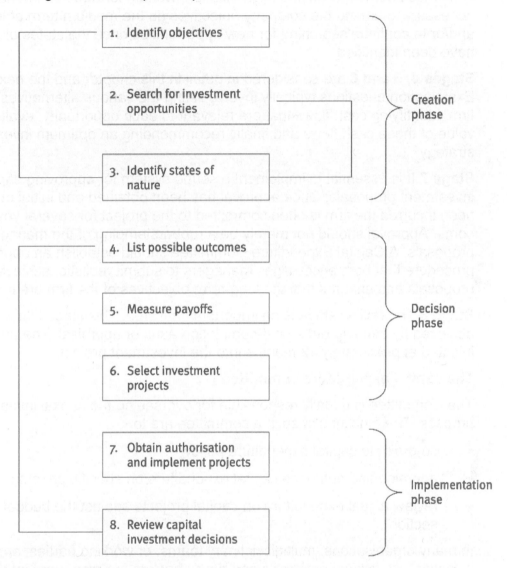

Stage 1 indicates the objectives or goals of the organisation. Most organisations pursue a variety of goals, for example maximisation of profits, maximisation of sales, survival of the firm, achieving satisfactory profits and obtaining the largest share of the market. Achieving profit maximisation in the long term will ensure maximisation of the market value of the shareholders' wealth. The capital investment process seeks to achieve maximisation of wealth by maximising the net present value of future net cash inflows.

Stage 2 involves the search for investment opportunities. Without a proactive, deliberate search for creative projects and opportunities, even the most sophisticated evaluation techniques are worthless. A firm's prosperity is dependent upon its ability to create investment opportunities.

Stage 3 requires data to be gathered about possible future environments that may affect the outcomes of the project. Examples of states of nature include economic booms/recessions, high inflation, world shortages etc. It may be necessary to amend the company objectives (in the medium term at least) and/or to continue searching for new opportunities once the states of nature have been identified.

Stages 4, 5 and 6 are considered in detail in this chapter and the next chapter. Examination questions typically involve listing the various alternatives open to a firm, identifying cash flows that are relevant to each opportunity, evaluating the value of these cash flows and finally recommending an optimum investment strategy.

Stage 7 It is essential to implement a sound system for approving capital investment proposals. Once approval has been obtained and initial outlays have been incurred the firm is often committed to the project for several years to come. Approval should not merely be a rubberstamping of the managers' proposals. A Capital Expenditure Committee should establish an approval procedure that both encourages managers to submit realistic, achievable proposals and ensures that the long-term objectives of the firm are being met.

Stage 8 The review stage is an important final step. This stage is usually achieved by carrying out a post-completion audit or appraisal. The audit is often initiated approximately 12 months into the investment project.

The capital expenditure committee

The Committee is usually responsible for overseeing the capital investment process. The functions of such a committee are to:

- co-ordinate capital expenditure policy

- appraise and authorise capital expenditure on specific projects

- review actual expenditure on capital projects against the budget (see next section).

In many organisations, multidisciplinary teams, or working parties, are set up to investigate individual proposals and report back to top management on their findings.

Such a team might comprise:

- project engineer

- production engineer

- management accountant

- relevant specialist, e.g. personnel officer, for a project involving sports facilities or canteens, safety officers, etc.

In capital investment appraisal, we initially assume that:

1   All cash inflows and outflows are known with certainty.

2   Sufficient funds are available to undertake all profitable investments.

3   There is zero inflation.

4   There is zero taxation.

These assumptions are all considered again in the next chapter.

3   The time value of money

 Money received today is worth more than the same sum received in the future, i.e. it has a **time value**.

For example, if offered the choice between a certain sum of $100 now, or the expectation of $100 in a year's time, then most (all) people will prefer the $100 now. However, what if the choice is between $100 now and $105 in one year or $110 or...?

Suppose you are indifferent between $100 now or the expectation of $112 in one year – this would indicate that your time value of money can be expressed as an interest rate of 12% per annum.

Discounted cash flow (DCF) techniques take account of this time value of money when appraising investments.

The time value of money

There are three main reasons for the time value of money:

Consumption preferences

There is a strong preference for the immediate rather than delayed consumption. Investors would typically prefer to receive returns sooner rather than later. They may even be willing to receive smaller returns now. Money, like any other desirable commodity, has a price. Given the choice of $100 now or the same amount in one year, it is always preferable to take the $100 now because it could be invested over the next year at say 10% interest rate to produce $110 at the end of the year.

Impact of inflation

In most countries, in most years, prices rise as a result of inflation. Therefore funds received today will buy more than the same amount a year later, as prices will have risen in the meantime. The funds are subject to a loss of purchasing power over time.

Risk

The earlier cash flows are due to be received, the more certain they are – there is less chance that events will prevent payment. Earlier cash flows are therefore considered to be less risky.

4 Compound interest

A sum invested today will earn interest. Compounding calculates the future value (or **terminal value**) of a given sum invested today for a number of years.

To compound a sum, the figure is increased by the amount of interest it would earn over the period.

FORMULA FOR COMPOUNDING

$$V = X(1 + r)^n$$

Where V = Future value

X = Initial investment (present value)

r = Interest rate (expressed as a decimal)

n = Number of time periods

Compounding

$100 is invested in an account for five years. The interest rate is 10% per annum.

The value of the account after five years can be calculated as follows:

$$V = 100 (1.10)^5 = \$161.05$$

Similarly, if your time value of money is 10% per annum, then you would be indifferent between receiving $100 now or $161.05 in five years' time. They would have the same value to you.

Example 1: Compounding

$450 is invested in an account earning 6.25% interest p.a. Calculate the fund value after 12 years.

5 Discounting

Discounting performs the opposite function to compounding. Compounding finds the future value of a sum invested now, whereas discounting considers a sum receivable in the future and establishes its equivalent value today. This value in today's terms is known as the **Present Value (PV)**.

In potential investment projects, cash flows will arise at many different points in time. Calculating the present value of future flows is a key technique in investment appraisal decisions.

FORMULAE FOR DISCOUNTING

Present value = Future value × discount factor **LEARN**

Where: Discount factor = $\frac{1}{(1+r)^n}$ or $(1+r)^{-n}$ **GIVEN**

Where: r is the interest rate expressed as decimal

N is the number of time periods

$(1 + r)^{-n}$ can be looked up in discounting tables. It is known as the discount factor.

 Illustration 1 – Discounting

$5,000 is required in 10 years. $x is invested in an account earning 5% interest p.a.

The value of $x may be established as follows:

We know that $V = X(1+r)^n$

And we know that V = $5,000

r = 5%

n = 10

So we can insert these values into the formula as follows:

$5,000 = X(1 + 0.05)^{10}$

$X = \$5,000/1.05^{10}$

$x = \dfrac{5,000}{1.05^{10}} = \$3,070$

 Example 2: Discounting I

Calculate the present value of $25,000 receivable in six years' time, if the interest rate is 10% p.a.

 The cost of capital

In the above discussions we referred to the rate of interest. There are a number of alternative terms used to refer to the rate a firm should use to take account of the time value of money:

- cost of capital

- discount rate

- required rate of return.

Whatever term is used, the rate of interest used for discounting reflects the cost of the finance that will be tied up in the investment.

There are four widely used appraisal methods:

(1) The Net Present Value, (NPV) that considers the time value of money and uses discounted cash flow techniques

(2) The Internal Rate of Return (IRR), that also considers the time value of money and uses discounted cash flow techniques

(3) The Payback period, reviewed in the next chapter

(4) The Accounting Rate of Return (ARR), reviewed in the next chapter.

6   Net present value (NPV)

The net present value (NPV) is the net benefit or loss of benefit in present value terms from an investment opportunity.

NPV is the 'difference between the sum of the projected discounted cash inflows and outflows attributable to a capital investment or other long-term project' (Official CIMA Terminology).

 The NPV represents the surplus funds (after funding the investment) earned on the project. This means that it tells us the impact on shareholder wealth. Therefore:

Decision criteria

• Any project with a positive NPV is viable.

• Projects with a negative NPV are not viable.

• Faced with mutually-exclusive projects, choose the project with the highest NPV.

Note: the NPV is a surplus. If the NPV is zero or tiny then the project is still providing the required rate of return. A positive NPV is desirable and the bigger it is the better, but it doesn't have to be more than zero.

Illustration 2 – What does the NPV actually mean?

NPV is defined as the:

difference between the sum of the projected discounted cash inflows and outflows attributable to a capital investment or other long-term project.

(CIMA Official Terminology)

However, it is often easier to understand it as the surplus of funds available to the investor.

Suppose, in an investment problem, we calculate the NPV of certain cash flows at 12% to be ($97), and at 10% to be zero, and yet at 8% the NPV of the same cash flows is + $108. Another way of expressing this is as follows.

- If the company's cost of capital is 12% the investor would be $97 out of pocket – i.e. the investment earns a yield below the cost of capital.

- If the company's cost of capital is 10% the investor would break even – i.e. the investment yields a return equal to the cost of capital.

- If the company's cost of capital is 8% the investor would be $108 in pocket – i.e. the investment earns a return in excess of the cost of capital.

In other words, an NPV of zero indicates that the project generates an acceptable rate of return and is, therefore, worth accepting because shareholder wealth is being maintained. A positive NPV indicates that the rate offered exceeds the required rate and so shareholder wealth increases. A negative NPV indicates that the project does not earn an acceptable rate of return and so it would reduce shareholder wealth.

Assumptions used in NPV

- All cash flows occur at the start or end of a year.

Although in practice many cash flows accrue throughout the year, for discounting purposes they are all treated as occurring at the start or end of a year. Note also that if today (T_0) is 01/01/20X0, the dates 31/12/20X1 and 01/01/20X2, although technically separate days, can be treated for discounting as occurring at the same point in time, i.e. at T_1.

- Initial investments occur at once (T_0), other cash flows start in one year's time (T_1).

In project appraisal, the investment needs to be made before the cash flows can accrue. Therefore, unless the examiner specifies otherwise, it is assumed that investments (including any working capital requirement) occur in advance. The first cash flows associated with running the project are therefore assumed to occur one year after the project begins, i.e. at T_1.

Example 3: Wilson NPV

Wilson Ltd is considering a capital investment in new equipment. The estimated cash flows are as follows.

Year	Cash flow $
0	(240,000)
1	80,000
2	120,000
3	70,000
4	40,000
5	20,000

The company's cost of capital is 9%.

Calculate the NPV of the project to assess whether it should be undertaken.

Example 4: Mickey Ltd

Mickey Ltd is considering two mutually-exclusive projects with the following details:

Project A

Initial investment	$450,000	
Scrap value at the end of year 5	$20,000	

Year:	1	2	3	4	5
Annual cash flows ($000)	200	150	100	100	100

Project B

Initial investment	$100,000	
Scrap value at the end of year 5	$10,000	

Year:	1	2	3	4	5
Annual cash flows ($000)	50	40	30	20	20

Assume that the initial investment is at the start of the project and the annual cash flows are at the **end** of each year.

Required:

Calculate the Net Present Value for Projects A and B if the relevant cost of capital is 10%.

Year	Discount factor 10%	Project A Net cash flow $000	PV $000	Project B Net cash flow $000	PV $000
0					
1					
2					
3					
4					
5					

Calculate which project has the highest NPV.

Advantages and disadvantages of NPV

When appraising projects or investments, NPV is considered to be superior (in theory) to most other methods. This is because it:

- considers the time value of money – discounting cash flows to PV takes account of the impact of interest, inflation and risk over time. (See later sessions for more on inflation and risk.) These significant issues are ignored by the basic methods of payback and accounting rate of return (ARR)

- is an absolute measure of return – the NPV of an investment represents the actual surplus raised by the project. This allows a business to plan more effectively. Neither ARR nor payback is an absolute measure

- is based on cash flows not profits – the subjectivity of profits makes them less reliable than cash flows and therefore less appropriate for decision making

- considers the whole life of the project – methods such as payback only consider the cash flows prior to the payback. NPV takes account of all relevant cash flows

- should lead to maximisation of shareholder wealth. If the cost of capital reflects the investors' (i.e. shareholders') required return, then the NPV reflects the theoretical increase in their wealth. For a company, this is considered to be the primary objective of the business.

However, there are some potential drawbacks:

- It is difficult to explain to managers. To understand the meaning of the NPV calculated requires an understanding of discounting. The method is not as intuitive as techniques such as payback.

- It requires knowledge of the cost of capital. The calculation of the cost of capital is, in practice, more complex than identifying interest rates. It involves gathering data and making a number of calculations based on that data and some estimates. The process may be deemed too protracted for the appraisal to be carried out.

- It is relatively complex. For the reasons explained above, NPV may be rejected in favour of simpler techniques.

7 Internal rate of return (IRR)

The IRR is the rate of return at which the project has a NPV of zero.

Decision criteria

- If the IRR is greater than the cost of capital, the project should be accepted. If the IRR is less than the cost of capital, the project should be rejected.

 Further explanation of IRR

Using the NPV method, PVs are calculated by discounting cash flows at a given cost of capital, and the difference between the PV of costs and the PV of benefits is the NPV. In contrast, the IRR method of analysis is to calculate the exact rate of return that the project is expected to achieve.

If an investment has a positive NPV, it means it is earning more than the cost of capital. If the NPV is negative, it is earning less than the cost of capital. This means that if the NPV is zero, it will be earning exactly the cost of capital.

Conversely, the percentage return on the investment must be the rate of discount or cost of capital at which the NPV equals zero. This rate of return is called the IRR and if it is higher than the target rate of return then the project is financially worth undertaking.

Calculating the IRR (using linear interpolation)

The steps in linear interpolation are:

1 Calculate two NPVs for the project at two different costs of capital

2 Use the following formula to find the IRR:

 FORMULA FOR IRR

$$IRR = L + \frac{N_L}{N_L - N_H} \times (H - L)$$

where:

L = Lower rate of interest   H = Higher rate of interest

N_L = NPV at lower rate of interest N_H = NPV at higher rate of interest.

 Accuracy of the formula

The formula makes an approximation of the IRR by assuming that the NPV will move downward in a straight line. In reality the NPV line is curved and therefore there will be an element of error in the IRR estimation. The choice of rates to estimate the IRR can affect the answer provided by the formula.

Ideally you should aim to satisfy two criteria:

- do not use rates which are too far apart. A 5% difference should be sufficient. The further the rates are away from each other than the greater the amount of error in the IRR calculation.

- For a 'normal' project, using one positive and one negative NPV will result in the IRR being over estimated. Using two positive NPVs, or two negative NPVs, will result in the IRR being under estimated. The only way to get accuracy is to have both, or at least one guess pretty close to the answer. The interpolation formula can cope with any combination.

Example 5: Mickey IRR

(a)   Calculate the internal rate of return of Project A.

Year	Discount factors at ?%	Project A Net cash flow $000	PV $000
0		(450)	
1		200	
2		150	
3		100	
4		100	
5		120	

(b)   Calculate the internal rate of return of Project B.

You are given the following:

At 10% the NPV was $33,310

At 20% the NPV is $8,510

At 30% the NPV is ($9,150)

Illustration 3 – Calculating the IRR using a graph

The IRR may be calculated by a linear interpolation, i.e. by assuming a linear relationship between the NPV and the discount rate. Plotting a graph would give an approximate IRR, but the same point can also be found using a formula.

Step 1   Calculate two NPVs for the project at two different costs of capital. You can choose any costs of capital and get a fair result. However, it helps to find two costs of capital for which the NPV is close to 0, because the IRR will be a value close to them. Ideally, you should use one cost of capital where the NPV is positive and the other cost of capital where the NPV is negative, although this is not essential. You should not waste time in the exam.

Step 2   Once the two NPVs have been calculated, they and their associated costs of capital can be used to calculate the IRR. In other words, we can estimate the IRR by finding the point where a line joining these points would cross the x-axis (the point where the NPV is zero) in a graph plotting the project NPV against various discount rates.

To calculate the exact IRR requires a more complex technique, best carried out using an Excel spreadsheet. This will not be expected in the exam.

Example 6: Potential Project

A potential project's predicted cash flows give a NPV of $50,000 at a discount rate of 10% and ($10,000) at a rate of 15%.

Calculate the internal rate of return (IRR).

Example 7: IRR and decision making

A business undertakes high-risk investments and requires a minimum expected rate of return of 17% pa on its investments. A proposed capital investment has the following expected cash flows:

Year	$
0	(50,000)
1	18,000
2	25,000
3	20,000
4	10,000

State, on financial grounds alone, whether this project should go ahead.

Note: you should calculate the NPV of the project at a cost of capital of 15% and 20%.

IRR where there are annuities/perpetuities

Calculating the IRR of a project with even cash flows

There is a simpler technique available, using annuity tables, if the project cash flows are annuities i.e. where it equal annual cash flows from year 1 onwards.

1   Find the cumulative discount factor, Initial investment ÷ Annual inflow.

2   Find the life of the project, n.

3   Look along the n year row of the cumulative discount factor until the closest value is found.

4   The column in which this figure is found is the IRR.

Illustration: Find the IRR of a project with an initial investment of $1.5 million and three years of inflows of $700,000 starting in one year.

NPV calculation:

		Cash flow $000	DF (c) %	PV $000
Time				
0	Investment	(1,500)	1	(1,500)
1 – 3	Inflow	700	(b)	(a)
NPV				Nil

- The aim is to find the discount rate (c) that produces an NPV of nil.

- Therefore the PV of inflows (a) must equal the PV of outflows, $1,500,000.

- If the PV of inflows (a) is to be $1,500,000 and the size of each inflow is $700,000, the DF required (b) must be 1,500,000 ÷ 700,000 = 2.143.

- The discount rate (c) for which this is the 3-year factor can be found by looking along the 3-year row of the cumulative discount factors shown in the annuity table.

- The figure of 2.140 appears under the 19% column suggesting an IRR of 19% is the closest.

Calculating the IRR of a project where the cash flows are perpetuities

$$\text{IRR of a perpetuity} = \frac{\text{Annual inflow}}{\text{Initial investment}} \times 100$$

Illustration – Calculating IRR where cash flows are perpetuities

Find the IRR of an investment that costs $20,000 and generates $1,600 for an indefinitely long period.

Solution

$$\text{IRR} = \frac{\text{Annual inflow}}{\text{Initial investment}} \times 100 = \frac{\$1,600}{\$20,000} \times 100 = 8\%$$

Advantages and disadvantages of IRR

Advantages:

- IRR considers the time value of money. The current value earned from an investment project is therefore more accurately measured. As discussed above this is a significant improvement over the basic methods.

- IRR is a percentage and therefore easily understood. Although managers may not completely understand the detail of the IRR, the concept of a return earned is familiar and the IRR can be simply compared with the required return of the organisation.

- IRR uses cash flows not profits. These are less subjective as discussed above.

- IRR considers the whole life of the project rather than ignoring later flows (which would occur with payback).

- The IRR can be calculated when the cost of capital is unknown (say, if finance for a project has yet to be determined). It therefore may provide a useful benchmark for appraising potential sources of capital.

- A firm selecting projects where the IRR exceeds the cost of capital would normally increase shareholders' wealth. This holds true provided the project cash flows follow the typical pattern of an outflow followed by a series of inflows, as in the investment examples above.

However there are a number of difficulties with the IRR approach:

- It is not a measure of absolute profitability. A project of $1,000 invested now and paying back $1,100 in a year's time has an IRR of 10%. If a company's required return is 6%, then the project is viable according to the IRR rule but most businesses would consider the absolute return too small to be worth the investment.

- Interpolation only provides an estimate (and an accurate estimate requires the use of a spreadsheet programme). The cost of capital calculation itself is also only an estimate and if the margin between required return and the IRR is small, this lack of accuracy could actually mean the wrong decision is taken.

  For example if the cost of capital is found to be 8% (but is actually 8.7%) and the project IRR is calculated as 9.2% (but is actually 8.5%) the project would be wrongly accepted. Note that where such a small margin exists, the project's success would be considered to be sensitive to the discount rate (see session 12 on risk).

- Non-conventional cash flows may give rise to no IRR or multiple IRRs. For example a project with an outflow at T0 and T2 but income at T1 could, depending on the size of the cash flows, have a number of different profiles on a graph (see below). Even where the project does have one IRR, it can be seen from the graph that the decision rule would lead to the wrong result as the project does not earn a positive NPV at any cost of capital.

For example, a project with an immediate outflow of $10m, followed by an inflow of $90m in one year's time and a final outflow of $100m would have the following NPVs:

Discount rate	NPV ($m)
10%	−10.8
29.85%	0
60%	7.2
670.5%	0
1000%	−2.64

The NPV starts off negative, then at rates above 30% will become positive, before becoming negative again at rates above 670.5%. This could be represented by the dark line in the diagram/graph below:

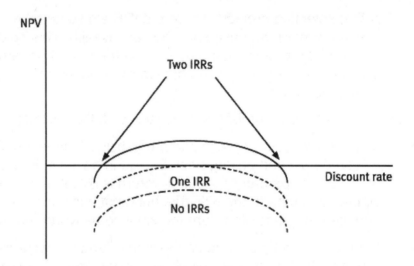

As the size of the project flows reduce the NPV would likewise reduce and the NPV line fall (as in the lower dashed lines). It can therefore be seen that there might only be one NPV (if the line just touches the zero NPV point) or no IRR's at all if the project has negative NPVs at all discount rates.

Note: multiple IRRs are usually associated with two or more periods when the project has an outflow. The problem doesn't arise if there is a traditional project with an initial investment, followed by annual inflows. It is also highly unlikely to arise if the second outflow is small and/or in the very distant future. For example, a project might have very small closure costs at the end, in which case it is still unlikely that there will be more than one IRR.

NPV versus IRR

Both NPV and IRR are investment appraisal techniques which discount cash flows and are superior to the basic techniques discussed in the previous session. However only NPV can be used to distinguish between two mutually-exclusive projects, as the following diagram demonstrates.

Explanation of the principle

NPV and IRR may sometimes give conflicting advice and recommend different projects.

Consider the following two projects:

	Initial investment ($m)	Year 1 flow ($m)	Year 2 flow ($m)	NPV ($m) @ 10%	IRR
Project A	(10)	0	25	10.7	58.1%
Project B	(10)	10	12	9.0	70.4%

Project A has the higher NPV but the lower IRR. The choice of project appraisal method would therefore affect the choice of project.

The NPV of these projects could be represented diagrammatically as follows:

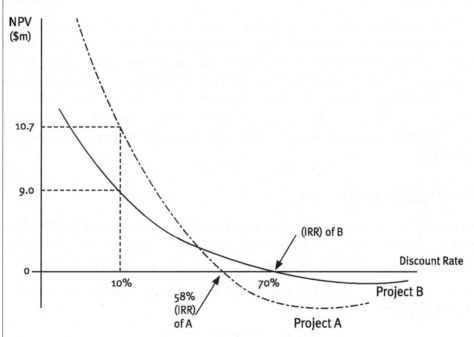

It can be seen that the NPV curves cross. But the vital piece of information is the firm's cost of capital. This is the actual cost of financing the project (i.e. it is the cost that the company will have to pay for financing the initial $10m investment). Once this cost is met, the remaining project surplus (the NPV) can be returned to shareholders. It is therefore the NPV information which will be of more concern to investors or shareholders.

> The IRR is not an actual cost of capital. It instead tells us the cost of capital at which the project will break even. This cost of capital might never arise.
>
> The IRR is a useful piece of information when we are examining one project. It allows us to determine the highest acceptable cost of capital. But when comparing one project to another, the NPV figure is based on a more appropriate cost of capital. Therefore the NPV of projects should be used when deciding which project in which to invest.

The advantage of NPV is that it tells us the absolute increase in shareholder wealth as a result of accepting the project, at the current cost of capital. The IRR simply tells us how far the cost of capital could increase before the project would not be worth accepting.

Attitudes to risk

> The general decision rule in DCF analysis is that where mutually exclusive projects are being considered, the one with the highest NPV is preferred. However, some caution should be exercised in the use of this rule. Our earlier exploration of attitude to risk indicated that a low-risk project with a lower expected NPV may be preferred to a high risk project with a higher NPV.
>
> IRR is normally reported as part of a project appraisal. However, since it is a relative measure which lacks an element of scale it should not be used to select between alternatives. A large project with a high NPV will normally be preferred to a small project with a lower NPV but a higher IRR. A tiny project can have a very high IRR. But IRR can still be informative since it offers insights into the return that alternative uses for capital offer and this can be a guide to future strategy and decision-making.

8 The Modified IRR

A more useful measure is the modified internal rate of return or MIRR. This measure has been developed to counter the above problems since it is unique, gives a measure of the return from a project, and is a simple percentage.

It is therefore more popular with non-financially minded managers, as a simple rule can be applied:

$$MIRR = Project's\ return$$

If Project return > company cost of finance → Accept project

The interpretation of MIRR

MIRR measures the economic yield of the investment under the assumption that any cash surpluses are reinvested at the firm's current cost of capital.

Although MIRR, like IRR, cannot replace net present value as the principal evaluation technique, it does give a measure of the maximum cost of finance that the firm could sustain and allow the project to remain worthwhile. For this reason it gives a useful insight into the margin of error, or room for negotiation, when considering the financing of particular investment projects.

Calculation

There are several ways of calculating the MIRR, but the following formula is usually used:

Formula:

MIRR = [(Terminal value of inflows/Present Value of outflows)$^{1/n}$] – 1

where 'n' represents the number of future time periods.

Example 8: Alpine Ltd

A project with the following cash flows is under consideration in a company called Alpine Ltd:

$000	T0	T1	T2	T3	T4
	(20,000)	8,000	12,000	4,000	2,000

Cost of capital 8%

Calculate the MIRR.

---

9   NPV and IRR with equal cash flows

Discounting annuities

 When a project has equal annual cash flows the annuity factor may be used to calculate the NPV (and hence the IRR).

An annuity is a constant annual cash flow for a number of years.

 The **annuity factor** (AF) is the name given to the sum of the individual DF.

The PV of an annuity can therefore be quickly found using the formula:

PV = Annual cash flow × AF

As when calculating a discount factor, the annuity factors (AF) can be found using an annuity formula or annuity tables (cumulative present value tables).

Annuity factor formula

The formula is:

$$AF = \frac{1 - (1 + r)^{-n}}{r}$$

Where

r = cost of capital

n = the number of periods

For example, for a six-year annuity at 10%:

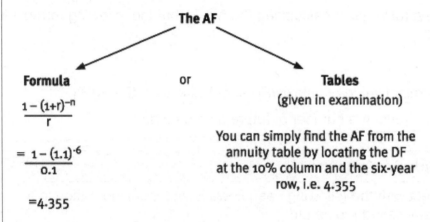

The AF

Formula   or   **Tables**
(given in examination)

$$\frac{1 - (1+r)^{-n}}{r}$$

You can simply find the AF from the annuity table by locating the DF at the 10% column and the six-year row, i.e. 4.355

$$= \frac{1 - (1.1)^{-6}}{0.1}$$

=4.355

Note: there is a small difference due to roundings.

Note: annuity tables are titled cumulative present value tables in the exam.

Illustration 4 – Annuities

Pluto Ltd has been offered a project costing $50,000. The returns are expected to be $10,000 each year for seven years. Cost of capital: 10%.

To decide whether the project be accepted:

Year	Cash flow	Discount factor	Present value
	$		$
0	(50,000)	1.000	(50,000)
1–7	10,000	4.868	48,680
			(1,320)

The project should therefore be rejected.

The IRR of the project may be calculated as follows:

$10,000 × annuity factor = $50,000   Annuity factor = 5

Using tables and a life of seven years, the closest annuity factor to 5 is 5.033. This means the IRR is approximately 9%.

Discounting perpetuities

 A **perpetuity** is an annual cash flow that occurs forever.

 It is often described by examiners as a cash flow continuing 'for the foreseeable future'.

The PV of a perpetuity is found using the formula:

$$PV = \frac{\text{Cash flow}}{r}$$

'r' in the formula is the company's required rate of return (or cost of capital).

or

$$PV = \text{cash flow} \times \frac{1}{r}$$

$\frac{1}{r}$ is known as the 'perpetuity factor'.

 Illustration 5 – Perpetuities

An investment of $50,000 is expected to yield $5,670 per annum in perpetuity.

The net present value of the investment opportunity if the cost of capital is 9% can be calculated as follows:

NPV = ($50,000) + $5,670 ÷ 0.09 = $13,000

 Example 9: Present Value, annuities, perpetuities

Calculate the present value of the following cash flows:

1   A fifteen year annuity of $300 starting at once. Interest rates are 6%.

2   A perpetuity of $33,000 commencing immediately. Interest rates are 22%.

Annuities/perpetuities in advance

The use of annuity factors and perpetuity factors both assume that the first cash flow will be occurring in one year's time. If this is not the case, you will need to adjust your calculation.

Advanced annuities and perpetuities

Some regular cash flows may start now (at T_0) rather than in one years time (T_1).

Calculate the PV by ignoring the payment at T0 when considering the number of cash flows and then adding one to the annuity or perpetuity factor.

Illustration – Advanced annuities and perpetuities

A 5-year $600 annuity is starting today. Interest rates are 10%. Find the PV of the annuity.

Solution

This is essentially a standard 4-year annuity with an additional payment at T_0. The PV could be calculated as follows:

	T_0	T_1	T_2	T_3	T_4
CF	600	600	600	600	600
PV	600 +		600 × 4-year 10% AF		

PV = 600 + 600 × 3.17 = 600 + 1902 = $2,502

The same answer can be found more quickly by adding 1 to the AF:

PV = 600 × (1 + 3.17) = 600 × 4.17 = $2,502.

Illustration – Advanced perpetuities

A perpetuity of $2,000 is due to commence immediately. The interest rate is 9%. What is the PV?

Solution

This is essentially a standard perpetuity with an additional payment at T_0. The PV could be calculated as follows:

T_0	T_1	T_2	T_3	T_4 .....
2,000	2,000 → ∞			

PV (2,000) + (2,000 × 9% perpetuity formula)

Again, the same answer can be found more quickly by adding 1 to the perpetuity factor.

$$2,000 \times \left(1 + \frac{1}{0.09}\right) = 2,000 \times 12.11 = \$24,222$$

Annuities/perpetuities in arrears

Delayed annuities and perpetuities

Some regular cash flows may start later than T_1.

These are dealt with by:

1   applying the appropriate factor to the cash flow as normal

2   discounting your answer back to T_0.

Illustration – Delayed annuities and perpetuities

What is the PV of $200 incurred each year for four years, starting in three year's time, if the discount rate is 5%?

Solution

Method: A four-year annuity starting at T_3
$$(1-4)$$

T_0	T_1	T_2	T_3	T_4	T_5	T_6
			200	200	200	200

PV   2.   1.

Step 1   Discount the annuity as usual

200 × 4 yr 5% AF = 200 × 3.546 = 709.2

Note that this gives the value of the annuity at T_2

Step 2   Discount the answer back to T_0

709.2 × 2 yr 5% DF = 709.2 × 0.907 = $643

Annuity or perpetuity factors will discount the cash flows back to give the value one year before the first cash flow arose. For standard annuities and perpetuities this gives the present (T_0) value since the first cash flow started at T_1.

However for delayed cash flows, applying the factor will find the value of the cash flows one year before they began, which in this example is T_2. To find the PV, an additional calculation is required – the value must be discounted back to T_0.

Care must be taken to discount back the appropriate number of years. The figure here was discounted back two years because the first step gave the value at T_2. It can help to draw a timeline as above and mark on the effect of the first step (as shown with a 1. here) to help you remember.

10 Changing discount rates

Throughout this chapter, we have assumed that a company will have a constant discount rate. This allows us to use the tables of discount rates that are provided in the exam. However, in reality discount rates might change from year to year. For example, in the next chapter we will see that inflation affects discount rates, and because inflation is not constant discount rates will not be constant.

In these instances, we cannot use the tables that we are provided with, and instead we must calculate each year's discount factor individually using the discounting formula from the start of this chapter.

Illustration 6 – Changing discount rates

A company is considering a four year investment. Its cost of capital during this period is expected to rise each year as interest rates and inflation rates rise in the economy. It expects its cost of capital to be as follows:

Year 1	10%
Year 2	12%
Year 3	15%
Year 4	16%

Calculate the discount rate that should be used for each year.

Answer

Because the cost of capital is changing each year, we cannot use the tables that we are provided with. Instead, we have to calculate the discount rate for each year individually.

The best way to do this is to divide the discount factor for the previous year by (1 + the cost of capital for the year in question). This can be shown as follows:

	Calculation	Discount factor
Year 0		1.000
Year 1	1.000/1.10	0.909
Year 2	0.909/1.12	0.812
Year 3	0.812/1.15	0.706
Year 4	0.706/1.16	0.608

These are the discount factors that would be used in any PV calculation employed by the company.

Note: this means that the cash flow in year 3, say, has to be discounted on the basis that we need a 10% return for year 1, followed by 12% for year 2, followed by 15% for year 3.

This technique can be very important when dealing with inflation in the next chapter.

11 Dealing with non annual periods

In some instances we may have to deal with cash flows which are not in annual terms – for example, costs might be paid in 6 monthly blocks. In this case, we need to pro-rate the discount rate to match the period of the cash flows.

Illustration 7 – Dealing with non-annual periods

If, say, we are given an annual discount rate of 10% but cash flows are received in non-annual instalments, in order to calculate the appropriate cost of capital to use for calculations we would need to pro-rate the 10% as follows:

Cash flows are in...	Pro-rata formula	Calculation	Appropriate discount rate
Quarters	$(1 + i)^{1/4} - 1$	$(1.10)^{1/4} - 1$	2.41 % per quarter
6 monthly periods	$(1 + i)^{1/2} - 1$	$(1.10)^{1/2} - 1$	4.88% per 6 months
Months	$(1 + i)^{1/12} - 1$	$(1.10)^{1/12} - 1$	0.8% per month
2 yearly instalments	$(1 + i)^2 - 1$	$(1.10)^2 - 1$	21 % per two years

12 Capital rationing

If investment funds are unlimited, then all projects with a positive NPV should be undertaken. Capital rationing occurs when insufficient funds are available to undertake all beneficial projects.

Hard and soft capital rationing

The term soft capital rationing is often used to refer to situations where for various reasons the firm internally imposes a budget ceiling on the amount of capital expenditure. If the capital is restricted because of external constraints such as the inability to obtain funds from the financial markets, the term hard capital rationing is used. The type of rationing imposed on a firm will not, however, affect our analysis.

The objective of all capital rationing exercises is the maximisation of the total NPV of the chosen projects' cash flows at the cost of capital. Thus it becomes necessary to rank projects to enable the optimum combination to be undertaken.

Underlying assumptions:

* Individual projects are divisible. The resulting NPV will be pro-rated. For example, if only 25% of the capital is available for a project only 25% of its NPV will be earned.

* Annual cash flows cannot be delayed or brought forward.

* Capital funds are restricted in just one period (year 0).

The decision aims to maximise NPV given a single limiting factor. As with other decisions with one scarce resource, the opportunities should be ranked according to NPV per $1 invested. This measure is called the profitability index (PI).

$$\text{Profitability index} = \frac{\text{NPV of project}}{\text{Initial cash outflows}}$$

LEARN

The optimal investment plan is determined by:

1 calculating a PI for each project

2 ranking the projects according to their PI

3 allocating funds according to the projects' rankings until they are used.

Example 10: Capital Rationing

A company may undertake any of the following investment projects.

Project	Investment required	Net Present value
	$000	$000
A	3,400	850
B	2,750	825
C	2,000	720
D	3,400	680
E	860	430
F	950	400
G	1,250	350

In the next budget period there is only $9 million available for capital expenditure projects. Each project is divisible.

Required:

(a) If the company ranks the projects according to highest NPVs, which projects will be undertaken? Calculate the total NPV.

(b) If the company selects projects according to their profitability index, calculate which projects will be undertaken. Calculate the total NPV now.

13 Discounted Payback Profitability Index (DPBI)

Alternatively, the index may be shown as a 'discounted payback index' (DPBI):

$$DPBI = \frac{\text{Present Value of net cash inflows}}{\text{Initial cash outlay}}$$

LEARN

This is a measure of the number of times a project recovers the initial funds invested, something that is particularly important if funds are scarce.

The higher the figure, the greater the returns. A DPBI of less than 1 indicates a negative NPV, i.e. that the present value of the net cash inflows is less than the initial cash outlay.

Dealing with indivisible projects

There may be scenarios where 'common sense' has to come into play and this general rule has to be ignored. Consider the following example:

Example

A company has an investment limit of $800,000 and has to choose between the following three projects:

Project	Investment	Inflow PV	NPV	PI	Rank
A	600,000	700,000	100,000	0.17	1
B	500,000	560,000	60,000	0.12	3
C	300,000	345,000	45,000	0.15	2

On the basis of the general rule, Project A only would be selected since it has the highest PI. But this precludes any other projects, generating an NPV of $100,000 and leaving $200,000 of the capital limit uncommitted. Consequently, NPV is maximised by adopting two projects (B and C) both of which have lower PIs than A. By adopting these two projects we raise total NPV to $105,000.

In these circumstances, the objective can only be achieved by selecting from amongst the available projects on a trial and error basis. Because of the problem of indivisibility this may leave some funds unutilised. Consider another example:

Example

PQ has $50,000 available to invest. Its cost of capital is 10 %. The following indivisible projects are available.

Project	Initial outlay	Return p.a. to perpetuity
	$	$
1	20,000	1,500
2	10,000	1,500
3	15,000	3,000
4	30,000	5,400
5	25,000	4,800

Solution

The first stage is to calculate the NPV of the projects.

Project	Initial outlay	PV of cash flows	NPV
	$	$	$
1	20,000	15,000	(5,000)
2	10,000	15,000	5,000
3	15,000	30,000	15,000
4	30,000	54,000	24,000
5	25,000	48,000	23,000

The approach is then one of considering all possible combinations of projects under the investment limit of $50,000.

The optimum selection of projects is as follows:

Project	Initial outlay	NPV
	$	$
2	10,000	5,000
3	15,000	15,000
5	25,000	23,000
	50,000	43,000
Unused funds	Nil	
Funds available	50,000	

14 Identifying real options in investment appraisal

- Flexibility adds value to an investment.

  - For example, if an investment can be staggered, then future costs can be avoided if the market turns out to be less attractive than originally expected.

  - The core to this value lies in reducing downside risk exposure but keeping upside potential open – i.e. in making probability distributions asymmetric.

  - Financial options are an example where this flexibility can be valued.

  - A call option on a share allows an investor to 'wait and see' what happens to a share price before deciding whether to exercise the option and will thus benefit from favourable price movements without being affected by adverse movements.

- Real options theory attempts to classify and value flexibility in general by taking the ideas of financial options pricing and developing them.

  - A financial option gives the owner the right, but not the obligation, to buy or sell a security at a given price. Analogously, companies that make strategic investments have the right, but not the obligation, to exploit these opportunities in the future.

  - As with financial options most real options involve spending more up front (analogous to the option premium) to give additional flexibility later.

- Conventional investment-appraisal techniques typically undervalue flexibility within projects with high uncertainty.

  - High uncertainty within a NPV context will result in a higher discount rate and a lower NPV. However, with such uncertainty any embedded real options will become more valuable.

There are many different classifications of real options:

Options to delay/defer

The key here is to be able to delay investment without losing the opportunity, creating a call option on the future investment.

Illustration 8 – Identifying real options – Delay/Defer

For example, establishing a drugs patent allows the owner of the patent to wait and see how market conditions develop before producing the drug, without the potential downside of competitors entering the market.

Options to switch/redeploy

It may be possible to switch the use of assets should market conditions change.

Illustration 9 – Identifying real options – switch/redeploy

For example, traditional production lines were set up to make one product. Modern flexible manufacturing systems (FMS) allow the product output to be changed to match customer requirements.

Similarly a new plant could be designed with resale and/or other uses in mind, using more general-purpose assets than dedicated to allow easier switching.

Illustration 10 – Identifying real options – Switch/redeploy

For example, when designing a factory management can choose whether to have higher or lower operating gearing. By having mainly variable costs, it is financially more beneficial if the factory does not have to operate every month.

Options to expand/contract

It may be possible to adjust the scale of an investment depending on the market conditions.

Illustration 11 – Identifying real options – expand

For example, when looking to develop their stadiums, many football clubs face the decision whether to build a one- or a two-tier stand:

- A one-tier stand would be cheaper but would be inadequate if the club's attendance improved greatly.

- A two-tier stand would allow for much greater fan numbers but would be more expensive and would be seen as a waste of money should attendance not improve greatly.

Some clubs (e.g. West Bromwich Albion in the UK) have solved this problem by building a one-tier stand with stronger foundations and designed in such a way (e.g. positioning of exits, corporate boxes, etc.) that it would be relatively straightforward to add a second tier at a later stage without knocking down the first tier. Such a stand is more expensive than a conventional one-tier stand but the premium paid makes it easier to expand at a later date when (if) attendance grows.

Illustration 12 – Identifying real options – expand

Amazon.com undertook a substantial investment to develop its customer base, brand name and information infrastructure for its core book business.

This in effect created a portfolio of real options to extend its operations into a variety of new businesses such as CDs, DVDs, etc.

Options to abandon

If a project has clearly identifiable stages such that investment can be staggered, then management have to decide whether to abandon or continue at the end of each stage.

Relevant costs and the decision to abandon

During our initial consideration of project appraisals, it was noted that past costs were irrelevant to any decision regarding the future of a project. This remains true for those occasions when the company has already started a project and wishes to establish whether it should continue with it, or whether it should abandon the project part way through its life.

The only relevant costs are future costs: these will be compared with future revenues to decide the viability of abandonment. Management is often reluctant to take a decision to abandon a project half-way through, as it is often considered to reflect a poor past decision; however true this may be, it would be even worse to compound the error by making another poor decision. Projects must, therefore, be kept constantly under review.

Factors in the decision to abandon

The following considerations must be taken into account in deciding whether to continue or abandon a project:

- future cash outflows associated with the project

- future cash inflows associated with the project

- revenues/costs that would arise if the project were abandoned

  - other projects, which may be:

    alternatives to the project under consideration

    more profitable uses of funds tied up in the project under review.

Each of these factors must be consciously assessed at each stage of the project's life and, if it is seen that abandoning the project would be more beneficial than proceeding with it, then an abandonment decision must be made.

During a post-completion appraisal it may be realised that the project is not likely to be so profitable as first thought and the possibility of abandoning it or terminating it early should be considered. Past cash flows are, of course, irrelevant to the decision – only future cash flows need to be considered. Abandoning the project is only necessary when the net discounted expected future cash flow of the project becomes negative.

Illustration 13 – Project abandonment decisions

Case I

A project, P, has expected cash flows as follows:

Year	Cash flow	DF @ 10%	PV
$			$
0	(3,500)	1.000	(3,500)
1	2,000	0.909	1,818
2	2,000	0.826	1,652
3	2,000	0.751	1,502
NPV			+ 1,472

The initial investment of $3,500 in project P represents the purchase of a customised machine, the price of which is known with certainty. Because it is a customised machine its resale value is low; it can only be sold for $1,000 immediately after purchase. Once the machine is bought, therefore, the expected value of abandoning the project would be $1,000 (1.0 × $1,000). This must be compared with the expected value of continuing with the project, which is $4,972 ($1,818 + $1,652 + $1,502). In this case the expected benefits of continuing with the project far outweigh the returns from abandoning it immediately.

Case II

The decision to abandon a project will usually be made as a result of revised expectations of future revenues and costs. These revisions may be consistent with the data on which the original investment decision was based, or represent an alteration to earlier expectations. If the decision is consistent with the original data, the possibility, but not the certainty, that the project might have to be abandoned would have been known when the project was accepted. In these circumstances, project abandonment is one of a known range of possible outcomes arising from accepting the project.

In Case I, the cashflows for the project were based on expected value techniques. The expected cash flows and probabilities were as follows:

Year 0	Year 1		Year 2		Year 3	
$	p	$	p	$	p	$
3,500	0.33	3,000	0.33	3,000	0.33	3,000
	0.33	2,000	0.33	2,000	0.33	2,000
	0.33	1,000	0.33	1,000	0.33	1,000
Expected value		2,000		2,000		2,000

In year 0, the expected net cash inflow in each year of project P's 3-year life is $2,000. The actual outcome of any of the 3 years is unknown at this point, and each of the three possible outcomes is equally likely. The factors that will cause any one of these results to occur may differ each year, or they may be the same each year. In some instances, a particular outcome in the first year may determine the outcome of years 2 and 3 with certainty. For example, the outcome of $3,000 in year 1 may mean that this same outcome will follow with certainty in years 2 and 3. Similarly outcomes of $2,000 and $1,000 in year 1 may be certain to be repeated in years 2 and 3. In year 0, the investor can only calculate the expected net cash flow in years 2 and 3, but with perfect correlation of flows between years these future flows are known with certainty at the end of year 1. If the year 1 inflow is either $3,000 or $2,000, perfect correlation between years will ensure that the actual NPV of the project will be positive. But if the first year's outcome is $1,000, the investment will have a negative NPV of $1,014, that is ($[3,500] + $1,000 × 2.486).

Should the project be abandoned? The information is now certain and so the decision on whether to abandon should be made using a risk-free interest rate and not the company's normal cost of capital. If we assume that the risk-free rate is 5 per cent, the present value of continuing at the end of year 1 will be:

Year	Cash flow	DF @ 5%	PV
$		$	
0	(1,000)	1.000	(1,000)
1	1,000	0.952	952
2	1,000	0.907	907
PV of continuing after 1 year			+ 859

Clearly the project should not be abandoned.

Case III

Consider another project, Project X with the following expected cash flows:

Year	Discounted cash flow $m
1	(8)
2	(16)
3	(24)
4	55
NPV	+ 7

The company experienced great difficulty in implementing the project in year 1, and the actual costs incurred during that year were $16 m. The company must then ask itself whether the actual outcome in year 1 necessitates any revision in the expected outcomes of later years. If no revision is required, further costs of $40 m (year 0 values) must be incurred to secure inflows of $55 m (year 0 values). The expected net present value of continuing with project X beyond year 1 will thus be $15 m (year 0 values). (Note that adjusting the figures to year 1 values would increase the expected NPV slightly, strengthening the case for continuation.)

The overall result of the investment would, of course, be negative by $1 m, if years 2 – 4 costs and revenues are as forecast. The excess spend of $8m in year 1 is greater than the $7 m net present value originally predicted. However, at the end of year 1 the $16 m is a sunk cost and does not influence a decision on termination made at that time.

15 Post-completion audit

The post-completion appraisal of projects provides a mechanism whereby experience gained from current and past projects can be fed into the organisation's decision-making process to aid decisions on future projects. In other words, it aids organisational learning. A post-completion appraisal reviews all aspects of an ongoing project in order to assess whether it has fulfilled its initial expectations. It is a forward-looking rather than a backward-looking technique. The task is often carried out by the Capital Expenditure Committee, or an appointed sub-committee.

Further discussion on post-completion audits

Benefits of post-completion audit

1. If managers know in advance that projects are going to be subject to a post-completion appraisal they ensure that assumptions and plans for the project are more accurate and realistic.

2. If an appraisal is carried out before the project life ends, and it is found that the benefits have been less than expected because of management inefficiency, then steps can be taken to improve efficiency.

3. It might identify weaknesses in the forecasting techniques and the estimating techniques used to evaluate the project. The discipline and quality of forecasting for future investments can be improved.

4. Managers may be motivated to achieve the forecast results if they are aware of a pending post-completion appraisal.

5. The appraisal reveals the reliability and quality of contractors and suppliers involved in the project.

6. The appraisal may highlight the reasons for success or failure in previous projects – thereby providing a learning experience for managers to aid better decision making in the future.

Problems with post-completion audits

1. It may not be possible to identify separately the costs and benefits of any particular project.

2. It can be a time-consuming and costly exercise.

3. Applied punitively, post-completion appraisal may lead managers to becoming over-cautious and risk averse.

4. The strategic effects of a capital investment project may take years to materialise and it may never be possible to identify and quantify them correctly.

5. There are many uncontrollable factors in long-term investments. A post-completion appraisal will not help managers change these factors in the future.

Role of post-appraisal in project abandonment

Those intimately involved with a project may be reluctant to admit, even to themselves, that early problems with a project are likely to continue. When problems are being experienced in project implementation, those involved may be tempted to try to resolve the situation in one of two ways. They can make a change in the original plans and/or incur further expenditure in order to meet the original objective.

Whether either of these responses is appropriate will depend on the particular circumstances of the project but any significant changes or deviations should not be undertaken without the formal approval of higher management. The control systems in place will normally require changes of scope to be documented and approved before they are undertaken. It is usually the responsibility of the engineers associated with the project to ensure that this is done.

Expected project cost overruns should be highlighted by the routine monitoring of project expenditure by accounting staff, and formal approval should be obtained for the anticipated overspend. A prerequisite of approval by top management will often be the provision of the same level of detailed justification as was required when the initial funds were sanctioned. These controls ensure that significant changes to the character of a project cannot be made without top management's approval. However, they do not, of themselves, ensure that the option to terminate a project is considered, although it would be unlikely that management would fail to consider this possibility.

Some companies require an audit on all projects that need additional funds. The request for further funding would then be considered alongside the audit report. Routine monitoring of projects tends to focus almost exclusively on costs. An audit will review both costs and revenues, and, most importantly, focuses on the future. By checking the continuing validity of both forecast costs and revenues, the post-audit team is in a position to prepare a report to advise management on the wisdom of continuing with the project.

16 Practice Questions

Objective Test Question 1: Discounting II

Calculate how much should be invested now in order to have $250 in eight years' time? The account pays 12% interest per annum.

Objective Test Question 2: Allen Ltd

Allen Ltd is considering a project with a three-year life producing the following costs and revenues:

	$
Cost of machine	100,000
Depreciation of machine (for three years)	20,000 p.a.
Residual value of machine	40,000
Annual cost of direct labour	20,000
Annual charge for foreman (10% apportionment)	5,000
Annual cost of components required	18,000
Annual net revenues from machine	80,000
Cost of capital	20%

Identify which of the following is closest to the net present value of the machine:

A   ($13,000)

B   ($11,380)

C $11,610

D $22,370

Objective Test Question 3: IRR Multiple Choice

Identify the correct explanation of the internal rate of return – it is the interest rate that equates the present value of expected future net cash flows to:

A   the initial cost of the investment outlay

B   the depreciation value of the investment

C   the terminal (compounded) value of future cash receipts

D   the firm's cost of capital

Objective Test Question 4: Delayed Annuities

The financial director of A Co has prepared the following schedule to enable her to appraise a new project. Interest rates are 10%. She wants to calculate the PV of the cash flows using two different assumptions regarding the project duration.

The assumptions are as follows:

A   That the real annual cash flow will be $250,000 from Year 4 for the foreseeable future.

B   That the real annual cash flow will be $250,000 from Year 4 to Year 18.

Year	T_0	T_1	T_2	T_3	Assumption (A) T_4 onwards	Assumption (B) T_4–T_{18}
	$000	$000	$000	$000	$000	$000
Net cash flow	(2,000)	(440)	363	399	250	250

Required:

Calculate the NPV from the project under

Assumption A   [ ]

Assumption B   [ ]

Case Study Style Question: Pepper Studios

You are a Financial Manager employed by Pepper Studios ('Pepper'), a company that makes feature films. Pepper produces and distributes films globally, in partnership with external investors.

You receive the following email from the Finance Director:

> **From:** Finance Director
> **To:** Financial Manager
> **Date:** today
> **Subject:** film investments 2021
>
> We now have to finalise our decision on our next film production. While the additional marketing spend should generate future income it does affect our ability to invest in our original film choices for 2021. Our available budget for investment next year is now $420m.
>
> I have attached your original summary of our short listed films for the year. I would really like to be able to commit to all four as they all provide a good return, but I know that is not possible.
>
> There is the additional complication that there is a possibility that we could use the same lead actor for both **The Next Day of Summer** and **Lost Property 2**. Although this is not decided, I would like this to be taken account of when looking at our film choices for next year. I need you to prepare a detailed report so that we can make an informed decision about this at the next board meeting.

Attachment:

Potential investments in 2021				
	Production, $m	Marketing, $m	Total, $m	NPV, $m
'The Next Day Of Summer'	120	80	200	450
'Lost Property 2'	160	60	220	460
'7 Sleeps'	220	170	390	890
'Mashatac'	140	80	220	440

Prepare a report presenting an analysis of the figures provided, including a recommendation as to what film or films Pepper Studios should invest in this year.

You should provide an analysis for the same lead actor being used in 'The Next Day of Summer' and 'Lost Property 2' and an analysis where different lead actors are used. Please advise on other factors which should be considered in making this decision, including a brief explanation of capital rationing.

Answers to examples and objective test questions

Example 1: Compounding

$V = 450(1.0625)^{12} = \$931.45$

Example 2: Discounting I

$X = 25,000/(1.10)^6 = \$14,112$

Example 3: Wilson Ltd

Year	Cash flow $	DF at 9%	PV $
0	(240,000)	1.000	(240,000)
1	80,000	0.917	73,360
2	120,000	0.842	101,040
3	70,000	0.772	54,040
4	40,000	0.708	28,320
5	20,000	0.650	13,000
NPV			+ 29,760

The PV of cash inflows exceeds the PV of cash outflows by $29,760, which means that the project will earn a DCF return in excess of 9%, i.e. it will earn a surplus of $29,760 after paying the cost of financing. It should therefore be undertaken.

Example 4: Mickey NPV

Year	Discount factor	Project A Cash flow $000	Project A Present value $000	Project B Cash flow $000	Project B Present value $000
0		(450)	(450)	(100)	(100)
1	0.909	200	181.8	50	45.45
2	0.826	150	123.9	40	33.04
3	0.751	100	75.1	30	22.53
4	0.683	100	68.3	20	13.66
5	0.621	120	74.52	30	18.63
		NPV =	73.62	NPV =	33.31

Example 5: Mickey IRR

(a)

Year	Discount factors at 20%	Project A Net cash flow $000	PV $000
0	1.000	(450)	(450)
1	0.833	200	167
2	0.694	150	104
3	0.579	100	58
4	0.482	100	48
5	0.402	120	48
		NPV @ 20% =	(25)

$$IRR = L + \frac{N_L}{N_L - N_H} \times (H - L)$$

$$IRR = 10 + \frac{74}{74 - (-25)} \times (20 - 10)$$

$$IRR = 10 + \frac{74}{99} \times (10)$$

$$IRR = 10 + (0.747 \times 10)$$

IRR = 17.5%

(b) **Project B**

At 10% the NPV was $33,310

At 20% the NPV is $8,510

At 30% the NPV is ($9,150)

$$IRR = 20 + \frac{8,510}{8,510 - (-9,150)} \times (30 - 20)$$

$$IRR = 20 + \frac{8,510}{17,660} \times (10)$$

$$IRR = 20 + (0.482 \times 10)$$

IRR = 24.8%

Example 6: Potential project

$$IRR = 10\% + \frac{50,000}{50,000 - (-10,000)} \times (15\% - 10\%) = 14.17\%$$

Example 7: IRR and decision making

Year $	Cash flow	DF @ 15% $	PV @ 15%	DF @ 20% $	PV @ 20%
0	(50,000)	1.000	(50,000)	1.000	(50,000)
1	18,000	0.870	15,660	0.833	14,994
2	25,000	0.756	18,900	0.694	17,350
3	20,000	0.658	13,160	0.579	11,580
4	10,000	0.572	5,720	0.482	4,820
NPV			+ 3,440		(1,256)

The IRR is above 15% but below 20%. Using the interpolation method

1   The NPV is + 3,440 at 15%.

2   The NPV is – 1,256 at 20%.

3   The estimated IRR is therefore:

$$IRR = 15\% + \frac{3,440}{(3,440 - (-1,256))} \times (20 - 15)\%$$

$$= 15\% + 3.7\%$$

$$= 18.7\%$$

The project is expected to earn a DCF return in excess of the target rate of 17%, so on financial grounds (ignoring risk) it is a worthwhile investment.

Example 8: Alpine Ltd

MIRR = [(TV of inflows/PV of outflows)$^{1/n}$] – 1

Here, n = 4

The inflows occur at T_1, T_2, T_3 and T_4. With a cost of capital at 8%, their terminal value TV may be calculated as follows:

	T_1	T_2	T_3	T_4	Total
Cash inflow	8,000	12,000	4,000	2,000	
TV	8,000 × (1.08)^3	12,000 × (1.08)^2	4,000 × (1.08)	2,000	**30,395**
	= 10,078	= 13,997	= 4,320		

The Present Value of outflows is $20,000.

MIRR = [(TV of inflows/PV of outflows)$^{1/4}$] – 1

MIRR = [(30,395/20,000)$^{1/4}$] – 1

MIRR = 11.03%

Example 9: Present Values, Annuities and perpetuities

1   This is a standard 14-year annuity with one additional payment at T_0.

Step 1: Look up the 14-year AF →

AF = 9.295

Step 2: Add 1 → 9.295 + 1 = 10.295

Step 3: Calculate the PV → 300 × 10.295 = $3,088.50

2   This is simply a standard perpetuity with one additional payment at T_0.

Step 1: Calculate the perpetuity factor → 1/0.22 = 4.545

Step 2: Add 1 → 4.545 + 1 = 5.545

Step 3: Calculate the PV → 33,000 × 5.545 = $182,985

Example 10: Capital Rationing

Project	Investment Required	Net Present Value	NPV ranking	Profitability Index	Index ranking
	$000	$000			
A	3,400	850	1	0.25	6
B	2,750	825	2	0.30	4
C	2,000	720	3	0.36	3
D	3,400	680	4	0.20	7
E	860	430	5	0.50	1
F	950	400	6	0.42	2
G	1,250	350	7	0.28	5

(a)   If the company ranks the projects according to highest NPVs, it can invest in projects A, B, and C in full, a total investment of $3,400,000 + $2,750,000 + $2,000,000 = $8,150,000. Project D can be partially invested in for $9,000,000 – $8,150,000 = $850,000.

Total NPV = $850,000 + $825,000 + $720,000 + ($850,000/$3,400,000) × $680,000 = $2,565,000.

(b)   If the company selects projects according to their profitability index, it can invest in projects E, F, C, B, G, a total investment of $7,810,000. Project A can be partially invested in for $1,190,000.

Total NPV = $430,000 + $400,000 + $720,000 + $825,000 +$350,000 + ($1,190,000/$3,400,000) × $850,000 = $3,022,500.

Objective Test Question 1: Discounting II

Here, terminal (final) value 'V' = $250

$V = X(1 + r)^n$ so $250 = X (1.12)^8$

$X = \dfrac{\$250}{2.48}$ so X sum to invest today = $100.97

Objective Test Question 2: Allen Ltd

Total relevant cash flows between years 1 and 3 may be calculated as follows:

Annual net revenues from machine $80,000

Annual cost of components required ($18,000)

Annual cost of direct labour ($20,000)

A net total of $42,000, that needs discounting using an AF @ 20% for 3 years = 2.106 (from the tables)

Year	Cash flow $000		Discount factor	Present value
0	Initial cost	(100)		(100)
1 – 3	Annual cash	42	2.106	88.452
3	Residual	40	0.579	23.16
				11.612

Net present value = $11,612 so **Answer C**

Objective Test Question 3: IRR Multiple Choice

At the IRR, PV of future net cash flows = initial capital outlay.

Answer A

Objective Test Question 4: Delayed annuities

Year	T$_0$	T$_1$	T$_2$	T$_3$	T$_4$	Assumption (A) onwards	Assumption (B) T$_4$–T18
	$000	$000	$000	$000		$000	$000
Net cash flow	(2,000)	(440)	363	399		250	250
Perpetuity factor (here discounts the cash flow to T$_3$)						1 ÷ 0.1 = 10	
AF (here discounts the cash flow to T$_3$)							15-yr 10% AF =7.606
DFs @ 10%	1.000	0.909	0.826	0.751		0.751	0.751
PV	(2,000)	(400)	300	300		1,878	1,428
NPV (A)						78	
NPV (B)							(372)

Case Study Style Question: Pepper Studios

Date: Today

Subject: Film investments 2021

There is a short list of four potential films which we could decide to invest in in 2021:

- 'The next day of summer'
- 'Lost property 2'
- '7 sleeps'
- 'Mashatac'

The investment required to make all four films is estimated at $1,030m but the capital available for investment is $420m. The financial decision as to which film to invest in should focus on which investment or combination of investments would maximise the total NPV.

Different lead actors

Given the capital available, the possible investment combinations for 2021 assuming different lead actors in each film could be:

- Option 1: '7 sleeps' only (cost $390m)
- Option 2: 'The next day of summer' and 'Lost property 2' (cost $420m)
- Option 3: 'The next day of summer' and 'Mashatac' (cost $420m)

If we decide to make only '7 sleeps', the expected NPV generated would be $890m, whereas investing in 'The next day of summer' and 'Lost property 2' would generate a total NPV of $910m. If 'The next day of summer' is produced along with 'Mashatac' the total NPV would be $890m.

From this, the decision should be to invest in Option 2: 'The next day of summer' and 'Lost property 2' as this will maximise the NPV.

Same lead actor

If the same lead actor is used in 'The next day of summer' and 'Lost property 2' then these films become mutually exclusive. It is not possible to make both films at the same time. This means that option 2 above, our recommended option, is no longer possible. Options 1 and 3 both give the same NPV of $890m but Option 1 costs $390m compared to $420m for Option 3, therefore the decision in this case would be to make '7 sleeps' only.

Other factors to consider

Assuming different lead actors, investing jointly in 'The next day of summer' and 'Lost property 2' is financially the best decision as the NPV is $20m higher than the alternatives. However, the investment required for this combination is $420m which is at the top of our capital limit. This leaves us no contingency. This could cause a problem if either film was to overrun as this would cause the costs to come in over budget. We would be taking a big risk if we commit to this combination of investments as we may not have the capital available to complete one or both of them should additional funding be required but not available.

While the investment in '7 sleeps' would result in a lower NPV the investment in this film of $390m is $30m under our limit. This would give us a contingency budget for this film and could also leave capital available for other investments.

In addition we must consider the risk of taking on two films at the same time rather than focusing on one. It may be a better decision to use our resources to focus on one film rather than producing two at the same time. The same resources could be required in both films meaning delays in production.

Where the decision is made to use the same lead actor in 'The next day of summer' and 'Lost property 2' then the two possible investment options give the same NPV ($890m), but producing '7 sleeps' only would cost $30m less providing a contingency of $30m for the film or freeing up $30m which could be used on other projects.

This financial analysis and recommendation is based on the projected costs and NPVs for each project. Care should be taken as all figures used in this analysis are estimates. It is very difficult to accurately predict the costs and revenues for any film. Small changes in these estimates could result in a different recommendation and none of this analysis gives any guarantee of success.

Capital rationing

Each of the four short listed films has a positive NPV, therefore all are worth doing. This is because all investments with positive NPVs will increase shareholder value.

The reason that companies do not undertake all investments with a positive NPV is down to restrictions in the capital available. Where there is insufficient capital available to invest in all projects which generate a positive NPV, this is known as capital rationing.

There are two types of capital rationing, hard and soft:

- Hard capital rationing is an absolute limit on the amount of finance available and is often imposed by lenders and investors. Our films are generally financed in partnership with external investors. Where these investors were not available, or not willing to invest, we would have to finance our films from our own internal funds which would limit us to the funds were have available.

- Soft capital rationing is where a company imposes its own rationing on capital. While this is contrary to the rational view of shareholder wealth maximisation companies may choose not to spend up to the limit of available capital but to retain some capital for other future · projects or for contingency reasons.

Financial Manager

Investment appraisal – further aspects

Chapter learning objectives

Lead	Component
B1: Capital investment decision making	Apply the data required for decision making (a) Relevant cash flows (b) Non-financial information
B3: Apply investment appraisal techniques to evaluate different projects	(a) Payback (b) ARR (c) IRR (d) NPV

1 Chapter summary

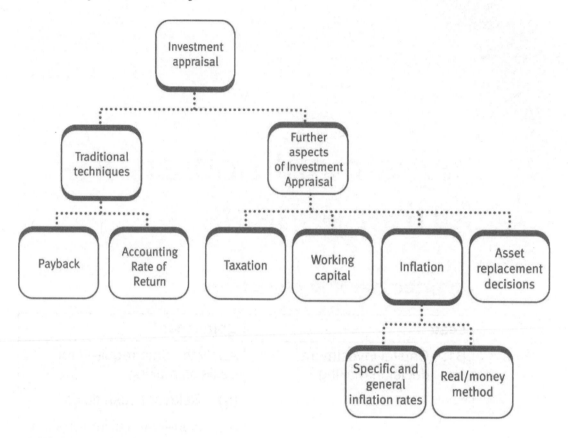

There are four widely used appraisal methods:

1 The payback period.

2 The Accounting Rate of Return (ARR)

3 The Internal Rate of Return (IRR)

4 The Net Present Value (NPV)

As seen in the previous chapter, NPV and IRR both consider the time value of money: they are discounted cash flow (DCF) techniques. In this chapter, we will introduce alternative investment appraisal techniques but we will also incorporate further complexities in NPV calculations – namely how we deal with tax, working capital and inflation issues.

2 Other investment appraisal techniques: the payback period

The payback period is the time a project will take to pay back the money spent on it. It is based on expected cash flows and provides a measure of liquidity and risk (the quicker that an investor can recover the initial investment the quicker they can reinvest it elsewhere and the lower the risk of this particular investment).

This is the time which elapses until the invested capital is recovered. It considers cash flows only.

Unlike DCF techniques, it is assumed that the **cash flows** occur evenly during the year.

Decision criteria

- Compare the payback period to the company's maximum return time allowed and if the payback is quicker the project should be accepted.

- Faced with a choice between mutually-exclusive projects, choose the project with the quickest payback (provided it meets the company's target payback period).

Calculation – constant annual cash flows

$$\text{Payback period} = \frac{\text{Initial investment}}{\text{Annual cash inflow}}$$

A payback period may not be for an exact number of years. To calculate the payback in years and months you should multiply the decimal fraction of a year by 12 to the number of months.

Illustration – Payback

An expenditure of $2 million is expected to generate net cash inflows of $500,000 each year for the next seven years.

The payback period for the project may be calculated as follows:

$$\text{Payback period} = \frac{\$2m}{\$500,000}$$

Payback period = 4 years

Example 1: Payback

A project requires an initial investment of $1,000,000 and then earns net cash inflows of $150,000 per year for 7 years.

What is the project's payback period?

Calculations – Uneven cash flows

However, if cash inflows are uneven, the payback has to be calculated by working out the cumulative cash flow over the life of a project.

Example 2: Target Payback

A business is considering a project which would last 5 years and have an initial investment of $40,000 in machinery. At the end of the project the machinery would have a scrap value of $4,000. The project would provide annual net cash inflows as follows:

Year	Net cash flow ($000)
1	16
2	20
3	12
4	12
5	10

The company has a target payback period of 2.5 years and new projects must also provide and average accounting rate of return of at least 15% p.a.

Advise the company on whether this project meets the company's targets.

Advantages and disadvantages of payback

Advantages

- Simplicity: as a concept, it is easily understood and is easily calculated.

- Improving investment conditions: When investment conditions are expected to improve in the near future, attention is directed to those projects that will release funds soonest, to take advantage of the improving climate.

- Payback favours projects with a quick return: it is argued that these are to be preferred because rapid project payback leads to rapid company growth (in fact, such a policy will lead to many profitable investment opportunities being overlooked if their payback period does not happen to be particularly swift).

  It is also argued that rapid payback reduces the risk of liquidity problems – but liquidity problems are best dealt with separately, through cash forecasting.

- Cash flows: cash flows are much more objective than accounting figures such as profit. Profit figures are easily manipulated using accounting policies, whereas this is not possible for cash flows.

> **Disadvantages**
>
> - Project returns may be ignored – In particular, cash flows arising after the payback period are totally ignored.
>
> - Timing ignored – Cash flows are effectively categorised as pre-payback or post-payback, but no more accurate measure is made. In particular, the time value of money is ignored. This problem can be overcome if the discounted payback method is used.
>
> - Lack of objectivity – There is no objective measure as to what length of time should be set as the minimum payback period. Investment decisions are therefore subjective.
>
> - Project profitability is ignored – Payback takes no account of the effects on business profits and periodic performance of the project, as evidenced in the financial statements. This is critical if the business is to be reasonably viewed by users of the accounts.

3 Accounting rate of return (ARR)

The ARR method calculates a percentage return provided by the accounting profits of the project.

The most common formula is:

$$ARR = \frac{\text{Average annual profit}}{\text{Average value of investment}} \qquad \textbf{LEARN}$$

Important notes to the formula:

- The 'average annual profit' is after depreciation.

- Net cash flow is normally equivalent to 'profit before depreciation'.

Average annual profit = Net cash flow less depreciation

- The average value of the investment represents the average capital employed over the life of the project.

$$\text{Average value of investment} = \frac{\text{Initial investment plus residual value}}{2} \qquad \textbf{LEARN}$$

Decision criteria

- The ARR for a project may be compared with the company's target return and if higher the project should be accepted.

- Faced with a choice of mutually-exclusive investments, the project with the highest ARR should be chosen (provided it meets the company's target return).

Example 3: Mickey ARR

Project A

Initial investment		$450,000			
Scrap value in year 5		$20,000			
Year:	1	2	3	4	5
Annual cash flows ($000)	200	150	100	100	100

Project B

Initial investment		$100,000			
Scrap value in year 5		$10,000			
Year:	1	2	3	4	5
Annual cash flows ($000)	50	40	30	20	20

Required:

Calculate the ARR for each project, and indicate which project should be chosen.

Example 4: ARR and Payback

$50,000 is to be spent on a machine having a life of five years and a residual value of $5,000. Operating cash inflows will be the same each year, except for year 1 when the figure will be $6,000. The accounting rate of return (ARR) is measured as average annual profit as a percentage of the initial investment. If the ARR is 30% then identify the payback period:

A   2.75 years

B   2.15 years

C   1.85 years

D   2.54 years

Advantages	Disadvantages
• Simple to understand: As with the payback period, it is easily understood and easily calculated.	• Ignores the time value of money.
• Widely used and accepted.	• Is not a measure of absolute profitability.
• It considers the whole life of the project.	• Does not consider cash flows. Uses subjective accounting profits, which include depreciation.
Link with other accounting measures – Return on capital employed, calculated annually to assess a business or sector of a business (and therefore the investment decisions made by that business), is widely used and its use for investment appraisal is consistent with that. The ARR is expressed in percentage terms with which managers are familiar. However, neither this nor the preceding point necessarily justify the use of ARR.	It fails to take account of either the project life or the timing of cash flows (and time value of money) within that life. For example, a project with a very long life which has a high ARR might be accepted before a project with a shorter life and marginally lower ARR. The NPV of the shorter project may actually be higher. In example 6, it can be seen that Project B has a much higher ARR but that Project A has a much higher NPV. Project A is the project that should be accepted by management on a financial basis.
	• It will vary with specific accounting policies, and the extent to which project costs are capitalised. Profit measurement is thus 'subjective', and ARR figures for identical projects could vary from business to business depending on the accounting policies used.
	• Like all rate of return measures, it is not a measurement of absolute gain in wealth for the business owners.
	• There is no definite investment signal. The decision to invest or not remains subjective in view of the lack of an objectively set target ARR.
	• It is concluded that the ARR does not provide a reliable basis for project evaluation.

Discounted payback

One of the major criticisms of using the payback period is that it does not take into account the time value of money. As seen in the previous chapter, the discounted payback technique attempts to overcome this criticism by measuring the time required for the **present values** of the cash inflows from a project to equal the present values of the cash outflows.

The techniques are identical but the present value of the cash flows is used to calculate the cumulative cash flow and to determine the payback period.

4   Dealing with taxation

Taxation may have a significant impact on the viability of a capital investment project. Taxation payments and savings in tax payments are clearly cash flows associated with the project. They are relevant, and should be included in investment appraisal.

There are two tax effects that we need to deal with in investment appraisal, which are the effects of corporation tax, and the impact of tax depreciation (also known as capital allowances).

Typical assumptions are that the taxable profits will be **the net cash flows from the project less any tax depreciation**.

We also make assumptions about the timing of the payments: corporation tax is usually paid in two instalments. Half the tax is payable in the year in which it arises, the balance is paid in the following year.

The corporation tax rate will be given in the question.

Taxation has the following effects on an investment appraisal problem:

- Project cash flows will give rise to taxation which itself has an impact on project appraisal. Normally we assume that tax is paid in two instalments, where half the tax is payable in the year in which it arises, and the balance is paid in the following year. However, it is possible for alternative assumptions to be made and so you should read any examination question carefully to ascertain precisely what assumptions are made in the question.

- Organisations benefit from being able to claim tax depreciation (also known as capital allowances) – a tax deductible alternative to depreciation. The effect of these is to reduce the amount of tax that organisations are required to pay. Again it is important to read any examination question carefully in order to identify what treatment is expected by the examiner. A common assumption is that tax depreciation is available on a 25% reducing balance basis.

Note that the **tax depreciation is not a cash flow** and to calculate the tax impact we have to multiply each year's tax depreciation by the corporation tax rate. The effect of tax depreciation is on the amount of tax payable, which is the relevant cash flow.

In dealing with these tax effects it is always assumed that:

- where a tax loss arises from the project, there are sufficient taxable profits elsewhere in the organisation to allow the loss to reduce any relevant (subsequent) tax payment (and it may therefore be treated as a cash inflow) and that the company has sufficient taxable profits to obtain full benefit from tax depreciation.

In practice, the effects of taxation are more complex, and are influenced by a number of factors including the following:

- the taxable profits and tax rate

- the company's accounting period and tax payment dates

- whether assets qualify for tax depreciation

- losses available for set-off.

A detailed knowledge of tax is not required for this paper. Assumptions and simplifications will be made. These will usually be set out clearly in each examination question. It is important to follow the instructions for the treatment of tax in the question being attempted.

Tax depreciation

Tax depreciation is used to reduce taxable profits, and the consequent reduction in a tax payment should be treated as a cash saving arising from the acceptance of the project. In this examination tax depreciation is generally allowed on the cost of plant and machinery at the rate of 25% on a reducing balance basis. It may also be possible to claim tax depreciation on the costs of installation, such as labour and overhead costs of removing an old machine and levelling the area for the new machine.

Balancing allowance (or charge)

When the plant is eventually sold, there may be a difference between the reducing balance amount and the selling price of the asset. An appropriate adjustment must be made to ensure that the company receives allowances equal to the total allowance allowed (i.e. purchase price less final value).

 Balancing allowances/charges

If a business buys a capital asset in one year and sells it several years later, the total tax relief it will receive is the tax on the cost of the asset less its eventual disposal value.

For example, if a business buys equipment for $100,000 in Year 0 and disposes of it in Year 5 for $20,000, it will receive tax relief on the net cost of $80,000. If the rate of corporation tax is 30%, the reduction in tax payments over the five years would be 30% × $80,000 = $24,000.

Balancing allowances are given as a final deduction to ensure the full fall in value has been allowed. Balancing charges occur where the total tax depreciation claimed exceeds the fall in value of the asset. The excess claimed is treated as a taxable amount in the year of disposal.

Timing of the tax savings associated with tax depreciation

The benefit of tax saved because of tax depreciation is received when the corporation tax should have been paid. Thus, half the tax is saved in the current year, and half is saved in the year following.

Illustration: Yuba Ltd

An asset is purchased for $72,500 by Yuba Ltd. At the end of the fourth year it will be sold for $10,000. Tax depreciation is available at 25 per cent reducing balance and corporation tax is payable at 30 per cent per annum.

Corporation tax is paid in two instalments, with half the tax payable in the year in which it arises, and the balance paid in the following year.

Required:

(a) Calculate the tax depreciation each year and the associated corporation tax saving.

(b) Illustrate the timing of the tax savings calculated in part (a).

(a) Tax depreciation and the associated savings can be calculated as follows:

Year	$	Tax depreciation $	Tax saved at 30% $
0 – Investment	72,500		
1 – Tax depreciation (@25%)	18,125	18,125	5,438
	54,375		
2 – Tax depreciation (@25%)	13,594	13,594	4,078
	40,781		
3 – Tax depreciation (@25%)	10,195	10,195	3,059
	30,586		
4 – Disposal	10,000		
4 – Balancing allowance	20,586	20,586	6,176
Total tax depreciation/tax saved		62,500	18,751

The total tax depreciation will equal the difference between the initial cost ($72,500) and the residual value ($10,000). The total tax saving will be 30% of the tax depreciation (30% × $62,500).

(b)

Year	Cash benefit received	Total
1	$5,438/2 = $2,719	**$2,719**
2	$2,719 + ($4,078/2) = $4,758	**$4,758**
3	$2,039 + $1,529	**$3,568**
4	$1,529 + $3,088	**$4,617**
5	$3,088	**$3,088**

 For tax purposes, care must be taken to identify the exact time of asset purchase.

- Assets are assumed to be bought at T_0.

- It should be assumed that the asset is bought at the start of the accounting period and therefore the first tax depreciation is offset against the year 1 net cash flows.

Example 5: Placer Ltd

An asset is bought by Placer Ltd for a project at a cost of $25,000. The asset will be used for four years before being disposed of for $5,000. Tax-allowable depreciation is available at 25% reducing balance and the tax rate is 30%.

(a) Calculate the tax allowable depreciation and hence the tax savings for each year if tax is paid (and saved) a year in arrears.

(b) How would your answer to the previous question change if the sales proceeds for the asset at the end of the project had been $15,000?

NPV with tax – Example pro forma (assume a two-year project)

	Year 0	Year 1	Year 2	Year 3
	$	$	$	$
Cash inflows		X	X	
Cash outflows		(X)	(X)	
		—	—	
Net cash flow		X	X	
Tax on net cash flow		(X)	(X)	(X)
Investment	(X)			
Scrap value			X	
Tax depreciation savings (which would need a separate working)		X	X	X
Working capital	(X)		X	
Net cash flows	(X)	X	X	X
Discount factor	1.00	x	x	x
Present value	PV	PV	PV	PV

Example 6: Amigo Ltd

Amigo Ltd is considering investing in a new machine which has a capital cost of $25,000. It has an estimated life of four years and a residual value of $5,000 at the end of four years. The machine qualifies for tax depreciation at the rate of 25% per year on a reducing balance basis.

An existing machine would be sold immediately for $8,000 if the new machine were to be bought. The existing machine has a tax written down value of $3,000.

The existing machine generates annual net contribution of $30,000. This is expected to increase by 40% if the new machine is purchased.

Amigo pays corporation tax on its profits at the rate of 30%, with half of the tax being payable in the year that the profit is earned and half in the following year. The company's after tax cost of capital is 15% per year.

Calculate whether the investment is worthwhile. Should Amigo invest in the new machine?

5 Working capital

Working capital is treated as an investment at the start of the project, like any other investment. Any additional working capital requirements are invested when required. **Only the change in working capital is treated as a cash flow.**

- Working capital does not qualify for tax relief – so is ignored in the taxation and tax depreciation calculations.

- At the end of the project the working capital is 'released'. This is treated as a cash inflow at the end of the project, equal to the total investment in working capital (unless told otherwise).

 For a short life project, with cash flows inflating at different rates, it is best to set the NPV calculation out with the cash flows down the side and the time across the top.

Example 7: Camp Ltd

Camp plc has produced and marketed sleeping bags for several years. The sleeping bags are much heavier than some of the modern sleeping bags being introduced to the market. The company is concerned about the effect this will have on its sales.

Camp plc are considering investing in new technology that would enable them to produce a much lighter and more compact sleeping bag. The new machine will cost $250,000 and is expected to have a life of four years with a scrap value of $10,000. In addition an investment of $35,000 in working capital will be required initially.

The following forecast annual trading account has been prepared for the project:

	$
Sales	200,000
Material	(40,000)
Labour	(30,000)
Variable overheads	(10,000)
Depreciation	(20,000)
Annual profit	100,000

The company's cost of capital is 10%. Corporation tax is charged at 30% and is paid in two instalments, with half the tax payable in the year in which it arises, and the balance paid in the following year. Tax depreciation of 25% on reducing balance is available on capital expenditure.

Required:

Calculate whether Camp plc should invest in the new technology.

Example 8: Smith Ltd

Smith Ltd has decided to increase its productive capacity to meet an anticipated increase in demand for its products. The extent of this increase in capacity has still to be determined, and a management meeting has been called to decide which of the following two mutually exclusive proposals – A or B – should be undertaken.

The following information is available:

	Proposal A $	Proposal B $
Capital expenditure		
Buildings	50,000	100,000
Plant	200,000	300,000
Installation	10,000	15,000
Net Income		
Annual pre-depreciation profits (note (1))	70,000	95,000
Other relevant income and expenditure		
Sales promotion (note (2))	–	15,000
Plant scrap value	10,000	15,000
Buildings disposable value (note (3))	30,000	60,000
Working capital required over the project life	50,000	65,000

Notes:

(1) The investment life is ten years.

(2) An exceptional amount of expenditure on sales promotion of $15,000 will have to be spent in year 2 of proposal B. This has not been taken into account in calculating pre-depreciation profits.

(3) It is the intention to dispose of the buildings in ten years' time.

Using an 8% discount rate, calculate which of the two alternatives should be chosen.

6 The impact of inflation on cash flows

If an exam question involves inflation, we normally have to either adjust the cash flows, or adjust the cost of capital.

 Where cash flows have not been increased for expected inflation they are known as **current cash flows, or real cash flows**.

 Where cash flows have been increased to take account of expected inflation they are known as **money cash flows**, or **nominal cash flows**. Remember, if they do take inflation into account, they represent expected flows of money, hence the term 'money cash flows'.

You can assume that cash flows you are given in the exam are the money cash flows, unless told otherwise.

If the examiner specifies that the **cash flows are in current terms** you will generally need to put these in money terms before you can discount them. For example, if the question tells you that sales for the next 3 years are $100 in current terms, but are expected to inflate by 10%, then what is actually meant is that the sales will be:

Year 1: $110

Year 2: $121   } i.e. these are the cash flows in money terms

Year 3: $133.10

Make sure you read the question carefully. Sometimes, you will be given the **cash flows in Year 1 terms** with subsequent inflation.

- For example, if the question says "Sales will be $100 in the first year, but are then going to inflate by 10% for the next two years", then the sales will be:

Year 1: $100

Year 2: $110   } compare these to the previous example – make sure
                              you understand why they are different!

Year 3: $121

Methods of dealing with inflation

The impact of inflation can be dealt with in two different ways – both methods give the same NPV.

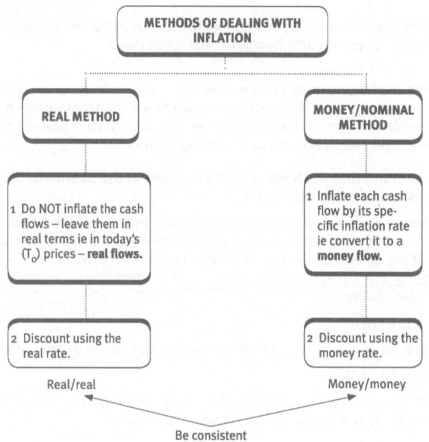

The real rate of return

If money is invested in an account, it will earn interest. However, inflation will have the effect of reducing the value of the return. By deflating the future cash (money) we can find the real return from the investment, i.e. the return at today's prices.

Formula

To find the real rate of return we can use the following formula:

$$(1 + r) = \frac{(1 + m)}{(1 + i)}$$

LEARN

This is where:

- **r** is the real rate of return

- **m** is the money cost of capital (this is the company's normal cost of capital)

- **i** is the rate of inflation.

Illustration

$1,000 is invested in an account that pays 10% interest per annum. Inflation is currently 7% per annum.

Calculate the real return on the investment.

After 1 year $1,000 will have compounded up to $1,000 × 1.10 = $1,100.

Now deflate this figure to find the real return on the investment:

$1,100 ÷ 1.07 = $1,028

Therefore, the $1,000 has increased by 2.8% in real terms. This is the real rate.

It can be calculated using the formula as follows:

$$(1 + r) = \frac{(1 + m)}{(1 + i)}$$

$$(1 + r) = \frac{(1 + 0.10)}{(1 + 0.07)}$$

$(1 + r) = 1.028$

$r \quad = 1.028 - 1$

$r \quad = 0.028 = 2.8\%$

Using the real rate of return in questions

If there is one rate of inflation in the question both the real and money method will give the same answer. However it is easier to adjust one discount rate, rather than all the cash flows over a number of years. This is particularly true where the cash flows are annuities. The real method is the only possible method where they are perpetuities.

Although it is theoretically possible to use the real method in questions incorporating tax, it is extremely complex. It is therefore much safer (and easier) to use the money/nominal method in all questions where tax is taken into account.

Example 9: Flo Ltd

A company has a money cost of capital of 21% per annum. The inflation rate is currently estimated at 9% per annum.

Identify the real cost of capital:

A   9%

B   11%

C   12%

D   14%

Example 10: Storm Ltd

Storm Ltd is evaluating project X which requires an initial investment of $50,000. Expected net cash flows are $20,000 per annum for 4 years at today's prices. However these are expected to rise by 5.5% per annum because of inflation. The firm's cost of capital is 15%. Calculate the NPV by:

(a) discounting money cash flows

(b) discounting real cash flows.

7 Specific and general inflation rates

The examples given above had all cash flows inflating at the general rate of inflation. In practice, inflation does not affect all costs to the same extent. In some investment appraisal questions you may be given information on more than one inflation rate. In these situations you will have information on both specific inflation rates and general inflation rates.

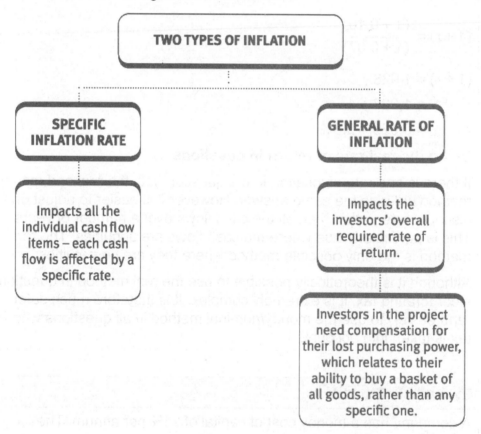

 Inflation can impact different types of products in different ways: prices don't all rise at exactly the same rate. In situations where you are given a number of specific inflation rates, the real method outlined above cannot be used.

Example 11: Andra Ltd

A company is considering a cost-saving project. This involves purchasing a machine costing $7,000, which will result in annual savings (in real terms) on wage costs of $1,000 and on material costs of $400.

The following forecasts are made of the rates of inflation each year for the next five years:

Wage costs	10%
Material costs	5%
General prices	6%

The cost of capital of the company, in real terms, is 8.5%.

Calculate the NPV of the project, assuming that the machine has a life of five years and no scrap value.

The following gives a useful summary of how to approach examination questions.

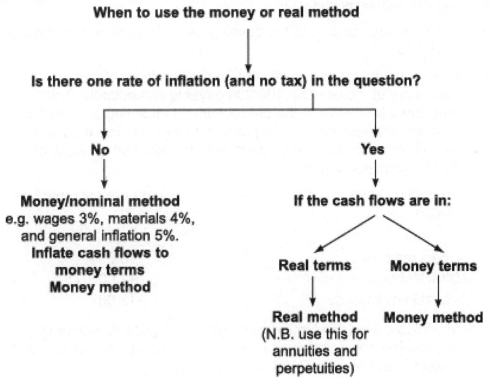

If a question contains both tax and inflation, it is advisable to use the money method.

The money method

To use the real method when cash flows inflate at different rates (specific rates) is extremely complex and would involve a lot of calculations. It is therefore advisable to always use the money method in these situations. This involves:

- inflating the cash flows at their specific inflation rates
- discounting using the money rate.

Very often the money rate will not be given in the question but will need to be calculated. This should be done using the real rate and the general inflation rate.

Example 12: Thunder Ltd

Thunder plc has just developed a new product to be called the Lightening and is now considering whether to put it into production. The following information is available:

(i) Costs incurred to date in the development of Lightening amount to $480,000.

(ii) Production of Lightening will require the purchase of new machinery at a cost of $2,400,000 payable immediately. This machinery is specific to the production of Lightening and will be obsolete and valueless when production ceases. The machinery has a production life of four years and a production capacity of 30,000 units per annum.

(iii) Production costs of Lightening (at year 1 prices) are estimated as follows:

	$
Direct material	8.00
Direct labour	12.00
Variable overheads	12.00

In addition, fixed production costs (at year 1 prices), including straight-line depreciation on plant and machinery specific to this project, will amount to $800,000 per annum.

(iv) The selling price of Lightening will be $80.00 per unit (at year 1 prices). Demand is expected to be 25,000 units per annum for the next four years.

(v) The retail price index is expected to be at 5% per annum for the next four years and the selling price of Lightening is expected to increase at the same rate. Annual inflation rates for production costs are expected to be as follows:

	%
Direct material	4
Direct labour	10
Variable overheads	4
Fixed costs	5

(vi) The company's cost of capital in money terms is expected to be 15%.

You may ignore the effects of taxation.

Unless otherwise specified all costs and revenues should be assumed to arise at the end of each year.

Required:

Calculate whether Thunder plc should produce Lightening on the basis of the information above.

Example 13: Leo

Leo is contemplating spending $400,000 on new machinery. This will be used to produce a revolutionary type of lock, for which demand is expected to last three years. Equipment will be bought on 31 December 20X5 and revenue from the sale of locks will be receivable on the 31 December 20X6, 20X7 and 20X8. Labour costs for the three years, payable in arrears, are estimated at $500,000 per annum in current terms. These figures are expected to rise at the rate of 10% per annum.

Materials required for the three years are currently in stock. They originally cost $300,000; they would cost $500,000 at current prices although Leo had planned to sell them for $350,000. The sales revenue from locks in the first year is projected at $900,000. This figure will rise by 5% per annum over the product's life.

If Leo has a money cost of capital of 13%, identify the net present value of the project (to the nearest $000).

A   ($130,000)

B   ($23,000)

C $52,000

D $126,000

Deflation

Many western economies have very low rates of inflation at present and some are even experiencing deflation. Deflation may also apply to certain hi-tech materials which get considerably cheaper when they go into mass production.

Deflation may affect business decision making in several ways:

- Investing in projects that have long payback periods may require some courage.

- Borrowing to finance the purchase of assets that are going to fall in value may also require some courage: money rates will be low, but real rates are higher.

- It may be difficult to reduce some costs – especially wages – in line with deflation.

- Consumers may defer purchasing decisions if they anticipate that prices will fall.

8 Dealing with questions with both tax and inflation

Combining tax and inflation in the same question does not make it any more difficult than keeping them separate.

Questions with both tax and inflation are best tackled using the money method.

- Inflate costs and revenues, where necessary, before determining their tax implications.

- Ensure that the cost and disposal values have been inflated (if necessary) before calculating tax depreciation.

- Always calculate working capital on these inflated figures, unless given.

- Use a post-tax money discount rate.

Example 14: Ackbono Ltd

Ackbono Co is considering a potential project with the following forecasts:

	Now	T	T	T
Initial investment ($million)	(1,000)			
Disposal proceeds ($million)				200
Demand (millions of units)		5	10	6

The initial investment will be made on the first day of the new accounting period.

The selling price per unit is expected to be $100 and the variable cost $30 per unit. Both of these figures are given in today's terms.

Tax depreciation is available at 25 per cent reducing balance and corporation tax is payable at 30 per cent per annum.

Corporation tax is paid in two instalments, with half the tax payable in the year in which it arises, and the balance paid in the following year.

The company has a real required rate of return of 6.8%.

General inflation is predicted to be 3% pa but the selling price is expected to inflate at 4% and variable costs by 5% pa.

Calculate the NPV of the project.

N.B. work in $ millions.

Example 15: R Ltd

November 20X7

In early November 20X7, R Ltd considered manufacturing a new product called Sparkle. Up to that time $750,000 had been spent on researching the product. The company estimated that it would take two further years to develop Sparkle to the point of production and by that time it would probably have a lead of 18 months over its chief competitor. R Ltd expected to launch Sparkle on 1 November 20X9 and to produce and sell 100,000 units in the first year if $1.5 million was spent on pre-launch advertising. During the first year of production, R Ltd planned to spend $750,000 on advertising; this level of expenditure would be maintained each year.

From the second year onwards, the market was expected to increase to between 160,000 and 200,000 units. Once the competitor entered the market, it was thought that the competitor would win 50% market share very quickly because of its reputation.

The development and engineering costs of Sparkle were estimated to be $6 million, $2 million of which would be incurred in the first year of development, 20X7/X8. A special piece of equipment costing $500,000 would be required for production and this was to be installed in the month prior to the commencement of manufacture.

R Ltd planned to set a selling price of $249 a unit on the basis that variable manufacturing and distribution costs were expected to be $122 per unit. The company normally sets selling prices so that the contribution/sales ratio is 50% or slightly more. The fixed administrative and space costs that relate to the product, and which would be incurred from the commencement of production, were estimated to be $7.5 million per annum. It was also estimated that working capital of $2.5 million would be needed at the start of production in November 20X9.

The product was expected to have a life span of about five years, at which time the equipment would be scrapped as having no value. The company estimated its cost of capital to be 12% per annum.

November 20Y0

Development of Sparkle took six months longer than planned. This was largely because it proved necessary to employ two extra members of staff in the engineering department for the technical aspects of the product development.

The engineering department did not have a budget for this in year 1 (20X7/X8) and so employment was delayed until the start of the second year, November 20X8, when the budget for the extra funds had been approved. This caused the planned expenditure on development for year 2 to be spread over the 18 month period from the start of year 2 to the middle of year 3. The two new members of staff were employed at salaries of $45,000 each and employment costs were estimated to be 100% of the first year's salary. As a result, production started six months late in May 20Y0, the pre-launch costs were delayed accordingly and only 55,000 units were sold in the year November 20X9 to October 20Y0.

As expected, the competitor has decided to enter the market and is launching its rival product Glitter this month, November 20Y0.

R Ltd now predicts the market for 20Y0/Y1 to be 150,000 units and its share of this to be 50%. Thereafter the market size will be as forecast previously, i.e. between 160,000 and 200,000 units each year, and the product life cycle will stop at the same date as planned previously. The monetary value of all expenditures and revenues to date has been very close to the estimates and there is no reason to revise future forecasts in this respect.

Required:

Using the case of Sparkle in the scenario:

(a) Calculate the net present value of the project as perceived at the beginning of November 20X7, when R Ltd decided to manufacture Sparkle. State clearly any assumptions you make.

(b) Calculate the revised net present value of the whole project as perceived at the beginning of November 20Y0.

(c) Describe the position revealed by the figures you have calculated in (a) and (b) and on the events which have taken place. Identify what the company should do now?

9 Capital asset replacement decisions

As the title suggests, this section considers the need to replace old, worn out capital assets within a firm.

There are two distinct types of decisions to consider:

1 Considering mutually-exclusive options with unequal lives.

2 Calculating an optimum replacement cycle.

We shall consider each in turn.

Mutually-exclusive options with unequal lives

Companies considering the replacement of an asset may be faced with alternatives where the life spans of the various machines differ, but the asset is required for the foreseeable future. The options must be evaluated over a comparable number of years.

In order to compare like with like we will calculate an equivalent annual cost. This is similar to an average annual cash flow. Once both machines' costs have been annualised the cheapest machine can be chosen by comparing annual costs.

FORMULA

$$\text{Equivalent annual cost} = \frac{\text{PV of costs}}{\text{Annuity factor for year n}}$$

LEARN

where n is the machine life time.

This is best explained by working through an example (the solution at the end of the chapter includes an explanation of the technique).

Example 16: Donald Ltd

Donald Ltd is considering replacing an asset with one of two possible machines:

Machine X	Initial cost	$120,000
	Life	3 years
	Running costs	$20,000 p.a.
	Residual value	nil
Machine Y	Initial cost	$60,000
	Life	2 years
	Running costs	Year 1: $40,000
		Year 2: $35,000
	Residual value	nil

The machines will be required into the foreseeable future. The company's cost of capital is 10%.

Required:

Calculate which machine should be purchased.

Lowest common multiple method

There is an alternative method for comparing machines with different lives known as the lowest common multiple method.

This is where we find the smallest number, which we can divide into by each of a set of numbers and evaluate the NPV cost over this period.

Example

If we look again at the decision faced in the previous 'Donald' example and apply the lowest common multiple method, we have two projects, one with a life of 2 years and one with a life of 3 years. The common multiple is 6 years. We then calculate the NPV of the two options over 6 years and compare the results as follows:

Machine X

Year	Description	Cash flow $	Discount rate 10%	Present value $
0	Outlay	120,000	1.000	120,000
1 – 3	Running cost	20,000	2.487	49,740
3	Replace	120,000	0.751	90,120
4 – 6	Running cost	20,000	1.868	37,360
			NPV =	**297,220**

Machine Y

Year	Description	Cash flow $	Discount rate 10%	Present value $
0	Outlay	60,000	1.000	60,000
1 – 2	Running cost	35,000	1.736	60,760
2	Replace	60,000	0.826	49,560
3 – 4	Running cost	35,000	1.434	50,190
4	Replace	60,000	0.683	40,980
5 – 6	Running cost	35,000	1.185	41,475
			NPV =	302,965

Machine X should be purchased as it has the least cost option (lowest NPV cost).

Optimum replacement cycles

Companies purchasing new plant and machinery must decide how often to replace them. Generally, as machinery ages its residual value decreases and the annual running costs increase. However, companies are unlikely to want to replace assets too frequently because of the capital outlay associated with the purchase.

In the next section we shall calculate the optimum replacement cycle in order to minimise long-term costs.

Factors in replacement decisions

The factors to be considered include the following:

- Capital cost of new equipment – the higher cost of equipment will have to be balanced against known or possible technical improvements.

- Operating costs – operating costs will be expected to increase as the machinery deteriorates over time. This may be the result of:

  - increased repair and maintenance costs

  - loss of production due to 'down-time' resulting from increased repair and maintenance time

  - lower quality and quantity of output.

- Resale value – the extent to which old equipment can be traded in for new.

- Taxation and investment incentives.

- Inflation – both the general price level change, and relative movements in the prices of inputs and outputs.

Method of solution

1   Consider each possible replacement cycle in turn: 1 year, 2 year, 3 year etc.

2   Calculate the PV of costs for each cycle.

3   Divide this PV by the annuity factor to find the equivalent annual cost.

4   Select the replacement cycle with the lowest equivalent annual cost.

Limitations of replacement analysis

The replacement analysis model assumes that the firm replaces like with like each time it needs to replace an existing asset.

However this assumption ignores

- changing technology – machines fast become obsolete and can only be replaced with a more up-to-date model which will be more efficient and perhaps perform different functions

- inflation – the increase in price over time increases the cost structure of the different assets, meaning that the optimal replacement cycle can vary over time

- change in production plans – firms cannot predict with accuracy the market environment they will be facing in the future and whether they will even need to make use of the asset at that time.

Example 17: Supermarket delivery vehicles

A supermarket is trying to determine the optimal replacement policy for its fleet of delivery vehicles. The total purchase price of the fleet is $220,000.

The running costs and scrap values of the fleet at the end of each year are:

	Year 1	Year 2	Year 3	Year 4	Year 5
Running costs	$110,000	$132,000	$154,000	$165,000	$176,000
Scrap value	$121,000	$88,000	$66,000	$55,000	$25,000

The supermarket's cost of capital is 12% per annum.

Ignore taxation and inflation.

Identify at the end of which year the supermarket should replace its fleet of delivery vehicles.

10 Practice Questions

Objective Test Question 1: Mickey Payback

Mickey Ltd is considering two mutually-exclusive projects with the following details:

Project A

Initial investment	$450,000				
Scrap value at the end of year 5	$20,000				
Year:	1	2	3	4	5
Annual cash flows ($000)	200	150	100	100	100

Project B

Initial investment	$100,000				
Scrap value at the end of year 5	$10,000				
Year:	1	2	3	4	5
Annual cash flows ($000)	50	40	30	20	20

Assume that the initial investment is at the start of the project and the annual cash flows are at the **end** of each year.

Which project should the company select, if the objective is to minimise the payback period?

A   Project A

B   Project B

C   Either project A or project B, as they have the same payback period

D   Neither project

Objective Test Question 2: Spring Ltd

The management of Spring Ltd are making a decision on whether or not to purchase a new piece of plant and machinery which costs $100,000. The new machine will generate a net cash flow of $30,000 each year for four years. At the end of the fourth year it will be sold for $20,000. The company's cost of capital is 5%. Tax depreciation is at 25% reducing balance and corporation tax is 30%. Corporation tax is payable in two instalments, with half paid in the current year and half paid in the following year.

Required:

Calculate the net present value of the project and advise management.

Objective Test Question 3: NPV

Spotty Ltd plans to purchase a machine costing $18,000 to save labour costs. Labour savings would be $9,000 in the first year and labour rates in the second year will increase by 10%. The estimated average annual rate of inflation is 8% and the company's real cost of capital is estimated at 12%. The machine has a two year life with an estimated actual salvage value of $5,000 receivable at the end of year 2. All cash flows occur at the year end.

What is the negative NPV (to the nearest $10) of the proposed investment?

A $50

B $270

C $380

D $650

Case Study Style Question – Apollonia Dental Care

Apollonia Ltd operates 30 dental practices in London. You are a financial manager in Apollonia's head office. Your primary responsibilities are associated with management accounting. You report to the senior financial manager, who reports directly to the finance director.

There has been lots of discussion as to whether buying or leasing new equipment (dentist chairs with lasered-powered drills attached) was preferable. You receive the following email from the senior financial manager:

> **From:** Senior Financial Manager
> **To:** Financial Manager
> **Date:** Today
> **Subject:** Acquisition of assets
>
> I have forwarded to you an email from Simon with regard to options for refreshing the assets at our practices. I've prepared the financial analysis (attached, you don't need to check the calculations), with the figures discounted at an appropriate cost, but would like you to put together some explanatory notes for me that I can take to the board.
>
> Please ensure that you cover an explanation of the figures used in the analysis, including explanations as to what has been included, why it is included and a recommendation about which option should be selected.

Purchase equipment							
	$m	$m	$m	$m	$m	$m	$m
Year	0	1	2	3	4	5	6
Purchase value	−20						
Sale value							
Tax depreciation tax savings		0.75	1.31	0.98	0.74	0.67	0.35
Maintenance costs		−0.2	−0.2	−0.2	−0.3	−0.4	
Net cash flows	−20	0.55	1.11	0.78	0.44	2.27	0.35
Discount factor	1	0.893	0.797	0.712	0.636	0.567	0.507
Present Value	−20	0.49	0.88	0.56	0.28	1.29	0.18
Net present costs	−16.32						
Equivalent annual cost	−4.53						
Lease equipment							
	$m	$m	$m	$m	$m	$m	$m
Year	0	1	2	3	4	5	6
Lease payments	−5	−5	−5	−5			
Tax savings		0.75	1.5	1.5	1.5	0.75	
Maintenance costs		−0.2	−0.2	−0.2	−0.2		
Net cash flows	−5	−4.45	−3.7	−3.7	1.3	0.75	0
Discount factor	1	0.893	0.797	0.712	0.636	0.567	0.507
Present Value	−5	−3.97	−2.95	−2.63	0.83	0.43	0
Net present costs	−13.29						
Equivalent annual cost	−4.38						

Answers to examples and objective test questions

Example 1: Payback

$$\text{Payback period} = \frac{\$1,000,000}{\$150,000 \text{ per year}}$$

Payback period = 6.67 years, that is 6 years and (0.67 × 12 months), so 6 years 8 months. 12%

Example 2: Target Payback

Payback period

After two years $36,000 of the initial $40,000 of the investment has been recovered. It will take one third of year 3 ($4,000 required/ $12,000 received in year 3) to recover the remaining investment.

So the payback period is 2.33 years, which satisfies the target of 2.5 years.

Accounting rate of return

$$\text{Average annual profit} = \frac{\text{Total net cashflows} - \text{Total depreciation}}{\text{Life of the project}}$$

$$= \frac{\$70,000 - \$36,000}{5 \text{ years}}$$

$$= \$6,800$$

$$\text{Average investment} = \frac{\text{Initial investment} + \text{Scrap value}}{2}$$

$$= \frac{\$40,000 + \$4,000}{2}$$

$$= \$22,000$$

$$\text{ARR} = \frac{\$6,800}{\$22,000}$$

ARR = 30.9% p.a.

This is above the target return of 15%.

Overall

The investment satisfies both target measures and should therefore be accepted.

Example 3: Mickey ARR

	Project A $000	Project B $000
Total profit before depreciation (total operating cash)	650	160
Less total depreciation	(430)	(90)
Total profit after depreciation	220	70
÷ number of years	5	5
Average annual profit	44	14
Average value of investment	235	55
Accounting rate of return	18.7%	25.5%

Conclusion: the firm should select project B.

Example 4: ARR and Payback

Average annual profit = $50,000 × 30%	$15,000
	× 5 yrs
Total profit	$75,000
Add back depreciation	$45,000
Total cash	$120,000
Less year 1 cash flow	(6,000)
	$114,000
Cash per annum (yrs 2–5) 114/4	$28,500
Outlay	$50,000
Cash inflow after 2 years 6,000 + 28,500	$34,500
Still required	$15,500
Proportion of year 3 to gain balance of cash =	15,500 ÷ 28,500 = 0.54
Hence payback period =	2.54 years

Answer D

Example 5: Placer Ltd

(a)

			tax rate 30%	1 year in arrears
t0	asset purchase 1st day of accounting period	25,000		
t1	1st tax-allowable depreciation 25%	6,250	1,875	t2
	tax written down value	18,750		
t2	2nd tax-allowable depreciation 25%	4,688	1,406	t3
	tax WDV	14,062		
t3	3rd tax-allowable depreciation 25%	3,516	1,055	t4
	tax WDV	10,546		
t4	sales proceeds	5,000		
	balancing allowance	5,546	1,664	t5

(b)

			tax rate 30%	1 year in arrears
	First three years as before			
	tax WDV	10,546		
t4	sales proceeds	**15,000**		
	balancing **charge**	(4,454)	(1,336)	t5

Example 6: Amigo Ltd

(W1) The incremental increase in contribution earned as a result of using the new machine is $30,000 × 40% = $12,000 per year.

(W2) Tax due/paid on incremental contribution earned:

Year	Incr. Contribution	Tax due (30%)	Year tax paid				
			1	2	3	4	5
1	12,000	3,600	1,800	1,800			
2	12,000	3,600		1,800	1,800		
3	12,000	3,600			1,800	1,800	
4	12,000	3,600				1,800	1,800
5	12,000	3,600					
			1,800	3,600	3,600	3,600	1,800

(W3) Tax depreciation/tax relief.

Existing machine

The sale of the existing machine leads to a balancing charge of $8,000 – $3,000 = $5,000. Tax payable on this is $5,000 × 30% = $1,500. Assume this is paid half in year 0 and half in year 1.

New machine

Year	Bal b/f	Tax depr (25%)	Tax relief (30%)	Your relief received				
				1	2	3	4	5
1	25,000	6,250	1,875	937	938			
2	18,750	4,688	1,406		703	703		
3	14,063	3,515	1,055			528	527	
4	10,547	5,547	1,664				832	832
				937	1,641	1,231	1,359	832

* Disposal = $5,000 when the TWDV was $10,547. Therefore the Balancing allowance = $5,547

All figures $	Year 0	Year 1	Year 2	Year 3	Year 4	Year 5
Existing machine sales proceeds	8,000					
Incremental contribution (W1)		12,000	12,000	12,000	12,000	
Capital	(25,000)				5,000	
Tax paid (W2)		(1,800)	(3,600)	(3,600)	(3,600)	(1,800)
Tax paid on existing machine (W3)	(750)	(750)				
Tax relief on new machine (W3)		937	1,641	1,231	1,359	832
Net cash flow	(17,750)	10,387	10,041	9,631	14,759	(968)
DCF @ 15%	1	0.870	0.756	0.658	0.572	0.497
Present values	(17,750)	9,037	7,591	6,337	8,442	(481)

Net present value = $13,176

The net present value is positive and therefore it is worthwhile purchasing the machine.

Example 7: Camp Ltd

Corporation tax

Depreciation is not an allowable expense.

Therefore, taxable profit = $100,000 + $20,000 = $120,000 p.a.

Corporation tax at 30% = $36,000 p.a.

Half payable in current year, half payable in year following.

Tax depreciation

Capital cost:	$250,000
Scrap value:	$10,000
Total tax depreciation:	$240,000

Year	Reducing balance	Tax depreciation	Tax saved (30%)	Benefit received	Total cash benefit
1	$187,500	$62,500	$18,750	$9,375	**$9,375**
2	$140,625	$46,875	$14,063	$9,375 + $7,032	**$16,407**
3	$105,469	$35,156	$10,547	$7,031 + $5,274	**$12,305**
4	$10,000	$95,469	$28,641	$5,273 + $14,321	**$19,594**
5				$14,320	**$14,320**

Net present value

Year	0	1	2	3	4	5
	$	$	$	$	$	$
Net inflows		120,000	120,000	120,000	120,000	
Corporation tax		(18,000)	(36,000)	(36,000)	(36,000)	(18,000)
Tax depreciation		9,375	16,407	12,305	19,594	14,320
Investment	(250,000)				10,000	
Working capital	(35,000)				35,000	
Total net flows	(285,000)	111,375	100,407	96,305	148,594	(3,680)
Discount factors	1.000	0.909	0.826	0.751	0.683	0.621
Present value	(285,000)	101,240	82,936	72,325	101,490	(2,285)

Net present value = $70,706

* working capital of $35,000 is injected in Year 0 and then released in Year 4.

Example 8: Smith Ltd

Since the decision has been made to increase capacity (i.e. 'to do nothing' is not an alternative), the easiest approach is to discount the incremental cash flows.

The tabular approach of the previous chapter is still appropriate particularly as the project lasts for ten years.

Time		A $000	B $000	B – A $000	8% DF/AF	PV $000
0	Capital expenditure	(260)	(415)	(155)	1	(155.00)
0	Working capital	(50)	(65)	(15)	1	(15.00)
2	Promotion	–	(15)	(15)	0.857	(12.86)
1–10	Net income	70	95	25	6.710	167.75
10	Scrap proceeds	40	75	35	0.463	16.21
	Net present value					1.10

The present value of proposal B exceeds that of proposal A at 8% and therefore proposal B is preferred.

Assumptions

- The disposal value of buildings is realistic and all other figures have been realistically appraised.

- Expenditure on working capital is incurred at the beginning of the project life and recovered at the end.

- Adequate funds are available for either proposal.

- All cash flows occur annually in arrears.

Example 9: Flo Ltd

B

1.21/1.09 = 1.11

Example 10: Storm Ltd

(a) **Discounting money cash flow at the money rate**

Year	Money cash flow $	Discount rate 15%	Present value $
0	(50,000)		(50,000)
1	21,100	0.870	18,357
2	22,261	0.756	16,829
3	23,485	0.658	15,453
4	24,776	0.572	14,172
		NPV =	14,811

(b) **Discounting the real cash flows at the real rate**

Calculate the real rate.

$$(1 + r) = \frac{(1 + m)}{(1 + i)}$$

$$(1 + r) = \frac{(1 + 0.15)}{(1 + 0.055)}$$

$$(1 + r) = 1.0900$$

$$\therefore r = 0.09, \text{ i.e. } 9\%$$

Year	Real cash flow $	Discount rate 9%	Present value $
0	(50,000)		(50,000)
1–4	20,000 p.a.	3.240	64,800
		NPV =	14,800

Example 11: Andra

Since the question contains both specific and general inflation rates, the money method should be used.

Step 1

The money method needs to be calculated using the information provided on the real rate of return and the general rate of inflation.

$(1 + i) = (1 + r)(1 + m)$

$(1.085)(1.06) = (1+m)$

$(1+m) = 1.1501$ so $m = 0.15$ or 15%

Step 2

Inflate the cash flows using the specific inflation rates and discount using the money rate calculated above.

	T₀ $	T₁ $	T₂ $	T₃ $	T₄ $	T₅ $
Investment	(7,000)					
Wages savings (inflating @ 10%)		1,100	1,210	1,331	1,464	1,610
Materials savings (inflating @ 5%)		420	441	463	486	510
Net cash flow	(7,000)	1,520	1,651	1,794	1,950	2,120
PV factor @ 15%	1.000	0.870	0.756	0,658	0.572	0.497
PV of cash flow	(7,000)	1,322	1,248	1,180	1,115	1,054

Therefore NPV = $(1,081) which suggests the project is not worthwhile.

Example 12: Thunder Ltd

Notes:

$480,000 development cost is a sunk cost.

Depreciation is not a cash flow and should be excluded from the fixed costs.

Depreciation = $2,400,000/4 years = $600,000 p.a.

Therefore relevant fixed cost = $800,000 – $600,000 = $200,000.

Year 1 cash flows are:

				$000
Revenue	25,000	×	$80	2,000 – rises at 5%
Direct material	25,000	×	$8	200 – rises at 4%
Direct labour	25,000	×	$12	300 – rises at 10%
Variable overheads	25,000	×	$12	300 – rises at 4%
Fixed costs				200 – rises at 5%

Year	0	1	2	3	4
			$000		
Capital	(2,400)				
Revenue		2,000	2,100	2,205	2,315
Direct material		(200)	(208)	(216)	(225)
Direct labour		(300)	(330)	(363)	(399)
Variable OH		(300)	(312)	(324)	(337)
Fixed cost		(200)	(210)	(221)	(232)
Net cash flow	(2,400)	1,000	1,040	1,081	1,122
15% disc. factor		0.870	0.756	0.658	0.572
Present value	**(2,400)**	**870**	**786**	**711**	**642**

The net present value is $609,000.

Therefore the company should invest in the project.

Example 13: Leo Ltd

All cash flows shown are money cash ($000)

Year	Capital	Labour	Material	Revenue	Net cash	13% factors	Present value
0	(400)		(350)		(750)		(750)
1		(550)		900	350	0.885	310
2		(605)		945	340	0.783	266
3		(665.5)		992	326.5	0.693	226
						NPV =	52

Net Present Value = $52,000

Answer C

Example 14: Ackbono Ltd

$ millions	T_0	T_1	T_2	T_3	T_4
Sales (W1)		520	1082	675	
Variable costs (W2)		(158)	(331)	(208)	
Net trading inflows		362	751	467	
Taxation (30%) – in year		(54)	(112)	(70)	
Taxation – in year (30%)			(55)	(113)	(70)
Initial investment	(1,000)				
Scrap proceeds				200	
Tax depreciation benefit (W3)		37	66	82	55
Net cash flows	(1,000)	345	650	566	(15)
DF @ 10% (W4)	1	0.909	0.826	0.751	0.683
PV	(1,000)	314	537	425	(10)
				NPV	266

(W1) Revenue

Revenue needs to be expressed in money terms.

Revenue at T_1 = 5m × $100 × (1.04) = $520m.

Revenue at T_2 = 10m × $100 × (1.04)^2 = $1,082m.

Revenue at T_3 = 6m × $100 × (1.04)^3 = $675m.

(W2) Costs

Costs need to be expressed in money terms.

Costs at T_1 = 5m × $30 × (1.05) = $158m.

Costs at T_2 = 10m × $30 × (1.05)^2 = $331 m.

Costs at T_3 = 6m × $30 × (1.05)^3 = $208m.

(W3) Tax depreciation ($m)

Year	Bal b/f	Tax depr (25%)	Tax relief (30%)	1	2	3	4
1	1,000	250	75	37	38		
2	750	188	56		28	28	
3	562	362	109			54	55
				37	66	82	55

(Year relief received columns: 1, 2, 3, 4)

*Disposal = $200m when the TWDV was $562m. Therefore the balancing allowance = $362.

(W4) Discount rate

(1 + m) = (1 + r) × (1 + i) = 1.068 × 1.03 = 1.10, giving a money rate (m) = 10%.

Example 15: R Ltd

(a) **Tip:** Set up a table of cash flows. Keep all workings separate from this table.

Year	Date	Advertising	Capital costs	Contri-bution	Working capital	Net cash flow	12% discount factor	Present value
		$000	$000	$000	$000	$000	$000	$000
0	1.11.07							
1	1.11.08		(2,000)			(2,000)	0.893	(1,786)
2	1.11.09	(1,500)	(4,500)		(2,500)	(8,500)	0.797	(6,775)
3	1.11.10	(750)		12,700		11,950	0.712	8,508
4	1.11.11	(750)		17,145		16,395	0.636	10,427
5	1.11.12	(750)		11,430		10,680	0.567	6,056
6	1.11.13	(750)		11,430		10,680	0.507	5,415
7	1.11.14	(750)		11,430	2,500	13,180	0.452	5,957
								27,803
			Less PV of fixed costs: 7,500 × (4.564 – 1.690)					(21,555)
			Net present value					6,24

Production:

Year

1	100,000	units
2	135,000	units*
3	90,000	
4	90,000	
5	90,000	
*(160 + 200)/2	180	
1st 6 months	90	
2nd 6 months	45	(50% because of competitor)
Total for year	135	

Contribution per unit: $249 – $122 = $127

Assumptions:

– The amount already spent is not relevant – it is a sunk cost.

– The sales figures are the average of the range and the competitor takes 50% of market share after 18 months of sales.

– The equipment has no scrap value after five years.

– Working capital is released immediately production ceases.

– Inflation has been ignored.

Conclusion: the NPV is $6,248,000. Hence the project should be accepted.

(b)

Year	Date	Fixed cost	Advertising	Capital costs	Contri-bution	Working capital	Net cash flow	12% discount factor	Present value
		$000	$000	$000	$000	$000	$000	$000	$000
0	1.11.07								
1	1.11.08			(2,000)			(2,000)	0.893	(1,786)
2	1.11.09			(2,847)		(2,500)	(5,347)	0.797	(4,262)
3	1.11.10	(3,750)	(1,875)	(1,923)	6,985		(563)	0.712	(401)
4	1.11.11	(7,500)	(750)		9,525		1,275	0.636	810.9
5	1.11.12	(7,500)	(750)		11,430		3,180	0.567	1,803
6	1.11.13	(7,500)	(750)		11,430		3,180	0.507	1,612
7	1.11.14	(7,500)	(750)		11,430	2,500	5,680	0.452	2,567
					Net present value				345.2

Development costs:

Year

1		= $2m
2	2/3 of $4m = $2.667m + $0.180	= $2.847m
3	1/3 of $4m = $1.333m + $0.090 + $0.5m	= $1.923m

Salary costs in Year 2: $180,000

Salary costs in Year 3: $90,000

Advertising in Year 3: $1.5m + $0.375 (50% of $750,000) = $1.875m

Example 16: Donald Ltd

Method and answer guide

Firstly calculate the NPV of costs:

Year	Discount factor	Machine X		Machine Y	
		Cash flow	Present value	Cash flow	Present value
		$000	$000	$000	$000
0		120	120	60	60
1	0.909	20	18	40	36
2	0.826	20	17	35	29
3	0.751	20	15		
Net present value			170		125

It is not appropriate to compare these two NPVs. Machine X shows three years of costs whereas Machine Y only has two years' worth of costs. Remember that the machines are needed into the foreseeable future, so do not pick the cheapest single purchase. The machine will be replaced many times over the next few years. Because of this we need to find a way of comparing the costs over an equal time period (not unequal years).

Machine X:

NPV of one life cycle	= $170k
EAC	= $170k ÷ 2.487
	= $68k p.a.

Machine Y:

NPV of one life cycle	= $125k
EAC	= $125k ÷ 1.736
	= $72k p.a.

Machine X is the cheapest.

Example 17: Supermarket delivery vehicles

		Replacement Cycle									
	Discount	1 year		2 year		3 year		4 year		5 year	
Year	Factor	Cash	PV	Cash	PV	Cash	PV	Cash	PV	Cash	PV
0		(220)	(220)	(220)	(220)	(220)	(220)	(220)	(220)	(220)	(220)
1	0.893	11	9.8	(110)	(98.2)	(110)	(98.2)	(110)	(98.2)	(110)	(98.2)
2	0.797			(44)	(35.1)	(132)	(105.2)	(132)	(105.2)	(132)	(105.2)
3	0.712					(88)	(62.6)	(154)	(109.6)	(154)	(109.6)
4	0.636							(110)	(70.0)	(165)	(104.9)
5	0.567									(151)	(85.6)
Net present value			(210.2)		(353.3)		(486.0)		(603.0)		(723.5)
÷ Annuity factor			÷ 0.893		÷ 1.690		÷ 2.402		+3.037		÷ 3.605
Equivalent annual cost			(235.4)		(209.1)		(202.3)		(198.6)		(200.7)

Notes:

- In year 0 the cost of the machine is shown

- In each year after that the cash column shows the running costs of the machine

- In the year of sale, net cash flow is scrap less running cost

- The PV (present value) column represents the cash column multiplied by the discount factor for that year

- The net present value is then the sum of the present values

- In order to compare net present values an equivalent annual cost is calculated by dividing the NPV by the annuity factor for the length of the investment. So, for example, the 4 year NPV of $603.0 is divided by the 4 year 12% annuity factor of 3.037 to give an annual equivalent cost of $198.6

- These equivalent annual costs are compared and the lowest one is the optimal replacement cycle.

Therefore, the most economical replacement cycle is four years.

Objective Test Question 1: Mickey Payback

Project A	Cashflow	Cumulative cash flow
Year 0	(450)	(450)
Year 1	200	(250)
Year 2	150	(100)
Year 3	100	0

Payback period = 3 years

Project B		
Year 0	(100)	(100)
Year 1	50	(50)
Year 2	40	(10)
Year 3	30	20

10/30 = 0.33333 of a year, i.e. 4 months

Therefore, payback is 2 years and 4 months.

Note:

The question states that cashflows only arise at year ends. If they were to arise evenly throughout the year then a more accurate payback period would be 2 years and 4 months.

Objective Test Question 2: Spring Ltd

Before you start a table of cash flows sort out corporation tax and tax depreciation benefits.

Corporation tax

30% of net cash flows (profits), i.e. 30% of $30,000 = $9,000.

Half is payable in the year of the profit, and half in the year following, i.e.:

Year	Corporation tax
1	$4,500
2	$9,000
3	$9,000
4	$9,000
5	$4,500

Tax depreciation

Capital cost: $100,000

Scrap value: $20,000

Total tax depreciation: $80,000

Year	Reducing balance	Tax depreciation	Tax saved (30%)	Benefit received	Total cash benefit
1	$75,000	$25,000	$7,500	$3,750	$3,750
2	$56,250	$18,750	$5,625	$3,750 + $2,813	$6,563
3	$42,188	$14,062	$4,219	$2,813 + $2,110	$4,922
4	$20,000	$22,188	$6,656	$2,110 + $3,328	$5,437
5				$3,328	$3,328

Now you can calculate the net cash flow each year, and discount:

Yr	Asset	Profits	Corporation tax	Tax dep'n benefit	Total net cash	Discount factor	Present value
	$	$	$	$	$		$
0	(100,000)				(100,000)		(100,000)
1		30,000	(4,500)	3,750	29,250	0.952	27,846
2		30,000	(9,000)	6,563	27,563	0.907	25,000
3		30,000	(9,000)	4,922	25,922	0.864	22,397
4	20,000	30,000	(9,000)	5,437	46,437	0.823	38,218
5			(4,500)	3,328	(1,172)	0.784	(919)
						NPV =	12,542

Objective Test Question 3: NPV

C

Money cost of capital = [(1.08 × 1.12) − 1] × 100 = 20.96%

Time	t0 $	t1 $	t2 $
Outlay	(18,000)		
Labour		9,000	9,900
Salvage			5,000
			14,900
20.96% discount factor	1	0.8267	0.6835
Present value	(18,000)	7,440	10,184

NPV = $(376) or
$(380) to nearest $10

Case Study Style Question – Apollonia Dental Care

From: Financial Manager

To: Senior Financial Manager

Date: Today

Subject: Investment appraisal

Analysis of lease versus buy options

Apollonia has two options, to purchase the equipment outright or to lease it. The analyses for both options include only the cash flows relevant to their acquisition and usage. We do not use an analysis of the profits from using the equipment for two reasons:

- Firstly, profits are not very useful for capital investment decision-making, as they are subjective and can be manipulated with changes in accounting policies, or tweaks in such things as accruals and prepayments.

- Secondly, because both options would generate the same (or very similar) profits it is most appropriate to compare the cash flows of acquiring the use of the assets when comparing the two options.

We consider all relevant cash flows of the two options so that we can make a direct comparison. Relevant cash flows are those cash flows directly affected by the option we are looking at. Negative numbers on the analyses represent cash outflows and positive numbers represent cash savings or cash inflows.

Purchase of equipment

Under this option, we would immediately have to spend $20m on the equipment, but we would recoup $4 million of this at the end of five years of operation. Purchasing the equipment would mean that we could claim tax savings against our company profits due to the tax depreciation that is allowable on the purchase, so those tax savings have been recorded as a benefit of ownership.

We will also incur maintenance costs on the equipment over the five years of its useful life to us, so these have been estimated and recorded as cash outflows.

Lease of equipment

The cash flows of leasing are straightforward. This would be a four-year lease, with payments made in advance each year of $5m, totalling $20m. This is a higher cost than the purchase price (once the scrap value is taken into account), but it is spread over four years instead of having to be paid in one instalment.

There are tax savings shown because the lease payments are tax deductible and so reduce the company tax bill annually.

Maintenance costs are included because they are slightly different to those under the purchase option, which has an extra year of such expenses. As they are different, they are relevant to our decision as to which option to choose.

Discounting

For both sets of figures, the total relevant costs for each year have been calculated and then a discount figure applied. This is because, on long-term investments like these, the time value of money is very important. Discounting reflects the fact that cash flows that occur in the future are worth less than cash flows that occur today. When the discount factor has been applied, all of the cash flows are stated in equivalent terms and we are able to calculate a total present value of costs. This simply means that the total net present cost figure has all the cash flows restated as though they were spent today – this provides a like- for-like comparison of the two sets of cash flows.

A discount figure is used that represents the business's cost of financing, otherwise known as the cost of capital.

Equivalent annual cost

As the two options last for different time periods, one more calculation is needed to ensure that the totals are comparable.

To purchase the equipment, we would be spending a present cost of $16.32 million but this would last for five years. To lease the equipment we would be spending less, at $13.29 million but the lease would only provide use of the equipment for four years.

The two present value calculations are therefore not comparable. Hence, an equivalent annual cost has been calculated. This is a conversion of the total cost into an equivalent annual spend, i.e. what would it cost us if we were to pay the same amount out every year for the asset? This final calculation makes the numbers genuinely comparable to each other, despite their differing lives.

As can be seen, the purchase option and the lease option have very similar equivalent annual costs of $4.53 million for purchasing the asset and $4.38 million for leasing. Thus, leasing is slightly cheaper but the figures are so close that other considerations may be taken into account.

Other considerations

For instance, the lease lasts for four years. It may be that technology has moved on in four years' time such that we would desire to replace the assets at that time rather than wait another year, as we would do under the purchase option.

It also gives us the opportunity to spread the cost of the lease without having to find separate borrowing to fund the purchase.

The pricing decision

Chapter learning objectives

Lead	Component
B4: Capital Investment Decision-Making	Discuss pricing strategies (a) Discuss pricing decisions (b) Discuss pricing strategies

1 Chapter summary

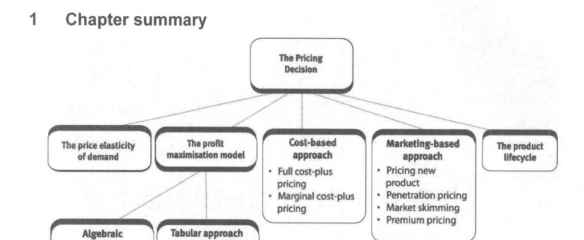

2 Introduction

In this chapter, we will learn about the alternative strategies that an organisation may adopt in the pricing of its products or services.

The price to be charged to customers for the business's products or services is often one of the most important decisions to be made by managers. Not all businesses are free to determine their own selling prices: for example, some are unable to influence the external price and are obliged to accept the prevailing market price for their goods. For these businesses cost control is an important factor in maintaining profitability.

Other businesses are in a position to select their selling price. The objectives that they pursue in their pricing policy will affect the price to be charged for each product or service. For example, the business may be concerned with profit maximisation: in this chapter you will see how managers can use cost and demand analysis to determine the theoretical profit-maximising price.

Other objectives may also affect a company's pricing policy. For example, the company may be seeking to maximise revenue, to gain the largest share of the market, to utilise spare capacity or merely to survive. In this chapter, we will be looking at many of the different aspects which influence a company's pricing strategy, beginning with the price elasticity of demand.

3 Knowledge brought forward

There is no knowledge brought forward from Subjects C01 and P1, but you may benefit from reading the Chapter on Cost Behaviour and Pricing Decisions from Certificate Level Subject C04.

4 Price elasticity of demand

Businesses make a profit by selling goods and services at a price that is higher than their cost. Profit is the result of the interaction between cost, volume and price:

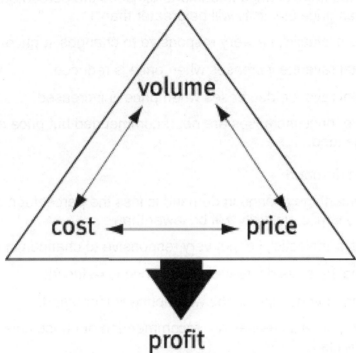

For instance, the volume of goods sold affects the cost per unit. If the volume increases, the fixed overheads are spread over more units, and so the cost per unit decreases. Lower costs give the seller the opportunity to reduce prices and so further increases volumes, or to increase profit margins. Cost is also influenced by price. This is discussed in target costing earlier in this text; the aim is to be able to produce at a target cost which is less than the target selling price. This chapter, however, concentrates on the link between price and volume, and its resulting effect on profit.

When a business proposes to change the price of a product or service, the key question is 'to what degree will demand be affected?'

The **price elasticity of demand** measures the change in demand as a result of a change in its price. It can be calculated as follows:

$$\text{Price elasticity of demand} = \frac{\text{Change in quantity demanded, as a percentage of demand}}{\text{Change in price, as a percentage of the price}}$$

Example 1: Elasticity

Assume that the sales of a retailer fall from 20 per day to 12 per day when the price of a chocolate bar goes up from 40c to 60c. What is the price elasticity of demand?

Interpretation of PED

Elastic demand

If the percentage change in demand exceeds the percentage change in price, then price elasticity will be greater than 1.

Demand is 'elastic', i.e. very responsive to changes in price.

- Total revenue increases when price is reduced.

- Total revenue decreases when price is increased.

Therefore, price increases are not recommended but price cuts are recommended.

Inelastic demand

If the percentage change in demand is less the percentage change in price, then price elasticity will be lower than 1.

Demand is 'inelastic', i.e. not very responsive to changes in price.

- Total revenue decreases when price is reduced.

- Total revenue increases when price is increased.

Therefore, price increases are recommended but price cuts are not recommended.

More on price elasticity

Pricing decisions have a major effect on volume sold and, as a consequence, on profit generated. One of the major considerations of a pricing decision is therefore the effect of a change in price will have on volume sold. If price is reduced, by how much will demand increase?

If price is increased, will a small or large decrease in demand occur? A complete answer to these questions, if such an answer does indeed exist, will involve a number of different factors in the total marketing mix, but the basic microeconomic analysis of demand is the fundamental starting point. There are two extremes of the price/demand trade off, represented graphically here:

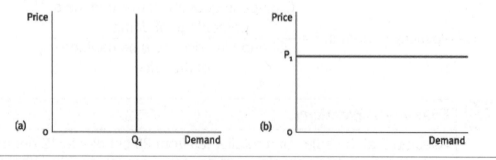

In (a), the same quantity, Q1, will be sold regardless of the selling price, as demand is completely unresponsive to changes in price. Demand is, therefore, completely inelastic, and the supplier would (theoretically) have unlimited scope, and considerable incentive, to increase price. In (b), demand is limitless at a particular price, P1, but it would vanish at prices above P1, that is demand is completely elastic. Under these circumstances there is obviously no point in reducing price below P1, as this will cause existing profits to fall. Needless to say, these two extremes are rarely seen in practice, and the more normal situation is represented by one of the following charts:

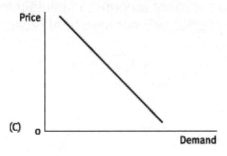 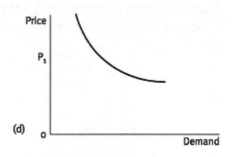

In both (c) and (d) the supplier is faced with a downward-sloping demand curve, in which reductions in price will result in increased demand and vice versa. This is a negative relationship, or negative correlation, as a decrease in price implies an increase in demand, and vice versa.

The slope of the line is the critical factor for a pricing decision, and is expressed by the following formula:

$$\text{Elasticity of demand} = \frac{-\%\ \text{change in quantity demanded}}{\%\ \text{change in price}}$$

The numerator and denominator are expressed in terms of percentage change rather than in any absolute amount, in order to avoid distortions caused by the use of different units of measurement. Given the slope of the curve, the negative sign in the numerator has the effect of making the outcome positive, which is generally considered a more convenient representation. If elasticity at a point on the curve is greater than 1, demand is considered elastic. This means that a fall in price increases demand considerably, so that total revenue increases, but an increase in price decreases demand substantially, so that total revenue falls. On the other hand, if point elasticity is less than 1 (i.e. it is inelastic) a fall in price will increase demand, but not by a sufficient amount to maintain the previous revenue level, yet a rise in price will increase total revenue:

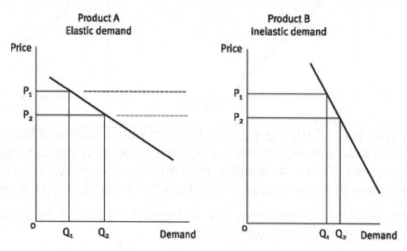

For product A, with elastic demand, a drop in price from P1 to P2 results in a relatively greater increase in sales volume. However, the same drop in price for product B, with inelastic demand, results in a far smaller change in volume.

Note that the formula measures movement between two discrete points on the curve, and that even though the slope itself is constant, elasticity will differ between different points on the curve:

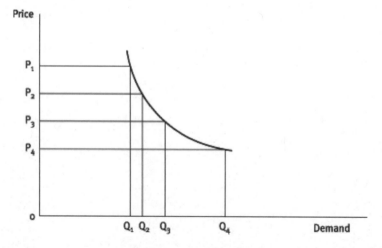

Note that although the price drops from P1–P2 to P3–P4 are equal, the impact on the quantity sold is greater with each fall in price.

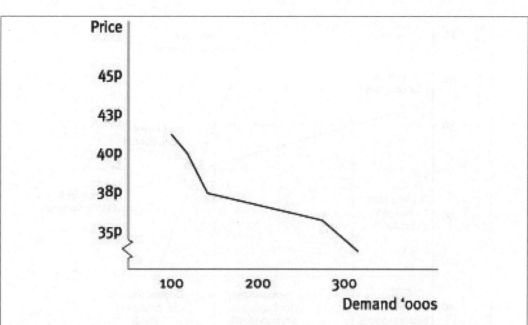

This is important information for an organisation. For example, when price elasticity is high (i.e. more than 1) the organisation will have difficulty in situations where cost inflation is higher than price inflation, because putting up prices in line with costs will cause a disproportionately large reduction in demand, and total revenues will decline. In times of inflation it is better to put up prices frequently by a small amount each time, as customers do not appear to notice the increases – or certainly do not react to them. If prices are held and then substantially increased in a single price rise, demand is likely to fall off sharply. In practice the prices of many products (e.g. consumer durable products) need to fall over time in order to increase demand. It is vital, therefore, to make costs fall by the same percentage if margins are to be maintained.

Different point elasticity can be seen in practice, as customers do not tend to react evenly to price increases. For example, $1 or $2 may be a psychological barrier and if price is increased over this level demand drops quite rapidly. If the product is sold in a supermarket the organisation needs to know how customers react to different prices in order to determine which price points are crucial. In the figure below, the rise between 38p and 40p triggers a large reduction in demand.

To complicate the issue an organisation does not decrease price with the aim of increasing volume in isolation. The effect on volume will depend on how competitors react to the price change, and on the price elasticity of the products.

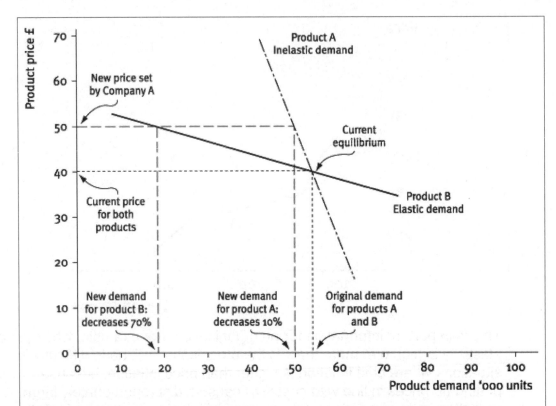

Different products in the same industry have different price elasticity because they are sold in slightly different markets due to product differentiation. This means that two or more products are sold that have different features, quality, sizes and so on. For example, a Volkswagen Golf GTI (the high-performance model) may enjoy lower price elasticity than the standard Golf 1.4E, so that the price of the former can be increased more safely than can that of the latter.

The figure above shows two companies. Company A's product A has a highly inelastic demand, while company B's product B has relatively elastic price elasticity:

In an industry in which costs of production are rising, the responsiveness of demand is an essential factor when deciding on price levels. In the above graph, the company producing product A could increase price by 25 per cent, from $40 to $50, with only a 10 per cent effect on volume (from about 54,000 down to 50,000 units). If the company that produces product B attempts to follow the price rise, its volume will fall from about 54,000 units to approximately 18,000 – the result of very elastic demand. In an industry where prices are falling, then the greater the price elasticity the greater the potential for increasing sales volume.

It is also important for an organisation to take account of expected competitors' reactions to any price increases the organisation makes.

One form of competitor reaction can be demonstrated with the kinked demand curve which shows 'price stickiness'. This occurs where competitors tend to follow price cuts with cuts of their own, but do not copy price rises. This is a pattern commonly found in the newspaper industry.

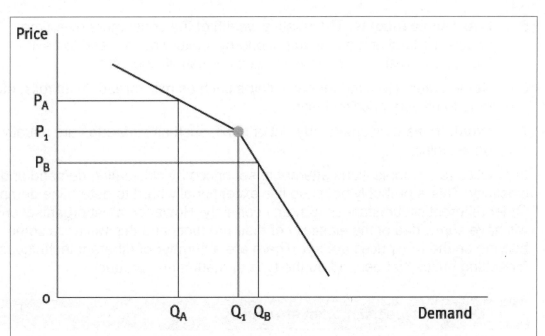

If the price is increased beyond the current price of P_1 to P_A, since competitors do not follow suit, demand will fall away sharply to Q_A (demand is elastic). If however, the price is dropped to P_B, competitors do follow, and little is gained in the way of extra sales (from Q_1 to Q_B) – demand is inelastic.

Where this occurs, firms may be reluctant to change their prices and the result is price stickiness.

5 Factors affecting price elasticity

When making decisions on products, markets and competitors, other factors, including the following, should be considered:

1   **Scope of the market.** The larger the defined market, the more inelastic is the demand for the broader definition of product. For example, the total market for transport is relatively inelastic, whereas the market for 21-speed pedal cycles is comparatively elastic.

2   **Information within the market.** Consumers may not know of the competing products in sufficient time to reassess their purchasing behaviour.

3   **Availability of substitutes.** The less the differentiation between competing products, the greater the price elasticity of those products. Differentiated products benefit from customer awareness and preference, so their demand patterns tend to be more inelastic.

4   **Complementary products.** The inter-dependency of products results in price inelasticity, because the volume sales of the dependent good rely on sales of the primary good. The consumer will make a purchase of the complementary product in order to achieve satisfaction from the primary good. For example, the purchase of a radio, remote control toy car or a torch, etc., all require the purchase of the complementary product – batteries.

5   **Disposable income.** The relative wealth of the consumers over time affects the total demand in the economy. Luxury goods tend to have a high price elasticity, while necessities are usually inelastic.

6   **Necessities.** Demand for basic items such as milk, bread, toilet rolls, etc., tend to be very price inelastic.

7   **Habit. Items** consumers buy out of habit, such as cigarettes are usually price inelastic.

In practice few organisations attempt to set prices by calculating demand and elasticity. This is probably because it is exceptionally hard to determine demand under different circumstances with any certainty. However, most organisations will have some idea of the elasticity of their products and this will have some bearing on the way prices are set. There are a number of different techniques for setting prices that depend on the type of market and product.

Different types of market structures

The price that a business can charge for its products or services will be determined by the market in which it operates.

In a **perfectly competitive** market, every buyer or seller is a 'price taker', and no participant influences the price of the product it buys or sells. Other characteristics of a perfectly competitive market include:

*   **Zero entry/Exit barriers** – It is relatively easy to enter or exit as a business in a perfectly competitive market.

*   **Perfect information** – Prices and quality of products are assumed to be known to all consumers and producers.

*   **Companies aim to maximise profits** – Firms aim to sell where marginal costs meet marginal revenue, where they generate the most profit.

*   **Homogeneous products** – The characteristics of any given market good or service do not vary across suppliers.

Imperfect competition refers to the market structure that does not meet the conditions of perfect competition. Its forms include:

(a)   **Monopoly**, in which there is only one seller of a good. The seller dominates many buyers and can use its market power to set a profit-maximising price. Microsoft is usually considered a monopoly.

(b)   **Oligopoly**, in which a few companies dominate the market and are inter-dependent : firms must take into account likely reactions of their rivals to any change in price, output or forms of non-price competition. For example, in the UK, four companies (Tesco, Asda, Sainsbury's and Morrisons) share 74.4% of the grocery market.

(c)   **Monopolistic competition**, in which products are similar, but not identical. There are many producers ('price setters') and many consumers in a given market, but no business has total control over the market price.

For example, there are many different brands of soap on the market today. Each brand of soap is similar because it is designed to get the user clean; however, each soap product tries to differentiate itself from the competition to attract consumers. One soap might claim that it leaves you with soft skin, while another that it has a clean, fresh scent. Each participant in this market structure has some control over pricing, which means it can alter the selling price as long as consumers are still willing to buy its product at the new price.

If one product costs twice as much as similar products on the market, chances are most consumers will avoid buying the more expensive product and buy the competitors' products instead. Monopolistic products are typically found in retailing businesses. Some examples of monopolistic products and/or services are shampoo products, extermination services, oil changes, toothpaste, and fast-food restaurants.

6 The profit-maximisation model

A mathematical model can be used to determine an optimal selling price. The model is based on the economic theory that profit is maximised at the output level where **marginal cost is equal to marginal revenue**.

Full use of the model requires a knowledge of calculus, which is outside the scope of your syllabus. However, you are expected to understand the following basic principles:

It is worthwhile a firm producing and selling further units where the increase in revenue gained from the sale of the next unit exceeds the cost of making it (i.e. the marginal revenue exceeds the marginal cost). However, if the cost of the next unit outweighs the revenue that could be earned from it (i.e. the marginal cost exceeds the marginal revenue), production would not be worthwhile.

A firm should therefore produce units up to the point where the marginal revenue equals the marginal cost: **MR = MC**

The basic price equation is given as $p = a + bx$

where

p = price

x = quantity demanded

a and b are constants, where b is the slope of the curve and is calculated as (change in price/change in quantity)

For example, if you are told that demand falls by 25 units for every increase in price of $1, then b = (−1/25) = −0.04

The **marginal revenue** equation can be found by doubling the value of b:

MR = a + 2bx

The marginal cost is the variable cost of production.

Illustration 1 – The MR = MC diagram

Marginal revenue is the additional revenue from selling one extra unit, for example:

Quantity	Price	Revenue	Marginal revenue
1	$70	$70	$70
2	$60	$120	$50
3	$50	$150	$30
4	$40	$160	$10
5	$30	$150	$(10)

Marginal cost is the cost from making one more unit. It is usually just the variable cost, e.g. MC = $30.

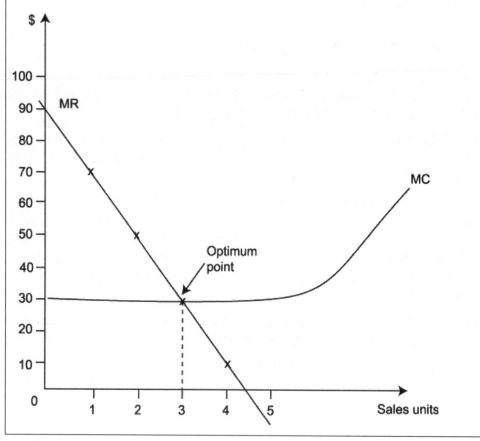

7 Procedure for establishing the optimum price of a product

This is a general set of rules that can be applied to most questions involving algebra and pricing.

1. Establish the linear relationship between price (P) and quantity demanded (Q). The equation will take the form:

$$P = a + bQ$$

where 'a' is the intercept and 'b' is the gradient of the line. As the price of a product increases, the quantity demanded will decrease. The equation of a straight line P = a + bQ can be used to show the demand for a product at a given price:

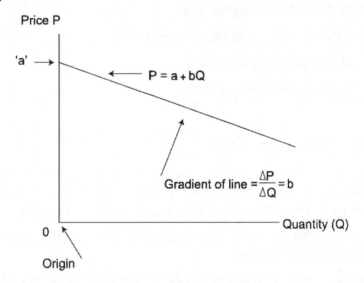

Note: 'b' is always negative because of the inverse relationship between price and quantity.

2. Double the gradient to find the marginal revenue: **MR = a + 2bQ**.

3. Establish the **marginal cost MC**. This will simply be the variable cost per unit.

4. To maximise profit, **equate MC and MR** and solve to find Q.

5. Substitute this value of Q into the price equation to find the optimum price.

6. It may be necessary to calculate the maximum profit.

Example 2: The algebraic approach

At a price of $200, a company will be able to sell 1,000 units of its product in a month. If the selling price is increased to $220, the demand will fall to 950 units. It is also known that the product has a variable cost of $140 per unit, and fixed costs will be $36,000 per month.

Required:

(a)   Find an equation for the demand function (that is, price as a function of quantity demanded)

(b)   Write down the marginal revenue function

(c)   Write down the marginal cost

(d)   Find the quantity that maximises profit

(e)   Calculate the optimum price

(f)   What is the maximum profit?

Example 3: Maximum profit

The total fixed costs per annum for a company that makes one product are $100,000, and a variable cost of $64 is incurred for each additional unit produced and sold over a very large range of outputs.

The current selling price for the product is $160. At this price, 2,000 units are demanded per annum.

It is estimated that for each successive increase in price of $5 annual demand will be reduced by 50 units. Alternatively, for each $5 reduction in price, demand will increase by $50 units.

Required:

(a)   Calculate the optimum output and price, assuming that if prices are set within each $5 range there will be a proportionate change in demand.

(b)   Calculate the maximum profit.

Example 4: Product K

Product K incurs a total cost of $10 per unit sold, as follows.

	$ per unit
Variable production cost	4
Variable selling cost	2
Fixed production cost	3
Fixed selling and administration cost	1
Total cost	**10**

The marginal revenue (MR) and demand functions for product K are:

MR = 200 – 0.4x

p = 200 – 0.2x

Where p – price, x = quantity demanded per period.

What is the profit-maximising selling price of product K, and what quantity will be sold per period at this price?

8 The tabular approach

When data in the exam is given in tabular form and there is no indication about the demand function, and/or when there is no simple linear relationship between output and profit – the tabular approach is likely to be the best to define optimum profit and the associated selling price.

Example 5: Tabular approach

XYZ Ltd is introducing a new product. The company intends to hire machinery to manufacture the product at a cost of $200,000 per annum. However, this will only enable 60,000 units per annum to be produced, although additional machines can be hired at $80,000 per annum. Each machine hired enables capacity to be increased by 20,000 units per annum, but it is not possible to increase production beyond 90,000 units because of shortage of space.

The minimum rental period is for one year and the variable cost is estimated to be $6 per unit produced. There are no other fixed costs that can be specifically traced to the product. Marketing management has estimated the maximum selling prices for a range of output from 50,000 units to 90,000 units. The estimates are as follows:

Units sold	50,000	60,000	70,000	80,000	90,000	90,000*
Selling price ($)	22	20	19	18	17	15

* At $15 demand will be in excess of 90,000 units but production capacity will limit the sales.

Required:

Present relevant financial information to management for the pricing and output decision.

Answer guide

	$	$	$	$	$	$
Price per unit	22	20	19	18	17	15
Variable cost per unit						
Contribution per unit						
Number of units sold	50,000	60,000	70,000	80,000	90,000	90,000
Total contribution ($000)						
Less fixed costs ($000)						
Net profit ($000)						

9 Limitations of the profit-maximisation model

The profit-maximisation model does make some attempt to take account of the relationship between the price of a product and the resulting demand, but it is of limited practical use because of the following limitations:

1 It is unlikely that organisations will be able to determine the demand function for their products or services with any degree of accuracy.

2 The majority of organisations aim to achieve a target profit, rather than the theoretical maximum profit.

3 Determining an accurate and reliable figure for marginal or variable cost poses difficulties for the management accountant.

4 Unit marginal costs are likely to vary depending on the quantity sold. For example bulk discounts may reduce the unit materials cost for higher output volumes.

5 Other factors, in addition to price, will affect the demand, for example, the level of advertising or changes in the income of customers.

10 Pricing strategies based on cost: Total cost-plus pricing

Cost-plus pricing involves adding a mark-up to the total cost of the product, in order to arrive at the selling price.

Unfortunately, since fixed costs are spread over the units of production, the full cost of a product will be a function of the number of units produced, which in turn will be a response to the number of units sold. Yet, sales quantity will depend on the price charged for the product, and so the argument is circular.

Where an order is placed with a jobbing company (a company that makes products to order) for a specific quantity of a product made to the customer's specification, cost-plus may be an acceptable pricing method. But for the majority of organisations this is not the case. Other factors will influence the pricing decision, such as competition and product differentiation. Nevertheless it is reassuring to have some knowledge of cost and price at particular volumes, even if the knowledge is not perfect.

If an organisation does use cost as the basis for pricing it has to decide whether to employ a standard mark-up or whether to vary the mark-up according to the market conditions, type of customer, etc. A standard mark-up is used by some organisations, such as government contractors and some job costing companies, but the majority of companies vary the percentage to reflect differing market conditions for their products. The example below demonstrates total cost pricing, using varying cost assumptions of total cost.

Total cost-plus pricing

A company is replacing product A with an updated version, B, and must calculate a base cost, to which will be added a mark-up in order to arrive at a selling price. The following variable costs have been established by reference to the company's experience with product A, although they may be subject to an error margin of + or – 10 % under production conditions for B:

	$
Direct material	4
Direct labour (1/4 hr @ $16/hr)	4
Variable manufacturing overheads (1/4 hr of machine time @ $8/hr)	2
Total variable cost per unit	**10**

As the machine time for each B would be the same as for A, the company estimates that it will be able to produce the same total quantity of B as its current production of A, which is 20,000 units. 50,000 machine hours may be regarded as the relevant capacity for the purposes of absorbing fixed manufacturing overheads. Current fixed costs are $240,000 for the production facilities, $200,000 for selling and distribution, and $180,000 for administration. For costing purposes, the 20,000 units of B can be assumed to consume 10 per cent of the total selling, distribution and administration costs.

Alternative 1, *using conventional absorption costing principles and building in the conservative error margin*

	$
Variable production costs (as above)	10
Add: allowance for underestimate 10%	1
Add: manufacturing cost 1/4 hour of machine time @ $4.80/hour ($240,000/50,000 hours)	1.2
Base cost	**12.2**

Alternative 2, *as 1 but including administrative costs*

	$
Base cost as under 1 above	12.2
Add: fixed administrative costs ($180,000 × 10% = $18,000/ 20,000 units)	0.9
Base cost	**13.1**

Alternative 3, *as 2 but including selling and distribution costs*

	$
Base cost as under 2 above	13.1
Add: fixed selling and distribution costs ($200,000 × 10% = $20,000/20,000 units)	1.0
Base cost	**14.1**

Depending on the analysis adopted, the base cost varies from $12.2 to $14.1. The base cost rises with each alternative, as an increasing proportion of the total costs is recovered. The profit mark-up built into the pricing formula is therefore likely to fall with each alternative from 1 to 3.

The profit mark-up needs to be based on some assumption. Normally it is fixed so that the company makes a specific return on capital based on a particular capacity utilisation.

A number of advantages are claimed for cost-plus pricing:

(i) The required profit will be made if budgeted sales volumes are achieved.

(ii) It is a particularly useful method in contract costing industries such as building, where a few large individual contracts can consume the majority of the annual fixed costs and the fixed costs are low in relation to the variable costs.

(iii) Assuming the organisation knows its cost structures, cost-plus is quick and cheap to employ. Its routine nature lends itself to delegation, thus saving management time.

(iv) Cost-plus pricing can be useful in justifying selling prices to customers; if costs can be shown to have increased, this strengthens the case for an increase in the selling price.

However, there are a number of **problems** with cost-plus pricing:

(i) There will always be problems associated with the selection of a 'suitable' basis on which to charge fixed costs to individual products or services. Selling prices can show great variation, depending on the apportionment basis chosen. This can lead to over-or under-pricing relative to competitors causing the firm to either lose business or make sales at an unintentional loss.

(ii) If prices are set on the basis of normal volume, and actual volume turns out to be considerably lower, overheads will not be fully recovered from sales and predicted profits may not be attainable.

(iii) Cost-plus pricing takes no account of factors such as competitor activity.

(iv) Cost-plus overlooks the need for flexibility in the different stages of a product's life cycle. It takes no account of the price customers are willing to pay and price elasticity of demand. The following example illustrates this point.

Illustration 2

The variable cost of product A is $10. Fixed manufacturing costs of $1 m are spread over an estimated production and sales volume of 200,000 units, i.e. $5 per unit. This gives a total cost of $15 per unit. The cost-plus approach used by the manufacturer of A, based on a standard mark-up of 40 per cent on the product's total cost, dictates a selling price of $21. Assuming all costs were as anticipated, and the company managed to sell 200,000 units at the fixed price of $21, a gross profit of $1.2m ($6 × 200,000) would be earned. Suppose, however, that a market survey had indicated the price elasticity of demand for the product shown in the table below:

Price ($)	Demand (units)
19	250,000
20	240,000
21	200,000
22	190,000
23	160,000

A more correct analysis of the pricing problem would have concentrated on maximising total contribution, and therefore total profitability as shown in this table:

Price ($)	Variable cost	Contribution	Demand	Total contribution	Profit
19	10	9	250,000	2.25	1.25
20	10	10	240,000	2.40	1.40
21	10	11	200,000	2.20	1.20
22	10	12	190,000	2.28	1.28
23	10	13	160,000	2.08	1.08

The decision to use a full cost-plus price of $21 has an associated opportunity cost. In failing to take into consideration the market conditions the organisation has forgone an extra profit of $200,000 and its market share is lower than it could have been.

11 Marginal cost-plus pricing

To the accountant, marginal cost is the same as variable cost. Some of the reasons for using it in preference to total cost are as follows:

1   It is just as accurate as total cost-plus pricing. A larger mark-up percentage is added because both fixed costs and profit must be covered, but the uncertainty over the fixed costs per unit remains in both pricing methods.

2   Knowledge of marginal cost gives management the option of pricing below total cost when times are bad, in order to fill capacity.

3   It is particularly useful in pricing specific one-off contracts because it recognises relevant costs and opportunity costs as well as sunk costs.

4   It also recognises the existence of scarce or limiting resources. Where these are used by competing products and services it must be reflected in the selling price if profit is to be maximised. If there is a scarce or bottleneck resource the aim must be to maximise the total contribution from the limiting factor. The contribution that each alternative product or service makes from each unit of the scarce resource must be calculated and a suitable profit margin added.

Marginal cost-plus pricing

A company has been producing A successfully for a number of years, and demand appears to be static into the foreseeable future at a market price of $15 per unit. A market has just developed in product B, which the company could produce without additional investment in plant, and without increasing or retraining the existing labour force. Unfortunately, however, B uses the same basic direct material as product A, material C – which is in short supply. The company must determine a minimum selling price for B, below which it would not be worthwhile to divert resources from A.

Costs for the two products are given in the table below:

	A		B
Direct material: 6 units of C @ $0 .60	$3.605 units of C @ $0.60		$3.00
Direct labour: 1/2 hour @ $6.00	$3.001/2 hour @ $6.00		$3.00
Variable overhead	$2.40		$1.00
	$9.00		$7.00
Selling price	$15.00		
Contribution	$6.00		

Contribution per unit of material C = $6/6 units = $1.

A produces a contribution of $6 using 6 units of C, that is, a contribution per unit of C, the limiting factor, of $1. B uses five units of C. The company must therefore seek a contribution of $5 (5 units of material C × $1). So the price must cover the cost of the unit and the lost contribution from C, i.e. be at least $7 + $5 = $12.

12 Criticism of marginal cost-plus pricing

Marginal costing as a basis for pricing has always had its sceptics. The main criticism is based on the following type of scenario:

There are two companies A and B competing with similar products in a market. The market is in recession and sales have decreased. Company A assesses its costs and lowers its price to below total cost, but well above marginal cost, in order to gain more market share. This tactic works; demand is elastic and so company A gains market share at the expense of company B. In order to get back its market share company B reduces its price below that of company A. Both companies now have their original market share but their margins are reduced. Company A then lowers the price again, etc. This continues, until one company is forced out of business. The remaining company now has to increase prices to the original level, which may well be difficult and can incur customer resistance.

13 Marketing-based pricing strategies

There are many different pricing strategies, and it may come as a surprise to would-be accountants that cost is only one of many methods and is certainly not universally used as the key method for pricing.

Premium pricing

Premium pricing is pricing above competition on a permanent basis. This can only be done if the product appears 'different' and superior to competition, which normally means establishing a brand name based on one of the following:

- Quality
- Image/style
- Reliability/robustness
- Durability
- After-sales service
- Extended warranties.

 Brands and premium pricing

In order to establish a brand, heavy initial promotion is required and the name must be constantly advertised or promoted thereafter. Brand names, such as, Levi, Mars, Coca-Cola, etc., require many millions of pounds spent on them each year. The benefit is a higher selling price generating a larger profit per unit and customer loyalty, making the product relatively price inelastic. These benefits must, of course, outweigh the cost of keeping the brand name in front of the customers.

Market skimming

Skimming is a technique where a high price is set for the product initially, so that only those who are desperately keen on the product will buy it. Then the price is lowered, making the product more accessible. When the next group of customers have had a chance to buy at that price, the price is lowered again, and so on. The aim of this strategy is usually to **maximise revenue**. But, on occasions, it is also used to prolong the life of older products.

Market skimming and consumer durables

Consumer durable companies tend to skim the market. This is done, to a certain extent, to recover large research and development costs quite quickly. But the products also lend themselves to this treatment as trend-setters are willing to pay a high price to own the latest gismo, and the rest of the population follow their example in later years. Books are also sold this way, with new novels published in hardback at a high price. The hard cover costs little more than a soft cover. Avid readers of that author will buy the hardback book at the high price. A year or so later the book is reissued with a soft cover at a much cheaper price in order to reach a wider audience.

Price skimming was probably first employed at the end of the eighteenth century by Josiah Wedgwood, the famous ceramics manufacturer. He made classical-shaped vases decorated with sprigs of decoration, which he sold to the rich and well-to-do. Naturally he priced his products accordingly. As the designs became old and well known he reduced the price on those lines and introduced new designs at the high price. Thus, he created different tiers of markets for his products, and people who were not so well off could afford a piece which had been in production for some years. This marketing technique helps to prolong a product's life and extracts the maximum profit from it.

If demand for a new or innovative product is relatively inelastic, the supplier has the chance of adopting a market skimming price strategy. It is usually much easier to reduce prices than increase them, so it is better to begin with a high price, and lower it if demand appears more elastic than anticipated. If profitable skimming is to be sustained beyond the introductory phase, there must be significant barriers to entry to the market, in order to deter too many potential competitors entering attracted by the high prices and returns. In the case of books only one company own the rights to publish. Wedgwood had created an image/brand among the rich and famous which others could not copy, especially if they wished to undercut his prices. Consumer durable products have high manufacturing costs that deter too many companies entering the industry.

Penetration pricing

Penetration pricing occurs when a company sets a very low price for the new product initially. The price will usually be below total cost. The aim of the low price is to establish a large market share quickly by encouraging customers to try the product and then to repeat buy. This type of tactic is used, therefore, where barriers to entry are low. It is hoped to establish a dominant market position, which will prevent new entrants coming into the market because they could not establish a critical mass easily with prices so low.

 Penetration pricing

In the past, companies used penetration pricing when they introduced a new product, such as a new spray polish, through supermarkets. The price would be, say, between 60 per cent and 80 per cent of the ultimate price. Customers would buy the new product largely because of its price and, it was hoped, repeat buy either because they did not notice the price increase or because they did not mind paying for a good product. If customers do notice the price increase they are likely to be put off further purchases if the increase is too large. If a company succeeds with this type of pricing it wins a large market share very quickly which competitors will find hard to break into.

Price differentiation

If the market can be split into different segments, each quite separate from the others and with its own individual demand function, it is possible to sell the same product to different customers at different prices. Marketing techniques can be employed to create market segmentation, if natural demarcation lines are not already in existence. Segmentation will usually be on the basis of one or more of the following:

- Time (e.g. rail travel is cheaper off-peak, hotel accommodation, telecommunications)

- Quantity (e.g. small orders at a premium, bulk orders at a discount)

- Type of customer (e.g. student and OAP rates)

- Outlet/function (e.g. different prices for wholesaler, retailer, end consumer)

- Geographical location (e.g. stalls and upper circle, urban and rural sites, wealthy and poor districts, different countries)

- Product content (e.g. sporty versions of a small car).

This type of pricing is of particular use where a service provider (theatre, leisure centre, train operator) has a high proportion of fixed costs. By attracting those willing and able to use the service at the less popular time/location will help to improve profitability.

Loss leader pricing

When a product range consists of one or more main products and a series of related optional 'extras', which the customer can 'add on' to the main product, the supplier can set a relatively low price for the main product and a high one for the 'extras'. Obviously, the aim is to stimulate sufficient demand for the former to ensure the target return from sales of the latter. The strategy has been used successfully by aircraft engine manufacturers, who win an order with a very competitively priced main product that can only be serviced by their own, highly priced spare parts.

Loss leader pricing – examples

Gillette did not invent the safety razor but the market strategy Gillette adopted helped to build market share. Gillette razors were sold at 1/5 of the cost to manufacture them but only Gillette blades fitted and these were sold at a price of 5 cents. The blades cost only 1 cent to manufacture and so Gillette made large profits once it had captured the customer. One of the best known uses of this technique in recent years has been the sale of printer ink for home printers.

Investigations by Which? and by Computeractive magazine showed that whilst the price of inkjet printers can be as little as $34, the cost of running the printer over an 18-month period could be up to $1,700. The top brand names for replacement ink cartridges cost more per millilitre than vintage champagne and even where the consumer only buys two replacement cartridges a year, the cost of the ink is likely to be significantly higher than the cost of the initial printer.

Discount pricing

Discount pricing is the long-term pricing strategy used by firms such as Ikea and Ryanair, based on low cost, high volume and low margins.

Products are priced lower than the market norm, but are put forward as being of comparable quality. The aim is that the product will procure a larger share of the market than it might otherwise do, thereby counteracting the reduction in selling price. However, care must be taken to ensure that potential customers' perceptions of the product are not prejudiced by the lower price. The consumer will often view with suspicion a branded product that is priced at even a small discount to the prevailing market rate.

Using discounts in pricing (short-term)

There are a number of reasons for using discounts to adjust prices:

1   To get cash in quickly. This is a not always a financially sound strategy as the firm may lose more in sales revenues from the discount, than they would lose in interest from a bank loan for the same amount.

2   To differentiate between different types of customer, wholesale, retail, etc.

3   To increase sales volume during a poor sales period without dropping the price permanently.

4   Some industries give discounts as normal practice, for example the antique trade, and some retail shops seem to have semi-permanent sales.

5   Perishable goods are often discounted towards the end of their life or the end of the day, or seconds are often sold off cheaply. This may not be a good strategy as it does not improve the company image, and some customers may get wise and delay their purchase until the end of the day when prices are cheaper.

Example 6: Pricing strategies

Place each of the following statements in a grey cell, against the pricing strategy to which it is most likely to relate:

Price differentiation on age	
Price differentiation on gender	
Skimming	
Volume discounting	
Loss leader pricing	
Penetration pricing	

Lower admission prices for children at certain sporting events.	This applies to a product with a short life cycle, and there is a need to recover its development costs quickly and make a profit.	Demand is very elastic, and would react well to low prices.
Lures the customer in with a relatively low priced product, in order to lock the customer in to subsequent additional purchases of different items that are relatively highly priced.	Offering a lower price per unit for customers who do not wish to place large individual orders, but who purchase large quantities over time.	Lower admission prices for females at some night clubs.

Controlled pricing

A significant proportion of the previously nationalised industries in the UK have been 'privatised' into the private sector, with a constraining influence usually called the industry 'regulator'. Examples of these regulating bodies are Oftel (telecommunications) and Ofwat (water).

Many of these companies are in a largely monopolistic situation and so regulation of these industries was perceived as desirable. Regulation largely takes the form of controlling price so that the monopolistic companies cannot exploit their unique position. The regulators use selling price as the means of controlling the volume of supply in the industry. They may also decide to specify the quality of the product or level of service that must be achieved or to prohibit the company operating in certain sectors.

When an industry is regulated on selling price, the elasticity is zero. No price change is allowed. Not only does this mean that 'small' customers pay less than they otherwise would, but large customers pay more than one might expect under more competitive positions. Over recent years all of the monopolistic industries have introduced some kind of discounted price for very large customers, which is beginning to allow genuine competition to enter the market. Gradually other billing companies have been allowed to enter the market and so price has become more flexible.

Product bundling

Bundling is putting a package of products together to make, for example, a complete kit for customers, which can then be sold at a temptingly low price. It is a way of creating value for customers and increasing company profits. It is a strategy that is often adopted in times of recession when organisations are particularly keen to maintain sales volume. One industry where this tactic started in the recession of the early 1990s is the computer industry. A manufacturer might decide to substantially reduce the profit margin on some hardware, such as printers. If, for example, only half its PC purchasers would also buy the company's model of printer, a bundled package which includes the PC and the printer for a lower combined price may well prove very successful. On the other hand, some customers will be put off by product bundling as they do not want the complete package; they will resent the increased price, however small it is.

Bundling

Bundling is profitable in situations in which some buyers value one of the items in a bundle relatively highly but the remainder slightly above or below cost price. Other buyers place a relatively high valuation on both or all of the items in the bundle. Four film exhibitors, A to D, are willing to pay the following prices for two films X and Y:

A values X at $16,000 and Y at $5,000

B values X at $14,000 and Y at $6,000

C values X at $11,000 and Y at $10,000

D values X at $10,000 and Y at $11,000

The distributor's marginal cost of supplying each film is $8,000.

The distributor offers X and Y separately at $14,000 and $8,000 respectively, or the pair as a package for $21,000. The result is that A, C and D hire the package and B hires film X only, as the cost of both the bundle and film Y exceed his particular valuations. The distributor's profit would be ($21,000 × 3) + ($14,000) − ($8,000 × 7) = $21,000.

However, A might also prefer to hire film X for $14,000, instead of taking the package, as the extra cost of the bundle exceeds his valuation of Y by $2,000. If A did choose this option, the distributor's profit would rise to $22,000, as he does not have to supply either A or B with film Y, which has a supply cost in excess of their valuations: ($21,000 × 2) × ($14,000 × 2) − ($8,000 × 6) = $22,000.

Bundling is a particularly efficient means of exploiting price differentiation. Buyers are offered a pricing structure in which they are charged higher prices for buying the items separately (X + Y = $22,000) than in a package (X + Y = $21,000). Bundling works as a discriminatory device by:

- Using the package to extract the most from those customers who value it most. (In our example C and D, who placed relatively high valuations on both films.)

- Charging a relatively high separate price for the item in the package that is valued very highly by some particular buyers. (In our example film X, which was valued very highly by both A and B.)

If the distributor did not bundle he would make a profit of $19,000, as A and B would purchase product X and C and D would purchase product Y.

Bundling: Amstrad

Bundling can be extremely successful, especially when tried on mature products for the first time. For instance, Amstrad had considerable success when it entered the hi-fi market and demystified the technology by being the first company to sell a complete package of amplifier, deck and speakers. This was more than just a pricing strategy: it was a complete marketing strategy. In recent years the telecommunications industry has successfully used this technique; first with TV channel packages, and then more recently extended to TV, broadband and phone bundles.

Whether a bundling strategy will succeed depends on the predicted increase in sales volume and the changes in margin. There are likely to be other cost changes such as savings in product handling, packaging and invoicing costs. Longer-term implications and competitors' reactions must not be ignored. For example, how will customers react when products are 'unbundled'? Will this result in a marked decline in sales? Will bundling be seen as an inferior product strategy which will have long-term implications for the brand's image? Will competitors retaliate by bundling their products? If they do this, will the strategy be successful?

Pricing with additional features

The decision to add extra features to a product is a similar decision to bundling products. Most people prefer to have extra features incorporated into the product but they may not be prepared to pay the extra price. Others do not require the extra features and view them as a definite disadvantage. This is likely to be the case with older customers and electrical or electronic equipment. Older people find mastering the equipment quite difficult and they do not want extra features that make operation even more difficult.

14 The product life cycle

Products and services, like human beings, have a life cycle. This is represented by the generic curve shown below:

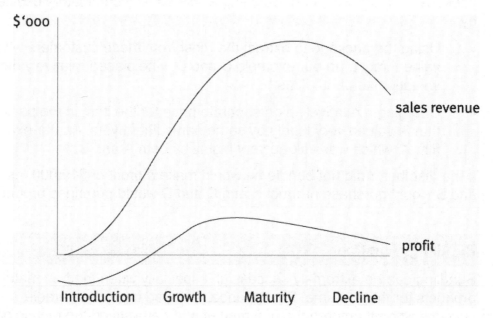

The length of the life cycle varies considerably from a year or so, for some children's toys, to hundreds of years, as in the case of binoculars, for example. The product life cycle is divided into four basic stages as shown in the figure above; each stage has different aims and expectations.

Price is a major variable over the product life cycle. Depending on market structure and demand, different pricing strategies will be appropriate for different stages in the cycle. The four stages in the life cycle and appropriate price strategies are described below:

(i) **Introductory phase**

Demand will be low when a product is first launched onto the market, and heavy advertising expenditure will usually be required to bring it to consumers' attention. The aim is to establish the product in the market, which means achieving a certain critical mass within a certain period of time. The critical mass is the sales volume that must be achieved in order to make the product viable in the medium term. Depending on the nature of the product, a price penetration (low entry price) policy may be adopted in order to reach the critical mass quickly. On the other hand the market may be skimmed (exploiting those purchasers keen to have the latest product such as plasma screen TVs) and so a high introductory price may be set.

(ii) **Growth**

Once the hurdle of the introductory stage has been successfully negotiated, the product enters the growth stage, where demand shows a steady and often rapid increase. The cost per unit falls because of economies of scale with the greater level of production. The aim at this stage is to establish a large market share and to perhaps become the market leader. Market share is easier to obtain during the growth stage because the market is growing and increased market share does not have to be gained by taking sales from another company. In a more mature market, market share has to be poached from competitors and their reaction may be unpleasant as they try to hold on to their market share. During the growth stage competitors will enter the market, some of which will not survive into the maturity stage. Despite the fact that competing products will be launched into the growing market and pricing is often keen in order to gain market share, it is usually the most profitable stage for the initial supplier.

(iii) **Maturity**

The increase in demand slows down in this stage, as the product reaches the mass market. The sales curve flattens out and eventually begins to fall. As market maturity is reached the organisation becomes more interested in minimising elasticity. Products have to be differentiated in order to maintain their position in the market and new users for mature products need to be found to keep demand high. Generally, profits will be lower than during the growth stage.

(iv) **Decline**

When the market reaches saturation point, the product's sales curve begins to decline. When the market declines price wars erupt as organisations with products which have elastic demand seek to maintain full utilisation of their production capacity.

Profits can still be made during the early part of this stage, and the products will be managed to generate cash for newer products. This will determine how prices are set. Eventually rapidly falling sales inevitably result in losses for all suppliers who stay in the market. This particular product has effectively come to the end of its life cycle, and alternative investment opportunities must be pursued.

Despite the recent general tendency to shorter life cycles, the length of any particular stage within the cycle and the total length of the life cycle itself will depend on the type of product or service being marketed. Although the curve will be characterised by a sustained rise, followed by levelling out and falling away, the precise shape of the curve can vary considerably. Life cycles are discussed further earlier in this text.

15   Practice questions

OT Question 1: Tabular Approach

ABC plc is about to launch a new product. Facilities will allow the company to produce up to 20 units per week. The marketing department has estimated that at a price of $8,000 no units will be sold, but for each $150 reduction in price one additional unit per week will be sold.

Fixed costs associated with manufacture are expected to be $12,000 per week.

Variable costs are expected to be $4,000 per unit for each of the first 10 units; thereafter each unit will cost $400 more than the preceding one. The most profitable level of output per week for the new product is:

A   10 units

B   11 units

C   13 units

D   14 units

E   20 units

OT Question 2: Delnorte Ltd optimum price

Market research by Delnorte Ltd has revealed that the maximum demand for product R is 50,000 units each year, and that demand will reduce by 50 units for every $1 that the selling price is increased. Based on this information, Delnorte Ltd has calculated that the profit-maximising level of sales for product R for the coming year is 35,000 units. The price at which these units will be sold is:

A $100

B $300

C $500

D $700 .

E $900

OT Question 3: Optimum price

Another product manufactured by Delnorte Ltd is product M. At a price of $700 for product M there would be zero demand, and for every $40 reduction in the selling price the demand would increase by 100 units. The variable cost of producing a unit of product M is $60.

Delnorte Ltd knows that if the demand equation for product M is represented by p = a – bx, where p is the selling price and x is the quantity demanded at price p, then the marginal revenue (MR) for product M can be represented by MR = a – 2bx.

The profit-maximising output of product M is:

A   100 units

B   700 units

C   800 units

D   1,600 units

E   1,750 units

OT Question 4: Fresno Optimum price

Fresno Ltd is considering the pricing of one of its products. It has already carried out some market research with the following results:

The quantity demanded at a price of $100 will be 1,000 units.

The quantity demanded will increase/decrease by 100 units for every $50 decrease/increase in the selling price. The marginal cost of each unit is $35.

Calculate the selling price that maximises company profit.

OT Question 5: Glenn Optimum price

Glenn Ltd is launching a new product which it expects to incur a variable cost of $14 per unit. The company has completed some market research to try to determine the optimum selling price with the following results.

If the price charged was to be $25 per unit, then the demand would be 1,000 units each period. For every $1 increase in the selling price, demand would reduce by 100 units each period. For every $1 reduction in the selling price, the demand would increase by 100 units each period.

Calculate the optimum selling price.

Data Set Question: AB Ltd

During the current year AB Ltd planned to produce 150,000 units of its main product, a cordless hand drill. Nearing the end of the current year, activity so far has corresponded to budget and it is anticipated that average costs for the whole year will be as shown below:

Average cost per unit (for 150,000 activity level)

	$
Direct material	18
Direct labour	10
Variable overhead	10
Fixed overhead	10
	48

The budget for next year is being developed and the following cost changes have been forecast:

Direct material: price increase of 33.3%

Director labour: rate increase of 10%

Variable overhead: increase of 5%

Fixed overhead: increase of 15%

The substantial price increase for materials is causing concern and alternative sources are being considered. One source quotes a material cost per unit of $20 but tests on samples show that the cheaper materials would increase labour costs by an additional 50c per unit and would lead to a reject rate of 5%. It would also be necessary to install a test and inspection department at the end of manufacturing to identify the faulty items. This would increase fixed costs by an additional $200,000 per year.

Selling prices are also considered when the budget is being developed. Normally, selling prices are determined on a cost-plus basis, the mark-up being 50% on unit cost, but there is concern that this is too inflexible as it would lead to a substantial price rise for next year. The sales director estimates that demand varies with price thus:

	$	$	$	$	$	$	$
Price/unit	64	68	72	76	80	84	88
Demand (000 units)	190	170	150	140	125	110	95

Calculate:

The **number of units** where the variable cost
saving is equal to the incremental fixed costs:

The selling price that would maximise profit for
next year $

The maximum profit achievable $

It has been realised that, through better organisation, it would be possible
to reduce the extra fixed costs of $200,000 originally estimated in
connection with the cheaper material.

Required:

The **increase** in fixed costs at which the $
company would be indifferent as to its choice
of suppliers for materials.

Case Study Style Question – CamLife Ltd

CamLife Ltd manufactures webcams, devices which can provide live video and audio streams via personal computers. You report to the senior financial manager, but you also regularly advise the marketing department on pricing matters.

You receive the following email from CamLife's Marketing Director:

> **From:** Marketing Director
> **To:** Management Accountant
> **Date:** xxxxxx
> **Subject:** Pricing Strategies
>
> As you know, we in CamLife have recently been suffering from liquidity problems. We, in the Marketing Department, hope that these will be eased by the launch of our new webcam, which has revolutionary audio sound and visual quality.
>
> The webcam is expected to have a product life cycle of two years. Market research has already been carried out to establish a target selling price and projected lifetime sales volumes for the product. Cost estimates have also been prepared, based on the current proposed product specification.
>
> CamLife uses life cycle costing to work out the target costs for its products, believing it to be more accurate to use an average cost across the whole lifetime of a product, rather than potentially different costs for different years. The average market price for a webcam is currently $150.
>
> I'd like to discuss the next step with you, as we have to decide on which pricing strategy to adopt.....Shall we do things differently, and go for skimming? Could you actually explain the price skimming pricing strategy and discuss whether this strategy may be more appropriate for CamLife than charging one price throughout the webcam's entire life?

Examples and objective test questions answers

Example 1: Elasticity

The price elasticity can be calculated as follows:

% change in price = (increase in price of 20/original price of 40) × 100 = + 50%

% change in demand = decrease in demand of –8/original demand of 20) × 100 = –40%

PED = –40/+50 = –0.8

The negative sign is usually ignored in the PED calculation and the PED = 0.8.

Example 2: The algebraic approach

(a) b = (220 – 200)/(950 – 1,000) = –0.4

200 = a –0.4 × 1,000

a = 200 + 400 = 600.

So the demand function is P = 600 – 0.4Q

(b) To find MR, just double the gradient so that MR = 600 – 0.8QMR = 600 – 0.8Q

(c) MC = 140

(d) The optimum quantity Q is achieved when the company produces units up to the point where marginal revenue equals marginal cost, i.e. when MR = MC

with MR = a + 2bQ

i.e. MR = $600 – 0.8Q

and MC = $140

so q is achieved when a + 2bQ = $140

i.e. when $600 – 0.8Q = $140

i.e. when Q = 575 units

(e) P= 600 – 0.4 × 575 = $370

(f) Revenue = Price × Quantity = $370 × 575 = $212,750

Cost = $36,000 + $140 × 575 = $116,500

Profit = $96,250

Example 3: Maximum profit

(a)   Let Q = quantity produced/sold

Gradient 'b'=

$$b = \frac{\text{Change in price}}{\text{Change in quantity}} = \frac{\$5}{\$50}$$

B = –0.1

Price = a – 0.1 Q; $160 = a – 0.1 (2,000) therefore **a = $360**

P = $360 – 0.1Q

MR = $360 – 0.2Q

MC = $64

(b)   To maximise profit, MR = MC.

Therefore, $360 – 0.2Q = $64

Q	= (360 – 64) ÷ 0.2	= 1,480	Units
P	= 360 * 0.1	= $212	
	(1,480)		
Revenue	= $212 × 1,480	= $313,760	
Less Costs	= ($64 × 1,480) + $100,000	= ($194,720)	
Maximum profit		= $119,040	

Example 4: Product K

Solution

Marginal cost per unit of product K = variable cost per unit = $6

Profit is maximised when marginal cost marginal revenue
i.e. when 6 = 200 – 0.4x

x = 485

When x = 485, p = 200 – (0.2 × 485) = 103

Therefore the profit-maximising selling price is $103 per unit, at which price 485 units will be sold per period.

Example 5: Tabular approach

	$	$	$	$	$	$
Price per unit	22	20	19	18	17	15
Variable cost per unit	(6)	(6)	(6)	(6)	(6)	(6)
Contribution per unit	16	14	13	12	11	9
Number of units sold	50,000	60,000	70,000	80,000	90,000	90,000
Total contribution ($000)	800	840	910	960	990	810
Less fixed costs ($000)	(200)	(200)	(280)	(280)	(360)	(360)
Net profit ($000)	600	640	630	680	630	450

To maximise profit, price should be $18, output 80,000 and 1 extra machine should be hired.

Example 6: Pricing strategies

Place each of the following statements in a grey cell, against the pricing strategy to which it is most likely to relate:

Price differentiation on age	Lower admission prices for children at certain sporting events.
Price differentiation on gender	Lower admission prices for females at some night clubs.
Skimming	This applies to a product with a short life cycle, and there is a need to recover its development costs quickly and make a profit.
Volume discounting	Offering a lower price per unit for customers who do not wish to place large individual orders, but who purchase large quantities over time.
Loss leader pricing	Lures the customer in with a relatively low priced product, in order to lock the customer in to subsequent additional purchases of different items that are relatively highly priced.
Penetration pricing	Demand is very elastic, and would react well to low prices.

OT Question 1: Tabular Approach

The best approach is to calculate the profit for a range of outputs from 10 units upwards, then select the output with the highest profit.

The answer is **B**

Units	Total variable costs	Selling price per unit (W1)	Total select revenue	Total contribution
10	$40,000	$6,500	$65,000	$25,000
11	$44,400	$6,350	$69,850	$25,540
12	$49,200	$6,200	$74,400	$25,200
13	$54,400	$6,050	$78,650	$24,250
14	$60,000	$5,900	$82,600	$22,600
20	$102,000	$5,000	$100,000	($2,000)

Working 1: Selling Price per unit

At $8,000, we sell no units, but for each $150 reduction in price one additional unit per week will be sold. This means that at $8,000 – $150 = $7,850, we will sell one unit.

At [$8,000 – ($150 × 2)] = $7,700, we will sell 2 units.

At [$8,000 – ($150 × 10)] = $6,500, we will sell 10 units.

At [$8,000 – ($150 × 11)] = $6,350, we will sell 11 units.

At [$8,000 – ($150 × 12)] = $6,200, we will sell 12 units.

At [$8,000 – ($150 × 13)] = $6,050, we will sell 13 units.

At [$8,000 – ($150 × 14)] = $5,900, we will sell 14 units.

At [$8,000 – ($150 × 20)] = $5,000, we will sell 20 units.

OT Question 2: Delnorte Ltd optimum price

Answer: **B**

In the demand equation p = a – bx

When price = 0, demand, x = 50,000 therefore 0 = a – 50,000b (i)

When price = 1, demand, x = 49,950 therefore 1 = a – 49,950b (ii)

Subtract 1 = 50b so b = 0.02

Substitute in (i) a = (50,000 × 0.02) so a = 1,000

The demand equation for product R is p = 1,000 – 0.02x

When x = 35,000 units, p = 1,000 – (0.02 × 35,000) = 300

OT Question 3: Optimum price

Answer: **C**

In the demand equation p = a – bx

When price = $700, demand = 0 therefore a = 700

When price = $660, demand = 100 therefore 660 = a – 100b

Substitute for a 660 = 700 – 100b therefore b = 0.4

The demand equation for product M is p = 700 – 0.4x

The marginal revenue equation is given by MR = 700 – 0.8x

Profit is maximised when marginal cost = marginal revenue, i.e. when 60 = 700 – 0.8x

i.e. **when x = 800**.

OT Question 4: Fresno Optimum price

Price at which demand equals zero = $100 + (1,000/100) × $50 = $600

P = $600 – 0.5x

MR = $600 – x

MC = $35

MC = MR

$35 = $600 2 x

x = $565

p = $600 – $(0.5 × 565)

p = $317.50

OT Question 5: Glenn Optimum price

Marginal cost (MC) = $14

Price (P) = $35 – 0.01q

Marginal revenue (MR) = $35 – 0.02q

So if MC = MR, then 14 = 35 – 0.02q

Q = 1,050

Price = $35 – (0.01 × 1,050) = $24.50

Data Set Question: AB Ltd

	Current material	Cheaper material
	$ per unit	$
Direct material	24.00	20.00
Direct labour	11.00	11.50
Variable overhead	10.50	10.50
Total variable cost	45.50	42.00

for 0.95 of a unit

$$\therefore \text{Cost per unit} = \frac{\$42}{0.95}$$

$$= \$44.21 \text{ per unit}$$

Fixed costs last year: $10 × 150,000 = $1,500,000

∴ Fixed cost in coming year: $1,500,000 × 1.15 = $1,725,000

If use cheaper material fixed costs increase by $200,000: $1,925,000

When the company switches from the current material to the cheaper material, the cost per unit will decrease but the fixed cost will increase.

At low levels of activity the cheapest material would be the current one, taking advantage of the low fixed cost.

However, as production increases the cheaper material becomes more attractive, as one wishes to take advantage of the lower unit cost. At high levels of activity the cheaper material is preferable, the lower unit cost more than compensates for the higher fixed cost.

So, in conclusion, the material choice is dependent upon the activity level.

Ascertain the level of activity where the purchaser would be **indifferent** between the two materials.

When switch from regular to cheaper:

Saving in variable cost is $45.50 – $44.21 = $1.29 per unit.

Increase in fixed cost is $200,000.

Therefore, the number of units where the variable cost saving is equal to the incremental fixed cost is:

$200,000 ÷ 1.29 = 155,038.8 units

Conclusion

If production is expected to be **155,038** units or less, use the regular supplier. If production is expected to be **155,039** or more, use the cheaper material.

Price	Demand	Variable cost per unit	Contribution per unit	Total contribution	Fixed costs	Profit
$	000s	$	$	$000	$000	$000
64	190	(44.21)	19.79	3,760.1	(1,925)	1,835.1
68	170	(44.21)	23.79	4,044.3	(1,925)	2,119.3
72	150	(45.50)	26.50	3,975.0	(1,725)	2,250.0
76	140	(45.50)	30.50	4,270.0	(1,725)	2,545.0
80	125	(45.50)	34.50	4,312.5	(1,725)	2,587.5
84	110	(45.50)	38.50	4,235.0	(1,725)	2,510.0
88	95	(45.50)	42.50	4,037.5	(1,725)	2,312.5

From the table above, it can be seen that profit is maximised when 125,000 units are sold for $80 each.

The maximum profit is $2,587,500.

The regular supplier should be retained.

At 125,000 units the saving in variable costs if the firm switches to the cheaper supplier is

125,000 × $1.29 = $161,250

The company would be indifferent between the two suppliers if fixed costs increased by $161,250.

New fixed cost level   = $1,725,000 + $161,250

= $1,886,250

From: Management Accountant

To: Marketing Director

Date: xxxxxx

Subject: Pricing Strategies

Thank you for your email, here are some elements of response which I hope will suit.

Market skimming is a strategy that attempts to exploit those areas of the market which are relatively insensitive to price changes. Initially, high prices for the webcam would be charged in order to take advantage of those buyers who want to buy it as soon as possible, and are prepared to pay high prices in order to do so.

The existence of certain conditions is likely to make the strategy a suitable one for CamLife. These are as follows:

- Where a product is new and different, so that customers are prepared to pay high prices in order to gain the perceived status of owning the product early. The webcam has superior audio sound and visual quality, which does make it different from other webcams on the market.

- Where products have a short life cycle this strategy is more likely to be used, because of the need to recover development costs and make a profit quickly. The webcam does only have a two year life cycle, which does make it rather short.

- Where high prices in the early stages of a product's life cycle are expected to generate high initial cash inflows. If this were to be the case for the webcam, it would be particularly useful for CamLife because of the current liquidity problems the company is suffering. Similarly, skimming is useful to cover high initial development costs, which have been incurred by CamLife.

- Where barriers to entry exist, which deter other competitors from entering the market; as otherwise, they will be enticed by the high prices being charged. These might include prohibitively high investment costs, patent protection or unusually strong brand loyalty. It is not clear from the information whether this is the case for CamLife.

- Where demand and sensitivity of demand to price are unknown. In CamLife's case, market research has been carried out to establish a price based on the customers' perceived value of the product. The suggestion therefore is that some information is available about price and demand, although it is not clear how much information is available.

It is not possible to say for definite whether this pricing strategy would be suitable for CamLife, because of the limited information available. However, it does seem unusual that a high-tech, cutting edge product like this should be sold at the same price over its entire, short life cycle. Therefore, price skimming should be investigated further, presuming that this has not already been done by CamLife.

Responsibility Centres

Chapter learning objectives

Lead	Component
C1: Managing and controlling the performance of organisational units	Analyse the performance of responsibility centres and prepare reports (a) Analyse the performance of cost centres, revenue centres, profit centres, and investment centres (b) Reports for decision-making
C2: Discuss various approaches to the performance and control of organisations	(a) Discuss budgets and performance evaluation (b) Discuss other approaches to performance evaluation

1 Chapter summary

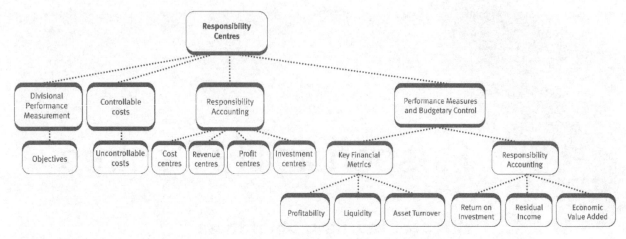

Decentralisation, which is also known as divisionalisation, seeks to overcome the problem of managing a large organisation by creating a structure based on several autonomous decision-making units.

The objectives of decentralisation can be listed as

(a) Ensure goal congruence

(b) Increase motivation of management

(c) Reduce head office bureaucracy

(d) Provide better training for junior and middle management.

The major disadvantage of decentralisation is the potential for dysfunctional decision making, i.e. where divisions make decisions **in their own best interests**, but which are not good from the overall company point of view.

The problem can be overcome by introducing a suitable system of performance evaluation, that has the following objectives:

1 Promote goal congruence

2 Encourage initiative and motivation

3 Provide feedback to management

4 Encourage long-term rather than short term views

These objectives can only be achieved with the introduction of **responsibility centres**.

2　Cost, revenue, profit and investment centres

In **responsibility accounting**, a specific manager takes responsibility for a particular aspect of the budget. Within the budgetary control system, he or she is then accountable for actual performance. Managers are accountable for their area of responsibility.

The area of operations for which a manager is responsible is called a responsibility centre. Within an organisation, there could be a hierarchy of responsibility centres.

- If a manager is responsible for a particular aspect of operating costs, the responsibility centre is a **cost centre**: 'a production or service location, function, activity or item of equipment for which costs are accumulated.' A cost centre could be large or small, such as an entire department or the activities associated with a single item of equipment.

- If a manager is responsible for revenue, the responsibility centre is a **revenue centre**: the division is only responsible for the generation of revenue. The best example of this is the sales department, where there is less focus on costs (sales managers aren`t held responsible for things like overhead cost reduction) and more focus on generating sales.

- If a manager is responsible for revenue as well as costs, the responsibility centre is a **profit centre**, and the manager responsible is held accountable for the profitability of the operations in his or her charge.

There could be several cost centres within a profit centre, with the cost centre managers responsible for the costs of their particular area of operations, and the profit centre manager responsible for the profitability of the entire operation.

- If a manager is responsible for investment decisions as well as for revenues and costs, the responsibility centre is an **investment centre**. The manager is held accountable not only for profits, but also for the return on investment from the operations in his or her charge. There could be several profit centres within an investment centre.

Each cost centre, profit centre, revenue centre and investment centre should have its own budget, and its manager should receive regular budgetary control information relating to the centre, for control and performance measurement purposes.

Example 1: Photocopiers

Bryn Ltd sells and repairs photocopiers. The organisation has operated for many years with two departments, the sales department and the service department, but the departments have no autonomy. The organisation is now thinking of restructuring, so that the two departments become profit centres and the managers of the departments are given autonomy. The individual salaries of the managers will be linked to the profits of their respective departments.

What are the likely consequences of structuring the departments as profit centres? Select ALL that apply.

- Improved decision making due to local knowledge.

- Departmental managers will become more motivated and more autonomous.

- Senior management will find the new structure more time-consuming to handle.

- Possible loss of control from senior management.

- Dysfunctional decision making.

- Possible duplication of functions and costs.

3 Responsibility accounting and controllability of costs

If the principle of controllability is applied, a manager should be made responsible and accountable only for the costs (and revenues) that he or she is in a position to control. A controllable cost is a cost 'which can be influenced by its budget holder'. Controllable costs are generally assumed to be **variable** costs, and **directly attributable fixed costs**. These are fixed costs that can be allocated in full as a cost of the centre.

It is important to make managers responsible and accountable for costs they can control. Without accountability, managers do not have the incentive to control costs and manage their resources efficiently and effectively.

If the principle of controllability is applied, control reports would make managers responsible for the variable costs and directly attributable costs of the centre.

A common assumption in management accounting is that controllable costs consist of variable costs and directly attributable fixed costs. Uncontrollable costs are costs that cannot be influenced up or down by management action.

This assumption is not entirely correct, and it should be used with caution.

Some items treated as variable costs cannot be influenced or controlled in the short term. Direct labour costs are treated as a variable cost, but in reality, the direct labour work force is usually paid a fixed wage for a minimum number of working hours each week. Without making some employees redundant, and unless there is overtime working, the direct labour cost cannot be reduced or increased in the short term because it is really a fixed cost item.

An item that is **uncontrollable** for one manager could be controllable by another. In responsibility accounting, it is important to identify areas of responsibility. In the long term, all costs are controllable. At senior management level, control should be exercised over long-term costs as well as costs in the short term.

The advantages of this approach to responsibility accounting are:

- profit centre managers are made aware of the significance of other overhead costs

- profit centre managers are made aware that they need to earn a sufficient profit to cover a fair share of other overhead costs.

The disadvantages of this approach are that:

- profit centre managers are made accountable for a share of other overhead costs, but they can do nothing to control them

- the apportionment of other overhead costs between profit centres, like overhead apportionment generally, is usually a matter of judgement, lacking any economic or commercial justification.

A useful distinction can be made between **committed** fixed costs, which are costs that are uncontrollable in the short term, but are controllable over the longer term; and **discretionary** fixed costs, which are costs treated as fixed cost items that can nevertheless be controlled in the short term, because spending is subject to management discretion.

Examples are advertising expenditure, and executive travel and subsistence costs.

Controllable and uncontrollable costs

A summarised report for the profit centres of an organisation might be:

	Centre A $	Centre B $	Centre C $	Total $
Revenue	300,000	260,000	420,000	980,000
Variable costs	170,000	100,000	240,000	510,000
Directly attributable costs	70,000	120,000	80,000	270,000
Controllable costs	**240,000**	**220,000**	**320,000**	**780,000**
Attributable gross profit	60,000	40,000	100,000	200,000
Other overhead costs				**(180,000)**
Net profit				20,000

A criticism of the controllability accounting principle is that managers are not encouraged to think about costs for which they are not responsible. In the example above, there are $180,000 of costs not attributable to any profit centre. These might be head office costs, for example, or marketing overheads.

- Within a system of responsibility accounting, there should be cost centre managers accountable for these costs.

- Even so, these overhead costs might be caused to some extent by the demands placed on head office administration or marketing services by the profit centre managers.

- When these costs are high, a further problem is that profit centre profits need to be large enough to cover the general non-allocated overhead costs.

An argument could therefore be made that profit centre managers should be made accountable for a share of overhead costs that are not under their control, and a share of these costs should be charged to each profit centre. Profit reporting would therefore be as follows:

	Centre A $	Centre B $	Centre C $	Total $
Revenue	300,000	260,000	420,000	980,000
Variable costs	170,000	100,000	240,000	510,000
Directly attributable costs	70,000	120,000	80,000	270,000
Controllable costs	**240,000**	**220,000**	**320,000**	**780,000**
Attributable gross profit	60,000	40,000	100,000	200,000
Other overhead costs	(50,000)	(50,000)	(80,000)	**(180,000)**
Net profit	10,000	(10,000)	20,000	20,000

Example 2: Controllability

The materials purchasing manager is assessed on:

- total material expenditure for the organisation

- the cost of introducing safety measures, regarding the standard and the quality of materials, in accordance with revised government legislation

- a notional rental cost, allocated by head office, for the material storage area.

Which of these costs are controllable by the manager, and should be used to appraise him/her? Select ALL that apply.

4 Pros and cons

The advantages of this approach to responsibility accounting are:

- Profit centre managers are made aware of the significance of other overhead costs.

- Profit centre managers are made aware that they need to earn a sufficient profit to cover a fair share of other overhead costs.

The disadvantages of this approach are that:

- Profit centre managers are made accountable for a share of other overhead costs, but they can do nothing to control them

- The apportionment of other overhead cost between profit centres, like overhead apportionment generally, is usually just a matter of judgement, lacking any economic or commercial justification.

Responsibility centres and internal markets (extract)

Bob Scarlett, Financial Management, April 2007

An objective must be set for an autonomous responsibility centre. Determining how far that objective has been achieved provides a performance measure for the centre. The system must be adapted to priorities and circumstances in each case. Accordingly, responsibility centres may be grouped under three main headings:

Cost centre (CC)

This is a responsibility centre to which costs are attributed, but not earnings or capital.

CCs can be designed in two alternative ways: either (a) the CC is given a fixed quantity of inputs and be required to maximise outputs, or (b) a required level of outputs is specified for the CC which must be achieved with minimum inputs.

An example of (a) is a public relations department, which is given a fixed budget to spend and has to use this to achieve the best possible result. An example of (b) is a cleaning department, which is given certain areas to clean and has to do this at minimum cost. In both cases, the CC manager is allowed a degree of autonomy in making decisions on how the operation is run. But the system guides the manager to act in a manner which is consistent with the interest of the organisation.

However, the CC offers one particular weakness insofar as it relies on the measurement of financial spend to assess performance. There is no direct incentive for the manager to enhance the quality of output. Costs can always be contained by reducing quality. In the case of a CC, quality reduction is not identified by the use of financial performance metrics.

Many organisations treat their IT departments as cost centres. This often has unfortunate consequences.

The idea that IT is a cost centre and carries no profit or loss is dangerous and should be opposed wherever it is encountered, according to Simon Linsley, head of consultancy, IT and development at Philips. Will Hadfield, Computer Weekly, 30 May 2006

This CW article describes how IT system installation projects were usually completed on time and within budget at the electronics firm Philips. However, the manner in which system projects were implemented often gave rise to serious disruption at the operational level, causing stress to the staff of client departments and degraded customer service.

Profit centres (PC)

This is a responsibility centre to which costs and revenues are attributed, but not capital.

In the case of a CC, the manager has autonomy as regards either (a) outputs or (b) inputs – but not both together. In the case of the PC, the manager has autonomy over both inputs and outputs. The objective of a PC is to maximise profit or achieve a profit target. The manager of the PC is allowed to make decisions concerning both the resources used and output (in terms of both quantity and price) achieved.

In the case of a PC, reliance on financial performance measures does not provide any incentive to lower quality. Lowering quality will impact on sales quantity and/or selling price, which will impact on profit. The PC may also induce other behaviour which is in the interests of an organisation. For example, unit costs within a CC may be minimised by use of long continuous production runs and this pattern of production may be favoured accordingly. But, it is a pattern of production which will result in high inventory holding and/or lowered response levels to individual customer requirements. These last features will adversely impact on profit and, therefore, a sub-optimum pattern of production is less likely to be induced within a PC.

An IT department within an organisation may be organised as a profit centre. Typically, this will involve invoicing client departments for its services and inviting competition from outside consultants for system installation projects.

IT directors should push for the IT function in their organisation to be treated as a profit centre rather than a cost to the business. This was the key message from Glenn Martin, managing director and chief technology officer at financial services firm Cazenove, speaking to the City IT financial services technology forum last week. Christian Annesley, Computer Weekly, 15 November 2005

Rather than forcing through system installations in a manner which minimises costs, IT managers are now incentivised to allow for the full operational requirements of client departments when organising projects.

The logic behind responsibility centres suggests that an organisation should be split into decoupled internal components with decision rights in each given to its own management, within certain parameters. Each component trades its services with the others on an arm's length basis, giving rise to an 'internal market'.

This concept was applied widely in the British public sector in the 1990s. The BBC under Director General John Birt introduced an internal market amongst its different components – Technology, Production, News and so on. The development of an internal market has also been a feature of NHS reform, whereby different units within the NHS have the character of buyers and providers of services.

So much for the theory. Practical experience has introduced organisations to a concept known as 'failure of the internal market'. For example, the BBC Gramophone Library was rated as the greatest sound archive in the world and it was traditionally run as a cost centre. During the reforms of the 1990s, it became a profit centre and was required to charge user departments in the BBC for the issue of recordings.

Music that was previously provided free by the Library now came with a charge and it wasn't cheap. Which is why all the music shops in Oxford Street were busy with BBC researchers buying far cheaper commercial CDs. At the prestigious Radio 4 daytime current affairs programmes, The World at One and PM, staff were barred from using any material from the BBC's gramophone library because the cost was too high. Netribution, 'BBC axes Producer Choice', March 2006

The BBC's internal market was deeply unpopular and produced unintended effects in the way that managers behaved. It has been largely abandoned in recent years. The reality was that the BBC's Gramophone Library was a vital resource that had to be seen as a cost centre and nothing other than that.

Responsibility centres and internal markets have much to offer. But insensitivity in their use, or their use in inappropriate circumstances, can result in them doing more harm than good.

5 Key performance indicators

An organisation and its divisions should have certain targets for achievement. Targets can be expressed in terms of key metrics. The term 'metric' is now in common use within the context of measurement of performance. It is a basis for analysing performance (both budgeted and actual).

A budget should not be approved by senior management unless budgeted performance is satisfactory, as measured by the key metrics. Actual performance should then be assessed in comparison with the targets. The expression **'key performance indicators'** might be used.

Profitability and liquidity are key areas of financial performance.

Profitability

Return on Capital Employed (ROCE)

A key metric for profitability might be the **operating profit/sales ratio** (profit margin), or the contribution/sales ratio (contribution margin).

We use the operating profit as a percentage of the capital employed. The ROCE shows the operating profit that is generated from each $1 of assets employed.

If operating profit (profit before finance charges and tax) is not given in the question, use net profit instead.

A high ROCE is desirable. An increase in ROCE could be achieved by:

- Increasing operating profit e.g. through an increase in sales price or through better control of costs

- Reducing capital employed, e.g. through the repayment of long term debt.

Senior management might set a target for a minimum profit/sales ratio for the budget period, and refuse to authorise a budget unless this minimum target is met in the plan.

The ROCE can be understood further by calculating the operating profit margin (operating profit/sales × 100) and the asset turnover.

The operating profit margin: operating profit/turnover

The operating profit equals the gross profit less indirect costs incurred, such as administrative salaries. The operating profit is often expressed as a percentage of the selling price, known as the operating profit margin: in simple terms, the higher the better.

Poor performance is often explained by prices being too low, or costs being too high. By analysing the operating profit margin, the reader can determine how well the business has managed to control its indirect costs during the period.

When interpreting operating profit margin, it is advisable to link the result back to the gross profit margin. For example, if gross profit margin deteriorated in the year, it would be expected that operating margin would also fall. However, if this is not the case, or the fall is not so severe, it may be due to good indirect cost control or perhaps there could be a one-off profit on disposal of a non-current asset distorting the operating profit figure.

The asset turnover: turnover/capital employed

Asset turnover shows how efficiently management have utilised assets to generate revenue. When looking at the components of the ratio a change will be linked to either a movement in revenue, a movement in net assets, or both.

There are many factors that could both improve and deteriorate asset turnover. For example, a significant increase in sales revenue would contribute to an increase in asset turnover or, if the business enters into a sale and operating lease agreement, then the asset base would become smaller, thus improving the result.

Triangulation

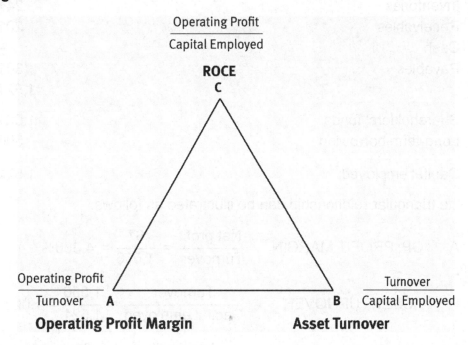

There is a direct relationship between the three figures; All figures are used twice, meaning A × B = C

$$\frac{\text{Operating Profit}}{\text{Turnover}} \times \frac{\text{Turnover}}{\text{Capital employed}} = \frac{\text{Operating Profit}}{\text{Capital employed}}$$

Operating Profit margin × Asset turnover = ROCE

Capital employed = equity + long-term finance

Note that we assume that the 'Capital Employed' at the start of the year is the one that was used to generate the profits at the end of the year. Therefore the opening capital employed is generally used in OT calculations, unless the question directs you otherwise.

Triangulation [DuPont model of measurement]

Extracts from the accounts of The Beta Company read as follows:

The Beta Company

Income Statement extracts $000

Sales/Revenue	1,556
Operating profit	67

Statement of Financial Position extracts $000

Non-current assets	1,380
Inventories	241
Receivables	201
Cash	–
Payables	(301)
	1,521
Shareholders' funds	1,021
Long-term borrowing	500
Capital employed	1,521

The triangular relationship can be illustrated as follows:

A   OP. PROFIT MARGIN $\dfrac{\text{Net profit}}{\text{Turnover}} = \dfrac{67}{1,556} = 4.306\%$

B   ASSET TURNOVER $\dfrac{\text{Turnover}}{\text{Capital employed}} = \dfrac{1,556}{1,521} = 1.023 \text{ times}$

C   ROCE $\dfrac{\text{Net profit}}{\text{Capital employed}} = \dfrac{67}{1,521} = 4.405\%$

Liquidity

Liquidity means having cash, or ready access to cash. Liquid assets are therefore cash and short-term investments that can be readily sold if the need arises. In addition, liquidity is improved by unused bank borrowing facilities.

Liquidity is improved through efficient cash management, and an important element of good cash management is control over inventory, trade receivables and trade payables.

A key metric for liquidity might therefore be the **current ratio** (which is the ratio of current assets to current liabilities), or the **quick ratio** or acid test ratio (which is the ratio of current assets excluding inventories to current liabilities).

$$\text{Current ratio} = \frac{\text{Current assets}}{\text{Current liabilities}}$$

$$\text{Quick ratio (acid test)} = \frac{\text{Current assets} - \text{inventory}}{\text{Current liabilities}}$$

A low liquidity ratio could indicate **poor liquidity and a risk of cash flow difficulties**. The appropriate minimum value for a liquidity ratio varies from one industry to another, because the characteristics of cash flows vary between different industries. As a broad rule, however, a current ratio below 2.0 times and a quick ratio below 1.0 times might be considered low.

Within a budgeting system, senior management might set a target for liquidity, in the form of a maximum and minimum acceptable current ratio and/or quick ratio. A current ratio or quick ratio that declines from one year to the next could indicate deteriorating liquidity and greater risk.

On the other hand, a business can have **excessive liquidity, with too much capital tied up in working capital**. The current ratio and quick ratio should therefore not be expected to rise above a maximum acceptable level.

We have seen also that an important element of good cash management is control over the various parts of working capital, in particular inventory, trade receivables and trade payables.

6 Divisional performance measurement

Type of division	Description	Typical measures used to assess performance
Cost centre	Division incurs costs, but has no revenue stream, e.g. the IT support department of an organisation.	<ul><li>Total cost and cost per unit.</li><li>Cost variances.</li><li>Non-financial performance indicators (NFPIs) related to quality, productivity & efficiency.</li></ul>
Revenue centre	Division is only responsible for the generation of revenue.	Total revenue and revenue per unit. Revenue (sales) variances.

Profit centre	Division has both costs and revenue. Manager does not have the authority to alter the level of investment in the division.	All of the above PLUS: • Total sales and market share. • Profit. • Sales variances. • Working capital ratios (depending on the division concerned). • Non-financial performance indicators (NFPIs) e.g. related to productivity, quality and customer satisfaction.
Investment centre	Division has both costs and revenue. Manager does have the authority to invest in new assets or dispose of existing ones.	All of the above PLUS: • Return On Investment (ROI) • Residual Income (RI). These measures are used to assess the investment decisions made by managers and are discussed in more detail below.

Important point: For each of these care must be taken to assess managers on controllable factors only. So for example, the manager of a cost centre should only be assessed on controllable costs.

7 Return On Investment (ROI)

ROI is a similar measure to ROCE, but is used to appraise the investment decisions of an individual department.

$$\text{ROI/ROCE} = \frac{\text{Divisional controllable profit before interest and tax}}{\text{Capital employed}} \times 100\%$$

Profit can be measured in relation to the financial resources it uses, the 'Capital Employed'. ROCE is common at the overall corporate level, whereas ROI is more commonly used for investment appraisal and for divisional performance.

- 'Controllable profit' is usually taken after depreciation but before tax. However, in the exam you may not be given this profit figure and so you should use the profit figure that is closest to this. Assume the profit is controllable, unless told otherwise.

- Capital employed is total assets less current liabilities or total equity plus long term debt. Use net assets if capital employed is not given in the question.

- Non-current assets might be valued at cost, net replacement cost or net book value (NBV). The value of assets employed could be either an average value for the period as a whole or a value as at the end of the period. An average value for the period is preferable. However, in the exam you should use whatever figure is given to you.

Example 3: ROI calculation

An investment centre has reported a profit of $28,000. It has the following assets and liabilities:

	$	$
Non-current assets (at NBV)		100,000
Inventory	20,000	
Trade receivables	30,000	
		50,000
Trade payables	8,000	
		42,000
		142,000

The ROI for the division is $_____%.

Additional example on ROI

Division A of Babbage Group had investments at the year end of $56 million. These include the cost of a new equipment item costing $3 million that was acquired two weeks before the end of the year. This equipment was paid for by the central treasury department of Babbage, and is recorded in the accounts as an inter-company loan.

The profit of division A for the year was $7 million before deducting head office recharges of $800,000.

Required:

What is the most appropriate measure of ROI for Division A for the year?

Solution

Since the new equipment was bought just two weeks before the year end, the most appropriate figure for capital employed is $53 million, not $56 million.

The figure for profit should be the controllable profit of $7 million.

ROI = $7 million/$53 million = 13.2%

Evaluation of ROI as a performance measure

ROI is a popular measure for divisional performance. However, it has some serious failings which must be considered when interpreting results.

Advantages

- It is widely used and accepted, since it is line with ROCE, and ROCE is frequently used to assess overall business performance.

- As a relative measure, the ROI enables comparisons between divisions or companies of different sizes.

- It can be broken down into secondary ratios for more detailed analysis, i.e. profit margin and asset turnover.

Disadvantages

- It may lead to dysfunctional decision making, e.g. a division with a current ROI of 30% would not wish to accept a project offering a ROI of 25%, as this would dilute its current figure. However, the 25% ROI may meet or exceed the company's target.

- ROI increases with the age of the asset if NBVs are used, thus giving managers an incentive to hang on to possibly inefficient, obsolescent machines.

- It may encourage the manipulation of profit and capital employed figures to improve results, e.g. in order to obtain a bonus payment.

- Different accounting policies can confuse comparisons (e.g. depreciation policy).

Example 4: Disadvantages of ROI

Nielsen Ltd has two divisions with the following information:

	Division A	Division B
	$	$
Profit	90,000	10,000
Capital employed	300,000	100,000
ROI	30%	10%

Division A has been offered a project costing $100,000 and giving annual returns of $20,000. Division B has been offered a project costing $100,000 and giving annual returns of $12,000. The company's cost of capital is 15%. Divisional performance is judged on ROI and the ROI – related bonus is sufficiently high to influence the managers' behaviour.

Required:

(a) What decisions will be made by management if they act in the best interests of their division (and in the best interests of their bonus)?

(b) What should the managers do if they act in the best interests of the company as a whole?

8 Residual income (RI)

Residual income is profit (controllable profit, at divisional level), less an imputed interest charge for invested capital.

RI = Controllable profit – Notional interest on capital

- Controllable profit (i.e. controllable profit, at divisional level) is calculated in the same way as for ROI.

- The notional interest on capital (sometimes called the 'imputed interest charge') is the capital employed in the division, multiplied by a notional cost of capital or interest rate.

  - Capital employed is calculated in the same way as for ROI.

  - The selected cost of capital could be the company's average cost of funds (cost of capital). However, other interest rates might be selected, such as the current cost of borrowing, or a target ROI. (You should use whatever rate is given in the exam).

Example 5: RI calculation

An investment centre has net assets of $800,000, and made profits before interest and tax of $160,000. The notional cost of capital is 12%.

Calculate and comment on the RI for the period.

Example 6: RI Increase

The manager of the 'D' Division is considering investing in a replacement machine at the beginning of next year, 2020.

If the investment does not go ahead, then the divisional results for 'D' in 2020 will be (in $000):

Sales	420
Cost of sales	310
Gross Profit	110
Other operating costs	85.2
Pre-tax operating profits	24.8
Capital invested	212

> If the investment **does** go ahead, then the divisional results for 'D' in 2020 will be:
>
> | Sales | 420 |
> |---|---|
> | Cost of sales | 279 |
> | Gross Profit | 141 |
> | Other operating costs | 97.2 |
> | Pre-tax operating profits | 43.8 |
> | | |
> | Capital invested | 260 |
>
> The divisional cost of capital is 8% per annum.
>
> **Should the divisional manager choose to go ahead with the investment, the increase in Residual income for the 'D' division amounts to:**
>
> A $7,840
>
> B $15,160
>
> C $23,000
>
> D $25,180

Evaluation of RI as a performance measure

Compared to using ROI as a measure of performance, RI has several advantages and disadvantages:

Advantages

- It encourages investment centre managers to make new investments if they add to RI. A new investment might add to RI but reduce ROI. In such a situation, measuring performance by RI would not result in dysfunctional behaviour, i.e. the best decision will be made for the business as a whole.

- Making a specific charge for interest helps to make investment centre managers more aware of the cost of the assets under their control.

- Risk can be incorporated by the choice of interest rate used: different interest rates for the notional cost of capital can be applied to investments with different risk characteristics.

Disadvantages

- It does not facilitate comparisons between divisions since the RI is driven by the size of divisions and of their investments.

- It is based on accounting measures of profit and capital employed which may be subject to manipulation, e.g. in order to obtain a bonus payment.

9 Comparing ROI and RI

Compared to using ROI (or ROCE) as a measure of performance, RI has several advantages and disadvantages.

Advantages

1   RI resolves the dysfunctional aspect of the ROI measure.

2   RI reduces ROCE's problem of rejecting projects with a ROCE in excess of the company's target, but lower than the division's current ROCE.

3   The cost of financing a division is brought home to divisional managers.

Disadvantages

1   RI does not facilitate comparisons between divisions.

2   RI does not relate the size of a division's profit to the assets employed in order to obtain that profit.

3   RI can also mislead, as it increases over time.

Additional example on ROI and RI

Two divisions of a company are considering new investments.

	Division X	Division Y
Net assets	$1,000,000	$1,000,000
Current divisional profit	$250,000	$120,000
Investment in project	$100,000	$100,000
Projected project profit	$20,000	$15,000

Company's required ROI = 18%

Required:

Assess the projects using both ROI and RI.

Solution

Consider divisional performance:

Without project

	Division X	Division Y
Divisional ROI	25%	12%
Divisional RI ($)	+ 70,000	– 60,000
With project		
Investment ($)	1,100,000	1,100,000
Profit ($)	270,000	135,000
ROI	24.5%	12.3%
RI ($)	72,000	– 63,000
Project in isolation		
ROI	20%	15%
RI ($)	+ 2,000	– 3,000

Based on ROI, Division X will reject its project as it dilutes its existing ROI of 25%. This is the wrong decision from the company perspective as the project ROI of 20% beats the company hurdle of 18%.

Likewise, Division Y will accept its project, which should be rejected as it fails to hit the company target.

In each case there is a conflict between the company and divisional viewpoints.

RI does not have this problem as we simply add the project RI to the divisional figures.

Example 7: ROI vs RI

An investment centre has net assets of $800,000, and made profits before interest of $160,000. The notional cost of capital is 12%. This is the company's target return.

An opportunity has arisen to invest in a new project costing $100,000. The project would have a four-year life, and would make profits of $15,000 each year.

Required:

(a) What would be the ROI with and without the investment? (Base your calculations on opening book values). Would the investment centre manager wish to undertake the investment if performance is judged on ROI?

(b) What would be the average annual RI with and without the investment? (Base your calculations on opening book values). Would the investment centre manager wish to undertake the investment if performance is judged on RI?

Divisional performance can be compared in many ways. ROI and RI are common methods but other methods could be used.

- Variance analysis – is a standard means of monitoring and controlling performance. Care must be taken in identifying the controllability of, and responsibility for, each variance.

- Ratio analysis – there are several profitability and liquidity measures that can be applied to divisional performance reports.

- Other management ratios – this could include measures such as sales per employee or square foot as well as industry specific ratios such as transport costs per mile, brewing costs per barrel, overheads per chargeable hour.

- Other information – such as staff turnover, market share, new customers gained, innovative products or services developed.

> **Example 8: Comparing divisional performance**
>
> Comment on the problems that may be involved in comparing divisional performance.

10 Economic value added (EVA®)

Economic value added (EVA) is a measure of performance similar to residual income, except the profit figure used is the ECONOMIC profit and the capital employed figure used is the ECONOMIC capital employed. It is argued that the 'profit' and 'capital employed' figures quoted in the financial statements do not give the true picture and that the accounting figures need to be adjusted to show the true underlying performance.

The basic concept of EVA is that the performance of a company as a whole, or of investment centres within a company, should be measured in terms of the value that has been added to the business during the period. It is a measure of performance that is directly linked to the creation of shareholder wealth.

The measurement of EVA is conceptually simple. In order to add to its economic value, a business must make an economic profit in excess of the cost of the capital that has been invested to earn that profit.

Calculation:

1	PAT is adjusted to give the Net Operating Profit after tax (NOPAT)	X
2	Deduct the economic value of the capital employed(*) × cost of capital	(X)
		X

(*) The calculation should be based on **opening** capital employed. We assume that the 'Capital Employed' at the start of the year is the one that was used to generate the profits during the year. Therefore the opening capital employed is generally used in calculations, unless the question directs you otherwise.

In more detail:

1	NOPAT is calculated from PAT		X
	Add back items that are non-cash, such as:		
	Accounting depreciation	Note 1	XX
	Provision for doubtful debts	Note 2	XX
	Non-cash expenses	Note 3	XX
	Interest paid net of tax	Note 4	XX
	Add back items that add value, such as:		
	Goodwill amortised	Note 5	XX
	Development costs	Note 6	XX
	Operating leases	Note 7	XX
	Take off:		
	Economic depreciation	Note 8	(X)
	Any impairment in the value of goodwill		
	= NOPAT in cash flow terms		XX

2 Deduct the charge for the cost of capital

Opening capital employed

Add adjustments to allow for the net replacement cost of tangible non-current assets

= Capital invested

3 Multiply capital invested by the cost of capital x%

= Charge for the cost of capital	(X)
= EVA	(XX)

More on EVA – Notes on the above calculation

Note 1 – Accounting depreciation: We add this back to PAT, because EVA is calculated after profits have been charged with economic depreciation (not accounting depreciation).

Note 2 – Provision for doubtful debts: Where a company had made a provision for doubtful debts, this should be reversed. Any adjustment in the income statement for an increase or decrease in the provision for doubtful debts should be reversed.

Note 3 – Non cash expenses: These were charged to profit, but must be added back because we want NOPAT in cash flow terms. Examples of non-cash expenses include depreciation and capitalised development costs.

Note 4 – Interest paid net of tax: if tax is at 35%, take interest payments and multiply by 0.65.

Adding this back results in profits that would have been reported had all the companies' capital requirements been financed with ordinary shares. A charge for interest and the tax effect of actual gearing are incorporated into the weighted average cost of capital (so if we leave the interest charge within the NOPAT number it will be double counted). It is the net interest i.e. interest after tax that is added back to reported profit because interest will already have been allowed as an expense in the computation of the taxation liability.

Note 5 – Goodwill: Goodwill is a measure of the price paid for a business in excess of the current cost of the net separable assets of the business. Payments in respect of goodwill may be viewed as adding value to the company. Therefore any amounts in respect of goodwill amortisation appearing in the income statement are added back to reported profit since they represent part of the intangible asset value of the business.

Note 6 – Development costs: Spending by the company on development costs should not be charged in full against profit in which the expenditure occurs. Instead, it should be capitalised because it has added value to the economic value of capital employed. The adjustment can be made by:

- Increasing NOPAT by the net increase in capitalised development costs, and

- Increasing the economic value of capital employed by the same amount.

Note 7 – Leases

All leases should be capitalised. Finance leases will have already been capitalised but operating leases should be capitalised too. The economic value of the capital employed increased to include the current value of the operating lease. The capitalised cost should then be amortised. The value of NOPAT should be increased by the operating lease charge and reduce by the amortisation charge. The net effect to increase NOPAT by the implied interest cost of the operating lease.

Note 8 – Economic depreciation

Considered to be a measure of the economic use of assets during a year. Involves a process of valuation. It is the period by period change in the market value of the asset.

Example 9: Economic Value Added

A company with several divisions has a cost of capital of 6%. An excerpt from Division B's accounting summary for the period is shown below:

	$
Revenue	1,000,000
Cost of sales	450,000
Gross profit	550,000
General administration costs	300,000
Depreciation	50,000
Provision for bad and doubtful debts*	25,000
Loan interest @ 5%	5,000
Net profit	170,000
Net assets at net book value**	500,000
Bank loan	100,000

The value of closing Capital Employed is $525,000.

* Taking total provision to $50,000.

** Replacement cost has been estimated at $700,000. If assets had been valued at replacement cost the depreciation charge would have been $70,000.

Ignore taxation, what is the economic value added (EVA) of the investment centre?

A $142,500

B $138,000

C $135,000

D $148,500

Advantages of EVA

The advantages of EVA are as follows.

- It is a performance measure that attempts to put a figure to the increase (or decrease) that should have arisen during a period from the operations of a company or individual divisions within a company.

- Like accounting return and residual income, it can be measured for each financial reporting period.

- It is based on economic profit and economic values of assets, not accounting profits and asset values.

Measuring and using EVA

The principle underlying EVA can be stated as follows.

- The objective of a company is to maximise shareholder wealth.

- The value of a company depends on the extent to which shareholders expect future economic profits to exceed the cost of the capital invested.

- A share price therefore depends on expectations of EVA.

- Current performance (EVA) is reflected in the current share price, so in order to increase the share price a company must achieve a sustained increase in EVA.

Peter Drucker has written: 'Until a business returns a profit that is greater than its cost of capital, it operates at a loss. Never mind that it pays taxes as if it had a genuine profit. The enterprise still returns less to the economy than it devours in resources.... Until then, it does not create wealth, it destroys it.'

Measuring EVA

The difficulties in applying EVA in practice arise from the problem of establishing the economic profit in a period, and the economic value of capital employed. These values are estimated by making adjustments to accounting profits and accounting capital employed.

- Accounting profits are based on the accruals concept of accounting, whereas NOPAT for EVA is based on cash flow profits. Adjustments have to be made to convert from an accruals basis to a cash flow basis.

- Depreciation of non-current assets is a charge in calculating EVA as well as accounting profit. Economic depreciation is the fall in the economic value of an asset during the period.

    - It might be assumed that the accounting charge for depreciation is a good approximation of the economic cost of depreciation, in which case no adjustment to accounting profit is necessary.

    - Alternatively, it might be assumed that the economic value of the assets are their net replacement cost, in which case economic depreciation will be based on replacement cost. An adjustment to accounting profit should then be made for the amount by which economic depreciation exceeds the accounting charge for depreciation.

- Similarly, an adjustment might be necessary for intangible non-current assets such as goodwill.

- Where a company had made a provision for doubtful debts, this should be reversed. Any adjustment in the income for an increase or decrease in the provision for doubtful debts should be reversed, and NOPAT increased or reduced accordingly.

- Spending by the company on development costs should not be charged in full against profit in the year the expenditure occurs. Instead, it should be capitalised because it has added to the economic value of capital employed, and it should then be amortised over an appropriate number of years. In practice, the adjustment can be made by:

  - increasing NOPAT by the net increase in capitalised development costs, and

  - increasing the economic value of capital employed by the same amount.

- All leases should be capitalised. Finance leases will have been capitalised already, but operating leases should be capitalised too, and the economic value of capital employed increased to include the current value of operating leases. Stern Stewart amortise this capitalised cost over five years. In adjusting from accounting profit to NOPAT, the value of NOPAT should be increased by the operating lease rental charge, and reduced by the amount of the amortisation charge. (The net effect is to increase NOPAT by the implied interest cost of the operating lease.)

Using EVA

Economic value added can be used to:

- set targets for performance for investment centres (divisions) and the company as a whole

- measure actual performance

- plan and make decisions on the basis of how the decision will affect EVA.

When EVA is used to measure performance, Stern Stewart have recommended that divisional managers should be:

- given training to understand the principles of EVA. Stern Stewart have found than non-accountants find the concept of EVA fairly easy to understand, and they see the link between EVA and changes in shareholder value

- informed about the interest cost that will be applied for the capital charge

- taught how to calculate EVA for decision-making purposes

- given a pay incentive based on a bonus for achieving or exceeding a target EVA.

- EVA can also be used for control purposes, by encouraging managers to:

  - identify products and services that provide the greatest EVA, and concentrate resources on those

  - identify customers who provide the greatest EVA, and give priority to serving them

  - identify and eliminate activities that do not add to EVA

  - identify capital that is not providing a sufficient return to cover its capital cost (such as excess equipment) and seek to reduce the capital investment.

11 Reports for decision making

Report visualisation, along with the advancement of multimedia technology over recent years, has become a very powerful means of sharing and providing insight around business performance, which can be easily digested by the recipient.

Report visualisation, through the use of data analytics in performance management, is the process of presenting report formats that represent data and information in a pictorial or graphical format . Visualisation helps the recipient to understand the significance of the content more easily than if presented in a traditional report format.

In today's modern business environment, the volume of data is far larger than ever. Therefore, the art of report visualisation has become increasingly important, as we become overwhelmed by both data and information.

In recent years, technology providers have embraced the market and developed new tools to assist in the production of high-impact visual reports. In parallel, progress in desktop and mobile technology have enabled visualisation to be truly interactive and dynamic.

A key role of the management accountant is to support effective decision making by presenting relevant, timely and accurate information in a manner that enables informed dialogue and decision making.

Reporting for each type of responsibility centre

For effective decisions to be taken, the information presented must focus on the right key performance indicators (KPIs) that drive true business performance. The overriding principle in deciding how to present data is that **one size does not fit all**.

Whether reporting is produced at responsibility centre (=divisional) level, or in Head Office, two key areas are fundamental to quality reporting:

1   Data and master data that are subject to robust control which ensures reporting integrity.

2   Standards in reporting that drive commonality across the whole organisation and aid assimilation to the consumer. For example, if 'red' is consistently used to display an adverse variance, then the reader is not having to ask the question every time.

The five principles for effective report visualisation

The following five key principles should always be considered:

1   **Ensure data is optimised for report visualisation**

Once the right measures that are to be reported have been identified, the relevant data sources, which might be more than one for each report, also need locating. Key points to consider per data source are:

- Where is the data source?

- Can the data be refreshed in time to make the report relevant?

The second area to consider is the creation of structure or hierarchies within the data that facilitates drill down to the reader. This is especially important if using tools such as mobile technology where the user is encouraged to drill to the next level with the touch of a finger.

For example, imagine a report on an iPad showing a map of the world featuring a big red variance for sales in Europe. To investigate the sales variances, different divisional managers may want to drill down by:

- Country or region

- Product/service

- Distribution channel.

This is facilitated by creating a dimensional structure that stores data against reporting hierarchies.

2   **The relevant visualisation tool must be applied**

The principal factor in choosing the relevant report visualisation technique will undoubtedly be driven by what the user for the report feels comfortable with.

However, there are a few common guiding principles that can be used to help match the visualisation to the requirement:

- Variance analysis is often depicted by using **waterfall charts**, commonly known as **bridges**. The key benefit delivered is that the size of the steps in the bridge are to scale, so the eye naturally focuses on the significant movements first.

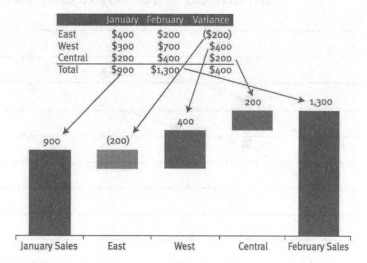

- In providing an overview of a business area, **dashboards** can provide a relevant summary. The key to delivering a useful dashboard is identifying what are the four or five relevant key drivers that can be reported on one page or screen. Dashboards provide a summary and often lead to a drill down to the next level, which is likely to be a different report:

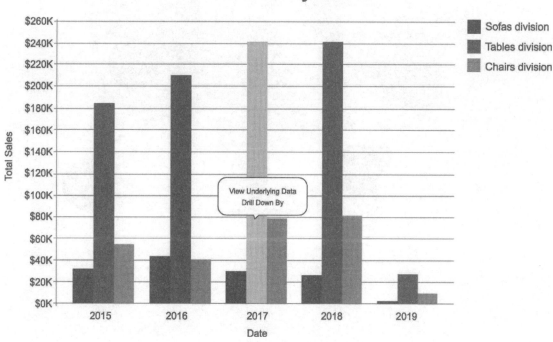

- Trend analysis or time-based results are generally shown using **line charts**. Modern planning solutions can also use line charts as the visual interface to plan for future periods by establishing a baseline and then allowing the planner to drag the chart, which then models the underlying data.

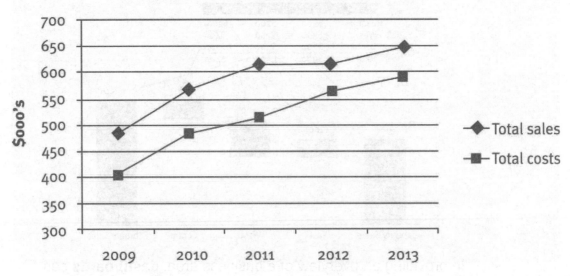

Total Sales and Total Costs

- Where organisations are built up of business areas or regions, **mapping charts** are useful, especially when presented on an interactive interface such as a tablet:

Division Gamma - Sales Units by Region

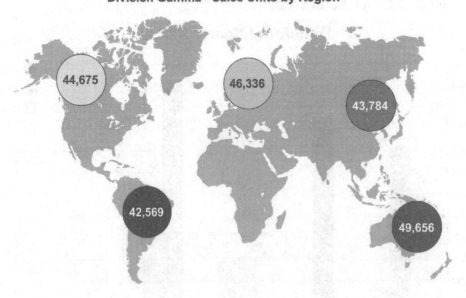

- When comparing data sets that are built up from component parts, then a bar chart or **side by side pie chart** brings the message to life:

3 An appropriate report layout must be chosen

As visualisation skills become more and more important for the management accountant, he or she must think of designing a report from the perspective of the graphic designer too. Consider the following:

- Layout – a simple and clean layout will always deliver a more impactful report than a report with too much information. Clear headings should be used that help explain what data is being presented.

- If the report is 'to be delivered digitally', then the visible area of the page should match the screen, as scrolling is not desirable.

- Positioning – the reader's eye naturally starts to read reports from the left-hand corner of the page and continues to the right or down. Therefore, if there is a key message, this should be positioned towards this area to gain optimum impact.

Colours – the first area to think through with colours is whether the colours you have used make the report attractive to the eye, which engages the reader.

The second use of colours is to assist in telling the story. 'Red' and 'green' are used universally to depict 'positive' and 'negative', so consider conditional formatting if appropriate. Colours in related charts should always be consistent -for example, if a product or channel is shown in blue in one chart, it should be shown in blue in the next chart too. Finally, although colours enliven a chart, it is not a good idea to use too many as the chart will look messy.

- Scaling – make scaling appropriate to the data and be wary of hiding the story through scaling. If your report contains multiple charts, try not to mix different scales on the same page, as this can confuse the reader.

4   **The reader experience must be optimised**

Engaging with the report user is key to ensuring the message is transmitted effectively from the paper or screen. When reporting in paper, think about the size and weight of the pack and consider dividers to help readers switch between sections.

For online reporting, there are many more options available to deliver a better user experience:

- Personalised – personalised reporting is key to engaging with users. This can be as simple as offering 'bookmarks' or 'favourites', or as complicated as the reporting solution making intelligent reporting suggestions based on the reader's history or security access.

- Intuitive – navigating searching around an online report should be intuitive and as familiar as searching the web or using a smartphone. Many reporting suites will include home buttons or searches similar to Google to assist in the familiar user experience. A few reporting software providers utilise 'Gamer Influenced Design' principles in designing a user experience consistent with a video game.

- Interactive – with touchscreen computers, tablets and smartphones more commonly being used for business, it is often desirable to use touch in an interactive report. Whether choosing the next report or drilling down to the next level, it is much more intuitive to swipe than it is to click the mouse.

- Customised – a certain group of report users, may want to customise their own reports, and this is facilitated by certain software vendors. They can then create their own user experience, but care must be taken to ensure the underlying data model is robust and does not allow the misrepresentation of data by custom-built reports.

5   **Visualisation to the appropriate delivery channel must be optimised**

Reports can be delivered via many different channels, such as desktops, laptops, tablets, mobile devices or paper. It is clear that a mobile phone is considerably smaller than an A4 sheet of paper and therefore logical that in order to produce a powerful report, the design will need to change.

Many software providers support functionality that automatically renders the report and layout based on the delivery device. This is termed 'author-once/run everywhere'.

Whilst these tools can help, it is important to consider other aspects, such as the user experience.

For example, the smaller the screen, the less you can show on the start page. However, you can provide drill paths and filter options to dig into the next level as required.

You should also consider the urgency of the report requirement. Urgent notifications can be sent to mobiles but in order to fully analyse the detail, it might be acceptable to wait until the user is in front of a computer.

The previous visualisation principles become even more important when thinking of various delivery channels. Technology is just the enabler to appropriately satisfy these.

Case Study: A global industrial manufacturer

Problem statement:

The organisation had grown significantly through mergers and acquisitions. As a result, it had multiple reporting solutions delivering output that satisfied divisional reporting requirements only.

The company had recently formed a group reporting function tasked with providing the CEO and CFO with the insight to drive the whole business. Previously, reports had been pulled together in MS Excel from divisional reporting which led to inconsistencies in data and definitions. These reports were in a traditional row and column tabular format, which required user interpretation.

Approach

To address the issue, a summary set of KPIs was developed that linked divisional performance to satisfy the strategic goals of the organisation. These KPIs were then expanded into more detailed measures that could be reported on by the divisions to explain variances in performance.

A mobile dashboard was created that started with a single screen reporting the six strategic goals of the organisation and then enabled the user to swipe into further information on a detailed measures (swipe left) view or a divisional (swipe right) view.

From each view, drop downs were also created to intuitively navigate between different views. Conditional formatting and interactive graphs were used to draw the viewer to the issue quickly.

Benefits

Providing a consistent view of the group and divisional performance based on common KPIs was a giant leap forward for the company.

The interactive way of viewing performance was seen by all users as a much more intuitive method than sifting through paper reports.

The conditional formatting, along with the graphical techniques, removed the need to analyse the numbers, allowing managers to take action more quickly. By being on mobile devices, managers now had instant access to financial performance at their fingertips.

12 Practice Questions

Objective Test Question 1: Non-controllable costs

Bitluns is a holiday company, that operates more than 100 all-inclusive resorts. The performance of the manager of each resort is evaluated using financial measures.

Many of the resort managers are not very happy, because their profit reports, that they are assessed on, include a share of head office costs and other costs that they cannot control.

Use the words and phrases in the table provided below to complete the following paragraphs:

controllable	costs	unfair
control	performance	profit
uncontrollable	fair	responsibility

Uncontrollable costs may be included in the performance report of a _____ centre so that the report shows the final _____ of that centre. This is sometimes done to make the manager aware of the other _____ involved in running the business.

However, from a performance measurement perspective, if it is the _____ of the manager that is being measured, then it is _____ to measure their performance on results that include items that are beyond their _____

The solution to this is to include the _____ items in a separate section of the report, and to measure the manager's performance based only on the _____ items.

Objective Test Question 2: Controllable RI

The manager of a trading division has complete autonomy regarding the purchase and use of non-current assets. The division operates its own credit control policy in respect of customers but the group operates a central purchasing function through which the division places all orders with suppliers and invoices are paid by head office.

Inventories of goods for sale are kept in central stores, from which local divisions call off requirements for local sales on a monthly basis into a local inventory.

Divisional performance is assessed on the basis of controllable Residual Income. The company requires a rate of return of 'R'.

Using the following symbols:

Divisional non-current assets	N
Apportioned net book value of central stores	S
Divisional working capital	
Receivables	D
Local Inventory	I
Bank	B
Payables	(P)
	___
	W
	___
Divisional net assets	T
	___
Divisional contribution	C
Controllable fixed costs	(F)
Head Office charges	(H)
	___
Divisional net income	G
	___

Which ONE of the following formulae calculates the division's controllable residual income?

(i) $[C - F] - [(N + D + B) \times R]$

(ii) $[C - F] - [(N + D + I + B) \times R]$

(iii) $C - [(N + D) \times R]$

(iv) $G - (T \times R)$

A (i) only

B (ii) only

C (iii) only

D (i) and (iv) only

Objective Test Question 3: EVA

A division has a reported annual profit of $27m. This was after charging $6m for the development and launch costs of a new product which is expected to have a life of 3 years.

The division has a risk adjusted cost of capital of 10% per annum, but it has a large bank loan, which incurs annual interest charges of 8%.

The net book value of the division's net assets is $85m. The replacement cost of the assets is estimated to be $96m.

Ignore the effects of taxation. The Division's EVA is:

$m

Data Set Question: Key metrics and depreciation

Tweedle Ltd has two divisions, Division Dee and Division Dum. Tweedle founded Dee on 1 January 2013. Dum was an independent business that had been formed some years before. Tweedle purchased Dum as a going concern in August 2013. Tweedle's directors are keen to benchmark the two divisions, because they produce similar products.

Details for the two companies for the year ended 31 December 2013 are as follows (in $000):

	Dee	Dum
Revenue	1,650	1,000
Cost of sales:		
Variable production costs	400	400
Fixed production costs (including depreciation, see note 2)	800	390
	1,200	790
GROSS PROFIT	**450**	**210**
Administration costs (fixed)	120	80
OPERATING PROFIT	**330**	**130**
Non-current assets:		
Cost	2,500	2,000
Depreciation	500	1,367
	2,000	633
Net current assets	200	150
Capital employed	2,200	783
Performance measures		
Return on Capital Employed (ROCE)	15.0%	16.6%
Operating profit margin	20.0%	13.0%
Asset turnover	0.8	1.3

Notes

1   Dee and Dum use different depreciation policies. Dee depreciates its non-current assets using straight-line depreciation, at the rate of 20% of cost with no residual value. Dum uses the reducing balance method of depreciation at the rate of 25% per annum.

2   Included in the fixed element of cost of sales for the year ended 31 December 2013 is depreciation of $500,000 for Dee and $200,000 for Dum.

3   Dee's assets are newer.

Tweedle's management team in charge of Dee have argued that it is unfair to compare them with Dum, because the two entities have different depreciation policies and Dum's assets are newer.

The parent company directors have agreed to restate Dee's results so that the assets are assumed to be the same age as Dum's, and the depreciation policy is the same.

After aligning Dee's operating profits and capital employed, as well as its performance measures, restate, for Dee:

Its operating profit, in $.

Its capital employed, in $.

Its (revised) ROCE, in %.

Its (revised) operating profit margin, in %.

Its (revised) asset turnover.

Case Study Style Question: GS

GS Ltd has recently decided to enter into a joint venture with Garvs Ltd, with the newly formed company being named ABG Ltd and manufacturing and selling high-end sports clothes in Nordland.

ABG Ltd has been trading for two full accounting periods. The majority of its assets are non-current and comprise plant and machinery. The machinery was acquired two years ago and has not been replaced yet, although this will be done in the next 12 months. The heavy investment demanded more cash than initially expected and so loans were agreed with the bank on a variable rate.

Sales were initially limited to retail partners in Nordland's capital city, although the retail partner base is increasing gradually to other cities. Prices have remained stable, although they may rise in the future to try and increase profitability. The main materials used to make the clothing are imported from a neighbouring country, Exland, and paid for in Euros.

When ABG Ltd was incorporated two years ago, external consultants were used to help set up the production systems in the first year. Having trained the newly employed staff, the consultants' costs could not be justified and so we did not renew their contract.

You have been called to a meeting with Joe Froome.

"We have had the first two years' trading results in for ABG Ltd and I have made a copy for you to look at. We are encouraged to see that it is making a profit, however the board thought that after two years the results would be looking better. They would like us to draft a brief report that comments on the financial performance and position to date and suggests what the future could hold for ABG Ltd. Here are some ratios that I have calculated for us to consider but, as I am needed in another meeting, I need you to put the analysis together. I think you will find these extracts from the management commentary about ABG Ltd useful.

Remember that there is more market share to gain as we are starting to notice an increase in competition. As you know, when we first entered the market, we were the only manufacturer in Nordland, but now that we have started to find success there, competitors have also started manufacturing there and selling to the Nordland market.

Please could you review these calculations and provide me with a brief analysis for me to take to the board."

ABG Ltd – financial statements from the first two years of trading:

	Year 2	Year 1
Revenue	$130 million	$90 million
Market share	8%	5%
Gross profit margin	32%	35%
Return on capital employed	17.6%	9.8%
Operating profit margin	6.9%	5.9%
Asset turnover	2.55 times	1.66 times
Gearing (Debt/Debt + Equity)	55%	65%

Answers to examples and objective test questions

Example 1: Photocopiers

All statements are true.

Example 2: Controllability

- Total material expenditure for the organisation FALSE.

  The total material expenditure for the organisation will be dependent partly on the prices negotiated by the purchasing manager and partly by the requirements and performance of the production department. If it is included as a target for performance appraisal the manager may be tempted to purchase cheaper material which may have an adverse effect elsewhere in the organisation.

- The cost of introducing safety measures, regarding the standard and the quality of materials, in accordance with revised government legislation TRUE.

  The requirement to introduce safety measures may be imposed but the manager should be able to ensure that implementation meets budget targets.

- A notional rental cost, allocated by head office, for the material storage area. FALSE.

  A notional rental cost is outside the control of the manager and should not be included in a target for performance appraisal purposes.

Example 3: ROI calculation

ROI : $28,000/$142,000 = 19.7%.

Example 4: Disadvantages of ROI

If he/she acts in the best interests of their own division, only the manager of Division B will want to accept the project offered to him/her.

- If managers want to act in the best interests of the business as a whole, only the manager of Division A should accept the project offered to him/her.

(a)

	Division A	Division B
	$000	$000
Old ROI	90/300	10/100
	= 30%	= 10%
New ROI	(90 + 20)/(300 + 100)	(10 + 12)/(100 + 100)
	= 27.5%	= 11%
Will manager want to accept project?	No	Yes

The manager of Division A will not want to accept the project as it lowers her ROI from 30% to 27.5%. The manager of Division B will like the new project as it will increase their ROI from 10% to 11%. Although the 11% is bad, it is better than before.

(b) Looking at the whole situation from the group point of view, we are in the ridiculous position that the group has been offered two projects, both costing $100,000. One project gives a profit of $20,000 and the other $12,000. Left to their own devices then the managers would end up accepting the project giving only $12,000. This is because ROI is a defective decision-making method and does not guarantee that the correct decision will be made.

Workings:

	Division A	Division B
	$000	$000
Old ROCE		
Profit	90	10
Capital employed	300	100
Old ROCE	30%	10%
New ROCE		
Profit	90 + 20	10 + 12
	300 + 100	100 + 100
New ROCE	27.5%	11%
Will manager want to accept project?	No	Yes

The manager of division A will not want to accept the project as it lowers the divisional ROCE from 30% to 27.5%. The manager of division B will like the new project as it will increase their ROCE from 10% to 11%. Although the 11% is bad, it is better than before.

Looking at the whole situation from the group point of view, we are in the ridiculous position that the group has been offered 2 projects, both costing $100,000. One project gives a profit of $20,000 and the other $12,000. Left to their own devices then the managers would end up accepting the project giving only $12,000. This is because ROCE is a defective decision making method and does not guarantee that the correct decision will be made.

There are a number of different ways of making the correct decision. The simplest way is to calculate the ROCE of the project itself.

Example 5: RI calculation

If performance is measured by RI, the RI for the period is:

	$
Profit before interest and tax	160,000
Notional interest (12% × $800,000)	96,000
RI	64,000

(Note: Capital employed is not available in this question and therefore net assets should be used as a substitute value).

Investment centre managers who make investment decisions on the basis of short-term performance will want to undertake any investments that add to RI, i.e. if the RI is positive.

Example 6: RI increase

The answer is B.

Residual income (RI) = Divisional profit – (cost of capital × net assets)

RI **without** the machine = $24,800 – 8% × $212,000 =$ 7,840

RI **with** the machine = $43,800 – 8% × $260,000 =$ 23,000

Difference = $15,160

Example 7: ROI vs RI

(a) **ROI**

	Without the investment	With the investment
Profit	$160,000	$175,000
Capital employed	$800,000	$900,000
ROI	20.0%	19.4%

ROI would be lower; therefore the centre manager will not want to make the investment. since his performance will be judged as having deteriorated. However, this results in dysfunctional behaviour since the company's target is only 12%.

(b) **RI**

		Without the investment		With the investment
Profit		$160,000		$175,000
Notional interest	($800,000 × 12%)	$96,000	($900,000 × 12%)	$108,000
RI		$64,000		$67,000

The investment centre manager will want to undertake the investment because it will increase RI. This is the correct decision for the company since RI increases by $3,000 as a result of the investment.

Example 8: Comparing divisional performance

Problems may include:

- Divisions may operate in different environments. A division earning a ROI of 10% when the industry average is 7% may be considered to be performing better than a division earning a ROI of 12% when the industry average is 15%.

- The transfer pricing policy may distort divisional performance.

- Divisions may have assets of different ages. A division earning a high ROI may do so because assets are old and fully depreciated. This may give a poor indication of future potential performance.

- There may be difficulties comparing divisions with different accounting policies (e.g. depreciation).

- Evaluating performance on the basis of a few indicators may lead to manipulation of data. A wider range of indicators may be preferable which include non-financial measures. It may be difficult to find non-financial indicators which can easily be compared if divisions operate in different environments.

Example 9: Economic Value Added

	$
Accounting profit	170,000
Add back accounting depreciation	50,000
Deduct economic depreciation	(70,000)
Add back increase to doubtful debt provision	25,000
Add back interest	5,000
NOPAT (ignoring tax)	180,000
Replacement cost of assets	700,000
Total bad debt provision	50,000
Economic value of capital employed	750,000
Cost of capital charge at 6%	45,000
NOPAT	180,000
Less capital charge	(45,000)
EVA	**135,000**

Option A uses the bank loan cost of 5% instead of the cost of capital. Option B fails to add back the bad debt provision to the value of assets, and Option D makes the error of using the value of closing capital employed in the capital charge calculation.

Objective Test Question 1: Non-controllable costs

Uncontrollable costs may be included in the performance report of a responsibility centre so that the report shows the final profit of that centre. This is sometimes done to make the manager aware of the other costs involved in running the business.

However, from a performance measurement perspective, if it is the performance of the manager that is being measured, then it is unfair to measure their performance on results that include items that are beyond their control.

The solution to this is to include the uncontrollable items in a separate section of the report, and to measure the manager's performance based only on the controllable items.

Objective Test Question 2: Controllable RI

Answer B (ii) only.

Objective Test Question 3: EVA

Calculation of NOPAT

	$m
Accounting operating profit	27
Add back development and launch costs	6
Less one year's amortisation of development and launch costs	(2)
	31

Calculation of value of capital employed

	$m
Replacement cost of net assets	96
Add back increase in capitalised launch and development costs	4
	100

Calculation of EVA

The correct figure to use for calculating the capital charge is the cost of capital, i.e. the 10%. The 8% is a distracter.

	$m
NOPAT	31
Capital charge (10% × $100m)	10
EVA	21

Data Set Question: Key metrics and depreciation

Its operating profit, in $.	$566,000
Its capital employed, in $.	$991,000
Its revised ROCE, in %.	57.15%
Its revised operating profit margin, in %.	34.32%
Its revised asset turnover.	1.66

Approach:

First, we have to recalculate Dee's operating profit if the depreciation charge contained in the fixed production costs had been calculated using a reducing balance method, which is the method used by Dum.

At the moment, depreciation for Dee is $500,000 using straight line depreciation at 20%. This means $500,000 depreciation charge every year for 5 years, and the assets were originally $2.5 m = the assets in Dee are only 1 year old.

Calculating the age of assets in Dum:

In Dum, accumulated depreciation is $1,367,000. This represents 4 years' worth of depreciation. (W1), and Dum's assets are therefore 4 years old.

We then need to 'pretend' that Dee's assets are also 4 years old in order to align their age with that of Dum's assets. At the moment, depreciation of $500,000 is included in the fixed element of the cost of sales.

What would Dee's depreciation charge for the year be if we used a reducing balance method of depreciation at the rate of 25% per annum?

	Depreciation charge for the year @ 25%	NBV	Accumulated depreciation
Year 1	625	1,875	625
Year 2	469	1,406	1,094
Year 3	352	1,055	1,445
Year 4	**264**	791	1,709

Dee's depreciation charge for the year (if we used a reducing balance method of depreciation at the rate of 25% per annum) would be $264,000. At the moment, the depreciation charge amounts to $500,000. The difference of $236,000 comes to inflate the operating profit for Dee, which becomes $330,000 + $236,000 = $566,000.

The divisional Fixed Assets will also change their value. Instead of an accumulated depreciation charge of $500,000, we now have an accumulated depreciation of $1,709,000. Therefore, the value of fixed assets becomes $791,000 and not $2m as per the question.

This represents a reduction in fixed assets value of $1,209,000, and capital employed becomes $991,000.

Therefore, ROCE = ($566,000/$991,000) = 57.15%

Operating profit margin = ($566,000/$1,650,000) = 34.32%

Asset turnover = ($1,650,000/$991,000) = 1.66

Working 1 (in $000)

	Depreciation charge for the year @ 25%	NBV	Accumulated depreciation
Year 1	500	1,500	500
Year 2	375	1,125	875
Year 3	281	844	1,156
Year 4	211	633	**1,367**

Case Study Style Question: GS

ABG Ltd has been trading for two years and its revenue has increased by 44.4%. This is impressive for a business over its first two years.

Revenue growth may come from increases in sales volume and/or price. The extracts suggest that the sales prices have remained stable and so the increase is down to higher sales volumes being made. The increase in market share supports this too. The increase in revenues would improve further with a higher market share.

The gross profit margin has reduced slightly over the two years despite the operating profit margin increasing slightly. Sales prices have remained stable so the reduction in the gross profit margin is due to an increase in the cost of sales. The raw materials are bought from an overseas supplier and the price will change if there are fluctuations in the exchange rate between $ and Euros. The figures suggest that either the price of material has increased or that the exchange rate has moved against ABG Ltd. As the business grows, there will be economies of scale and ABG Ltd's purchasing director should negotiate discounts for buying in bulk. This will reduce the price per unit and should improve margins.

The fact that the operating profit margin has increased despite the reduction in gross margin is positive. The main reason for this difference seems to be that in year 1 an external consultant was used whereas in year 2 it may be that the staff took over the role they were performing when the consultants' contracts were not renewed. This may have given rise to cost savings and therefore increased the operating profit. Further cost savings and efficiencies in the future should improve this ratio further, especially if improvements can be made to the gross profit margin.

The return on capital employed (ROCE) has improved this year. This will be due in part to the increase in the operating profit from the savings made with external consultants. In addition, as the machinery gets older, its carrying value reduces through depreciation. This in turn, reduces the capital employed and so ROCE will increase. When the new machines are bought the ratio may worsen unless there is a significant improvement in operating profit.

A higher **asset turnover** ratio year-on-year implies that the company is more efficient at using its **assets**; it would be even more interesting to know how our asset turnover ratio compares with our competitors'.

Gearing ratio has reduced this year. This tells us that the level of debt compared to equity has reduced. This could be because the level of equity is increasing with more profits each year and/or some of the debt has been paid back. As the gearing level reduces this makes ABG Ltd look more attractive to future investors. Garvs and GSC will not want to issue more shares as they will lose control of ABG Ltd but there may be a need for more debt to help with the investment of replacement machinery. ABG Ltd will need to make sure that gearing levels do not climb high enough for the banks to raise concerns.

Finance Manager

Alternative measures of performance

Chapter learning objectives

Lead	Component
C1: Managing and controlling the performance of organisational units	Analyse the performance of responsibility centres and prepare reports
	(a) Analyse the performance of cost centres, revenue centres, profit centres, and investment centres
	(b) Reports for decision-making
C2: Discuss various approaches to the performance and control of organisations	(a) Discuss budgets and performance evaluation
	(b) Discuss other approaches to performance evaluation

1   Chapter summary

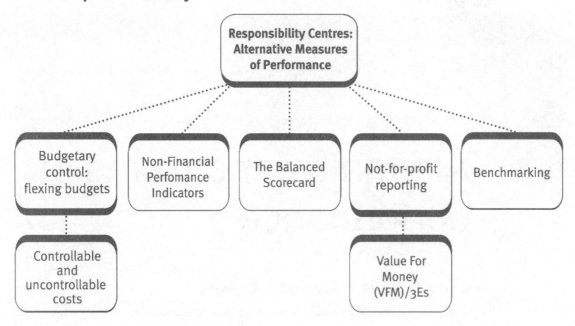

2   Budgetary control: flexing budgets to measure performance

 A fixed budget is a budget produced for a single level of activity. A fixed budget will remain the same no matter the volume of sales or production. A fixed budget is not particularly useful for control; it is predominantly used in the planning stage of budget preparation and is often referred to as the original budget.

 A flexible budget is one which, by recognising cost behaviour patterns, is designed to change as volume of activity changes. A flexible budget should represent what the costs and revenues were expected to be at different activity levels. It is particularly useful for control as the original (fixed) budget can be flexed to show the costs and revenues for the actual level of activity.

The key points to note are:

- A fixed budget is set at the beginning of the period, based on estimated production. This is the original budget. At the same time a flexible budget may be produced at a range of activity levels.

- Actual results are compared with the relevant section of the flexible budget, that which corresponds to the actual level of activity. This is usually referred to as the flexed budget.

Budgetary control and responsibility accounting are linked: it is important to ensure that each manager has a well-defined area of responsibility and the authority to make decisions within that area, and that no parts of the organisation remain as 'grey' areas where it is uncertain who is responsible for them. If this is put into effect properly, each area of the organisation's activities is the responsibility of a manager. This structure should then be reflected in the organisation chart.

Each centre has its own budget, and the manager receives control information relevant to that budget centre. Costs (and revenue, assets and liabilities where applicable) must be traced to the person primarily responsible for taking the related decisions, and identified with the appropriate department.

Example 1: Wye Group

Division A of the Wye Group manufactures one product and when operating at 100% capacity can produce 5,000 units per period, but for the last few periods has been operating below capacity.

Below is the flexible budget prepared at the start of last period, for three levels of activity at below capacity:

Level of activity (units)	3,500	4,000	4,500
	$	$	$
Direct materials	7,000	8,000	9,000
Direct labour	28,000	32,000	36,000
Production overheads	34,000	36,000	38,000
Administration, selling and distribution overheads	15,000	15,000	15,000
Total cost	84,000	91,000	98,000

In the event, the last period turned out to be even worse than expected, with production of only 2,500 units. The following costs were incurred:

	$
Direct materials	4,500
Direct labour	22,000
Production overheads	28,000
Administration, selling and distribution overheads	16,500
Total cost	71,000

Required:

Use the information given above to prepare the following.

(a) A flexed budget for 2,500 units.

(b) A budgetary control statement.

Example 2: Bug Ltd

Bug Ltd manufactures one uniform product. Activity levels in the assembly department are an average level of activity of 20,000 units production per four-week period. The actual results for four weeks in October are:

	Budget 20,000 units	Actual 17,600 units
	$	$
Direct labour	20,000	19,540
Direct expenses	800	1,000
Direct material	4,200	3,660
Depreciation	10,000	10,000
Semi-variable overheads	5,000	4,760
	40,000	38,960

Assume that at a level of production of 15,000 units, semi-variable overheads are forecast to be $4,500.

Produce a budgetary control statement showing the actual costs, flexed costs and variances produced.

Controllable and uncontrollable costs

Controllable costs and revenues are those costs and revenues which result from decisions within the authority of a particular manager or unit within the organisation. These should be used to assess the performance of managers.

Over a long time-span most costs are controllable by someone in the organisation. For example – rent may be fixed for a number of years but there may eventually come an opportunity to move to other premises as such:

- rent is controllable in the long term by a manager fairly high in the organisation structure if the opportunity arises to move premises or negotiate with the land lord

- but in the short term rent is uncontrollable even by senior managers.

There is no clear-cut distinction between controllable and non-controllable costs for a given manager. There may be joint control with another manager. The aim under a responsibility accounting system will be to assign and report on the cost to the person having primary responsibility.

Illustration 1 – Controllable and uncontrollable costs

An example of the two different approaches to controllable and uncontrollable costs is provided by raw materials. The production manager will have control over usage, but not over price, when buying is done by a separate department. For this reason the price and usage variances are separated and, under the first approach, the production manager would be told only about the usage variance, a separate report being made to the purchasing manager about the price variance. The alternative argument is that if the production manager is also told about the price variance, he may attempt to persuade the purchasing manager to try alternative sources of supply.

It is recognised that in-correct allocation of costs to managers could result in a lowering of morale and a reduction of motivation.

To be fully effective, any system of financial control must provide motivation and incentives. If this requirement is not satisfied, managers will approach their responsibilities in a very cautious and conservative manner. It is often found that adverse variances attract investigation therefore failure to distinguish controllable from uncontrollable costs can alienate managers as potentially adverse variances will occur that appear to be under their control but are not.

When adverse variances are reported this implies poor performance by the managers. If they are unable to correct or explain the adverse variances, then they may suffer negative sanctions. They may miss out on a salary increase, or they may be demoted. Positive inducements may be offered to encourage managers to avoid adverse variances. A manager who meets budget may be granted a performance related salary bonus or promotion. If a cost is not controllable by a manager they could be incorrectly penalised or incorrectly rewarded.

It has been seen that an essential element in budgetary control is performance evaluation. Actual results are compared with budget or standard in order to determine whether performance is good or bad. What is being evaluated is not just the business operation but the managers responsible for it. The purpose of budgetary control is to encourage managers to behave in a manner that is to the best advantage of the organisation. Compliance with budget is enforced by a variety of negative and positive sanctions so it is essential that costs allocated to managers are controllable by those managers.

Planning and operational variances

The standard is set as part of the budgeting process which occurs before the period to which it relates.

This means that the difference between standard and actual may arise partly due to an unrealistic budget and not solely due to operational factors. The budget may need to be **revised** to enable actual performance to be compared with a standard that reflects these changed conditions.

Traditional variance

– Compares actual results with the original (flexed) budget.

Planning variance

– Compares the revised (flexed) budget and the original (flexed) budget.

– Often deemed to be uncontrollable. Management should not be held accountable.

Operational variance

– Compares actual results with the revised (flexed) budget.

– Deemed controllable. Management held responsible for operational variances.

Planning and operational variances may be calculated for sales, materials and labour; the operating statement would include a separate line for each variance calculated.

Benefits and problems of planning and operational variances

Benefits of planning and operational variances

- In volatile and changing environments, standard costing and variance analysis are more useful using this approach.

- Operational variances provide up to date information about current levels of efficiency.

- Operational variances are likely to make the standard costing system more acceptable and to have a positive effect on motivation.

- It emphasises the importance of the planning function in the preparation of standards and helps to identify planning deficiencies.

Problems of planning and operational variances

- There is an element of subjectivity in determining the ex-post standards as to what is 'realistic'.

- There is a large amount of labour time involved in continually establishing up to date standards and calculating additional variances.

- There is a great temptation to put as much as possible of the total variances down to outside, uncontrollable factors, i.e. planning variances.

- There can then be a conflict between operating and planning staff, each laying the blame at each other's door.

On the face of it, the calculation of operational and planning variances is an improvement over the traditional analysis. However, you should not overlook the considerable problem of data collection for the revised analysis: where does this information come from, and how can we say with certainty what should have been known at a particular point in time?

3 Shortcomings of financial indicators

The use of traditional financial performance metrics is widespread, but the practice has its problems. For example:

1 They only tell what has happened over a limited period in the immediate past.

2 They give no indication of what is going to happen in the future.

3 They are vulnerable to manipulation and to the choice of accounting policy on matters such as depreciation and inventory valuation.

4 They do not relate to the strategic management of the business and may induce 'short-term ism', at the expense of motivation, quality and efficiency.

4   Non-Financial Performance Indicators

So, if we wish to obtain a fuller evaluation of performance, then we have to turn to a range of non-financial performance indicators (NFPIs).

Non-financial performance indicators are **'measures of performance based on non-financial information that may originate in, and be used by, operating departments to monitor and control their activities without any accounting input.'** (CIMA Official Terminology)

Non-financial performance measures may give a more timely indication of the levels of performance achieved than financial measures do, and may be less susceptible to distortion by factors such as uncontrollable variations in the effect of market forces on operations.

Certain academic writers have developed models of performance evaluation for strategic advantage. The general thrust behind these is that performance indicators should be developed that relate to the long-term strategic development of the organisation. This follows the principle advocated by management guru/writer Tom Peters: **'What gets measured gets done'.**

The performance indicators adopted for a given business or business segment should relate to its key success factors – those things that are most likely to determine its success or failure. NFPIs can be expressed in either quantitative or qualitative terms. For example, it might be reported that we have a 5 per cent market share (a quantitative measure) and we are first supplier of preference to almost all our established customers (a qualitative measure).

Let us consider a number of NFPIs, how they might be expressed and relevant information relating to them might be gathered.

Competitiveness

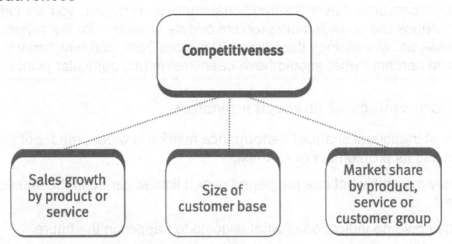

Regular market surveys drawing on both internal and external sources of information can be used to compile reports.

Activity level

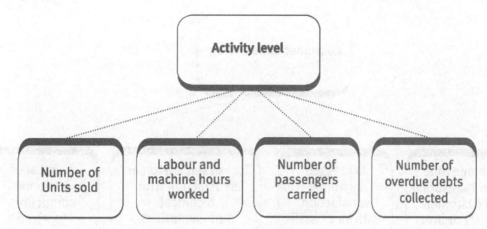

Relevant information could be drawn mainly from internal sources, with appropriate checks to ensure accuracy.

Productivity

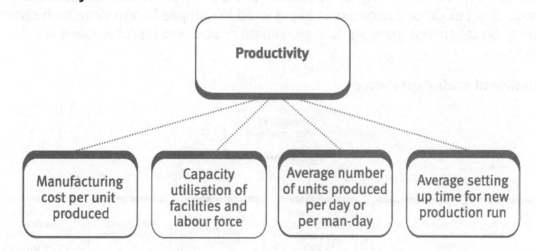

Again, most of this information could be drawn from internal sources.

Quality of service

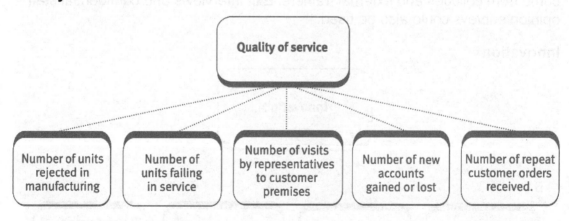

Again, most relevant information would be available from internal sources but this could be reinforced by periodic customer surveys.

Customer satisfaction

Relevant information would have to come mainly from customer surveys although some internal sources could be selectively used. Customer surveys can be carried out on a regular structured basis or on an occasional informal basis. If a sample of customers is being used to compile information, then care has to be taken that the sample is significant in size and representative in structure.

Quality of staff experience

Some information could be taken from internal sources but much would have to come from colleges and external trainers. Exit interviews and confidential staff opinion surveys could also be used.

Innovation

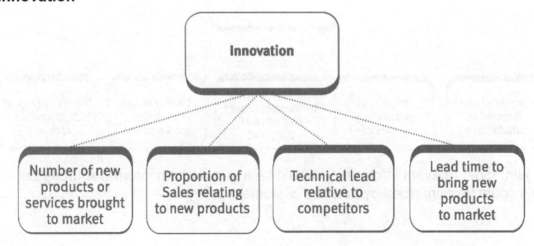

This kind of information would have to be taken from a variety of internal and external sources. The slightly subjective nature of what constitutes a 'new product' is such that this may be an area where an external assessor or consultant might be used to prepare the report.

These sort of performance indicators have the advantage of being 'forward looking'. That is, they are likely to address factors that relate to how well or badly the business will perform in the future.

For example, a service business with a high staff turnover rate is at a disadvantage. If experienced and qualified staff are constantly leaving and being replaced, then this may not contribute to the quality of service being offered to customers. We have all experienced visits to a shop, travel agent or garage where we have been served by an inexperienced and obviously new member of staff – who is unfamiliar with our account history and appears to have limited knowledge of the products that he or she is trying to sell. We find it much more satisfactory to be served by an experienced member of staff who knows his or her customers and products.

Yet, a deterioration in the standard of staff being employed (as evidenced by the indicators listed above under quality of staff experience) would not impact greatly on current period ROCE. A focus on current ROCE might actually induce a business to make greater use of poorly paid, junior staff in order to minimise operating costs. The impact of this on the business might be felt only in the long term.

As with any performance indicator, an NFPI has to be viewed in some context in order to be most meaningful. A good control report will express indicators in terms of a deviation from plan, relative to an industry benchmark or as part of a trend analysis covering comparable earlier periods.

Further, it is best to consider performance indicators as part of a package giving a multi-dimensional impression of how the organisation is performing.

Illustration 2 – BAA

One example of the use of NFPIs frequently reported in management literature is that of BAA plc (formerly the British Airports Authority). This is the case of a service company that attempts to evaluate its own performance in terms of the quality it is able to offer to customers.

It has identified about 12 key success factors which include access, aesthetics, cleanliness, comfort, staff competence, staff courtesy, reliability, responsiveness and security. These take on board the factors that customers appreciate when using an airport – short distances to walk from point of arrival to point of departure, safety from attack or robbery, easy availability of luggage trolleys and wheel chairs and so on.

BAA carries out regular surveys involving interviews with customers, consultant reports, analysis of operational data, and monitoring customer feedback. Appropriate indicators for each factor are reported and studied through comparison between different airports and trend analysis over time. For example, if airport A persistently reports a higher level of theft from customers than other airports – then this might prompt the introduction of additional security measures at airport A. If complaints about staff courtesy at airport D have been on a persistent upward trend over time, then this might prompt enquiries into staff supervision at that site and/or additional staff training.

A customer survey might include a question as follows:

'Your impression of the service available in the cafeterias at Airport B is best described as

A   Most satisfactory

B   Satisfactory

C   Acceptable

D   Less than acceptable

E   Unsatisfactory.

Answering this involves a qualitative judgement on the part of the customer, but the survey results can be reported and evaluated in quantitative terms. For example, if 80% of customers offered A or B answers to this question, then the impression given is that the standard of service at Airport B cafeterias is not a problem– and it may even serve as a model of best practice for other airports.

This line of discussion leads us into more modern models of performance evaluation.

5   Reports in a not-for-profit organisation

Not-for-profit organisations such as local authorities and charities have their own rules and requirements in terms of accounting. Some of the financial measures we have looked at so far (gross margin, contribution, ROCE) will not always be appropriate in a not-for-profit organisation.

There are two main problems involved in assessing performance of these organisations:

- the problem of identifying and measuring objectives
- the problem of identifying and measuring outputs.

Objectives

One of the issues in performance evaluation, in any sector, is defining organisational objectives. Once that is done, performance indicators can be devised that indicate the extent to which such objectives have been achieved.

In not-for-profit organisations the objectives may be much more varied, reflecting the variety of organisations included in the sector:

- charities

- professional institutions

- educational establishments

- government bodies.

Although the detail will vary depending on the organisation involved, we could suggest that the general objective of not-for-profit organisations is to provide the best possible service within a limited resource budget:

- **Charities** will have a limited amount of funds available – they will seek to use these funds to provide services to as many of their beneficiaries as possible. It will be important not to waste money or any other resources.

- A central **government department** (health or education for example) or a local authority typically has a limited amount of finance available. Its objective will be to provide the best possible service to the community with the financial constraints imposed upon it.

The problems of output measurement

Outputs of organisations in these sectors are often not valued in monetary terms. How do we measure the output of a school or hospital?

Output targets can be set in these situations, but they will always be open to debate and argument.

The not-for-profit sector incorporates a diverse range of operations including national government, local government and charities etc. The critical thing about such operations is that they are **not** motivated by a desire to maximise profit.

Many, if not all, of the benefits arising from expenditure by these bodies are non-quantifiable (certainly not in monetary terms, e.g. social welfare). The same can be true of costs. So any cost/benefit analysis is necessarily quite judgemental, i.e. social benefits versus social costs as well as financial benefits versus financial costs. The danger is that if benefits cannot be quantified, then they might be ignored.

Another problem is that these organisations often do not generate revenue but simply have a fixed budget for spending within which they have to keep.

> ### Illustration 3 – Output measures of schools
>
> In many countries, governments set targets for schools in the form of examination pass rates – a form of output for the school. League tables are then published which rank schools based on their pupils' examination results but:
>
> - There are many people who argue that the output of a school cannot be measured by examination results. They argue the output is a wider concept than this such as the concept of value added education. This would look at the improvement in knowledge and ability of pupils over their life at the school. But how do we measure this?
>
> - Comparing schools performance by publishing league tables of examination results is also open to question. It is of course an attempt to carry out comparative analysis of performance allowing one school to be measured against another. However, many people make the point that the tables do not compare like with like. Different schools have children from different social backgrounds for example, which may be reflected in examination results.

The 3Es concept

The 3Es concept is also known as the value for money (VFM) concept. This has been developed as a useful means of assessing performance in an organisation which is not seeking profit.

The value for money in these organisations is measured through the 3Es, as follows:

- **Economy** (an input measure). This measures the relationship between money spent and the inputs. Are the resources used the cheapest possible for the quality required?

- **Efficiency** (link inputs with outputs). This measures whether the maximum output is being achieved from the resources used.

- **Effectiveness** (links outputs with objectives). This measures to what extent the outputs generated achieve the objectives of the organisation.

You should note that VFM still focuses on financial performance. Not-for-profit organisations will also need to consider non-financial performance measurements, particularly quality.

Illustration 4 – Examples of performance measures using the 3Es

Hospitals

(1) **Economy**

Comparing the standard cost of drugs used in treatments with the actual cost of drugs.

(2) **Efficiency**

Comparing the number of beds in use in a ward with the number of beds available in the ward.

(3) **Effectiveness**

Comparing the current waiting time for patients with the desired waiting time for patients.

Colleges or universities

(1) **Economy**

Comparing the standard cost of tutors with the actual cost of the tutors.

(2) **Efficiency**

Comparing actual tutor utilisation in hours with planned tutor utilisation in hours.

(3) **Effectiveness**

Comparing actual exam results (% over a certain grade or percentage passes) with desired exam results.

Example 3: Average class sizes

A government is looking at assessing state schools by reference to a range of both financial and non-financial factors, one of which is average class sizes.

Which of the three E's best describes the above measure?

A   Economy

B   Effectiveness

C   Efficiency

D   Externality

6   Benchmarking

Benchmarking is a technique that is increasingly being adopted as a mechanism for continuous improvement. CIMA's Official Terminology reads as follows:

> The establishment, through data gathering, of targets and comparators, that permit relative levels of performance (and particular areas of underperformance) to be identified. The adoption of identified best practices should improve performance.

It is a continuous process of measuring a firm's products, services and activities against other best-performing organisations, either internal or external to the firm. The idea is to ascertain how the processes and activities can be improved. Ideally, benchmarking should involve an external focus on the latest developments, best practice and model examples that can be incorporated within various operations of business organisations. It therefore represents the ideal way of moving forward and achieving high competitive standards.

In addition to monitoring performance through variance analysis, or as an alternative to variance reporting, organisations might use benchmarking to monitor their performance, and set targets for improved performance.

The basic idea of benchmarking is that performance should be assessed through a comparison of the organisation's own products or services, performance and practices with 'best practice' elsewhere.

The reasons for benchmarking may be summarised as:

- To receive an alarm call about the need for change
- Learning from others in order to improve performance
- Gaining a competitive edge (in the private sector)
- Improving services (in the public sector).

Different types of benchmarking

It is important to remember that in order to use benchmarking, it is necessary to gather information about best practice. This leads on to the problem of how much information is available and where it can be obtained.

Benchmarking can be categorised according to what is being benchmarked and whose performance is being used for comparison (as 'best in class').

- **Internal benchmarking.** With internal benchmarking, other units or departments in the same organisation are used as the benchmark. This might be possible if the organisation is large and divided into a number of similar regional divisions. Internal benchmarking is also widely used within government. In the UK for example, there is a Public Sector Benchmarking Service that maintains a database of performance measures. Public sector organisations, such as fire stations and hospitals, can compare their own performance with the best in the country.

- **Competitive benchmarking.** With competitive benchmarking, the most successful competitors are used as the benchmark. Competitors are unlikely to provide willingly any information for comparison, but it might be possible to observe competitor performance (for example, how quickly a competitor processes customer orders). A competitor's product might be dismantled in order to learn about its internal design and its performance: this technique of benchmarking is called reverse engineering.

- **Functional benchmarking.** In functional benchmarking, comparisons are made with a similar function (for example selling, order handling, despatch) in other organisations that are not direct competitors. For example, a fast food restaurant operator might compare its buying function with buying in a supermarket chain.

- **Strategic benchmarking.** Strategic benchmarking is a form of competitive benchmarking aimed at reaching decisions for strategic action and organisational change. Companies in the same industry might agree to join a collaborative benchmarking process, managed by an independent third party such as a trade organisation. With this type of benchmarking, each company in the scheme submits data about their performance to the scheme organiser. The organiser calculates average performance figures for the industry as a whole from the data supplied. Each participant in the scheme is then supplied with the industry average data, which it can use to assess its own performance.

7 Kaplan and Norton – The balanced scorecard

The joke

You're at the airport and there's a little while to your flight. You have a drink to pass the time and a person in uniform comes and sits next to you at the bar and after a while you get chatting and you find out that she is the pilot of the aeroplane that you are about to catch. You say that it must be very difficult flying an aeroplane with all those dials and knobs and switches and meters and things, and she says, 'No, not really. All I look at is the speedometer and I figure that if I get my speed right then things are fine.' You look at her a bit funny and you say, 'Well, what about the fuel gauge? Isn't that important?' She says, 'Yes, you're right, it is important and I used to look at it, but now I just look at the speedometer'. Then you say, 'Well what about the altimeter? Surely that's important?' She replies, 'Well, yes it is, but I try and focus on one thing at a time. Once I'm happy with my airspeed then in a few flights' time I might concentrate on altitude'

The question Kaplan and Norton now ask is would you catch that aeroplane?

The point that Kaplan and Norton are trying to make (in the unlikely event that you missed it) is that you cannot fly an aeroplane with only one instrument. Nor can you run a business by looking at one performance measure. Kaplan and Norton's Balanced Scorecard focuses on four different perspectives.

The balanced scorecard

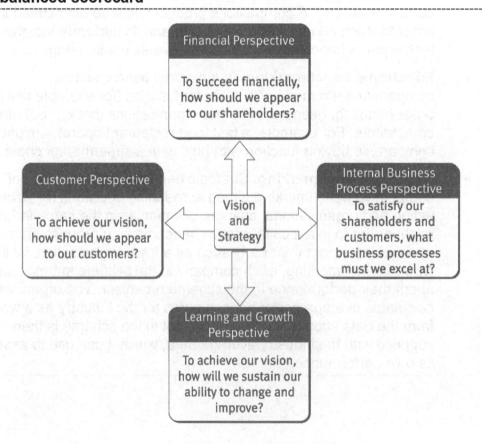

Robert Kaplan and David Norton published the original article (The Balanced Scorecard – Measures That Drive Performance) in the Harvard Business Review in January/February 1992. It has become one of the most requested HBR reprints.

The traditional performance measure for a business is of course financial, but one problem is that the financial measures relate to the past. Another is that the financial accounting model does not adequately consider the value to a company of its intangible assets such as a happy and loyal customer base, well-motivated, well trained and efficient staff and good quality products or services. The Balanced Scorecard incorporates non-financial measures of the drivers of future performance as well as financial measures of past performance.

In their 1996 book Kaplan and Norton state that 'Several critics have advocated scrapping financial measures entirely to measure business unit performance. They argue that in today's technologically and customer-driven global competition, financial measures provide poor guidelines for success. They urge managers to focus on improving customer satisfaction, quality, cycle times, and employee skills and motivation. According to this theory, as companies make fundamental improvements in their operations, the financial numbers will take care of themselves.' Kaplan and Norton reply that the use of financial measures still serves a purpose as it is not enough to improve quality and customer satisfaction and generate new products, etc., in the end these improvements have to be converted to financial advantage.

Kaplan and Norton also ask in their 1996 book are 4 perspectives sufficient? They answer their own question by saying that there is no rule that says that every organisation in the world should use exactly the 4 perspectives, and nothing else, but that in general across a variety of companies and industries the 4 perspectives do seem to work. They say that some companies do incorporate extra perspectives such as an environmental perspective, but they have yet to see a company use less than 4.

It can be seen from the diagram above that a vital part of the Balanced Scorecard is the company strategy and the starting point for the creation of a Balanced Scorecard is a company's mission statement or vision.

Measures for the balanced scorecard

The following lists give examples of possible measures:

Financial perspective

Goals would be set in terms of 3 main areas and the measures would relate to those areas.

- Survival   Cash flow, gearing

- Success   Monthly or quarterly sales growth and operating income

- Prosperity   Increase in market share and ROI.

Customer perspective

- Customer profitability
- Customer retention
- Customer satisfaction
- Customer acquisition
- Market share
- Percentage of sales from new products
- Percentage of on-time deliveries
- Preferred supplier status
- Lead time from receipt of order to delivery
- No of customer complaints.

Internal business process perspective

- Percentage of sales from new products
- Percentage of sales from proprietary products
- New product introduction versus competitors also new product introduction versus plan
- Manufacturing process capabilities
- Time to develop next generation of products
- Cycle time
- Unit cost
- Efficiency.

Learning and growth perspective

- Employee satisfaction
- Employee retention
- Employee productivity
- Time to market
- Percentage of products giving 80% of sales.

In practice: The Balanced Scorecard (CGMA cost management Model)

Implementation of the Balanced Scorecard and an alternative costing system at the Royal Botanic Garden Edinburgh (CIMA case study, 2010)

The Royal Botanic Garden Edinburgh (RBGE) first adopted the Balanced Scorecard (BSC) in 2004. The Senior Management Group (SMG),which was responsible for strategy development, used the BSC to answer the 'who, what, why, where, when' questions prompted by the four perspectives as they related to the services that the RBGE provides to external stakeholders.

The original BSC created by the RBGE was employed as the basis of strategy and performance reviews. However, the prospect of a strategic review by an international peer group, along with an imperative to demonstrate alignment to the Scottish Government's National Outcomes, prompted a deeper look at the organisation's strategic objectives and underlying perspectives. The ensuing revisions included improved alignment between the RBGE's 'impact' perspective and its 'activity' perspective. This review also led to the development of an objective costing system linked to an existing performance management system that improved monitoring of performance against strategic objectives.

Lessons learned

- The Balanced Scorecard can be adapted to suit an individual organisation.

- The effort and commitment required from senior management to transform strategic management processes should not be underestimated.

- Resistance to change may result as individuals become more accountable for their actions.

- Management accountants are well-placed in the organisation to become very involved in the development of the Balanced Scorecard and implementation process, thereby becoming an important strategic partner in the business.

Performance evaluation in the not-for-profit sector

An NFP organisation exists to achieve certain objectives and an evaluation of its performance in achieving those objectives must have regard to a combination of efficiency and effectiveness factors. The organisation should achieve the maximum output from the resources at its disposal (efficiency) and at the same time it should organise those resources in a manner that achieves a given result by the cheapest route (effectiveness).

Many of the performance indicators considered above can be applied to NFPs. For example, in evaluating the performance of a local authority one might consider:

1   Cost per km of road maintained

2   Cost per child in school

3   Cost per square metre of grass verge mown

4   Cost per tonne of sewage disposed of.

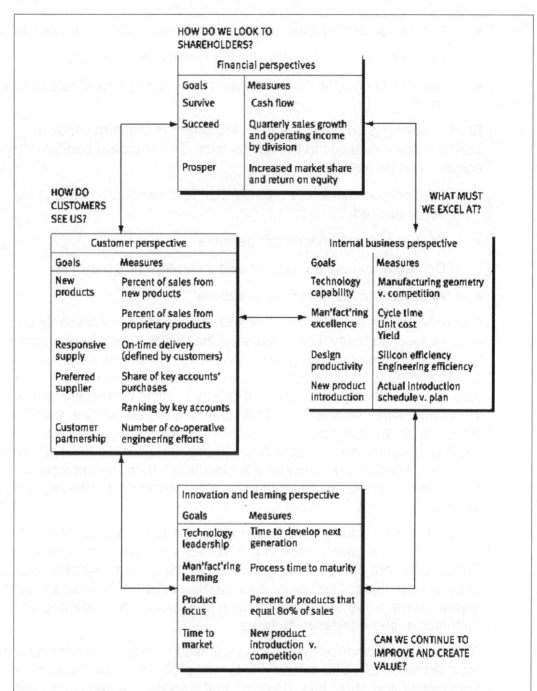

HOW DO WE LOOK TO SHAREHOLDERS?

Financial perspectives

Goals	Measures
Survive	Cash flow
Succeed	Quarterly sales growth and operating income by division
Prosper	Increased market share and return on equity

HOW DO CUSTOMERS SEE US?

Customer perspective

Goals	Measures
New products	Percent of sales from new products
	Percent of sales from proprietary products
Responsive supply	On-time delivery (defined by customers)
Preferred supplier	Share of key accounts' purchases
	Ranking by key accounts
Customer partnership	Number of co-operative engineering efforts

WHAT MUST WE EXCEL AT?

Internal business perspective

Goals	Measures
Technology capability	Manufacturing geometry v. competition
Man'fact'ring excellence	Cycle time Unit cost Yield
Design productivity	Silicon efficiency Engineering efficiency
New product introduction	Actual introduction schedule v. plan

Innovation and learning perspective

Goals	Measures
Technology leadership	Time to develop next generation
Man'fact'ring learning	Process time to maturity
Product focus	Percent of products that equal 80% of sales
Time to market	New product introduction v. competition

CAN WE CONTINUE TO IMPROVE AND CREATE VALUE?

These are all quantitative measures and care should be taken in their interpretation. For example, town A's sewage disposal cost might be half that of town B. Does that mean that A is more efficient than B? Not necessarily, because A might be pumping raw sewage direct into the sea whereas B treats sewage and transports it for disposal. If A is a resort town then its 'efficiency' in disposing of sewage might have a variety of adverse knock-on effects. In considering performance one has to consider qualitative factors. A variety of qualitative indicators might also be considered in tandem with the quantitative ones listed above:

- Number of claims made by motorists arising from pot holed roads

- Number of local children obtaining 2 A level GCEs or equivalent

- Rating of local road system by the Automobile Association

- Number of complaints from visitors concerning smell/taste of sea water.

Benchmarking is probably the most important recent innovation in performance evaluation in the NFP sector. The standard benchmarking practice can be used to:

- Study processes in the organisation and select which are to be benchmarked

- Secure suitable benchmark partners

- Compare appropriate figures and indicators with partners

- Adopt and implement 'best practices'.

A benchmark partner for one local authority need not necessarily be another local authority. For example, if the activity being benchmarked is 'office costs', then one could bench-mark against an insurance company or a mail order company. However, while such benchmark partners might give a local authority an idea about its efficiency in certain areas, they would offer little guidance on effectiveness. If the authority is seeking guidance on the appropriate combination of spend on police, social services, housing and so on in order to provide a certain level of welfare for elderly residents (a quest for effectiveness), then the appropriate benchmark partners would have to be other authorities providing a similar service.

In the United Kingdom, benchmarking and its associated concept of 'best practice' are now widely used in public sector performance evaluation. The Department of the Environment rates all local authorities on the basis of periodic reviews. The use of appropriate performance indicators are a central element in these reviews. Such indicators have regard to both quantitative and qualitative factors.

As with all performance evaluation exercises, it must be appreciated that the calculation of a particular indicator will probably mean little unless it is set in some sort of context. Calculating the value of a particular indicator means little, until it is **compared with** a budget, set in a trend or set against a best practice benchmark.

One final comment in this area should be made. You are reminded of the **Peter** principle – *'What gets measured gets done'*.

If a performance evaluation is based on an incorrect or incomplete range of metrics, then the system can induce the wrong things to get done. For example, in the late 1990s the performance of hospitals was judged on the length of their waiting lists. Specifically, the average time taken for a referred patient to have a first consultation was adopted as a key performance indicator. It is claimed that this induced hospitals to concentrate on patients with minor illnesses since they could be treated quickly and cleared off the list. The small number of patients requiring major treatments often had to wait longer than was the case before the performance indicator was adopted.

Hospital waiting lists were reduced, but not in a wholly neutral manner. Some people gained and some lost as a result of the system. That was never the intention.

8   Practice Questions

Objective Test Question 1: Balanced scorecard

Suggest performance indicators to include in the Balanced Scorecard of a credit card company.

Financial indicators of performance:	'Customers' indicators of performance:
Learning and growth indicators of performance:	**Internal processes indicators of performance:**

Data Set question: Faster Pasta

Faster Pasta is an Italian fast food restaurant that specialises in high quality, moderately priced authentic Italian pasta dishes and pizzas. The restaurant has recently decided to implement a balanced scorecard approach and has established the following relevant goals for each perspective:

Perspective	Goal
Customer perspective	• To increase the number of new and returning customers
	• To reduce the % of customer complaints
Internal	• To reduce the time taken between taking a customer's order and delivering the meal to the customer
	• To reduce staff turnover
Innovation and learning	• To increase the proportion of revenue from new dishes
	• To increase the % of staff time spent on training
Financial	• To increase spend per customer
	• To increase gross profit margin

The following information is also available for the year just ended and for the previous year.

	20X8	20X9
Total customers	11,600	12,000
– of which are new customers	4,400	4,750
– of which are existing customers	7,200	7,250
Customer complaints	464	840
Time between taking order and customer receiving meal	4 mins	13 mins
% staff turnover	12%	40%
% time staff spend training	5%	2%
Revenue	$110,000	$132,000
– revenue from new dishes	$22,000	$39,600
– revenue from existing dishes	$88,000	$92,400
Gross profit	$22,000	$30,360

Task: Answer 'TRUE' or 'FALSE' to the following assertions that Faster Pasta has achieved its goals of:

Increasing the number of new and returning customers

Decreasing the % customer complaints

Reducing the time taken between taking the customer's order and delivering the meal to the customer

Reducing staff turnover

Increasing the proportion of revenue from new dishes

Increasing the % of staff time spent on training

Increasing the spend per customer

Increasing gross profit margin

Case Study Style question – Benchmarking

PRE-SEEN MATERIAL

You work as Financial Controller for E5E. E5E is a charity concerned with heart disease. Its mission statement is as follows:

'To fund world class research into the biology and the causes of heart disease; To develop effective treatments and improve the quality of life for patients; To reduce the number of people suffering from heart disease; To provide authoritative information on heart disease.'

E5E obtains funding from voluntary donations from both private individuals and companies, together with government grants. Much of the work it does, in all departments, could not be achieved without the large number of voluntary workers who give their time to the organisation and who make up approximately 80% of the workforce.

E5E does not employ any scientific researchers directly, but funds research by making grants to individual medical experts employed within universities and hospitals. In addition to providing policy advice to government departments, the charity's advisors give health educational talks to employers and other groups.

You have just received the following email from the Board's spokesperson:

> **From:** Pablo Perez, Managing Director
> **To:** A.N. Accountant
> **Date:** 02.07.2014
> **Subject:** Benchmarking
>
> The Board recognises the need to become more professional in the management of the organisation. It feels that this can be best achieved by conducting a benchmarking exercise. However, it recognises that the introduction of this process may make some members of the organisation, particularly the volunteers, unhappy.
>
> Could you prepare a report for us, that discusses the advantages and disadvantages of benchmarking for E5E? We would also welcome advice on the stages in conducting a benchmarking exercise in the context of E5E , and on how those implementing the exercise should deal with the concerns of the staff, particularly the volunteers.
>
> Thank you

Answers to examples and objective test questions

Example 1: Wye Group

Solution:

(a) Flexed budget for 2,500 units

	$
Direct materials (W1) (2,500 × $2)	5,000
Direct labour (W2) (2,500 × $8)	20,000
Production overheads (W3)	30,000
Administration, selling and distribution overheads (W4)	15,000
Total cost	70,000

Workings:

(W1) Material is a variable cost – $2 per unit

$$\text{Variable material cost} = \frac{\$7,000}{\$3,500} = \$2 \text{ per unit}$$

(W2) Labour is a variable cost – $8 per unit.

$$\text{Variable Labour cost} = \frac{\$28,000}{\$3,500} = \$8 \text{ per unit}$$

(W3) Production overheads are semi-variable. Using the high/low method, the variable cost is $4 per unit, the fixed cost is $20,000. The cost for 2,500 units therefore = $20,000 + (2,500 × $4) = $30,000.

$$\text{Variable cost per unit} = \frac{\$(38,000 - 34,000)}{\$4,500 - 3,500} = \$4 \text{ per unit}$$

Total fixed cost by substituting at high activity level:

Total cost = $38,000

Total variable cost = 4,500 × $4 = $18,000

Fixed cost = $38,000 – $18,000 = $20,000

(W4) Other overheads are fixed.

(b)   Budgetary control statement

	Flexed budget 2,500 units	Actual 2,500 units	Variance
	$	$	$
Direct materials	5,000	4,500	500 (F)
Direct labour	20,000	22,000	2,000 (A)
Production overheads	30,000	28,000	2,000 (F)
Administration, selling and distribution overheads	15,000	16,500	1,500 (A)
Total cost	70,000	71,000	1,000 (A)

Example 2: Bug Ltd

1   Identify the cost behaviours and calculate the cost per unit based on budget

	Behaviour	Cost per unit
Direct labour	variable	20,000/20,000 = $1
Direct expenses	variable	800/20,000 = $0.04
Direct material	variable	4,200/20,000 = $0.21
Depreciation	fixed	n/a
Semi-variable overheads	semi variable	see working

Working for semi-variable overhead (high low method)

Variable cost = change in cost/change in activity

= ($5,000 – $4,500)/(20,000 – 15,000)

= $0.10

Fixed cost = total cost – total variable cost

= $5,000 – ($0.10 × 20,000)

= $3,000

2 **Produce the budget control statement**

	Actual 17,600 units $	Flexed 17,600 units $	Variance
Direct labour	19,540	17,600	1,940 A
Direct expenses	1,000	704	296 A
Direct material	3,660	3,696	36 F
Depreciation	10,000	10,000	–
Semi-variable overheads (W)	4,760	4,760	–
	38,960	36,760	2,200 A

Working for semi-variable overheads

Variable element 17,600 × $0.10 = $1,760

Fixed element $3,000

Total cost = $1,760 + $3,000 = $4,760

Example 3: Average class sizes

C

Class sizes are the result of the number of pupils educated (output), the number of teachers employed (input) and how well the timetable is organised in using those teachers. Therefore this is a measure of efficiency.

Objective Test Question 1: Balanced scorecard

Financial indicators of performance:	**'Customers' indicators of performance:**
Increase market share year-on-year	Wean businesses off cheque books
Increase cardholder's spending	Get banks to switch cards
Increase % fee	Focus on big spenders
Reduce debt	Issue more cards
	Maintain image
	Add reward programmes
Learning and growth indicators of performance:	**Internal processes indicators of performance:**
Outsource IT jobs	Increased marketing spend
Acquire other companies	Offer more products
Improve staff training levels	Achieve economies of scale

Data Set Question: Faster Pasta

Increasing the number of new & returning customers [TRUE]

Measure: The number of new customers has increased year on year from 4,400 to 4,750. This is an 8.0% increase. The number of returning customers has also increased slightly from 7,200 to 7,250, i.e. a 1.0% increase.

Comment: The company has achieved its goal of increasing the number of new and existing customers. It is worth noting that the proportion of customers who are returning customers has fallen slightly from 62.1 % to 60.4% of the total customers. This could indicate a small drop in the level of customer satisfaction.

Decreasing the % customer complaints [FALSE]

Measure: The percentage of customer complaints has increased from 4% (464 ÷ 11,600) to 7% (840 ÷ 12,000).

Comment: Faster Pasta should investigate the reasons for the increase in customer complaints and take the required action immediately in order to ensure that it can meet this goal in the future.

Reducing the time taken between taking the customer's order and delivering the meal to the customer [FALSE]

Measure: The time taken has more than tripled from an average of 4 minutes in 20X8 to an average of 13 minutes in 20X9.

Comment: Customers may place a high value on the fast delivery of their food. The increase in time may be linked to the increased number of customer complaints. If this continues customer satisfaction, and therefore profitability, will suffer in the long-term. The restaurant should take steps now in order to ensure that this goal is achieved going forward.

Reducing staff turnover [FALSE]

Measure: This has risen significantly from 12% to 40% and hence the business has not achieved its goal.

Comment: The reasons for the high staff turnover should be investigated immediately. This may be contributing to longer waiting times and the increase in customer complaints. This will impact long-term profitability.

Increasing the proportion of revenue from new dishes [TRUE]

Measure: This has increased year on year from 20% ($22,000 ÷ $110,000) in 20X8 to 30% ($39,600 ÷ $132,000) in 20X9. Therefore, the restaurant has achieved its goal.

Comment: This is a favourable increase and may have a positive impact on long-term profitability if the new products meet the needs of the customers.

Increasing the % of staff time spent on training | FALSE |

Measure: This has fallen significantly from 5% to only 2% and hence the company is not achieving its goal.

Comment: Staff may be unsatisfied if they feel that their training needs are not being met. This may contribute to a high staff turnover. In addition, staff may not have the skills to do the job well and this would impact the level of customer satisfaction.

Increasing the spend per customer | TRUE |

Measure: Spend per customer has increased from $9.48 ($110,000 ÷ 11,600) to $11.00 ($132,000 ÷ 12,000), i.e. a 16.0% increase.

Comment: This is a favourable increase. However, the issues discussed above must be addressed in order to ensure that this trend continues.

Increasing gross profit margin | TRUE |

Measure: The gross profit margin has increased year on year from 20% ($22,000 ÷ $110,000) to 23% ($30,360 ÷ $132,000).

Comment: This is a favourable increase. However, the issues discussed above must be addressed in order to ensure that this trend continues.

Case Study Style question – Benchmarking

REPORT

From: A.N.A.

To: Pablo Perez, The Board

Date: 02.07.2014

Subject: Benchmarking

It is undeniable that in practice, differences between charities and their aims make benchmarking principles difficult to apply.

However, advantages of benchmarking for a charity like ours may be listed as follows:

- A better understanding of the charity's position
- Highlights particular areas that need changing
- Can identify problem areas in advance
- Can be integrated into target-setting, performance appraisal and bonuses
- Could highlight areas where other charities are much more effective so perhaps E5E should stop those activities

- Can be used to overcome complacency

- Should be particularly useful in improving economy and, to some extent, efficiency – all charities have financial constraints and benchmarking would highlight areas for improvement

- Enables better information to be provided to stakeholders – particularly useful in supporting applications for government funds.

However, some **disadvantages** are also present:

- Time consuming and expensive to implement

- Finding suitable comparisons can be difficult

- Not so useful in improving effectiveness as the stated objectives are very difficult to measure:

    - 'To fund world class research into the biology and the causes of heart disease.' What is 'world-class'?

    - 'To develop effective treatments and improve the quality of life for patients.' How do you measure 'quality of life'?

    - 'To reduce the number of people suffering from heart disease.' Cause and effect can be difficult to match – can reductions in mortality rates be traced directly to E5E's work?

    - 'To provide authoritative information on heart disease.' How to measure what is 'authoritative'?

- Not a competitive industry – does it matter if another charity is more effective in certain areas?

- Danger of information overload

- Problems gathering information when so many staff are volunteers – there may be a need for extra training here as well

- Can be de-motivating if the organisation fails to meet benchmarks.

In summary benchmarking may help the charity become more economic and efficient but will not aid effectiveness.

Stages in conducting a benchmarking exercise

There is no universally agreed set of steps to follow when conducting a benchmarking exercise – the following is just one suggested answer.

E5E could use the following steps to conduct a benchmarking exercise:

1 **Planning**

- Decide what you wish to benchmark – for example, fund raising, % of funds passed on to recipients, % of funds raised from government, % of staff who are volunteers, funds raised per person, etc.

- Decide against whom you want to benchmark – this could include internal benchmarks (difficult), competitive benchmarks (e.g. other health research charities such as cancer research), activity benchmarks (e.g. universities to assess the educational aspects of E5E) and generic benchmarks (e.g. other communications organisations such as newspapers).

- Identify outputs required – e.g. a breakdown of funds collected, feedback on talks given.

- Determine data collection methodologies – e.g. should volunteers record information, should standard forms be prepared for talks, etc.

2 **Data collection**

- Secondary/background research – getting comparators.

- Primary research – from the benchmark.

3 **Analysis**

- Of the gaps – are they significant?

- Of the factors that create the gaps (enablers) – E5E would need to discuss findings with the relevant staff to understand why there are differences. For example, the benchmarking charity may have been much larger than E5E.

4 **Implementation of improvement programmes**

- Implementation planning – for example, visiting best in class and observing their methods.

- Roll-out of new modus operandi (changes) – for example, setting up new training programmes for volunteer staff, designing new advertising, training speakers, etc.

5 **Monitoring results**

- The process should be continuous.

Dealing with the concerns of staff

In each of the above stages the concerns of voluntary staff should be taken into account:

- E5E should have meetings to explain to staff why benchmarking is being introduced, its benefits and potential problems.

- Staff should be reassured of senior management commitment to the process.

- They should be consulted when deciding what to benchmark and what measures to use.

- They should be asked to help design new forms if they will be using them.

- They should be asked if they have any experience of benchmarking – just because they are volunteers does not mean that they have not had jobs where such experience may be gained.

- Emphasis should be on improvements of the processes rather than criticising staff.

I trust the above helps.

With regards

AN.

Transfer pricing

Chapter learning objectives

Lead	Component
C3: Managing and controlling the performance of organisational units	Explain the behavioural and transfer pricing issues related to the management of responsibility centres
	(a) Explain behavioural issues
	(b) Use and ethics of transfer pricing

1 Chapter summary

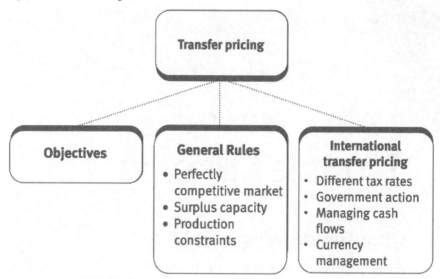

2 Performance management: behavioural consequences

When an organisation is structured into profit centres or investment centres, authority is delegated to the profit centre or investment centre managers. These managers are given the authority to take decisions at a local level, without having to wait for instructions from head office.

Control is applied from head office through performance measurement: centre managers are held accountable for the profits or returns that they make.

The purposes of decentralisation should be to:

1   give autonomy to local centre managers in decision-making

2   motivate centre managers to improve performance: with profit centres and investment centres, this includes motivating them to increase profitability

3   through performance enhancement at a profit centre level, to achieve better results for the organisation as a whole.

Decentralisation can create tension between local centre managers and head office management.

The performance of the managers of profit centres and investment centres will be assessed, and the managers themselves will be rewarded, on the basis of the results of their particular centre. Profit centre managers will therefore be motivated to optimise the results of their own division, regardless of other profit centres and regardless of the organisation as a whole.

When head office management believe that a profit centre manager is taking decisions that improve the profit centre performance, but are damaging for the interests of the organisation as a whole, they might want to step in and either:

1   alter the decisions that have been made at profit centre level, or

2   make new decisions for the profit centre.

However, if head office interferes in decision-making at profit centre level, local autonomy in decision making is lost.

3 Transfer pricing

In an organisation with profit centres and investment centres, there will almost certainly be some inter-connection between different centres. Some profit centres will supply goods and services to others.

When *inter-divisional* (inter-company) trading takes place between profit centres, the centre providing the goods or services to the other will want to earn income from the transfer. Unless it receives income from the transfer, it will make a loss on the transaction.

For example, if Division A provides items to Division B that cost $10 each to make, Division A must earn at least $10 from the transfer, otherwise it will make a loss. If decision making is delegated to profit centre management, the manager of Division A would refuse to supply Division B unless it is allowed to earn income of at least $10 for each unit.

Inter-divisional transfers must therefore be priced. The price of the transfer is the **transfer price**.

- The transfer is treated as an internal sale and an internal purchase within the organisation. It provides sales income to the supplying division and is a purchase cost for the receiving division.

- The sales income of one division is offset by the purchase cost of the other division. The transfer therefore affects the profits of the two divisions individually, but has no effect on the profit of the organisation as a whole.

Setting a transfer price: Inter-divisional trading policy

The transfer price for inter-divisional transactions is significant because:

- it determines how the total profit is shared between the two divisions, and

- in some circumstances, it could affect decisions by the divisional managers about whether they are willing to sell to or buy from the other division.

Both divisions must benefit from the transaction if inter-divisional sales are to take place.

- A selling division will not agree to sell items to another division unless it is profitable for the selling division to do so.

- Similarly, a buying division will not wish to purchase items from another division unless it is profitable for the division.

Transfer prices have to be established and agreed. They could be decided either centrally or locally.

- They could be imposed by head office.

- Alternatively, they could be decided by commercial negotiation between the profit centre managers.

- If decentralisation is to allow the power of decision making to profit centre managers, they should have the authority to agree transfer prices by discussion or negotiation between themselves.

Inter-divisional trading should take place within a broad company policy, that:

- for a 'selling division', given the choice between making a sale to an external customer or supplying goods or services to another division within the group, **the preference should be to sell internally**

- for a 'buying division', given the choice between purchasing from an external supplier or from another division within the company, the **preference should be to purchase internally**.

However, a division should be allowed to sell externally rather than transfer internally, or buy externally rather than internally, if it has a good commercial reason. Good commercial reasons would include an external customer offering a higher price, or an external supplier offering a lower price.

Example 1: Inter-divisional trading

A company has two profit centres, Centre A and Centre B. Centre A supplies Centre B with a part-finished product. Centre B completes the production and sells the finished units in the market at $35 per unit.

Budgeted data for the year:

	Division A	Division B
Number of units transferred/sold	10,000	10,000
Materials costs	$8 per unit	$2 per unit
Other variable costs	$2 per unit	$3 per unit
Annual fixed costs	$60,000	$30,000

Required:

Calculate the budgeted annual profit of each profit centre and the organisation as a whole if the transfer price for components supplied by Division A to Division B is:

(a) $20

(b) $25

4 Objectives of transfer pricing

1 Goal congruence

Within a divisionalised company, divisional managers will have responsibility for and will be judged on their division's performance. They will act independently, autonomously and selfishly in the best interests of their own division. They neither know nor care what is happening in other divisions.

It is the task of the management accounting system in general and the transfer pricing policy in particular to ensure that what is good for an individual division is good for the company as a whole.

2 Performance measurement

The transfer pricing system should result in a report of divisional profits that is a reasonable measure of the managerial performance.

3 Maintaining divisional autonomy

One of the purposes of decentralisation is to allow managers to exercise greater autonomy. There is little point in granting additional autonomy and then imposing transfer prices that will affect the profitability of the division.

4 Minimising the global tax liability

When a divisionalised company operates entirely within one tax regime the transfer pricing policy will have a minimal impact on the corporate tax bill. However multinational companies can and do use their transfer pricing policies to move profits around the world and thereby minimise their global tax liabilities.

5 Recording the movement of goods and services

In practice, an extremely important function of the transfer pricing system is simply to assist in recording the movement of goods and services.

6 A fair allocation of profits between divisions

Most of the advantages claimed for divisionalisation are behavioural. Insofar as transfer pricing has a material effect on divisional profit it is essential that managers perceive the allocation of corporate profit as being fair if the motivational benefits are to be retained.

Needless to say, a number of these objectives can conflict with each other, and prove difficult to achieve in practice. It is highly unlikely that any one method would meet all the firm's requirements in all circumstances the best that can be hoped for is a reasonable compromise.

Bases for setting a transfer price

In broad terms, there are three bases for setting a transfer price:

1   market-based prices

2   cost-based prices

3   negotiated prices.

A market-based transfer price might be agreed when there is an intermediate market for the transferred item. An intermediate market is a term to describe an external market for the goods or services of the selling division. The selling division can therefore make its profits either by transferring the goods or services internally, or selling them in the external market.

A **market-based** transfer price could be:

- the price for the item in the external market ('intermediate market'), or at a discount to the external market price, to allow for a share of the savings in selling costs that the selling division enjoys by transferring internally rather than selling externally. For example, packaging, distribution and warranty costs may be saved by transferring internally.

A **cost-based** transfer price could be:

- the marginal cost to the selling division of making the product or providing the service

- the selling division's marginal cost plus a mark-up for profit

- the full cost to the selling division of making the product, or

- the selling division's full cost plus a mark-up for profit.

When a transfer price is based on cost, it could be actual cost or budgeted cost. The most suitable basis would be budgeted cost (or standard cost).

- Standard costs or budgeted costs are known in advance; therefore transfers can be priced as they occur. The selling division can invoice the buying division immediately for all items transferred.

- Actual costs are not known until after the end of the accounting period. There would consequently be a delay in pricing transfers and issuing invoices.

- If transfers are at standard or budgeted cost, the selling division's manager could be motivated to improve profits by keeping actual costs below the standard or budgeted amount.

The intermediate market

The intermediate market for the products or services of a selling division could be:

- perfect
- imperfect, or
- non-existent.

A perfect intermediate market

If the intermediate market is perfect, all suppliers to the market are able to sell all their output at the prevailing market price. There are no restrictions on sales demand at that price, and no individual supplier dominates market supply.

When a selling division has a perfect external market for its output, it is therefore able to:

- sell all its output on the external market at the market price, and
- provided that it can sell at a price above its marginal cost, the only limitation on profitability from external sales is the output capacity of the division.

An imperfect intermediate market

An intermediate market is imperfect when the selling division is unable to sell all its output externally at the same market price. This can happen when the division is a dominant influence in the market, and monopoly or oligopoly conditions apply. In order to sell larger volumes of output in the intermediate market, the division is therefore required to reduce the sales price.

When there is an imperfect intermediate market, the problem of identifying a suitable transfer price for inter-divisional sales becomes fairly complex.

It might be possible to establish for the intermediate market a 'demand curve', showing the volume of sales demand at different prices. Demand curves are difficult to establish in practice, although some companies do use them. However, demand curves are common in the academic literature on transfer pricing and there could be examination questions on the topic.

A demand curve

The rule of market prices is that the total market demand for an item varies with the sales price. If the relationship between sales price and sales demand is linear, a demand curve could be expressed by the formula:

$P = a + bQ$

where

P is the sales price for all items sold

Q is the quantity of items sold

Values can be established for a and b. When the price is a, Q should be zero.

Example

Division X in Tropp Group has an imperfect intermediate market for its product B55. The demand curve for B55 is:

$P = 100 - 0.005Q$

This demand curve shows that:

- the maximum sales price is 100, but at this price sales demand would be zero

- for each reduction in price of 0.005, sales demand will increase by 1 unit

- at a price of 0, sales demand will be 20,000 units (= 100/0.005).

Marginal revenue

Marginal revenue is the extra revenue that will be earned by selling one additional unit in the market. In a perfect market, the marginal revenue for a company is always the market price of the item, because all output can be sold at the prevailing market price.

When the market is imperfect, marginal revenue is always lower than the market price.

If you are familiar with differentiation, you will no doubt know how to calculate marginal revenue from a demand curve. If you are not familiar with differentiation, the following rules should be learned:

- The demand curve gives a value for P: $P = a + bQ$

- Total revenue = $P \times Q$

- Substituting, we get: Total revenue = $(a + bQ) \times Q$

Total revenue = $aQ + bQ^2$

- Marginal revenue is found by differentiating $aQ + bQ^2$

Without going into the details of the arithmetic:

Marginal revenue (MR) = $a + 2bQ$

Example

The demand curve for product B55 is: $P = 100 - 0.005Q$

Total revenue (TR) from selling B55 = $(100 - 0.005Q) \times Q$

$TR = 100Q - 0.005 Q^2$

The marginal revenue from selling each extra unit of B55 is:

$MR = 100 - (2 \times 0.005)Q$

$MR = 100 - 0.010Q$

Maximising profit

In an imperfect market, profits are maximised by selling output up to a volume where marginal revenue = marginal cost.

The profit-maximising rule of MR = MC comes from economics and, in economics, cost includes an element for normal profit. However, the same rule can be applied in accounting, where marginal cost does not include a profit element.

This rule might have to be applied in order to determine the profit-maximising output for a company as a whole, and for a profit centre within the company.

5 Transfer Pricing: general rules

The general rule for decision-making is that all goods and services should be transferred at **opportunity cost**. For performance evaluation, the aim is to set a transfer price that will give a fair measure of performance in each division, i.e. profit.

There are 3 possible situations:

1 A situation where there is a competitive market for an intermediate product

2 A situation where the selling division has selling capacity

3 A situation where there are production constraints, and the selling division has no surplus capacity.

These will be detailed below in turn.

6 Transfer Pricing: a competitive market for an intermediate product

A perfect market means that there is only one price in the market, there are no buying or selling costs and the market is able to absorb the entire output of the primary division and meet all of the requirements of the secondary division.

OPTIMUM TP (DM) = MARKET PRICE + ANY SMALL ADJUSTMENTS

TP in a perfect intermediate market

Perfect intermediate market and no variable selling costs

Division A of the Robin Group makes a product A22, which it sells externally and to another division in the Group, Division B. Division B uses product A22 as a component in product B46, which it sells externally. There is a perfect external market for both A22 and B46.

Costs and sales prices are as follows:

	Division A Product A22	Division B Product B46
Variable production cost	$12 per unit	
Further variable costs		$15 per unit
Fixed costs	$200,000	$300,000
Sales price	$20 per unit	$45 per unit

Division A can either sell product A22 externally for $20, or transfer the product internally to Division B. Unless the transfer price is $20 or more, Division A will prefer to sell externally, in order to maximise its profit.

Division B can either buy product A22 from external suppliers at $20, or buy internally from Division A. If the transfer price exceeds $20, Division B will prefer to buy externally, in order to minimise its costs and so maximise its profit.

Conclusions

- The only transfer price at which Division A and Division B will be willing to trade with each other is $20, the **external market price**.

- At a transfer price of $20, each division would produce and sell up to its capacity. Each division would maximise its profit by making and selling as much as possible, and the total company profit would be maximised. Goal congruence would be achieved.

- In both Divisions A and B, the manager should be motivated to make and sell as much as possible, and to keep costs under control, in order to maximise profit.

- This price would probably be negotiated freely between the managers of Divisions A and B, without head office interference.

- The performance of each profit centre would be measured on a fair basis.

- If company policy is to encourage inter-divisional sales unless there is a good commercial reason for selling or buying externally, the two divisions should trade internally up to the output capacity of the lower-capacity division.

Another way of stating the ideal transfer price is:

	$
Marginal cost in Division A	12
Opportunity cost: contribution forgone from external sale by transferring a unit to Division B: ($20 – $12)	8
Ideal transfer price (= market price)	20

It can be seen that, in these circumstances, setting the transfer price as the market price satisfies all of the objectives of a transfer pricing system.

Perfect intermediate market, but with variable selling costs

If there are variable selling costs or buying costs in the intermediate market:

- it will cost the selling division more to sell externally than to transfer internally, or

- it will cost the buying division more to purchase from an external supplier than to buy internally.

It is therefore cheaper and more profitable to transfer internally than to sell or buy externally. The cost savings can be reflected in an adjustment to the transfer price, so that both divisions share the benefit.

Example

The example of divisions A and B of the Robin Group will be used again, except that the costs and sales prices are as follows:

	Division A Product A22	Division B Product B46
Variable production cost	$12 per unit	
Variable selling cost in the external market	$3 per unit	
Further variable costs		$15 per unit
Fixed costs	$200,000	$300,000
Sales price	$20 per unit	$45 per unit

Division A can either sell product A22 externally for $20 to earn a contribution of $5 per unit ($20 – $15) or transfer the product internally to Division B to earn a contribution of $8. The manager of Division A would prefer to sell to Division B because it is cheaper and more profitable. The lowest transfer price that Division A would accept is $17.

	$
External selling price	20
External variable selling cost	(3)
Minimum transfer price (= market price)	17

Division B can either buy product A22 from external suppliers at $20, or buy internally from Division A. If the transfer price exceeds $20, Division B will prefer to buy externally, in order to minimise its costs and so maximise its profit.

Conclusions

- There is **a range** of ideal transfer prices, between $17 and $20, at which Division A and Division B will be willing to trade with each other.

- If the transfer price is set between $17 and $20, each division would produce and sell up to its capacity. Each division would maximise its profit by making and selling as much as possible, and the total company profit would be maximised. Goal congruence would be achieved.

- In both Divisions A and B, the manager should be motivated to make and sell as much as possible, and to keep costs under control, in order to maximise profit.

> - This price would probably be negotiated freely between the managers of Divisions A and B, without head office interference. However, the manager of Division B might need to be aware that Division A is saving costs by selling internally, in order to extract a price concession in negotiations on the transfer price.
>
> - The performance of each profit centre would be measured on a fair basis.
>
> - If company policy is to encourage inter-divisional sales unless there is a good commercial reason for selling or buying externally, the two divisions should trade internally up to the output capacity of the lower-capacity division.
>
> It can be seen that there is a range of prices which will satisfy the general objectives of a transfer pricing system.

7 Transfer Pricing: the selling division has surplus capacity

A situation might arise where a profit centre has an intermediate market for its output, and also sells internally, but:

– there is a limit to the amount that it can sell externally, and

– it has spare capacity.

In such a situation, the opportunity cost of transferring units internally would be nil, and the ideal transfer price would be based on cost, not the external market price. The opportunity cost of transferring units internally is nil because the selling division can meet external demand in full, and still have excess capacity for making inter-divisional sales. The ideal transfer cost would therefore be marginal cost.

OPTIMUM TP (DM) = MARGINAL COST

Example 2: Spare capacity

Alameda Ltd has two divisions, Division Alpha and Division Beta. Division Alpha makes widgets, which it can sell externally for $45 as well as internally to Division Beta. The marginal cost of making a widget is $30 per unit in Division Alpha, and the division has spare capacity.

Division Beta turns widgets into another product, the bidget, at a marginal cost of $55 per unit. Division Beta can then sell bidgets externally for $120 per unit. External sales of widgets incur a variable distribution cost of $3 per unit:

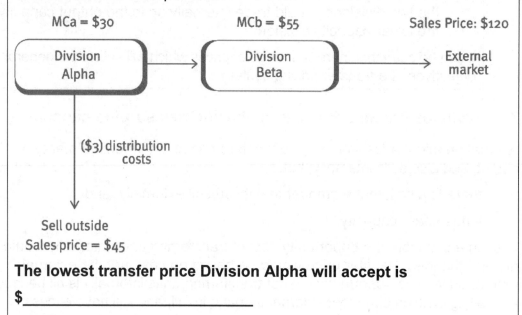

The lowest transfer price Division Alpha will accept is

$_____

The problem is that transferring at marginal cost is unlikely to be 'fair' to the supplying division.

There are three possible solutions:

(i) **2 part tariff**

The transfer price is marginal cost, but in addition a fixed sum is paid per annum or per period to the supplying division to go at least part of the way towards covering its fixed costs, and possibly even to generate a profit. A two-part tariff has a number of disadvantages:

– It may not provide motivation to the selling division manager.

– The measurement of the performance of the selling division may not be fair.

– The negotiation process may be time consuming and a fair profit may have to be imposed by head office.

Archer Group

Archer Group has two divisions, Division X and Division Y. Division X manufactures a component X8 which is transferred to Division Y. Division Y uses component X8 to make a finished product Y14, which it sells for $20. There is no external market for component X8.

Costs are as follows:

	Division X Component X8	Division Y Product Y14
Variable production cost	$5 per unit	$3 per unit*
Annual fixed costs	$40,000	$80,000

* Excluding the cost of transferred units of X8.

Under a two-part tariff transfer pricing arrangement, Division Y would pay:

1   a fixed fee of $40,000 each year plus possibly a negotiated mark up for profit, plus

2    $5 for each unit of component X8 transferred.

A two-part tariff should ensure that the selling division would not make a loss, and would make a profit if its actual costs are less than the agreed transfer price fixed fee and/or a profit mark-up has been allowed for in the fixed fee.

However, there is no incentive for the manager of Division X to produce more output.

(ii)   Cost-plus pricing

The transfer price is the marginal cost or full cost plus a mark-up. Using standard costs should be fair and up-to-date. If transfers are made at actual costs instead of standard costs, there is no incentive for the supplying division to control costs, as they can all be passed on to the receiving division.

(iii)   'Dual pricing'

Dual pricing is where one transfer price is recorded by the supplying division and a different transfer price is recorded by the buying division.

An adjustment account in the HQ books holds the differences between the divisions.

Fern Group

Fern Group has two divisions, Domestic and Business. Business Division manufactures computer desks for business customers. Its annual capacity is 15,000 desks, but currently annual demand is only 10,000 desks.

The marginal cost of making a desk in Business Division is $600, and the desks sell for $800. Fixed costs in the Business Division are $1,500,000.

Domestic Division makes and sells furniture items for retail customers. Its manager has seen an opportunity to make some alterations and additions to the Business Division computer desk, and sell it to retail customers as an IT desk for the home.

The extra cost of amending and improving the Business Division desk would be $200 per desk. The Domestic Division manager believes he could sell 5,000 desks for the home each year at $880 each. However, he would not want to pay Business Division more than $560 for each desk.

Required:

How might a dual transfer price arrangement help to reach an agreement between the two divisions?

Solution:

The first step with any transfer pricing problem is to establish what is in the best interests of the company as a whole.

In this example, it is in the interests of the company for Domestic Division to make and sell the 5,000 IT desks for the home.

Selling price	$880
Marginal cost in Business Division	$600
Marginal cost in Domestic Division	$200
Total marginal cost for each unit	$800
Contribution for each unit sold	$80
Total increase in annual contribution (5,000 units)	$400,000

The company should want the Domestic Division to make and sell the IT desks, and Business Division has sufficient spare capacity to meet the demand without affecting its own external sales of computer desks.

However, Business Division will not agree to a transfer price below marginal cost. At a transfer price of $560, it would lose $40 for each unit transferred.

Head office could try to persuade the manager of Domestic Division to agree to a transfer price at marginal cost plus. A transfer price between $600 and $680 would share the marginal profits between the two divisions.

If head office suggested a price above $600, the Domestic Division manager might decide to drop the plan to make and sell the IT desks, since the hoped-for extra profit might not be sufficient to justify the risk of offering a new product to the market. To get round the problem, head office might decide on **dual transfer prices**:

1   Domestic Division should buy desks from Business Division at $560 per unit.

2   Business Division should be paid in excess of marginal cost for supplying desks to Domestic Division. A transfer price of $610 might be offered.

3   The difference $50 ($610 – $560) between the two transfer prices would be a charge to head office.

4   With this arrangement, Business Division would supply 5,000 desks to Domestic Division.

5   Business Division would make additional annual profits of $10 per desk ($50,000 in total).

6   Domestic Division would make a contribution of $120 per desk sold ($880 – $200 – $560) and so increase annual profits by $600,000.

7   Head office would take a charge of $50 per desk or $250,000 in total.

8   The company as a whole would benefit by $50,000 + $600,000 – $250,000 = $400,000.

Example 3: Pool Group

Pool Group has two divisions that operate as profit centres. Each centre sells similar products, but to different segments of the market:

- Division P makes product P29 which it sells to external customers for $150. Variable costs of production are $45 per unit. The maximum annual sales demand for P29 is 5,000 units, although Division P has capacity for 7,000 units. Increasing output from 5,000 to 7,000 each year would result in additional fixed cost expenditure of $8,000.

- The manager of Division L has seen an opportunity to sell an amended version of Product P29 to its own customers, and is interested in buying 2,000 units each year to re-sell externally at $90 per unit. The costs of amending Product P29, for sale as Product L77, would be $25 per unit. However, the manager of Division L will not pay more than $40 per unit of Product P29.

> He argues that Division P will benefit from lower fixed costs per unit by working at full capacity. The manager of Division P refuses to sell at a price that does not cover the division's incremental costs.
>
> **Required:**
>
> Suggest a dual transfer pricing arrangement that might overcome the disagreement between the two divisional managers.

8 Transfer Pricing: Production constraints and the division has no surplus capacity

The shadow price is the opportunity cost of the lost contribution from the other product or it is the extra contribution that would be earned if more of the scarce resource were available.

OPTIMUM TP (DM) = MARGINAL COST + SHADOW PRICE

Example 4: No spare capacity

Alameda Ltd has two divisions, Division Alpha and Division Beta. Division Alpha makes widgets, which it can sell externally for $45 as well as internally to Division Beta. The marginal cost of making a widget is $30 per unit, and the division has **no** spare capacity.

Division Beta turns widgets into another product, the bidget, at a marginal cost of $55 per unit. Division Beta can then sell bidgets externally for $120 per unit. External sales of widgets incur a variable distribution cost of $3 per unit:

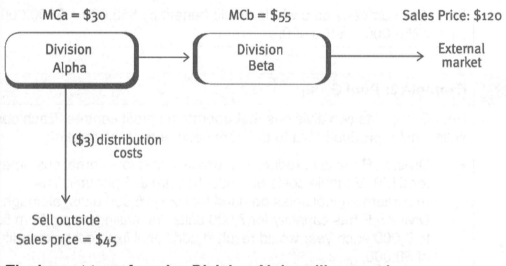

The lowest transfer price Division Alpha will accept is

$_____

Transfer pricing: Behavioural considerations

Transfer prices tend to vary over the product life cycle according to Cats-Baril et al. (1988). During the introductory phase, they suggest a cost plus fixed fee or cost plus a profit share. During the growth phase, they suggest a price related to the closest substitute and during maturity a price based on identical products. This is common sense to a large extent. It is probably only during the maturity stage that identical substitutes exist and during the introductory phase there may be no basis other than cost on which to base the price.

Using any actual cost or cost plus as a transfer price does not motivate the supplying division to act in the interest of the group. Standard or predetermined costs should always be used in place of actual cost. If actual cost is used, the supplying division is not encouraged to be efficient, and control costs as inefficiencies are passed on to the receiving division by way of a higher transfer price. It is even worse if a mark-up is used because the selling division is encouraged to push up the actual cost as this will increase the mark-up, and increase the division's profit. Standard costs are at least subject to scrutiny when they are set once a year and the receiving division has a chance to challenge them. If standard cost is used, the selling division has an incentive to control actual costs below that level and so increase its own profits.

It is usual to imagine transfer pricing taking place in vertically integrated manufacturing organisations. This is not the norm today. Transfer pricing takes place in many different types of organisation and it can have a profound effect on behaviour. For example, a garage carries out a number of different activities that are linked to the activities of another section. The activities include selling new cars, selling old cars, servicing cars sold, general repairs, repairing and servicing used cars accepted in part payment, providing financing and so on. A transfer price is used to transfer a used car accepted in part-payment for a new car between the new car sales and used car sales divisions. A transfer price will also have to be established for transferring the cost of servicing and repairing these cars for sale between the servicing division and the used car sales division. These prices will have considerable implications for the profitability of the different sections and on the actions of the employees when making sales deals. If performance measurement and assessment is to be fair, transfer prices need to be set carefully.

Transfer prices can also be used to deter competitors. If a vertically integrated company concentrates profits at the stage of production where there is least competition, competitors may be attracted to enter. On the other hand, competitors operating at the other stages may be disadvantaged by the low profits the vertically integrated company is taking and they may not be able to achieve a satisfactory return if they are only operating in a limited area of the value chain. Neghandhi (1987) cites cases of US oil companies and Japanese trading and manufacturing companies doing this.

9   International transfer pricing

Transfers within an international group will often be cross-border, between divisions in different countries. With international transfers and international transfer pricing, the issues already described in this chapter still apply. In addition, other factors need to be considered.

10   Different tax rates

A multinational company will seek to minimise the group's total tax liability. One way of doing this might be to use transfer pricing to:

- reduce the profitability of its subsidiaries in high-tax countries, and

- increase the profitability of its subsidiaries in low-tax countries.

Changes in the transfer price can redistribute the pre-tax profit between subsidiaries, but the total pre-tax profit will be the same. However, if more pre-tax profit is earned in low-tax countries and less profit is earned in high-tax countries, the total tax bill will be reduced.

Taxation and transfer pricing

Multinational organisations have a natural inclination to set transfer prices in order to minimise tax payments.

Taxation

If a group has subsidiaries that operate in different countries with different tax rates, the overall group corporation tax bill could be reduced by manipulating the transfer prices between the subsidiaries.

For example, if the taxation rate on profits in Country X is 25 per cent and in Country Y it is 60 per cent, the group could adjust the transfer price to increase the profit of the subsidiary in Country X and reduce the profit of the subsidiary in Country Y. Thus, if the subsidiary in Country X provides goods or services to the subsidiary in Country Y, the use of a very high transfer price would maximise the profits in the lower-tax country, and minimise the profits in the higher-tax country.

There is also the temptation to set up marketing subsidiaries in countries with low corporation tax rates and transfer products to them at a relatively low transfer price. When the products are sold to the final customer, a low rate of tax will be paid on the difference between the two prices.

The taxation authorities in most countries monitor transfer prices in an attempt to control the situation and in order to collect the full amount of taxation due. Double taxation agreements between countries mean that companies pay tax on specific transactions in one country only. However, if the company sets an unrealistic transfer price in order to minimise tax, and the tax authority spots this, the company will pay taxation in both countries, that is, double taxation. This additional payment can amount to millions of pounds and, as a result, is quite an effective deterrent. On the other hand, the gains of avoiding taxation may be even greater.

It appears that lax transfer pricing rules and legal accounting techniques let multinationals structure their businesses so that profits are moved to low or no-tax jurisdictions to reduce their liabilities. Losses can appear to be incurred in high-tax jurisdictions, like the UK, to increase allowable tax deductions.

For example, Starbucks' UK sales in 2011 were worth £398m. Costa's UK sales were worth £377m. But while Costa paid £15m in corporation tax in 2011/12, Starbucks paid nothing! How is this possible? Even though these 2011 sales were worth £398 million, its costs were recorded as £426.2m, giving a loss of £28.2m. Costa, by contrast, reported a taxable profit of £49.7m.

So how could reported UK losses be reconciled with an ongoing UK operation? The answer lies in transfer pricing. Whilst there is no evidence that the company had broken tax rules in any of the countries where it operated, Starbucks had used transfer pricing that routed profits to Switzerland to reduce their UK profits. The result was that despite Starbucks apparently being a highly successful UK operation, their UK tax liability was almost non-existent.

All of Starbucks' businesses worldwide, including in the UK, bought their coffee from its Switzerland office, which allegedly charged a 20% mark-up on the price at which it bought its coffee in the wholesale market. So, Starbucks bought coffee beans for the UK through a Swiss company, Starbucks Coffee Trading Co. Before the beans reached the UK, they were roasted at a Dutch subsidiary. Corporate profits were taxed at 24 percent in the UK and 25 percent in the Netherlands, whereas profits tied to international trade in commodities like coffee were taxed at rates as low as 5 percent in Switzerland.

The UK Public Accounts Committee doubted the 20% mark-up that the Netherlands based company paid to the Swiss based company on its coffee buying operations, with a further mark up before it sold to the UK, was reasonable. Starbucks agreed that it had a special tax arrangement with the Netherlands that made it attractive to locate business there, which the Dutch authorities allegedly asked Starbucks to hold in confidence, and that Switzerland offered a very competitive tax rate: and there we have the public's perception of transfer pricing, a device to remove profits from the UK to these areas with lower tax.

Starbucks declined to give details, or comment on what the charges indicated about the price its roaster paid its Swiss unit for coffee beans. It also declined to say what profit the Swiss coffee-buying unit made. Under Swiss law, the unit was not obliged to publish accounts.

What was clear was that while its UK subsidiary registered a loss, its Dutch roasting operation had only a small profit. In the previous three years, the Amsterdam unit had had an average annual turnover of 154 million euros but recorded average profit of 1.6 million euros, or 1 percent of that, according to its accounts.

Starbucks was the subject of a UK customs inquiry in 2009 and 2010 into the company's transfer pricing practices. This was "resolved without recourse to any further action or penalty", a Starbucks spokesman said.

Most countries now accept the Organisation for Economic Co-operation and Development's (OECD) guidelines. These guidelines were produced with the aim of standardising national approaches to transfer pricing as part of the OECD's charter to encourage the freedom of world trade. They provide guidance on the application of 'arm's length' principles. They state that where necessary transfer prices should be adjusted using an 'arm's length' price, that is, a price that would have been arrived at by two unrelated companies acting independently.

Example 5: Seacross

Seacross Group has two subsidiaries, UKD in the UK and GD in Germany.

UKD makes and sells Product S99. The variable cost of manufacture in the UK is £200 per unit and annual fixed costs are £210,000. Product S99 sells for £500 per unit in the UK market and annual demand is 800 units.

GD in Germany buys 400 units of S99 from UKD each year, adapts them for the German market, and sells them for the equivalent of £700 per unit. The variable costs of adapting the product and selling it in Germany are £50 per unit. The cost of shipping the 400 units to Germany is £6,000 and these are paid by GD. Fixed costs in GD are £24,000 each year.

The rate of taxation on company profits is 30% in the UK and 50% in Germany.

Required:

What would be the annual after-tax profits of the group if the transfer price for S99 is:

(a)   its UK market price, £500

(b)   its variable cost of manufacture, £200?

11   Government action on transfer prices

Governments are aware of the effect of transfer pricing on profits, and in many countries, multinationals are required to justify the transfer prices that they charge. Multinationals could be required to apply 'arm's length' prices to transfer prices: in other words, they might be required under tax law to use market-based transfer prices, to remove the opportunities for tax avoidance.

Multinationals might set up subsidiary companies in tax havens, trade through these companies, and hope to reduce their total tax liabilities. Tax avoidance, while legitimate, can be seen as aggressive when it involves using financial instruments and arrangements not intended as a way to obtain tax advantage. So it is also possible that some countries wishing to attract business might have tax laws that are very favourable to business. A country with the status of a 'tax haven' might offer:

- a low rate of tax on profits

- a low withholding tax on dividends paid to foreign holding companies

- tax treaties with other countries

- no exchange controls

- a stable economy

- good communications with the rest of the world

- a well-developed legal framework, within which company rights are protected.

Unlike tax evasion, tax avoidance is not illegal; it is operating within the letter, but perhaps not the spirit, of the law. Businesses may therefore be complying with the law – but is it ethical?

12   Transfer pricing to manage cash flow

Some governments might place legal restrictions on dividend payments by companies to foreign parent companies.

In this situation, it would be tempting for a multinational to sell goods or services to a subsidiary in the country concerned from other divisions in other countries, and charge very high transfer prices as a means of getting cash out of the country.

This tactic is not possible, however, when the country's tax laws require that transfer prices should be set on an arm's length basis.

13 Practice Questions

Objective Test Question 1: Transfer pricing

A professional firm has two divisions, a computer consultancy division (CSD) and a management advisory division (MAD). Each division provides consultancy and advisory services to clients and in the year just ended, the fees earned by CSD were $500,000 and the fees earned by MAD were $700,000. Establishment costs were $400,000 for the year in CSD and $500,000 for the year in MAD.

In providing services to their clients, each division obtains supporting services from the other division. During the year, CSD provided 5,000 hours of services to MAD and MAD provided 2,000 hours of services to CSD.

It has been agreed that the transfer prices for services should be $20 per hour for work done by CSD and $30 per hour for services provided by MAD.

Required:

The profit for the year reported by CSD was:

A $60,000

B $100,000

C $140,000

D $200,000

Objective Test Question 2: Transfer pricing

Hock Group has two divisions, Division P and Division Q. Division P manufactures an item that is transferred to Division Q. The item has no external market, and 60,000 units produced are transferred internally each year. The costs of each division are as follows:

	Division P	Division Q
Variable cost	$10 per unit	$12 per unit
Fixed costs each year	$120,000	$90,000

Head office management decides that a transfer price should be set that provides a profit of $30,000 to Division P. What should the transfer price per unit be?

Objective Test Question 3: Transfer pricing

An international group operates in four countries, the US, France, the UK and Malaysia. Its divisions in each country trade with each other. There are large differences between the countries in rates of taxation on corporate profits.

The company's management is reasonably confident that for the next year or so, it can predict which of its operating currencies (US dollars, euros, sterling and ringgitts) will rise in value against the others and which will fall.

Required:

In which currencies might the group's management wish to price inter-company sales within the group?

Objective Test Question 4: All That Jazz Ltd

All That Jazz Ltd (ATJ) has two divisions – the 'Gin' division and the 'Piano' division. Division 'Gin' manufactures a product called the aye and Division 'Piano' manufactures a product called the bee. Each bee uses a single aye as a component. 'Gin' is the only manufacturer of the aye and supplies both 'Piano' and outside customers. Details of Gin's and Piano's operations for the coming period are as follows:

	Division 'Gin'	Division 'Piano'
Fixed costs	$7,500,000	$18,000,000
Variable costs per unit	$280	$590 (*)
Capacity – Units	30,000	18,000

Note: exclude transfer costs

Market research has indicated that demand for ATJ Ltd's products from outside customers will be as follows in the coming period:

- the aye: at unit price $1,000 no ayes will be demanded but demand will increase by 25 ayes with every $1 that the unit price is reduced below $1,000

- the bee: at unit price $4,000 no bees will be demanded, but demand will increase by 10 bees with every $1 that the unit price is reduced below $4,000.

Required:

(a) Calculate the unit selling price of the bee (accurate to the nearest $) that will maximise ATJ Ltd's profit in the coming period.

(b) Calculate the unit selling price of the bee (accurate to the nearest $) that is likely to emerge if the Divisional Managers of 'Gin' and 'Piano' both set selling prices calculated to maximise divisional profit from sales to outside customers and the transfer price of ayes going from Gin to Piano is set at 'market selling price'.

(c) Explain why your answers to parts (a) and (b) are different, and propose changes to the system of transfer pricing in order to ensure that ATJ Ltd is charging its customers at optimum prices.

Data Set Question: Division A and Division B

Division A transfers 100,000 units of a component to Division B each year. The market price of the component is $25. Division A's variable cost is $15 per unit, and A's divisional's fixed costs are $500,000 each year.

What price would be credited to Division A for each component that it transfers to Division B under:

Dual pricing (based on marginal cost and market price)?

Two-part tariff pricing (where the Divisions have agreed that the fixed fee will be $200,000)?

Case Study Style Question: STK Transfer Pricing

STK Solutions (STK) is an IT service provider.

You have received the following email from the Finance Director:

From: Sarah Dentch
Date: Today
Subject: Restructuring and transfer pricing

As you are aware, STK is likely to go some major restructuring when lockdown ends and life at work returns to normal for our employees, most of whom will be encouraged to work from home from now on, whenever possible. It is anticipated that the restructuring plan may involve the consolidation of some business activities, changes in responsibility and more defined reporting lines within our management structure. This if course could result in a number of staff having to move to different areas of the company, re allocation of duties, the development of multi skilled teams and other staff being made redundant. Within STK employee relations have in the past been good, the CEO is aware that employees and any trade unions which represent their interests will be resistant to the changes that need to be made. The first stages of change will require skilful negotiation between the STK and unions on a range of issues relating to the movement of staff jobs, the proposed job losses and, specifically, the criteria for redundancy and the redundancy package.

As we have no HR professional to advise us the board have asked me to initially head up the negotiations on behalf of STK. I am concerned that my knowledge in this area is a little out of date and an unsure how to go about it.
In addition, in order to effectively assess the performance of each division to facilitate these decisions, we will need to introduce a transfer price from the Data Centre IT Staff to the Consultancy service areas for any time spent retraining or training consultants.

Could you please prepare a report for me which discusses the main objectives that should be considered when setting a transfer price. I would be grateful if you would suggest and discuss three different ways of setting a transfer price for this training / retraining service.

Test your understanding answers

Example 1: Inter-divisional trading

(a) If the transfer price is $20:

	Division A	Division B	Company as a whole
	$000	$000	$000
External sales	0	350	350
Inter-divisional transfers	200	0	0
	200	350	350
Costs			
Inter-divisional transfers	0	200	0
Other material costs	80	20	100
Other variable costs	20	30	50
Fixed costs	60	30	90
Total costs	160	280	240
Profit	40	70	110

(b) If the transfer price is $25:

	Division A	Division B	Company as a whole
	$000	$000	$000
External sales	0	350	350
Inter-divisional transfers	250	0	0
	250	350	350
Costs			
Inter-divisional transfers	0	250	0
Other material costs	80	20	100
Other variable costs	20	30	50
Fixed costs	60	30	90
Total costs	160	330	240
Profit	90	20	110

Conclusions from the example:

- The choice of transfer price does not affect the profit of the organisation as a whole, provided that there is agreement on the quantity of transfers.

- However, the choice of transfer price affects the profitability of the individual profit centres.

Example 2: Spare capacity

The lowest transfer price Division A will accept is $30.

Division A has spare capacity. It is already selling all it can to the external market, and can make extra widgets for B without losing external sales. Therefore, any transfer price must therefore cover A's marginal cost per unit, which is **$30**.

Example 3: Pool Group

It is in the interests of Pool Group for the additional units to be made and sold as Product L77.

The contribution per unit will be $90 – $45 – $25 = $20. The contribution from selling 2,000 units each year ($40,000) exceeds the additional fixed costs of $8,000.

To cover the incremental costs in Division P, the transfer price needs to be $45 + $(8,000/2,000 units) = $49.

Division L will not pay more than $40.

A dual transfer pricing arrangement that might win the agreement of both divisional managers is for Division P to receive $49 per unit of P29 and for Division L to pay $40. The difference of $9 per unit or $18,000 in total for the year would be a charge to head office.

Example 4: No spare capacity

The lowest transfer price Division A will accept is $42.

Division A has no spare capacity. Every unit A has to supply to B causes a loss of external net revenue. Therefore, the transfer price must be at least $42 to 'compensate' A (and the company) for its lost net revenue.

Example 5: Seacross

[Note: This example shows that when two profit centres are in different countries, it would be in the interests of the company as a whole to set transfer prices that keep a larger proportion of the total profit in the low-tax country.

In this example, the higher transfer price gives more profit to the UK division and less profit to the German division. The total pre-tax profit remains the same, but total tax charges are lower, giving a higher-total post-tax profit for the group.]

(a) **Transfer price = £500**

	UKD	GD	Company as a whole
	£	£	£
External sales	400,000	280,000	680,000
Inter-divisional transfers	200,000	0	0
	600,000	280,000	680,000
Costs			
Inter-divisional transfers	0	200,000	0
Other variable costs	240,000	20,000	260,000
Shipping costs	0	6,000	6,000
Fixed costs	210,000	24,000	234,000
Total costs	450,000	250,000	500,000
Pre-tax profit	150,000	30,000	180,000
Tax (30%:50%)	(45,000)	(15,000)	(60,000)
After-tax profit	105,000	15,000	120,000

(b) Transfer price = £200

	UKD	GD	Company as a whole
	£	£	£
External sales	400,000	280,000	680,000
Inter-divisional transfers	80,000	0	0
	480,000	280,000	680,000
Costs			
Inter-divisional transfers	0	80,000	0
Other variable costs	240,000	20,000	260,000
Shipping costs	0	6,000	6,000
Fixed costs	210,000	24,000	234,000
Total costs	450,000	130,000	500,000
Pre-tax profit	30,000	150,000	180,000
Tax (30%:50%)	(9,000)	(75,000)	(84,000)
After-tax profit	21,000	75,000	96,000

The American subsidiary requires 300,000 units however and the additional 100,000 units could only be supplied by reducing the supply to external customers. The minimum transfer price acceptable to the European subsidiary would be $95 as this would earn the same contribution per chip as external sales. At this price the American subsidiary would be paying $5 per chip more than from the external market and so would not be motivated to buy internally.

An average price for all 300,000 units could be set using $80 for the first 200,000 units and $95 for the remaining 100,000 units.

$200,000 \times \$80 + 100,000 \times \$95/300,000 = \$85$.

It has already been seen in part (b) that this is the minimum price the European subsidiary would consider if performance was measured on profit. The American subsidiary would be saving $5 per chip.

A better solution may be to transfer 200,000 chips internally and purchase the remaining 100,000 chips from the external supplier. Assuming the transfer price is set at $80 this would result in a profit for the European subsidiary of 600,000 × $45 + 200,000 × $30 − $26m = $7m. The American subsidiary would reduce costs by 200,000 × $15 = $3m. Group profits would increase by $3m, an increase of $1.5m compared to using a transfer price of $95 (see part a).

At $80 all of the profit increase was in the American subsidiary. Depending on where the transfer price is set in the range $80 to $90 the increase in profit can be divided more equitably between the two divisions.

Performance measures

If performance is measured using profit then any price above $85, (for 300,000 units), but below $90 would allow both subsidiaries to increase profits. If return on assets is used however the minimum price that would be acceptable to the European subsidiary would be $92 (part b). The American subsidiary would be unwilling to trade at that price. It would be impossible to set a transfer price that would be acceptable to both divisions.

Conclusion

It would be beneficial for the group if 200,000 chips were transferred internally rather than the current practise of external purchase. Providing the external supplier is willing to supply only 100,000 chips at $90 per unit this is the preferred option. A performance measurement system based on profit allows a transfer price to be set which would be acceptable to both subsidiaries. This is not the case if return on assets consumed is used.

(d) Multi-nationals may have some companies located in countries with high rates of corporate tax and others with lower rates. To reduce the overall tax charge the aim will be to keep profit as low as possible in high tax rate countries. This can be achieved by charging high transfer prices to companies in high tax countries purchasing goods and set low transfer prices for those companies in high tax countries supplying goods.

National tax authorities have taken action to discourage manipulation of profits. Internal transfers are examined closely and are expected to be at market prices, or where this is not possible, at cost. Heavy fines are imposed on companies suspected of deliberately manipulating transfer prices to avoid tax.

Objective Test Question 1: Transfer pricing

[Tutorial note: Only the profit reported by CSD is required. Total profit is shown here for information.]

	Company	MAD	Company
External sales	500,000	700,000	1,200,000
Internal transfers:			
5,000 × $20	100,000	–	–
Internal transfers:			
2,000 × $30	–	60,000	–
	600,000	760,000	1,200,000
Costs			
Transfers	60,000	100,000	0
Establishment costs	400,000	500,000	900,000
	460,000	600,000	900,000
Profit	**140,000**	**160,000**	**300,000**

The answer is **C**.

Objective Test Question 2: Transfer pricing

Target profit for Division P	$30,000
Fixed costs of Division P	120,000
Target contribution of Division P	$150,000

	$ per unit
Target contribution per unit (÷ 60,000)	$2.50
Variable cost	$10.00
Transfer price required	**$12.50**

Objective Test Question 3: Transfer pricing

Provided the arrangements are permitted by the tax regulations, the group should want to increase the chances of higher profits in lower-tax countries and lower profits in the higher-tax countries. The companies might agree prices for the year and:

- sales from a division in a higher-tax country might be priced in the weaker currency

- sales from a division in a lower-tax country might be priced in a stronger currency.

If exchange rates move as expected, profits of the companies in the higher-tax countries will be reduced and the companies in the lower-tax country will obtain the matching benefit.

Objective Test Question 4: All That Jazz Ltd

(a)

Division Gin	*Division Piano*
Capacity 30,000	Capacity 18,000
Marginal cost = $280	Marginal cost = $590
Fixed cost = $7.5 million	Fixed cost = $18 million
$P = 1,000 - 0.04Q$	$P = 4,000 - 0.1Q$
$MR = 1,000 - 0.08Q$	$MR = 4,000 - 0.2Q$

To maximise group profits from sales of bee:

Marginal revenue from bee	= Marginal cost of bee
$4,000 - 0.2Q$	$= 280 + 590$
Q	$= 15,650$
P	$= 4,000 - 0.1 \times 15,650$
	$= \$2,435$

Conclusion

A unit selling price of $2,435 per bee will maximise ATJ Ltd's profit in the coming period.

(b) Division Gin; for external sales of aye the division will ensure that:

Marginal revenue from aye	= Marginal cost of aye
$1,000 - 0.08Q$	= $280
Q	= 9,000
P	= $1,000 - 0.04 \times 9,000$
	= $640

This now becomes the internal transfer price and as such forms part of Division Piano's divisional marginal cost.

Division Piano; for sales of bee they will ensure their division MR = divisional MC

$4,000 - 0.2Q$	= 640 + 590
Q	= 13,850
P	= $4,000 - 0.1 \times 13,850$
	= $2,615

This now becomes the internal transfer price and as such forms part of Division Piano's divisional marginal cost.

(c) In part (a) of the question we establish that the group should sell 15,650 units of bee at $2,435 in order to maximise group profits. Under part (b) of the question the manager of Gin is not using a transfer price that will bring about this decision (goal congruency).

As the divisions are acting autonomously, it is understandable that the manager of Gin will aim to earn a divisional contribution from internal sales of aye. As he sells externally at a price of $640 he may consider that this seems to be a fair price for internal sales.

However, this internal transfer price then forms part of Division Piano's marginal costs. The divisional marginal costs at this point ($640 + $590) are NOT the same as the true marginal cost of a bee ($280 + $590). The manager of Piano ensures his divisional profits are maximised, however, this does not coincide with the group objective as the wrong cost data is essentially being used.

To overcome this problem, Head Office could impose a transfer price. Given the surplus capacity at Gin division, the TP to guarantee goal congruency should be the Marginal Cost of an aye, that is $280. At this transfer price the manager of Piano will record a divisional marginal cost of $870 ($280 + $590) and will happily operate at the optimum level, selling 15,650 bees at $2,435.

However, at a TP of marginal cost the manager of Gin is likely to become demotivated as his division receives no reward or benefit for work on internal transfers. Additionally, if divisional profit is used as a performance indicator, the system will fail to measure the performance of division Gin adequately.

So, as an alternative to the relevant cost being used for the TP, a cost based price could be used. Three methods may be employed:

– cost plus price. Here a mark-up could be added to the marginal cost

– two part tariff. This is where the marginal cost is used as the UNIT price of an aye, but a fixed fee is paid to Division A from Div B each period

– dual pricing system could be implemented. Division A sells ayes internally recording one TP (say $640 – the external market price of an aye) and Division B records purchases of aye at a different transfer price. Div B could use a TP of $280 – the MC of an aye. Under this system Division B would operate at the optimum level for the group, and Division A would earn a contribution on internal sales. Head office would reconcile the discrepancies with a reconciliation account.

Data Set Question: Division A and Division B

Dual price transfer price from division A's point of view is market price $25. This ensures that the supplying division can earn a profit.

The two-part tariff transfer price per unit is marginal cost $15.

Case Study Style Question: STK Transfer Pricing

From: Management Accountant

To: Sarah Dentch, Finance Director

Date: Today

Subject: Transfer Pricing

Dear Sarah,

In response to your query:

Transfer pricing objectives

When selecting an appropriate transfer price STK should consider the following objectives:

Goal Congruence

They should ensure that the transfer price leads to goal congruent decisions by each division. For example, if the transfer price is too high then the Consultancy service areas may be discouraged from sending their consultants for training and as a result the level of service offered to clients may be adversely affected.

If the transfer price is too low then the consultancy divisions may use the Data Centre extensively in times when they are short of work without considering whether the training time is completely necessary.

Performance measurement

By setting it transfer price it should be possible to identify periods when a considerable number of hours training have been provided by the Data Centre and the level of support that they are providing can be recognised.

Fair allocation of profit

If transfer prices are set at a level which is too high then this could make it appear that consultancy divisions are under performing because their profits will be reduced. At the same time the Data Centre would benefitting from higher revenue.

If the transfer prices are too low then the Data Centre may be appearing to underperform as the consultancy divisions benefits instead from lower charges.

Maintain Divisional Autonomy

If an appropriate transfer price has been set then each division should be able to make a choice regarding the amount of training that is requested from the consultancy divisions or whether the training is carried out from the Data Centre.

This would reduce the need for the senior management team to be involved in each decision.

Minimise Tax Liabilities

Currently this is not an option as the all divisions operate under the same company which is registered in Kayland.

Recording the level of service supplied

Setting a transfer price will ensure that the time spent training consultants in the Data Centre is recorded and will help to monitor the amount of time required to perform this support activity.

Informed decisions can then be made regarding the amount of resources that need to be available in the Data Centre.

Transfer pricing options

Optimum transfer pricing policy

The optimum transfer pricing policy usually occurs when the transfer price charged when there is available capacity recovers the marginal costs involved in providing the service and then the transfer price is increased once the supplying division is at full capacity to reflect any opportunity cost that has been incurred as a result of lost external sales.

This however may not be appropriate for this service: it is unlikely we'll face many marginal costs associated with the provision of training services, as the majority of costs will be fixed. There also does not appear to be any potential opportunity costs, as the services are not offered to external customers.

Cost plus pricing

The transfer price could be set by calculating the average cost of the Data Centre for each support hour that is provided. Full cost pricing is likely to be preferred to marginal costs as a majority of the costs are likely to be fixed. A mark-up could then be added to the costs to ensure that the Data Centre is not only recovering their costs but also has an opportunity to create a profit for the division.

However, if the mark-up is too high then this may discourage users from requesting training services. As this would then reduce the number of support hours that the Data Centre provides it will also increase the average cost per hour, pushing the transfer price up further. This would then further discourage users from requesting the service and could create a perpetual problem.

Market rate

There may be an option for the consultancy divisions to use external training providers to train their consultants, paying a market rate for the service.

If this is the case then it is likely that this market rate would be higher than the cost of providing the service internally. In this case, there is a risk that the consultancy divisions could make a decision which is not goal congruent if they send their staff on external training courses.

Conclusion and recommendation:

To avoid this lack of congruency, I recommend that the transfer price should be set at somewhere below the market rate, in order to encourage the consultancy divisions to use the internal support activity for any training requirements.

Management Accountant

11

The treatment of uncertainty and risk in decision making

Chapter learning objectives

Lead	Component
D1: Risk and Control	Risk and uncertainty associated with medium-term decision-making (a) Conduct sensitivity analysis (b) Conduct analysis of risk

1 Chapter summary

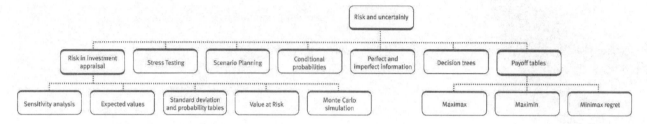

2 Risk and uncertainty

Decision making problems (such as whether to launch new products, whether to buy machines, choosing between products, **etc.**) typically involve an element of risk and uncertainty. This chapter looks at how the decision making process can take account of risk and uncertainty. This is often achieved by building in probabilities for possible outcomes and using expected values and decision trees to assess the problem.

Forecasting and decision making often include an element of risk or uncertainty. Because they look to the future, these decisions often involve estimates of future costs and benefits. Events in the future can be predicted, but managers can rarely be 100% confident that these predicted future events will actually arise. As actual results emerge, managers are likely to discover that they have achieved better or worse results than those predicted originally.

There are several ways of dealing with this variability of outcomes. Here, we consider several different possible outcomes that may arise. It is common in practice to consider three possible outcomes; the most likely outcome, the pessimistic (worst possible) outcome and the optimistic (best possible) outcome. Analysts may consider more than these three possibilities, but more information will become more complicated and cumbersome to analyse and understand. Examination questions will generally provide all the different possible outcomes that may arise, together with the associated chance (probability) of the outcome occurring. It is our task to analyse the information given, recommend an appropriate strategy for management to follow and finally to highlight the potential risk involved in the various choices.

The difference between risk and uncertainty

The decision making process faces the following problems:

- all decisions are based on forecasts
- all forecasts are subject to uncertainty
- this uncertainty needs to be reflected in the financial evaluation.

The decision maker must distinguish between:

- **risk** – quantifiable – possible outcomes have associated probabilities, thus allowing the use of mathematical techniques

- **uncertainty** – unquantifiable – outcomes cannot be mathematically modelled.

Illustration 1 – on risk and uncertainty

Risk: there are a number of possible outcomes and the probability of each outcome is known.

For example, based on past experience of digging for oil in a particular area, an oil company may estimate that they have a 60% chance of finding oil and a 40% chance of not finding oil.

Uncertainty: there are a number of possible outcomes but the probability of each outcome is not known.

For example, the same oil company may dig for oil in a previously unexplored area. The company knows that it is possible for them to either find or not find oil but it does not know the probabilities of each of these outcomes.

One possible approach to dealing with risk is to deploy sophisticated modelling techniques in an attempt to improve the reliability of business forecasts. The use of trend analysis, encountered earlier in this text, is one possibility. The key point is to develop a mathematical model to predict how future costs will behave having regard to labour becoming more adept at tasks (and hence unit resource requirements falling) the more times they are repeated.

3 Dealing with risk in investment appraisal decisions

Investment appraisal often involves a degree of uncertainty and risk. This may be dealt with in a number of ways:

- Adding a risk premium to the discount rate in order to compensate for risk: A premium may be added to the usual discount rate to provide a safety margin. The premium may vary from project to project to reflect the different levels of risk.

- Payback period: Estimates of cash flows several years ahead are quite likely to be inaccurate and unreliable. It may be difficult to control capital projects over a long period of time. Risk may be limited by selecting projects with short payback periods (though this might also induce short-termism into the decision making process and longer-term value-adding projects may be rejected unnecessarily).

- Sensitivity Analysis – explored in this chapter.

- Using probability distributions to give an indication of risk – explored in this chapter.

- Monte Carlo simulation – a computerised system that extends sensitivity analysis – also explored in this chapter.

4 Sensitivity analysis

Sensitivity analysis in NPV questions typically involves posing 'what if' questions. The NPV is recalculated under different conditions, e.g. what would happen if demand fell by 10%, how would the result be affected if variable costs are 5% higher, etc.

Alternatively, we may wish to discover the maximum possible change in one of the parameters before the opportunity becomes non-viable.

This maximum possible change is often expressed as a percentage:

$$\text{Sensitivity margin} = \frac{\text{NPV}}{\text{PV of flow under consideration}}$$

LEARN

This formula works for total cash flows. It cannot be used for individual units, selling prices, variable cost per unit, etc. Have a go at the following example.

Example 1: Amador Ltd

Amador Ltd is considering investing $120,000 in equipment that has a life of 15 years. Its final scrap value is $25,000.

The equipment will be used to produce 15,000 deluxe pairs of rugby boots per annum, generating a contribution of $2.75 per pair. Specific fixed costs are estimated at $18,000 per annum. The firm has a 15% cost of capital.

Required:

(a) Calculate the NPV of the project.

(b) Calculate the sensitivity of your NPV to the:

  (i) initial investment

  (ii) annual contribution

  (iii) annual fixed costs.

(c) Identify the minimum annual sales required to ensure that the project at least breaks even.

Pros and cons of sensitivity analysis

Strengths of sensitivity analysis

- No complicated theory to understand.

- Information will be presented to management in a form which facilitates subjective judgement to decide the likelihood of the various possible outcomes considered.

- Identifies areas which are crucial to the success of the project. If the project is chosen, those areas can be carefully monitored.

- Indicates just how critical some of the forecasts which are considered to be uncertain are.

Weaknesses of sensitivity analysis

- It assumes that changes to variables can be made independently, e.g. material prices will change independently of other variables. This is unlikely. If material prices went up the firm may be able to increase selling price at the same time and there would be little effect on NPV. A technique called simulation (discussed earlier) allows us to change more than one variable at a time.

- It only identifies how far a variable needs to change. It does not look at the probability of such a change. In the above analysis, sales volume appears to be the most crucial variable, but if the firm were facing volatile raw material markets a 65% change in raw material prices would be far more likely than a 29% change in sales volume.

- It is not an optimising technique. It provides information on the basis of which decisions can be made. It does not point directly to the correct decision.

5 Probabilities and expected values

An expected value summarises all the different possible outcomes by calculating a single weighted average. It is the long run average (mean).

The expected value is not the most likely result. It may not even be a possible result, but instead it finds the average outcome if the same event was to take place thousands of times.

Expected value formula

$$EV = \Sigma px$$ **LEARN**

where x represents the future outcome

and p represents the probability of the outcome occurring

Example 2: Ventura Ltd expected values

Ventura Ltd is considering launching a new product. It will do so if the expected value of the total revenue is in excess of $1,000. It is decided to set the selling price at $10. After some investigation a number of probabilities for different levels of sales revenue are predicted; these are shown in the following table:

Units sold	Revenue $	Probability	Pay-off $
80	800	0.15	120
100	1,000	0.50	500
120	1,200	0.35	420

The expected sales revenue at a selling price of $10 per unit is
$_____

Example 3: Dralin Distribution Co

Dralin Distribution Co is considering an investment of $460,000 in a non-current asset expected to generate substantial cash inflows over the next five years. Unfortunately, the annual cash flows from this investment are uncertain, but the following probability distribution has been established:

Annual cash flow $	Probability
50,000	0.3
100,000	0.5
150,000	0.2

At the end of its five-year life, the asset is expected to sell for $40,000. The cost of capital is 5%.

Calculate whether the investment should be undertaken.

Furthermore, not all decision-makers will have the same attitude towards risk. There are three main types of decision-makers:

- **Risk neutral** decision-makers consider all possible outcomes and will select the strategy that maximises the expected value or benefit.

- **Risk seekers** are likely to select the strategy with the best possible outcomes, regardless of the likelihood that they will occur. They will apply the maximax criteria (covered later).

- **Risk averse** decision-makers try to avoid risk. They would rather select a lower, but certain, outcome than risk going for a higher pay-off which is less certain to occur. They will apply the maximin criterion or the minimax regret approach (both covered later).

Illustration 2

For instance, after investigation in the above 'Ventura Limited' example (example 2), the predicted revenues might have been different. They might have been as follows:

Units sold	Revenue $	Probability	Pay-off $
40	400	0.15	60.00
100	1,000	0.50	500.00
137	1,370	0.35	479.50
		1.00	EV = 1,039.50

Both situations give rise to the same expected sales revenue of $1,040 (to the nearest $), but the two situations are not the same. The second involves a wider dispersal of possible outcomes; hence it involves higher risk.

If the decision-makers are risk neutral, their decision making will not be affected by the degree of risk in the different situations; these investors would be indifferent between situations of equal expected payoffs, even if one situation (situation 2) is riskier than the other.

If the decision-makers are risk averse, they will judge the range of possible outcomes described in the second situation to be worse than the first.

If the decision-makers are risk seekers, they may prefer the second situation, because of the higher outcome in the best possible situation. However, in this case, the dire downside of $400 may put them off. Whatever the case it can be seen that the evaluation of the options solely on the basis of their expected value may not always be appropriate.

Example 4: Cement Co part I

Cement Co is a listed company specialising in the manufacture of cement, a product used in the building industry. The company has been a major player in the construction sector of European country, Q, since its formation in 1997. It is passionate about customer care and proud of its active approach to safety and sustainability (recognising the need to minimise any adverse environmental impact of its operations).

The company operates in a very traditional industry but profits can be volatile. Q's economy has been in recession for the last three years and this has had a direct impact on Cement Co's profitability. Shareholders are concerned about this fall in profit and have expressed their desire for a secure return. Competitors, keen to find ways of increasing profit and market share, in these difficult economic circumstances, have started to increase the level of investment in research and development, ensuring their products anticipate and meet the needs of its customers.

When Q entered recession, many workers left the country in search of more lucrative and secure work. This has had a significant impact on Cement Co which is now facing labour shortages and increased labour costs. At the same time, suppliers have also increased their prices putting further pressure on Cement Co's margins.

The company has found that when weather conditions are good, the demand for cement increases since more building work is able to take place. Last year, the weather was so good, and the demand for cement was so great, that Cement Co was unable to meet demand. Cement Co is now trying to work out the level of cement production for the coming year in order to maximise profits. The company doesn't want to miss out on the opportunity to earn large profits by running out of cement again. However, it doesn't want to be left with large quantities of the product unsold at the end of the year, since it deteriorates quickly and then has to be disposed of. The company has received the following estimates about the probable weather conditions and corresponding demand levels for the coming year:

Weather	Probability	Demand
Good	25%	350,000 bags
Average	45%	280,000 bags
Poor	30%	200,000 bags

Each bag of cement sells for $9 and costs $4 to make. If cement is unsold at the end of the year, it has to be disposed of at a cost of $0.50 per bag.

Cement Co has decided to produce at one of the three levels of production to match forecast demand. It now has to decide which level of cement production to select.

As an incentive to increase profitability a new bonus scheme has just been introduced for a select group of Cement Co's directors. A bonus will be received by each of these directors if annual profit exceeds a challenging target.

Required:

Identify the risks facing Cement Co and assess the impact of different risk appetites of managers and shareholders on their response to these risks.

Illustration 3 – Further expected value examples

Situation 1

A company buys in sub-assemblies in order to manufacture a product. It is reviewing its policy of putting each sub-assembly through a detailed inspection process on delivery, and is considering not inspecting at all. Experience has shown that the quality of the sub-assembly is of acceptable standard 90 per cent of the time. It costs $10 to inspect a subassembly and another $10 to put right any defect found at that stage. If the sub-assembly is not inspected and is then found to be faulty at the finished goods stage the cost of rework is $40.

Required:

Advise the company whether or not they should change their policy.

Solution

Four outcomes are possible:

(i) Inspect and find no problems – cost $10.

(ii) Inspect and find problems – cost $20.

(iii) Do not inspect and no problems exist – no cost.

(iv) Do not inspect and problems do exist – cost $40.

If sub-assemblies achieve the required standard 90 per cent of the time then there is a 10 per cent chance that they will be faulty.

The expected value of the cost of each policy is as follows:

Inspect $\quad\quad\quad$ [09 × $10] + [01 × $20] = $11
Do not inspect $\quad$ [0.9 × $0] + [0.1 × $40] = $4

Taken over a long enough period of time, a policy of not carrying out an inspection would lead to a saving in cost of $7 per sub-assembly. On a purely quantitative analysis, therefore, this is the correct policy to adopt.

However, in the real world such a high level of failures is incompatible with a requirement for a 'quality product', and the concept of continuous improvement. It would be more useful to ask the supplier some basic questions regarding his quality management, in order to bring about a fundamental shift towards outcome (iii), rather than simply implementing a policy on the basis of such an uncritical analysis of the situation.

Situation 2

An individual is considering backing the production of a new musical in the West End. It would cost $100,000 to stage for the first month. If it is well received by the critics, it will be kept open at the end of the first month for a further 6 months, during which time further net income of $350,000 would be earned. If the critics dislike it, it will close at the end of the first month. There is a 50:50 chance of a favourable review.

Required:

Should the individual invest in the musical?

Solution

The expected value of backing the musical is:

$[0.5 \times \$250,000] - [0.5 \times \$100,000] = \$75,000$

As this provides a positive return it would be accepted on the basis of expected values as the alternative yields zero. However, the expected value can be misleading here as it is a one-off situation and the expected profit of $75,000 is not a feasible outcome. The only feasible outcomes of this project are a profit of $250,000 or a loss of $100,000.

While almost everybody would welcome a profit of $250,000, not many individuals could afford to sustain a loss of $100,000 and they would place a high utility on such a loss. Many investors would be risk averse in such a situation because they would not consider that a 50 per cent chance of making $250,000 was worth an equal 50 per cent risk of losing $100,000; the loss might bankrupt them. On the other hand, if the individual were a multi-millionaire the return of 250 per cent would be very appealing and the loss of a mere $100,000 would have a low utility attached to it.

The two exercises have only had single-point outcomes, that is conformity or otherwise with a pre-set quality standard and a successful show or a flop. It is obvious that the two outcomes of the first exercise represent the only possible alternatives and so quantification of the related pay-offs along the lines of the example appears reasonable. It is also obvious that the profit of $250,000 predicted for a successful show in the case of the second exercise is far too precise a figure. It would be more realistic to assume a range of possible successful pay-offs, which will vary, according to the number of seats sold and the price of the seats. If probabilities are attached to each estimate, the expected value of a successful outcome will take account of the range of possible outcomes, by weighting each of them by its associated probability. The range of possible outcomes might be as follows.

Profit ($)	Probability	Expected value ($)
(100,000)	0.5000	(50,000)
200,000	0.1750	35,000
250,000	0.2000	50,000
300,000	0.0750	22,500
350,000	0.0500	17,500
	1.0000	75,000

The statement of a range of possible outcomes and their associated probabilities is known as a probability distribution. Presenting the distribution to management allows two further useful inferences to be drawn:

- *The most likely successful outcome.* That is the successful outcome with the highest probability (a profit of $250,000).

- *The probability of an outcome being above or below a particular figure.* The particular figure will either be the expected value or a figure of consequence, such as zero profit, where a lesser outcome might have dire consequences. By summing the probabilities for pay-offs of $200,000 and $250,000, it can be concluded that there is a 37.5 per cent probability that profits will be $250,000 or less if the musical is successful. By summing those for $300,000 and $350,000 it can be determined that the probability of a profit of $300,000 or more in the event of success is only 12.5 per cent.

Advantages and disadvantages of EVs

Advantages:

- Takes risk into account by considering the probability of each possible outcome and using this information to calculate an expected value.

- The information is reduced to a single number resulting in easier decisions.

- Calculations are relatively simple.

Disadvantages:

- The probabilities used are usually very subjective.

- The EV is merely a weighted average and therefore has little meaning for a one-off project.

- The EV gives no indication of the dispersion of possible outcomes about the EV, i.e. the risk.

- The EV may not correspond to any of the actual possible outcomes.

Utility theory

Utility is another important aspect of risk and uncertainty. The basis of the theory is that an individual's attitude to certain risk profiles will depend on the amount of money involved. For example, most people would accept a bet on the toss of a coin, if the outcome were that they would win $6 if it came down heads and if it came down tails they would pay $4. The average person would be happy to play secure in the knowledge that they would win if the game were repeated over a long enough period; if not it would still be a good bet. But if the stakes were raised so that the win was $6,000 on a single toss coming down heads and a loss of $4,000 if it came down tails, the average person might think twice and reject the bet as being too risky. Utility theory attaches weights to the sums of money involved; these are tailor-made to the individual's attitude towards winning and losing certain sums of money.

Therefore, considering a proposed option solely on the basis of its expected value ignores the range of possible outcomes.

6 Standard Deviation

In order to measure the risk associated with a particular project, it is helpful to find out how wide ranging the possible outcomes are. The conventional measure is the standard deviation. The standard deviation compares all the actual outcomes with the expected value (or mean outcome). It then calculates how far on average the outcomes deviate from the mean. It is calculated using a formula.

The basic idea is that the standard deviation is a measure of volatility: the more that actual outcomes vary from the average outcome, the more volatile the returns and therefore the more risk involved in the investment/decision.

Illustration 4 – Further details on standard deviations

The standard deviation is calculated using the following formula:

$$\sigma = \sqrt{\frac{\Sigma(X - \overline{X})^2}{n}}$$

σ = standard deviation Σ = sum of

x = each value in the data set

$\overline{X}$ = mean of all values in the data set

n = number of value in the data set

Let's examine how standard deviations are calculated and used by considering the following illustration:

A company is considering whether to make product X or product Y. They cannot make both products. The estimated sales demand for each product is uncertain and the following probability distribution of the NPVs for each product has been identified.

Product X

NPV ($)	Probability	Expected value ($)
3,000	0.10	300
3,500	0.20	700
4,000	0.40	1,600
4,500	0.20	900
5,000	0.10	500
	1.00	4,000

Product Y

NPV ($)	Probability	Expected value ($)
2,000	0.05	100
3,000	0.10	300
4,000	0.40	1,600
5,000	0.25	1,250
6,000	0.20	1,200
	1.00	4,450

Using an expected value approach the company's decision would be to produce product Y. However, let's consider the standard deviation calculations for each product:

Product X

NPV Deviation from expected value	Squared deviation	Probability	Weighted amount ($)
3,000 – 4,000 = –1,000	1,000,000	0.10	100,000
3,500 – 4,000 = –500	250,000	0.20	50,000
4,000 – 4,000 = 0	0	0.40	0
4,500 – 4,000 = 500	250,000	0.20	50,000
5,000 – 4,000 = 1,000	1,000,000	0.10	100,000
Sum of weighted squared deviation			300,000
Standard deviation			547.72
Expected value			4,000

Product Y

NPV Deviation from expected value	Squared deviation	Probability	Weighted amount ($)
2,000 − 4,450 = −2,450	6,002,500	0.05	300,125
3,000 − 4,450 = −1,450	2,102,500	0.10	210,250
4,000 − 4,450 = −450	202,500	0.40	81,000
5,000 − 4,450 = 550	302,500	0.25	75,625
6,000 − 4,450 = 1,550	2,402,500	0.20	480,500

Sum of weighted squared deviation	1,147,500
Standard deviation	1,071.21
Expected value	4,450

The expected net present value for each product gives us an average value based upon the probability associated with each possible profit outcome. If net present value is used for decision-making, then on that basis Product Y would be produced as it yields the highest return.

However, the net present value for each product does not indicate the range of profits that may result. By calculating the standard deviation, this allows us to identify a range of values that could occur for the profit for each product. Product Y has a higher standard deviation than Product X and is therefore more risky. There is not a significant difference in net present value for each of the products. However, Product X is less risky than Product Y and therefore the final selection will depend on the risk attitude of the company.

The coefficient of variation

If we have two probability distributions with different expected values their standard deviations are not directly comparable.

We can overcome this problem by using the coefficient of variation (the standard deviation divided by the expected value) which measures the relative size of the risk.

For example, the standard deviation of the numbers 2, 7 and 9 is 2.94. The mean is 6 {(2 + 7 + 9)/3}. The standard deviation is calculated by taking the squares of the three deviations from the mean (16 + 1 + 9 = 26) and then calculating the square root of their average ($\sqrt{(26/3)}$ = 2.94).

In this case, equal weighting is given to the three figures. The coefficient of variation is the standard deviation of the series divided by its mean which is 0.49 in this case (2.94/6).

The standard deviation of a range of numbers gives a measure of the associated level of uncertainty. The measure is an absolute one and in order to allow comparison of two different series where the mean values of the two differ significantly, then the coefficient of variation is used.

Expected values, standard deviations or coefficient of variations are used to summarise the outcomes from alternative courses of action. However, it must be remembered that they do not provide all the relevant information to the decision maker.

The probability distribution will provide the decision maker with all of the information they require. It would be appropriate to use expected values, standard deviations or coefficient of variations for decision making when there are a large number of alternatives to consider i.e. where it is not practical to consider the probability distributions for each alternative.

Example 5: Marin Ltd standard deviation

Marin Ltd is considering investing in one of the following projects.

Project	Expected value $000	Standard deviation $000
A	850	500
B	1,200	480
C	150	200
D	660	640

It wishes to select the project with the lowest risk factor (coefficient of variation). Identify which project should it select:

A Project A

B Project B

C Project C

D Project D

7 Monte Carlo Simulation

Monte Carlo Simulation is a computerised system that extends sensitivity analysis. Simulation is a modelling technique that shows the effect of more than one variable changing at the same time.

It is often used in capital investment appraisal.

The Monte Carlo simulation method uses random numbers and probability statistics. It can include all random events that might affect the success or failure of a proposed project – for example, changes in material prices, labour rates, market size, selling price, investment costs or inflation.

The model identifies key variables in a decision: costs and revenues, say. Random numbers are then assigned to each variable in a proportion in accordance with the underlying probability distribution. For example, if the most likely outcomes are thought to have a 50% probability, optimistic outcomes a 30% probability and pessimistic outcomes a 20% probability, random numbers, representing those attributes, can be assigned to costs and revenues in those proportions.

A powerful computer is then used to repeat the decision repeatedly (thousands or even millions of times), until the outcome starts to 'settle down' and give management a view of the likely range and level of outcomes. Depending on the management's attitude to risk, a more informed decision can be taken.

This helps to model what is essentially a one-off decision using many possible repetitions. It is only of any real value, however, if the underlying probability distribution can be estimated with some degree of confidence.

Monte Carlo Illustration 5 – MP Organisation

The MP Organisation is an independent film production company. It has a number of potential films that it is considering producing, one of which is the subject of a management meeting next week. The film which has been code named CA45 is a thriller based on a novel by a well-respected author.

The expected revenues from the film have been estimated as follows: there is a 30% chance it may generate total sales of $254,000; 50% chance sales may reach $318,000 and 20% chance they may reach $382,000.

Expected costs (advertising, promotion and marketing) have also been estimated as follows: there is a 20% chance they will reach approximately $248,000; 60% chance they may get to $260,000 and 20% chance of totalling $272,000.

In a Monte Carlo simulation, these revenues and costs could have random numbers assigned to them:

Sales Revenue	Probability	Assign Random Numbers (assume integers)
$254,000	0.30	00 – 29
$318,000	0.50	30 – 79
$382,000	0.20	80 – 99
Costs		
$248,000	0.20	00 – 19
$260,000	0.60	20 – 79
$272,000	0.20	80 – 99

A computer could generate 20-digit random numbers such as 98125602386617556398. These would then be matched to the random numbers assigned to each probability and values assigned to 'Sales Revenues' and 'Costs' based on this. The random numbers generated give 5 possible outcomes in our example:

Random number	Sales revenue in $000	Random Number	Costs in $000	Profit
98	382	12	248	134
56	318	02	248	70
38	318	66	260	58
17	254	55	260	(6)
63	318	98	272	46

8 Value at Risk (VaR)

Value at risk (VaR) is a measure of how the market value of an asset or of a portfolio of assets is likely to decrease over a certain time, the **holding period** (usually one to ten days), under 'normal' market conditions.

VaR is measured by using normal distribution theory. It is typically used by investment banks to measure the market risk of their asset portfolios.

VaR = amount at risk to be lost from an investment under usual conditions over a given holding period, at a particular 'confidence level'.

Confidence levels are usually set at 95% or 99%. For example, for a 95% confidence level, the VaR will give the amount that has a 5% chance of being lost.

Illustration 6

A bank has estimated that the expected value of its portfolio in two weeks' time will be $50 million, with a standard deviation of $4.85 million.

Required:

Using a 95% confidence level, identify the value at risk.

Solution

A 95% confidence level will identify the reduced value of the portfolio that has a 5% chance of occurring.

From the normal distribution tables, 1.65 is the normal distribution value for a one-tailed 5% probability level. Since the value is below the mean, − 1.65 will be needed.

$z = (x − \mu)/\sigma$

$(x − 50)/4.85 = −1.65$

$x = (−1.65 \times 4.85) + 50 = 42$

There is thus a 5% probability that the portfolio value will fall to $42 million or below.

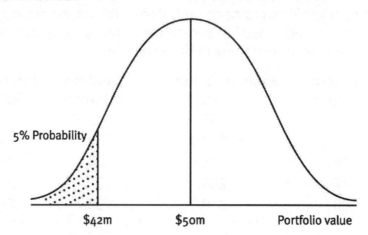

5% Probability

$42m $50m   Portfolio value

A bank can try to control the risk in its asset portfolio by setting target maximum limits for value at risk over different time periods (one day, one week, one month, three months, and so on).

Link between Monte Carlo Simulation and VaR

In the above Illustration, the expected portfolio value in two weeks' time was presented as a normal distribution with a mean of $50m.

This distribution may well have been created by running a Monte Carlo simulation on the likely outcome over the next two weeks.

Alternatively, the future expected value may have been forecasted by using historical data.

Example 6: Value at risk

A bank has estimated that the expected value of its portfolio in 10 days' time will be $30 million, with a standard deviation of $3.29 million.

Required:

Using a 99% confidence level, identify the value at risk.

9   Pay off tables and decision criteria

When evaluating alternative courses of action, management's decision will often depend upon their attitude towards the risk. To consider the risk borne by each alternative it is necessary to consider ALL the different possible profits/losses that may arise. A pay off table is simply a table that illustrates all possible profits/losses.

Illustration 7 – Two way data tables

Two way data tables are used to represent inter-related data in an easy to understand manner.

For example, consider a company who are unsure about both selling price and variable cost. They believe that selling price may be either $40 or $50 depending on differing market conditions, and that variable production cost will be either $20 or $30 depending on wage negotiations currently taking place. The company has therefore got a number of potential contributions per unit that could be represented in a two way table as follows:

		Selling price	
		$40	$50
Variable production cost			
$20		$20	$30
$30		$10	$20

A user can interpret the table quickly and easy. It can be seen, for example, that if selling price is $40 and variable production costs are $30, then the contribution per unit will be $10.

Two way data tables can be expanded to calculate expected contribution from different volume levels. This will be explored further in the following illustration.

Illustration 8

Geoffrey Ramsbottom runs a kitchen that provides food for various canteens throughout a large organisation. A particular salad is sold to the canteen for $10 and costs $8 to prepare. Therefore, the contribution per salad is $2.

Based upon past demands, it is expected that, during the 250-day working year, the canteens will require the following daily quantities:

On 25 days of the year	40 salads
On 50 days of the year	50 salads
On 100 days of the year	60 salads
On 75 days	70 salads

Total 250 days

The kitchen must prepare the salad in batches of 10 meals and it has to decide how many it will supply for each day of the forthcoming year.

Constructing a pay-off table:

- If 40 salads will be required on 25 days of a 250-day year, the probability that demand = 40 salads is:

  P(Demand of 40) = 25 days ÷ 250 days

  P(Demand of 40) = 0.1

- Likewise, P(Demand of 50) = 0.20; P(Demand of 60 = 0.4) and P (Demand of 70 = 0.30).

- Now let's look at the different values of profit or losses depending on how many salads are supplied and sold. For example, if we supply 40 salads and all are sold, our profits amount to 40 × $2 = 80.

- If however we supply 50 salads but only 40 are sold, our profits will amount to 40 × $2 – (10 unsold salads × $8 unit cost) = 0.

- Note too that there is an upper limit to the potential profit in some instances. If, for example, we supply 60 salads then the maximum we can sell is 60 salads with a profit of $2 per unit (and $120 overall). If demand reaches 70 salads we can still only sell 60 salads and therefore the maximum profit we can make from supplying 60 salads is $120.

Solution

The payoff table would appear as follows:

| | | Probability | Daily supply | | | |
			40 salads	50 salads	60 salads	70 salads
	40 Salads	0.10	$80	$0	($80)	($160)
	50 Salads	0.20	$80	$100	$20	($60)
Daily demand	60 Salads	0.40	$80	$100	$120	$40
	70 Salads	0.30	$80	$100	$20	$140

This could then be used to determine the expected value from each daily supply level:

EV (of supplying 40 salads) = 0.10(80) + 0.20(80) + 0.40(80) + 0.30(80) = 80

EV (of supplying 50 salads) = 0.10(0) + 0.20(100) + 0.40(100) + 0.30 (100) = 90

EV (of supplying 60 salads) = 0.10(–80) + 0.20(20) + 0.40(120) + 0.30 (120) = 80

EV (of supplying 70 salads) = 0.10(–160) + 0.20(–60) + 0.40(40) + 0.30 (140) = 30

On the basis of expected values, the best strategy would be to supply 50 salads and gain an EV of 90.

10 Maximax, maximin and minimax regret

When probabilities are not available, there are still tools available for incorporating uncertainty into decision making.

Maximax

 The maximax rule involves selecting the alternative that maximises the maximum pay-off achievable.

This approach would be suitable for an optimist who seeks to achieve the best results if the best happens.

 Illustration 9 – The 'Maximax' rule

Let's apply the maximax rule to the previous illustration on Geoffrey Ramsbottom

Geoffrey Ramsbottom's table looks as follows:

| | | Probability | Daily supply | | | |
			40 salads	50 salads	60 salads	70 salads
	40 Salads	0.10	$80	$0	($80)	($160)
	50 Salads	0.20	$80	$100	$20	($60)
Daily demand	60 Salads	0.40	$80	$100	$120	$40
	70 Salads	0.30	$80	$100	$120	$140

The manager who employs the maximax criterion is assuming that whatever action is taken, the best will happen; he/she is a risk-taker.

Here, the highest maximum possible pay-off is $140. We should therefore decide to supply 70 salads a day.

Example 7: Product Fishy – Maximax

Product 'Fishy' is a highly perishable commodity which can be sold on the retail market for $20 per case, or for animal food at $1 per case. 'Fishy' costs $10 per case from the wholesale market, and is only suitable for sale at the retail market for up to 24 hours after purchase. Orders for 'Fishy' must be placed in advance each day.

Vincent, a market stall owner, has kept the following records of sales of the 'Fishy' over the past 50 days, and correctly set up the following payoff table of his profits:

| | **Supply of cases** | | |
Daily demand	10 cases	20 cases	30 cases
10 cases	$100	$10	($80)
20 cases	$100	$200	$110
30 cases	$100	$200	$300

On the basis of using the maximax criteria, Vincent should supply _____ cases of 'Fishy'.

Maximin

The maximin rule involves selecting the alternative that maximises the minimum pay-off achievable.

This approach would be appropriate for a pessimist who seeks to achieve the best results if the worst happens.

Illustration 10 – The 'Maximum' rule

Geoffrey Ramsbottom's table looks as follows:

| | | Probability | **Daily supply** | | | |
			40 salads	50 salads	60 salads	70 salads
	40 Salads	0.10	$80	$0	($80)	($160)
	50 Salads	0.20	$80	$100	$20	($60)
Daily demand	60 Salads	0.40	$80	$100	$120	$40
	70 Salads	0.30	$80	$100	$120	$140

If we decide to supply 40 salads, the minimum pay-off is $80.

If we decide to supply 50 salads, the minimum pay-off is $0.

If we decide to supply 60 salads, the minimum pay-off is ($80).

If we decide to supply 70 salads, the minimum pay-off is ($160).

The highest minimum payoff arises from supplying 40 salads.

Example 8: Product Fishy – Maximin

Product 'Fishy' is a highly perishable commodity which can be sold on the retail market for $20 per case, or for animal food at $1 per case. 'Fishy' costs $10 per case from the wholesale market, and is only suitable for sale at the retail market for up to 24 hours after purchase. Orders for 'Fishy' must be placed in advance each day.

Vincent, a market stall owner, has kept the following records of sales of the 'Fishy' over the past 50 days, and correctly set up the following payoff table of his profits:

Daily demand	Supply of cases		
	10 cases	20 cases	30 cases
10 cases	$100	$10	($80)
20 cases	$100	$200	$110
30 cases	$100	$200	$300

On the basis of using the maximin criteria, Vincent should supply _____ cases of 'Fishy'.

The minimax regret rule

The minimax regret strategy is the one that minimises the maximum regret. It is useful when probabilities for outcomes are not available or where the investor is risk averse and wants to avoid making a bad decision. Essentially, this is the technique for a 'sore loser' who does not wish to make the wrong decision.

'Regret' in this context is defined as the opportunity loss through having made the wrong decision.

Illustration 11 – The 'Minimax Regret' rule

Following up from the pay-off table example, Geoffrey Ramsbottom's table looks as follows:

		Probability	Daily supply 40 salads	50 salads	60 salads	70 salads
	40 Salads	0.10	$80	$0	($80)	($160)
	50 Salads	0.20	$80	$100	$20	($60)
Daily demand	60 Salads	0.40	$80	$100	$120	$40
	70 Salads	0.30	$80	$100	$120	$140

If the minimax regret rule is applied to decide how many salads should be made each day, we need to calculate the 'regrets'. This means we need to find the biggest pay-off for each demand row, then subtract all other numbers in this row from the largest number.

For example, if the demand is 40 salads, we will make a maximum profit of $80 if they all sell. If we had decided to supply 50 salads, we would achieve a nil profit. The difference, or 'regret' between that nil profit and the maximum of $80 achievable for that row is $80.

Regrets can be tabulated as follows:

		Daily supply 40 salads	50 salads	60 salads	70 salads
	40 Salads	$0	$80	$160	$240
Daily demand	50 Salads	$20	$0	$80	$160
	60 Salads	$40	$20	$0	$80
	70 Salads	$60	$40	$20	$0

Conclusion

If we decide to supply 40 salads, the maximum regret is $60. If we decide to supply 50 salads, the maximum regret is $80. For 60 salads, the maximum regret is $160, and $240 for 70 salads. A manager employing the minimax regret criterion would want to minimise that maximum regret, and therefore supply 40 salads only.

Example 9: Cement Co Part II

Cement Co is a listed company specialising in the manufacture of cement, a product used in the building industry. The company has been a major player in the construction sector of European country, Q, since its formation in 1987. It is passionate about customer care and proud of its active approach to safety and sustainability (recognising the need to minimise any adverse environmental impact of its operations).

The company operates in a very traditional industry but profits can be volatile. Q's economy has been in recession for the last three years and this has had a direct impact on Cement Co's profitability. Shareholders are concerned about this fall in profit and have expressed their desire for a secure return. Competitors, keen to find ways of increasing profit and market share, in these difficult economic circumstances, have started to increase the level of investment in research and development, ensuring their products anticipate and meet the needs of its customers.

When Q entered recession, many workers left the country in search of more lucrative and secure work. This has had a significant impact on Cement Co which is now facing labour shortages and increased labour costs. At the same time, suppliers have also increased their prices putting further pressure on Cement Co's margins.

The company has found that when weather conditions are good, the demand for cement increases since more building work is able to take place. Last year, the weather was so good, and the demand for cement was so great, that Cement Co was unable to meet demand. Cement Co is now trying to work out the level of cement production for the coming year in order to maximise profits. The company doesn't want to miss out on the opportunity to earn large profits by running out of cement again. However, it doesn't want to be left with large quantities of the product unsold at the end of the year, since it deteriorates quickly and then has to be disposed of. The company has received the following estimates about the probable weather conditions and corresponding demand levels for the coming year:

Weather	Probability	Demand
Good	25%	350,000 bags
Average	45%	280,000 bags
Poor	30%	200,000 bags

Each bag of cement sells for $9 and costs $4 to make. If cement is unsold at the end of the year, it has to be disposed of at a cost of $0.50 per bag.

Cement Co has decided to produce at one of the three levels of production to match forecast demand. It now has to decide which level of cement production to select.

As an incentive to increase profitability a new bonus scheme has just been introduced for a select group of Cement Co's directors. A bonus will be received by each of these directors if annual profit exceeds a challenging target.

Required:

Evaluate the proposed levels of cement production using methods for decision making under risk and uncertainty and assess the suitability of the different methods used.

11 Perfect and imperfect information

In many questions the decision makers receive a forecast of a future outcome (for example a market research group may predict the forthcoming demand for a product). This forecast may turn out to be correct or incorrect. The question often requires the candidate to calculate the value of the forecast.

Perfect information	The forecast of the future outcome is always a correct prediction. If a firm can obtain a 100% accurate prediction they will always be able to undertake the most beneficial course of action for that prediction.
Imperfect information	The forecast is usually correct, but can be incorrect. Imperfect information is not as valuable as perfect information. Imperfect information may be examined in conjunction with Decision Trees (see later in this chapter).

The value of information (either perfect or imperfect) may be calculated as follows:

Expected profit (outcome) WITH the information

minus

Expected profit (outcome) WITHOUT the information

Illustration 12 – The value of information

A new ordering system is being considered, whereby customers must order their salad online the day before. With this new system Mr Ramsbottom will know for certain the daily demand 24 hours in advance. He can adjust production levels on a daily basis. How much is this new system worth to Mr Ramsbottom?

	X	**P**	
Supply = demand	Pay off	Probability	px
40	$80	0.1	8
50	$100	0.2	20
60	$120	0.4	48
70	$140	0.3	42
			———
			118

E.V. with perfect information	= $118
E.V. without perfect information (from the original EV calculation)	= $90
	———
Value of perfect information	$28 per day
	———

12 Decision trees and multi-stage decision problems

A decision tree is a diagrammatic representation of a decision problem, where all possible courses of action are represented, and every possible outcome of each course of action is shown. Decision trees should be used where a problem involves a series of decisions being made and several outcomes arise during the decision-making process. In some instances it may involve the use of joint probabilities – where the outcome of one event depends of the outcome of a preceding event.

 Illustration 13 – Joint probabilities

So far only a very small number of alternatives have been considered in the examples. In practice a greater number of alternative courses of action may exist, uncertainty may be associated with more than one variable and the values of variables may be interdependent, giving rise to many different outcomes.

The following exercise looks at the expected value of a manufacturing decision, where there are three alternative sales volumes, two alternative contributions, and three alternative levels of fixed cost. The number of possible outcomes will be 3 × 2 × 3 = 18.

Example

A company is assessing the desirability of producing a souvenir to celebrate a royal jubilee. The marketing life of the souvenir will be 6 months only. Uncertainty surrounds the likely sales volume and contribution, as well as the fixed costs of the venture. Estimated outcomes and probabilities are:

Units sold	Probability	Cont'n per unit $	Probability	Fixed cost $	Probability
100,000	0.3	7	0.5	400,000	0.2
80,000	0.6	5	0.5	450,000	0.5
60,000	0.1			500,000	0.3
	1.0		1.0		1.0

The next table shows the expected value of the net contribution to be $49,000. Totalling up the joint probabilities for each set of sales shows the project has a 56.5 per cent chance of making a net contribution, a 33 per cent chance of making a loss, and a 10.5 per cent chance of making neither a net contribution nor a loss. (For example, to calculate the probability of making a loss: we can see from the next table that a loss will arise in 7 situations. So if we add the overall probability of this happening we add up the joint probabilities associated with each of these outcomes – 0.150 + 0.090 + 0.025 + 0.015 + 0.010 + 0.025 + 0.015 = 0.33).

Units sold	Cont'n per unit $ $	Total Cont'n $ a	Fixed Cost $ b	Probability	Joint Prob. c	EV of net cont. $ (a-b) x c
100,000	7	700,000	400,000	0.3×0.5×0.2=	0.030	9,000
	7	700,000	450,000	0.3×0.5×0.5=	0.075	18,750
	7	700,000	500,000	0.3×0.5×0.3=	0.045	9,000
	5	500,000	400,000	0.3×0.5×0.2=	0.030	3,000
	5	500,000	450,000	0.3×0.5×0.5=	0.075	3,750
	5	500,000	500,000	0.3×0.5×0.3=	0.045	0
80,000	7	560,000	400,000	0.6×0.5×0.2=	0.060	9,600
	7	560,000	450,000	0.6×0.5×0.5=	0.150	16,500
	7	560,000	500,000	0.6×0.5×0.3=	0.090	5,400
	5	400,000	400,000	0.6×0.5×0.2=	0.060	0
	5	400,000	450,000	0.6×0.5×0.5=	0.150	−7,500
	5	400,000	500,000	0.6×0.5×0.3=	0.090	−9,000
60,000	7	420,000	400,000	0.1 ×0.5×0.2=	0.010	200
	7	420,000	450,000	0.1 ×0.5×0.5=	0.025	−750
	7	420,000	500,000	0.1×0.5×0.3=	0.015	−1,200
	5	300,000	400,000	0.1×0.5×0.2=	0.010	−1,000
	5	300,000	450,000	0.1 ×0.5×0.5=	0.025	−3,750
	5	300,000	500,000	0.1 ×0.5×0.3=	0.015	−3,000
			1.0		1.0	49,000

Decisions like this can be quite hard to visualise and it may be more useful to use a decision tree to express the situation.

Three-step method

Step 1: Draw the tree from left to right showing appropriate decisions and events/outcomes.

Symbols to use:

☐ A square is used to represent a decision point. At a decision point the decision maker has a choice of which course of action he wishes to undertake.

◯ A circle is used at a chance outcome point. The branches from here are always subject to probabilities.

Label the tree and relevant cash inflows/outflows (discounted to present values if necessary) and probabilities associated with outcomes.

Step 2: Evaluate the tree from right to left carrying out these two actions:

Calculate an EV at each outcome point.

Choose the best option at each decision point.

Step 3: Recommend a course of action to management.

Illustration 14 – University Decision tree

A university is trying to decide whether or not to advertise a new post-graduate degree programme.

The number of students starting the programme is dependent on economic conditions:

- If conditions are poor, it is expected that the programme will attract 40 students without advertising. There is a 60% chance that economic conditions will be poor.

- If economic conditions are good, it is expected that the programme will attract only 20 students without advertising. There is a 40% chance that economic conditions will be good.

If the programme is advertised and economic conditions are poor, there is a 65% chance that the advertising will stimulate further demand and student numbers will increase to 50. If economic conditions are good there is a 25% chance the advertising will stimulate further demand and numbers will increase to 25 students.

The profit expected, before deducting the cost of advertising of $15,000, at different levels of student numbers are as follows:

Number of students	Profit in $
15	(10,000)
20	15,000
25	40,000
30	65,000
35	90,000
40	115,000
45	140,000
50	165,000

Demonstrate, using a decision tree, whether the programme should be advertised.

Answer – University advertising decision tree

Step 1: Draw the tree from left to right. A **square** is used to represent a decision point (i.e. whether to advertise the programme, or not advertise).

For both options, a **circle** is used to represent a chance point – a poor economic environment, or a good economic environment.

Label the tree and relevant cash inflows/outflows and probabilities associated with outcomes:

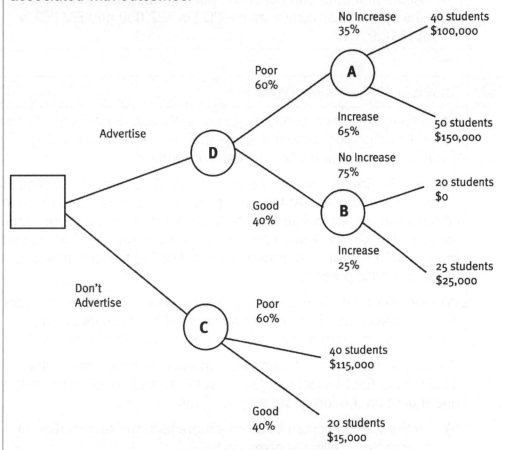

Note: The advertising costs have been deducted where relevant in arriving at the figures used on the tree.

For example, the gain for the top right outcome for 40 students = 115,000 – 15,000 = 100,000

Step 2: Evaluate the tree from right to left carrying out these two actions:

(a) Calculate an Expected Value at each outcome point. Working from top to bottom, we can calculate the EVs as follows:

EV (Outcome Point A) = (35% × $100,000) + (65% × $150,000) = $132,500

EV (Outcome Point B) = (75% × $0) + (25% × $25,000) = $6,250

EV (Outcome Point C) = (60% × $115,000) + (40% × $15,000) = $75,000

EV (Outcome Point D) = (60% × $132,500) + (40% × $6,250) = $82,000

(b)   Choose the best option at each decision point and **recommend** a course of action to management.

At the first (and only) decision point in our tree, we should choose the option to advertise as EV ('D') is $82,000 and EV ('C') is $75,000.

Example 10: Decision Trees

An oil company has recently acquired rights in a certain area to conduct surveys and geological test drillings that may lead to extracting oil where it is found in commercially exploitable quantities.

The area is already considered to have good potential for finding oil in commercial quantities. At the outset the company has the choice to conduct further geological tests or to carry out a drilling programme immediately. On the known conditions, the company estimates that there is a 70% chance of further tests indicating that a significant amount of oil is present.

Whether the tests show the possibility of oil or not, or even if no tests are undertaken at all, the company could still pursue its drilling programme or alternatively consider selling its rights to drill in the area.

Thereafter, however, if it carries out the drilling programme, the likelihood of final success or failure in the search for oil is considered dependent on the foregoing stages. Thus:

(i)   If the tests indicated that oil was present, the expectation of success in drilling is given as 80%.

(ii)   If the tests indicated that there was insufficient oil present, then the expectation of success in drilling is given as 20%.

(iii) If no tests have been carried out at all, the expectation of finding commercially viable quantities of oil is given as 55%.

Costs and revenues have been estimated for all possible outcomes and the net present value of each is given below:

Outcome	Net present value
	$ millions
Geological testing	(10)
Drilling cost	(50)
Success in finding oil	150
Sale of exploitation rights:	
Tests indicate oil is present	65
Tests indicate 'no oil'	15
Without geological tests	40

Required:

(a) Prepare a decision tree diagram to represent the above information.

(b) For the management of the company, calculate its best course of action.

(c) Explain the value of decision trees in providing management with guidance for decision making. Illustrate examples of any situations where you consider their use would be of benefit.

 More on decision trees

Decision trees force the decision maker to consider the logical sequence of events. A complex problem is broken down into smaller, easier-to-handle sections. The financial outcomes and probabilities are shown separately, and the decision tree is 'rolled back' by calculating expected values and making decisions. In the examination ensure that only relevant costs and revenues are considered, and that all cash is expressed in present value terms.

A number of other factors should be taken into account when considering decision tree-type problems:

* *Time value of money.* The time value of money should be incorporated in the calculations if the project is to last for more than one year. The time value of money is discussed in detail later in this text.

- *Assumes risk neutrality.* As mentioned under probability, some decision-makers do not choose options which give the greatest expected value, because they are either risk seekers or risk averse.

- *Sensitivity analysis.* The analysis depends very much on the values of the probabilities in the tree. The values are usually the subjective estimates of the decision-makers, and, no matter how experienced the people involved are, the values must be open to question. Sensitivity analysis can be used to consider 'break-even' positions for each variable – i.e. the value for a variable (such as probability) at which the decision would change. Sensitivity analysis is covered later in this chapter.

- *Oversimplification.* In order to make the tree manageable, the situation has often to be greatly simplified. This makes it appear far more discrete than it really is. In practice, it is much more likely that the outcomes would form a near continuous range of inflows and outflows. This cannot be shown on a decision tree, and so any decision tree usually represents a simplified situation.

Illustration 15 – make vs buy

A manager is considering a make v buy decision based on the following estimates:

	If made in-house	If buy in and re-badge
	$	$
Variable production costs	10	2
External purchase costs	–	6
Ultimate selling price	15	14

Identify the sensitivity of the decision to the external purchase price.

Step 1: What is the original decision?

Comparing contribution figures, the product should be bought in and re-badged:

	If made in-house	If buy in and re-badge
	$	$
Contribution	5	6

Step 2: Calculate the sensitivity (to the external purchase price).

For indifference, the contribution from outsourcing needs to fall to $5 per unit. Thus the external purchase price only needs to increase by $1 per unit (or $1/$6 = 17%).

If the external purchase price rose by more than 17% the original decision would be reversed.

13 Conditional probabilities

Conditional probability is the probability of an event whose calculation is based on the knowledge that some other event has occurred.

The symbol P(A|B) is read as 'the probability of A occurring given that B has already occurred', and we can say that:

P (A and B) = P (A|B) x P (B)

This formula can be rewritten in a variety of ways, depending on what you are trying to find out.

$$P(A \text{ and } B) = P(B|A) \times P(A) \qquad P(A|B) \times P(B) = P(B|A) \times P(A)$$

$$P(A/B) = \frac{P(A \text{ and } B)}{P(B)}$$

$$P(B/A) = \frac{P(B \text{ and } A)}{P(A)}$$

However, this can get a bit mind-boggling. An easier way to deal with this sort of problem is to use what is known as a **contingency table**.

Contingency tables

Contingency tables are created by taking the given probabilities, multiplying by some convenient number, typically 100 or 1,000 (to make the numbers easy to work with), then drawing a table to show the various combinations of factors which may exist.

Illustration 16 – Contingency tables

40% of the output of a factory is produced in workshop A and 60% in workshop B.

Fourteen out of every 1,000 components from A are defective and six out of every 1,000 components from B are defective.

After the outputs from A and B have been thoroughly mixed, a component drawn at random is found to be defective. What is the probability that it came from workshop B?

Solution

The problem will be solved by drawing a contingency table, showing defective and non-defective components and output from workshops A and B.

Consider 10,000 components. We know that of these 4,000 (40%) will be from workshop A and 6,000 (60%) from workshop B.

	Workshop A	Workshop B	Total
Defective			
Non-defective			
	___	___	___
Total	4,000	6,000	10,000

Of the 4,000 from workshop A, 14/1,000 – that is 56 – will be defective, and from workshop B 6/1,000 – that is 36 – will be defective. Hence, the table can be completed so far:

	Workshop A	Workshop B	Total
Defective	56	36	
Non-defective			
	___	___	___
Total	4,000	6,000	10,000

All the remaining figures can be completed as balancing figures, and the final contingency table looks like this:

	Workshop A	Workshop B	Total
Defective	56	36	92
Non-defective	3,944	5,964	9,908
	___	___	___
Total	4,000	6,000	10,000

The question was: what is the probability that a component came from workshop B, given that it is defective?

Given that it is defective, we know that we are dealing with one of the 92 components in the top row of the table. We can see that of these 92 components, 36 came from workshop B.

Hence

$$P(\text{came from workshop B given that it is defective}) = \frac{36}{92}$$

That is 0.39, or 39%.

There are other ways of solving such problems, but most students will find the contingency table method easier, and quicker.

Example 11: Conditional probabilities

30% of the new cars of a particular model are supplied from a factory X, the other 70% from factory Y. 10% of factory X's production has a major fault, 12% of factory Y's production has such a fault.

A purchaser's new car has a major fault: what is the probability that it was made at factory Y?

14 Stress testing

A stress test is a way of analysing a business to consider how well it could cope in difficult conditions. Stress testing is the process of assessing the vulnerability of a position against hypothetical events (a cyberattack, for example).

When a business is doing well, it can be difficult to identify how it would fare if there was a sudden downturn in the economic environment.

Illustration 17 – Bank of England

The Bank of England conducts annual stress tests on each of the major UK based banks.

The stress tests were brought in as a result of the financial crisis in 2008-2009, and the tests are designed to simulate scenarios that are similar or worse than what happened in the financial crisis. Some of the scenarios used in 2018 were:

- Property prices falling by 33%

- Interest rates rising to 4%

- UK GDP falling by almost 5%

The results are then published. If a bank fails the stress test, it has to face the reputational damage, and may be required to reduce dividend payments to shareholders to improve its capital position.

Example 12: Stress testing

A manufacturer is concerned about the potential loss of a major client. The manufacturer has already prepared the following budget for the year:

	$000
Revenue	480
Cost of sales	200
Other operating costs	80
Gross profit	200

The manufacturer wants to stress test the budget for the loss of the major customer who makes up 25% of its total sales. This customer provides a margin of 15% on sales.

What would be the revised budgeted profit if the customer's sales were lost?

A $182,000

B $80,000

C $110,000

D $150,000

Robert Simons, a Harvard business professor, suggested there are 7 questions that directors business should try to answer to check if their business is robust enough. The questions break down into 4 keys areas:

Prioritisation

- Who is your primary customer?

- How do your core values prioritise shareholders, employees, and customers?

Measurement

- What critical performance variables are you tracking?

- What strategic boundaries have you set?

Productivity

- How are you generating creative tension?

- How committed are your employees to helping each other?

Flexibility

- What strategic uncertainties keep you awake at night?

Stress testing – 4 key areas

Prioritisation

Simons' view is that people who work for the organisation cannot be customers, and to refer to any internal people/departments as a 'customer' means the organisation will lose focus on the true purpose.

Once your primary customer is established, the majority of resources should be used to make sure the company is delivering for their needs.

In a similar way, the core values of a business must be clearly defined and statements that list multiple desirable actions don't work. There is no right stakeholder to prioritise, but a company must decide who comes first: the shareholder, the customer, or the employees?

Measurement

There are various well known sayings: 'If it matters, measure it', 'what gets measured gets done', etc. The key is not to have too many measures on any scorecard. The business must identify the key factors that drive performance, and focus on those.

Productivity

The reference to creative tension is unusual, but the idea is that disagreement challenges the norms and can produce different ideas and outcomes. Diverse opinions and ideas lead to new ways of doing business. Idea generation is often associated with a positive outlook, but it can actually be the opposite. A positive outlook may be lead to people insisting that everything will eventually work out. The pessimistic view that 'things aren't working' can often lead to a positive change.

Commitment to mutual help links back to the theory of why organisations exist. Working effectively together enhances productivity. If employees trust they are being treated fairly, greater results are to be achieved.

Flexibility

Finally, as with any control system, flexibility is key. Customer preferences change, technology is moving at an incredible pace and business models require frequent updates.

Stress testing

Who is your primary customer?

M&S have always tried to appeal to a range of age groups, but M&S are struggling to keep pace with all the different clothing options. Shoppers are now confused by their range of brands and don't know what brands are aimed at them. Critics of M&S suggest this is one of their biggest issues, and, in order to turnaround their recent decline, they need to clearly define who they are selling to.

How do your core values prioritise shareholders, employees, and customers?

Shareholders

Many companies state in their mission that their purpose is to maximise shareholder wealth. Examples abound of companies who make reference to only one stakeholder in their mission, a clear prioritisation of shareholders.

Employees

Virgin's Richard Branson believes that the employee should be a company's number one priority. He says a happy and proud employee translates into excellent customer service, and, beyond, to shareholder satisfaction.

Customers

Google's mission statement since it started in 1998 has been "to organise the world's information and make it universally accessible and useful." Serving the end users has been at the heart of what Google do from the day it was founded and is one of the core reasons for the company's success.

What critical performance variables are you tracking?

In performance management, the advice is to focus on a few key metrics.

What strategic boundaries have you set?

Apple are well known using strategic boundaries, in 1998 Steve Jobs reduced the product portfolio by over 70%, so the business could focus on doing a few things very well. From a loss-making company in 1997, Jobs turned Apple into the biggest global brand. He famously said "Focus means saying no to the hundred other good ideas."

How are you generating creative tension?

The matrix structure is an example of how a company can develop creative tension. Having dual management means extra pressure on an employee to deliver. Many people find that pressure can help them perform and if managed well it can help companies succeed, many companies have used the matrix structure successfully (for example, P&G and Kraft).

How committed are your employees to helping each other?

While Henry Ford gets all the credit in all business strategy textbooks and articles, he had a team working with him. Clarence Avery was the lead developer, Peter Martin the head of assembly and Charles Sorensen was the assistant to Peter Martin. All these individuals combined to help create the assembly line that the model T car so famously came from.

What strategic uncertainties keep you awake at night?

When Alan Mulally became the CEO at Ford in 2006, the business was heading towards a $17 billion loss. He implemented a colour coding system for weekly meetings with his executives. As normal green meant good, yellow meant new issues, red meant problems. Mulally couldn't understand why all the charts were green at the first meeting, a company heading for a $17 billion loss could not all be green. One unit head put up a red chart and highlighted an issue he was having in Canada. Mulally applauded the unit head's honesty and then they discovered other areas were having the same issues. Through collaboration they were able to find a solution, and that changed the culture at Ford to one where people shared issues to find solutions.

---

15 Scenario Planning

Forecasts and analysis often focus on the 'most likely' potential future market state. Scenario planning is therefore often employed by organisations in order to force managers to think about other potential future market positions.

In scenario planning (or 'what-if' analysis), the key environmental factors (such as the state of the economy) are identified and the firm then considers how these might change in the future.

Plans are then considered for each of these eventualities.

The number of scenarios to plan for

The most common approach to scenario planning is to create three potential future scenarios:

- The most likely scenario – this reflects the majority of managements' expectations of the future possibilities for the market.

- The best case scenario – this reflects a position where the key environmental factors move in a favourable direction for the organisation (for example, if the product becomes fashionable, the economy improves, competitors fail to react to changing technology etc.).

- The worst case scenario – this reflects a position where the environment turns against the organisation (for example, if there were more entrants into the market or if the economy where to suffer a period of recession).

The organisation can then evaluate how it might react to these changes. Plans should be put in place for all potential scenarios. The organisation should model (I a spreadsheet, for example) how it would react to different scenarios and create key performance indicators or key risk indicators that indicate whether one scenario is becoming more likely than other expected scenarios.

However, many strategists suggest that having three alternatives, and in particular a most likely scenario, can render this analysis meaningless. They suggest that this will narrow managers' focus to this most likely scenario at the expense of the others. They therefore argue that it would be better to have only two potential future scenarios rather than distorting managers' mind-sets with a 'most likely' scenario.

Also, the scenarios should be plausible alternatives rather than a consideration of every potential eventuality that can be created by managers. Scenarios are also likely to consider the culmination (and interrelation) of changes in the environment rather than plan for each one discreetly. For example, it may plan for a change which results in legislation on imports coming together with problems in achieving domestic supplier agreements occurring at the same time rather than examining these separately if separate changes are unlikely to cause business problems.

This approach is particularly useful in environments that are unpredictable or which change quickly and in unexpected ways. But that is not to say that the managers are aiming to predict the unpredictable. The aim here is to help managers become more aware of what the key environmental factors are and how they might influence the organisation in the future.

16 Practice questions

Objective Test Question 1: Calculating an expected value

A company has identified four possible outcomes from a new marketing strategy as follows:

Outcome	Profit ($)	Probability
A	100,000	0.10
B	70,000	0.40
C	50,000	0.30
D	−20,000	0.20

The expected outcome of this strategy is $_____.

Objective Test Question 2: Hofgarten

- Hofgarten Newsagents stocks a weekly magazine which advertises local second-hand goods. Marie, the owner, can:

  - buy the magazines for 15c each

  - sell them at the retail price of 25c

- At the end of each week unsold magazines are obsolete and have no value.

1 Marie estimates a probability distribution for weekly demand which looks like this:

Weekly demand in units	Probability
10	0.20
15	0.55
20	0.25
	————
	1.00
	————

Required:

(i) The expected value of demand is _____ units.

(ii) If Marie is to order a fixed quantity of magazines per week, calculate how many that should be?_____ units.

Assume no seasonal variations in demand.

Objective Test Question 3: Three new products maximax

A company is choosing which of three new products to make (A, B or C) and has calculated likely pay-offs under three possible scenarios (I, II or III), giving the following pay-off table.

Profit (loss) Scenario	Product chosen A	B	C
I	20	80	10
II	40	70	100
III	50	(10)	40

Required:

Using maximax, which product would be chosen?

Objective Test Question 4: Three new products minimax regret

Required:

Using the information from 'Objective Test Question 3' above, apply the minimax regret rule to decide which product should be made.

Objective Test Question 5: Three new products maximin

Required:

Using the information from 'Objective Test Question 3' above, apply the maximin rule to decide which product should be made.

Objective Test Question 6: External consultant

Following on from the data provided in 'Objective Test Question 3' above, the company has made an estimate of the probability of each scenario occurring as follows:

Scenario	Probability
I	20%
II	50%
III	30%

However, an external consultant has some information about each likely scenario and can say with certainty which scenario will arise. Calculate the value of the external consultants' information:

$_____

Objective Test Question 7: Sensitivity analysis

A manager has identified the following two possible outcomes for a process.

Outcome	Probability	Financial implications ($000s)
Poor	0.4	Loss of 20
Good	0.6	Profit of 40

The expected value has been calculated as EV = (0.4 × –20) + (0.6 × 40) = +16. This would suggest that the opportunity should be accepted.

Required:

(a) Suppose the likely loss if results are poor has been underestimated. What level of loss would change the decision? In effect we want a break-even estimate.

(b) Suppose the probability of a loss has been underestimated. What is the break-even probability?

Objective Test Question 8: Imperfect information

Identify the correct description of imperfect information:

A   costs more to collect than its value to the business

B   is available only after preliminary decisions on a business venture have been taken

C   does not take into account all factors affecting a business

D   may contain inaccurate predictions

Objective Test Question 9: Three investments

Three investors are considering the same investments. The net returns from the investments depend on the state of the economy and are illustrated as follows:

State of the economy	Returns from investment			Probability of economic state
	A $	B $	C $	
Good	6,000	14,000	3,000	0.1
Fair	5,000	3,000	5,000	0.4
Poor	4,000	500	8,000	0.5

Details on the attitudes to risk of the three investors is as follows:

- Micah is risk neutral

- Zhang is a risk seeker

- Jill is risk averse and typically follows a minimax regret strategy with her investments.

Calculate which investment would be best suited to each investor's risk attitude.

Objective Test Question 10: CHARITY ORGANISATION

For the past 20 years a charity organisation has held an annual dinner and dance with the primary intention of raising funds.

This year there is concern that an economic recession may adversely affect both the number of people attending the function and the advertising space that will be sold in the programme published for the occasion.

Based on past experience and current prices and quotations, it is expected that the following costs and revenues will apply for the function:

			$
Cost:	Dinner and dance	Hire of premises	700
		Band and entertainers	2,800
		Raffle prizes	800
		Photographer	200
		Food at $12 per person (with a guarantee of 400 persons minimum)	
	Programme:	A fixed cost of $2,000 plus $5 per page	
Revenues:	Dinner and dance	Price of tickets	$20 per person
		Average revenue from:	
		Raffle	$5 per person
		Photographs	$1 per person
	Programme:	Average revenue from advertising	$70 per person

A sub-committee, formed to examine more closely the likely outcome of the function, discovered the following from previous records and accounts:

Number of tickets sold	Number of past occasions
250 to 349	4
350 to 449	6
450 to 549	8
550 to 649	2

Number of programme pages sold	Number of past occasions
24	4
32	8
40	6
48	2

Required:

Calculate the expected value of the profit to be earned from the dinner and dance this year.

Objective Test Question 11: RS Group

The RS Group owns a large store in Ludborough. The store is old-fashioned and profits are declining. Management is considering what to do. There appear to be three possibilities:

1   Shut down and sell the site for $15m.

2   Continue as before with profits declining.

3   Upgrade the store.

The Group has had problems in the past and experience suggests that when stores are upgraded, 60% achieve good results and 40% poor results.

Because of the doubts, management is considering whether to contact a leading market research company to carry out consumer research in Ludborough for $1m. It has been fortunate in obtaining details of the track record of the research company, as follows:

		Actual outcome	
		Good	Poor
Attitude predicted by research	Positive	0.85 *	0.10
	Negative	0.15	0.90

* This means that when the actual results were good the research had predicted this 85% of the time.

If the research indicates a positive attitude, management will consider deluxe upgrading which will generate more profit but will cost $12m, as compared with standard upgrading costing $6m.

If the research indicates a negative attitude, then management will consider standard upgrading compared with shutting down and selling the site.

The time scale for the analysis is 10 years and the following estimates of returns have been made:

With Deluxe upgrading: Good results $40m total present value

Poor results $20m total present value

With Standard upgrading: Good results $25m total present value

Poor results $10m total present value

If operations continue as before, returns over the next 10 years will be $13.03m in present value terms.

Required:

(a) prepare a decision tree to represent the above information.

Note: No discounting is necessary for this question as the values are already expressed in present value terms.

(b) calculate what decisions should be taken.

(c) explain the basis of your analysis.

Objective Test Question 12: X and Y

A company can make either of two new products, X and Y, but not both. The profitability of each product depends on the state of the market, as follows:

Market state	Profit from product		Probability of market state
	X $	Y $	
Good	20,000	17,000	0.2
Fair	15,000	16,000	0.5
Poor	6,000	7,000	0.3

Calculate the expected value of perfect information as to the state of the market.

A $0

B $600

C $800

D $1,000

Objective Test Question 13: Venus department store

The Venus Department Store operates a customer loan facility. If one of its new customers requests a loan then Venus either refuses it, gives a high loan limit, or gives a low loan limit. From a number of years past experience the probability that a new customer makes a full repayment of a loan is known to be 0.95, whilst the probability of non-repayment is 0.05 (these probabilities being independent of the size of loan limit). The average profit in $, per customer made by Venus is given by the following table.

	Loan limit	
	High	Low
Full-repayment	50	20
Non-repayment	−200	−30

Required:

(a) In the past the company has used a selection criterion that is totally arbitrary (i.e. it is not influenced by the customer's ability to repay).

   Prepare a decision tree to represent the information. Calculate the expected value and explain what the management of Venus should do if a new customer requests a loan?

(b) Venus can apply to an agency to evaluate the credit-rating of a customer. This agency would provide a rating for the customer as either a good risk or as a bad risk, this credit-rating being independent of the size of the loan being considered. Analysis of the last 1,000 customer ratings by this agency revealed the following information.

Agency	Type of customer		
Credit rating	Full-repayment	Non-repayment	Total
Good risk	790	10	800
Bad risk	160	40	200
Total	950	50	1,000

   Determine the value of this credit rating to Venus.

(c) The Venus management believe that this first agency is not very good at selecting full-payers and non-payers. It considers contacting a second agency which guarantees perfect information concerning the credit rating of the customers.

   Explain the meaning of the term 'perfect information' in the context of this question.

   Calculate the value of this perfect information.

Objective Test Question 14: Stress testing

An importer has produced the following budget for next month:

	$000
Sales	64
Material costs	(28)
Labour costs	(12)
Overhead costs	(18)
Gross profit	6

The importer wants to stress test the budget for a potential change in currency rates on the products that it imports. A currency change would increase material costs by 10%, only half of which could be passed on to the importers powerful customers.

The revised gross profit for the month would be $_____ (round to the nearest $)

Data Set Question: Two-stage process

A product is manufactured in a two-stage process, the stages being designated A and B.

Each process has two machines, named A1 and A2 for process A, and B1 and B2 for process B.

Each unit of finished product must pass through either one of the two machines in process A, and then through either one of the two machines in process B. (50% go through A1 and 50% through A2. Similarly for B1 and B2.)

How many different ways may a product be manufactured?

The probabilities of a defective product from each machine are as follows: 2% for A1, 6% for A2, 4% for B 1, 2% for B2. The defectives are thrown out as they occur.

What is the probability of a perfect item being produced?

The total production is 10,000 items started every year. The loss on each defective item is $10, and the profit on each item is $80.

The expected net profit is $

Case Study Style Question: Driverless buses

You receive the following email:

From: Sebastian Cohard
To: Financial manager
Subject: Driverless bus investment

Hi,

The board has decided that it would like to move forward with investing in driverless technology as they don't want Menta to be left behind in this potentially significant change to the market. However they are unsure as to the level of investment that should be made, given the risks involved.

The board is trying to decide between three options:
- Invest in a joint venture with Newtech to develop driverless technology by setting up a private company with equal share ownership by the two parties.
- Purchase a majority shareholding in a company (Robobus) that already has the driverless technology.
- Purchase a minority shareholding in a company (Robobus) that already has the driverless technology

The directors of Robobus (which is listed on the stock market) have indicated to us that they would be willing to consider either a majority or minority investment from Menta.

I have estimated the likely net present values of revenues and operating costs, excluding non-cash items such as depreciation, over the next five years for each of the three options. I have also included the capital investment costs on each branch. Our best understanding of industry prospects is that there is a high probability that demand for driverless buses will be slow to take off and a low (20%) probability that demand will be immediately strong.

I have summarised my projections in the form of a decision tree, attached. I made the mistake of giving this to the board without a narrative comment on the issues and now the board believes that we should undertake the majority investment in Robobus because that has an expected net present value of $4.0 million, compared to only $3.9 million if we undertake the joint venture with Newtech and even lower ($2.6m) if we make the minority investment in Robobus.

Please explain to the board how the use of expected values do not fully consider the options available and why it might be more appropriate to ignore it. Use the information given on the decision tree to support your explanation.

Sebastian

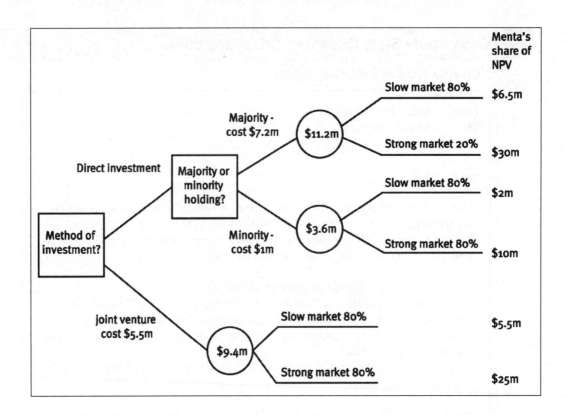

Answers to examples and objective test questions

Example 1: Amador Ltd

(a)

Year		Cash flow $	15% discount rate	Present Value
0	Investment	(120,000)		(120,000)
1–15	Contribution	41,250	5.847	241,189
1–15	Fixed costs	(18,000)	5.847	(105,246)
15	Scrap value	25,000	0.123	3,075
				19,018

Net Present Value = $19,018

(b) (i) If the capital outlay were to rise by more than $19,018 the project would cease to be viable. As a percentage increase this is:

$$\text{Sensitivity margin} = \frac{\$19,018}{\$120,000} \times 100\% = 15.85\%$$

(ii) If the PV of contribution were to fall by more than $19,018 the project would cease to be viable. As a percentage change this is:

$$\text{Sensitivity margin} = \frac{\$19,018}{\$241,189} \times 100\% = 7.89\%$$

(iii) If the PV of fixed costs were to rise by more than $19,018 the project would cease to be viable. As a percentage increase this is:

$$\text{Sensitivity margin} = \frac{\$19,018}{\$105,246} \times 100\% = 18.07\%$$

(c) The break-even point can be calculated as follows:

To remove the current NPV of $19,018, the PV of contribution would have to fall to $222,171 ($241,189 – $19,018). Calculating this as an annual amount can be done using the relevant annuity factor:

Annual cash amount = $222,171 ÷ 5.847 = $37,997

Let 'x' be minimum sales

Annual contribution = $2.75 × = $37,997

Therefore × = 13,817 units

Example 2: Ventura Ltd expected values

The expected sales revenue at a selling price of $10 per unit is $1,040, that is [800 × 0.15] + [1,000 × 0.50] + [1,200 × 0.35]. In preparing forecasts and making decisions management may proceed on the assumption that it can expect sales revenue of $1,040 if it sets a selling price of $10 per unit. The actual outcome of adopting this selling price may be sales revenue that is higher or lower than $1,040. And $1,040 is not even the most likely outcome; the most likely outcome is $1,000, since this has the highest probability.

Example 3: Dralin Distribution Co

Expected annual cash flows are:

Annual cash flow (x)	Probability (p)	PV
50,000	0.3	15,000
100,000	0.5	50,000
150,000	0.2	30,000

NPV calculation:

Time	Cash flow (x)	DF 5%	PV $
0	(460,000)	1	(460,000)
1–5	95,000	4.329	411,255
5	40,000	0.784	31,360
		NPV =	(17,385)

As the NPV is negative, the project should not be undertaken.

An alternative approach would be to calculate three separate NPVs and then combine them, giving the following figures:

Annual cash flow (x)	Probability (p)	NPV $
50,000	0.3	(212,190)
100,000	0.5	4,260
150,000	0.2	220,710
ENPV = 0.3 × (–212,190) + (0.5 × 4,260) + 0.2 × (220,710) =		(17,385)

Even though the NPV is negative these figures show that there is a 70% chance of the project giving a positive NPV. Some investors may consider the project acceptable on this basis.

Example 4: Cement Co Part I

The primary objective of Cement Co, a listed company, will be to maximise shareholder wealth. The directors should, in theory, be acting in the best interests of the shareholders. The shareholders appear to be reasonably risk averse at the moment since they have expressed concern over the fall in profit.

Cement Co is open to a lot of risk and uncertainty:

–   Firstly, Q's economy is in recession which will have a direct impact on Cement Co as house building falls and government contracts are cut.

–   At the same time, the company's costs are increasing due to increases in wages and in suppliers' prices.

–   Cement Co is risking falling behind its competitors who have increased investment in research and development. There is a risk that Cement Co will not be able to meet the needs of its customers as well as its competitors.

–   Cement Co does pride itself on its approach to sustainability and safety. However, the industry is characterised by its negative impact on the environment and poor safety record and therefore it is imperative that Cement Co does not lose focus on achieving their sustainability and safety targets.

–   Finally, volatile weather conditions can have a huge impact on the building industry and on Cement Co's profitability. The weather is clearly something that cannot be controlled but the risk should be appropriately managed.

Directors can take one of three approaches to managing risk:

- Risk averse directors – will assume the worst outcome and will seek to minimise its effect. Some of Cement Co's directors will be keen to take this approach in the hope of securing a satisfactory return for shareholders and securing their positions.

- Risk seeking directors – will assume the best outcome and will seek to maximise its effect. Some of the directors will be risk seeking, hoping to secure an outcome that will maximise profitability and their annual bonus.

- Risk neutral directors – these directors will be interested in the most probable outcome. This would be a sensible approach in situations where the risks remain unaltered and decisions are repeated many times.

Example 5: Marin Ltd standard deviation

Project B

Project	Expected value $000	Standard deviation $000	Coefficient of variation
A	850	500	0.59
B	1,200	480	0.40
C	150	200	1.33
D	660	640	0.97

Example 6: Value at risk

A 99% confidence level will identify the reduced value of the portfolio that has a 1% chance of occurring.

From the normal distribution tables, 2.33 is the normal distribution value for a one-tailed 1% probability level. Since the value is below the mean – 2.33 will be needed.

$z = (x - \mu)/\sigma$

$(x - 30)/3.29 = -2.33$

$x = (-2.33 \times 3.29) + 30 = 22.3$

There is thus a 1% probability that the portfolio value will fall to $22.3 million or below.

Example 7: Product Fishy Maximax

The maximax rule involves selecting the alternative that maximises the maximum pay-off achievable. Vincent would look at the best possible outcome at each supply level, then select the highest one of these.

If Vincent supplies 10 cases, the best possible outcome is a profit of $100.

If Vincent supplies 20 cases, the best possible outcome is a profit of $200.

If Vincent supplies 30 cases, the best possible outcome is a loss of $300.

Vincent would therefore opt for 30 cases when using the maximax criteria.

Example 8: Product Fishy Maximin

The maximin rule involves selecting the alternative that maximises the minimum pay-off achievable. Vincent would look at the worst possible outcome at each supply level, then select the highest one of these.

If Vincent supplies 10 cases, the worst possible outcome is a profit of $100.

If Vincent supplies 20 cases, the worst possible outcome is a profit of $10.

If Vincent supplies 30 cases, the worst possible outcome is a loss of $(80).

Vincent would therefore opt for 10 cases when using the maximin criteria.

Example 9: Cement Co Part II

Before any of the techniques for decision making under risk and uncertainty are applied, it will be necessary to construct a payoff table:

			SUPPLY		
DEMAND	Weather	Probability	350,000	280,000	200,000
			Profit $000	Profit $000	Profit $000
350,000	Good	0.25	1,750 (W1)	1,400	1,000
280,000	Average	0.45	1,085 (W2)	1,400	1,000
200,000	Poor	0.30	325	640	1,000

Workings:

Profit per bag sold in coming year = $9 – $4 = $5 Loss per bag disposed of = $4 + $0.50 = $4.50

(W1) 350,000 × $5 = $1,750,000

(W2) [280,000 × $5] – [70,000 × $(4.50)] = $1,085,000 etc.

We can now evaluate the proposed levels of cement production using four different methods:

Method 1: Expected Values

Use the probabilities provided in order to calculate the expected value of each of the supply levels.

Good: (0.25 × $1,750,000) + (0.45 × $1,085,000) + (0.30 × $325,000) = $1,023,250

Average: (0.7 × $1,400,000) + (0.3 × $640,000) = $1,172,000 Poor: 1 × $1,000,000 = $1,000,000

The expected value of producing 280,000 bags when conditions are average is the highest at $1,172,000, therefore this supply level should be chosen.

Method 2: Maximin

Identify the worst outcome for each level of supply and choose the highest of these worst outcomes.

	SUPPLY		
	350,000	280,000	200,000
	Profit $000	Profit $000	Profit $000
Worst	325	640	1,000

The highest of these is $1,000,000 therefore choose to supply only 200,000 bags to meet poor conditions.

Method 3: Maximax

Identify the best outcome for each level of supply and choose the highest of these best outcomes.

	SUPPLY		
	350,000	**280,000**	**200,000**
	Profit $000	**Profit $000**	**Profit $000**
Best	1,750	1,400	1,000

The highest of these is $1,750,000 therefore choose to supply 350,000 bags to meet good conditions.

Method 4: Minimax Regret

For each level of demand, identify the right decision (the supply level which results in the highest profit) and the regret for the other supply levels. Choose the maximum level of regret at each possible supply level and then choose the level of supply that minimises this maximum regret.

	SUPPLY		
DEMAND	**350,000**	**280,000**	**200,000**
	Regret $000	**Regret $000**	**Regret $000**
350,000	Right decision	350 (W3)	750
280,000	315 (W4)	Right decision	400
200,000	675	360	Right decision
Maximum regret	675	360	750

(W3) Regret (opportunity cost) = $1,750,000 − $1,400,000 = $350,000

(W4) Regret (opportunity cost) = $1,400,000 − $1,085,000 = $315,000

Suitability of the different methods

The **maximin** decision rule looks at the worst possible outcome at each supply level and then selects the highest one of these. It is used when the outcome cannot be assessed with any level of certainty. The decision maker therefore chooses the outcome which is guaranteed to minimise his losses. In the process, he loses out on the opportunity of making big profits. It is often seen as the pessimistic approach to decision-making (assuming that the worst outcome will occur) and is used by decision makers who are risk averse. It can be used for one-off or repeated decisions.

The **expected value** rule calculates the average return that will be made if a decision is repeated again and again. It does this by weighting each of the possible outcomes with their relative probability of occurring. It is the weighted arithmetic mean of the possible outcomes. Since the expected value shows the long run average outcome of a decision which is repeated time and time again, it is a useful decision rule for a risk neutral decision maker. This is because a risk neutral person neither seeks risk nor avoids it; they are happy to accept an average outcome. The problem often is, however, that this rule is often used for decisions that only occur once. In this situation, the actual outcome is unlikely to be close to the long run average. For example, with Cement Co, the closest actual outcome to the expected value of $1,172,000 is the outcome of $1,085,000. This is not too far away from the expected value but many of the others are significantly different.

The **maximax** decision rule looks at the best possible outcome at each supply level and then selects the highest one of these. It is used when the outcome cannot be assessed with any level of certainty. The decision maker therefore chooses the outcome which is guaranteed to maximise his gain. In the process, he risks making a lower profit. It is often seen as an optimistic approach to decision making (assuming the best outcome will occur) and is used by decision makers who are risk seeking. It can be used for one-off or repeated decisions.

The **minimax regret** decision rule looks at the maximum regret (opportunity cost) at each level of supply and aims to choose the level of supply which minimises the maximum regret. In the process, he risks making a lower profit. It is often seen as a technique for a 'sore loser' who doesn't want to make the wrong decision.

Example 10: Decision trees

(a) and (b)

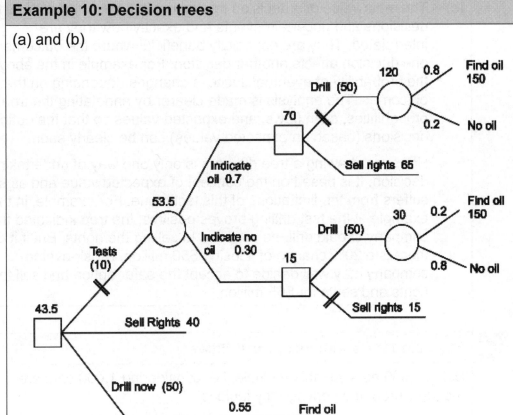

= Path to follow

Advice:

The company should undertake geological tests. If the tests indicate that oil is present then a drilling programme should be carried out. However, if the tests indicate that there is no oil then the company should sell the drilling rights.

This strategy will maximise expected returns at $43.5m.

(c) The main value of a decision tree is that it maps out clearly all the decisions and uncertain events and exactly how they are interrelated. They are especially beneficial where the outcome of one decision affects another decision. For example in the above, the probability of eventual success changes depending on the test outcomes. The analysis is made clearer by annotating the tree with probabilities, cash flows, and expected values so that the optimum decisions (based on expected values) can be clearly seen.

However, drawing a tree diagram is only one way of undertaking a decision. It is based on the concept of expected value and as such suffers from the limitations of this technique. For example, in this example, if the test drilling proves positive, the tree indicated the company should drill, as opposed to selling the rights. But if it does there is a 20% chance of it losing $50 million. A risk-averse company may well decide to accept the safer option and sell the rights and settle for $65 million.

Example 11: Conditional probabilities

Using 1,000 as a suitable multiple, i.e. considering 1,000 cars are manufactured, the contingency table is:

| | Made at factory..... | | Total |
	Factory X	Factory Y	Total
Has major fault	30	84	114
No major fault	270	616	886
Total	300	700	1,000

The question was: what is the probability that a car came from factory Y, given that it has a major fault?

Given that a major fault exists, we know that we are dealing with one of the 114 cars in the top row of the table. We can see that of these 114 cars, 84 came from Factory Y.

Hence P(made at factory Y|major fault exists) = 84/114

= 0.737

Example 12: Stress testing

A

Revised budget

	Original $000	Adjustment	Revised $000
Revenue	480	Less: 25% × 480k = 120k	360
Cost of sales	200	Less: 85% × 120k = 102k	98
Other operating costs	80		80
Gross profit	200		182

Alternatively:

Lost sales = 25% × 480k = 120k

Reduction in profit:= 15% × 120k = 18k

Revised profit = 200k − 18k = 182k

Objective Test Question 1: Calculating an expected value

Expected value calculation

Outcome	Profit ($)	Probability	Profit x Probability ($)
A	100,000	0.10	10,000
B	70,000	0.40	28,000
C	50,000	0.30	15,000
D	−20,000	0.20	− 4,000
Expected value			49,000

Expected profit is $49,000.

Objective Test Question 2: Hofgarten

(i) EV of demand = (10 × 0.20) + (15 × 0.55) + (20 × 0.25) = 15.25 units per week.

(ii) The first step is to set up a decision matrix of possible strategies (numbers bought) and possible demand, as follows:

Outcome	Strategy (number bought)		
(number demanded)	10	15	20
10			
15			
20			

The 'pay-off' from each combination of action and outcome is then computed:

No sale: cost of 15c per magazine.

Sale: profit of 25c – 15c = 10c per magazine

Pay-offs are shown for each combination of strategy and outcome.

Probability	Outcome (number demanded)	Decision (number bought)		
		10	15	20
0.20	10	100	25	(50)
0.55	15	100	150	75
0.25	20	100	150	200
1.00	EV	100c	125c	81.25c

Conclusion: The strategy which gives the highest expected value is to stock 15 magazines each week.

Workings:

(i) If 10 magazines are bought, then 10 are sold no matter how many are demanded and the payoff is always 10 × 10c = 100c.

(ii) If 15 magazines are bought and 10 are demanded, then 10 are sold at a profit of 10 × 10c = 100c, and 5 are scrapped at a loss of 5 × 15c = 75c, making a net profit of 25c.

(iii) The other contributions are similarly calculated.

Objective Test Question 3: Three new products maximax

Using maximax, an optimist would consider the best possible outcome for each product and pick the product with the greatest potential.

Here C would be chosen with a maximum possible gain of 100.

Objective Test Question 4: Three new products minimax regret

In the pay-off matrix above, if the market state had been scenario I:

The correct decision would have been:

B (net income $80)

If A had been chosen pocket instead:	The company would have been out of by $60 (i.e. 80 – 20)
If C had been chosen:	It would have been out of pocket by $70 (i.e. 80 – 10)

- The opportunity loss associated with each product is: A = $60, B = $0, C = $70.

Scenario II and III can be considered in the same way and the results can be summarised in a regret table.

The completed opportunity loss ('regret') table is thus as follows.

State	Decision		
	A	B	C
I	60	0	70
II	60	30	0
III	0	60	10
Maximum regret	60	60	70

The maximum regret value for:

A = $60

B = $60

C = $70

The minimum value of these is $60, hence the minimax regret strategy would be either A or B.

B would probably be adopted because its second-highest regret outcome ($30) is lower than the second-highest for A ($60).

Objective Test Question 5: Three new products maximin

- Using maximin, a pessimist would consider the poorest possible outcome for each product and would ensure that the maximum payoff is achieved if the worst result were to happen.

- Therefore, product A would be chosen resulting in a minimum pay-off of 20 compared to a minimum pay-off of (10) for product B and 10 for product C.

Objective Test Question 6: External consultant

Firstly, we have to calculate the expected value without the information.

EV (A) = 0.2(20) + 0.5(40) + 0.3(50) = 39

EV (B) = 0.2(80) + 0.5(70) + 0.3(−10) = 48

EV (C) = 0.2(10) + 0.5(100) + 0.3(40) = 64

So the company would choose project C, with an expected pay-off of 64.

If the company had perfect information it would act as follows:

Scenario indicated by perfect information	Company's decision*	Pay-off
I	Invest in product B	80
II	Invest in product C	100
III	Invest in product A	50

* this will be based on the highest expected pay-off in that scenario. For example, if scenario I is predicted the company will face a pay-off of 20 from product A, 80 from product B, and 10 from product C. It will therefore decide to invest in product B.

The expected value from these decisions would be:

EV (C) = 0.2(80) + 0.5(100) + 0.3(50) = 81

This is 17 higher than the expected value (64) when the company had no information. Therefore the information has a value of 17.

Objective Test Question 7: Sensitivity analysis

(a)   The EV would have to decrease by $16,000 before the original decision is reversed, i.e. this is the break-even point.

   –   Let the loss be L

   Currently, EV = (0.4 × L) + (0.6 × 40)

   If EV falls to zero:

   EV of 0 = (0.4 × L) + (0.6 × 40)

   0 = 0.4L + 24

   – 24 = 0.4L

   – 24/0.4 = L

   L = – 60

   –   The loss would have to increase from $20,000 to $60,000 before the decision is reversed. This is a 200% increase in the loss.

(b)   The EV would have to decrease by $16,000 before the original decision is reversed, i.e. this is the break-even point.

   –   Let the probability of a loss be P and the probability of a profit be 1 – P.

   Currently, EV = (P × –20) + [(1–p) × 40)]

   If EV falls to zero:

   EV of 0 = (P × –20) + [(1–p) × 40)]

   0 = –20P + 40 –40P

   60P = 40

   P = 40/60

   P = 0.67

   –   The probability of a loss would have to increase to 0.67 from 0.4 before the decision is reversed.

Objective Test Question 8: Imperfect information

D

Perfect information is certain to be right about the future. Imperfect information may predict wrongly.

Objective Test Question 9: Three investments

Micah

As a risk neutral investor Micah will base his decision on the expected value of each investment. These are calculated as follows:

Investment A = ($6,000 × 0.1) + ($5,000 × 0.4) + ($4,000 × 0.5) = $4,600

Investment B = ($14,000 × 0.1) + ($3,000 × 0.4) + ($500 × 0.5) = $2,850

Investment C = ($3,000 × 0.1) + ($5,000 × 0.4) + ($8,000 × 0.5) = $6,300

Micah will therefore choose to invest in Investment C as it has the highest overall expected value.

Zhang

As a risk seeker Zhang will ignore the expected values and probabilities, and she will focus solely on the pay-outs. She will apply the maximax criteria and consider where the highest pay-out might arise. The highest possible return is the $14,000 that arises in a good market state for Investment B. Zhang will therefore choose to invest in Investment B.

Jill

To apply the minimax regret criteria Jill will have to create a regret table as follows:

State of the economy	Regret		
	A $	B $	C $
Good	8,000	0	11,000
Fair	0	2,000	0
Poor	4,000	7,500	0
Maximum regret	8,000	7,500	11,000

Jill will therefore choose to invest in Investment B as it has the lowest maximum regret ($7,500) of the three investments.

Objective Test Question 10: Charity organisation

Revenue per person = $20 + $5 + $1

Number of tickets	Probability	Revenue	Food cost	Net benefit	Prob. × benefit
		$	$	$	$
300	0.2	7,800	(4,800)	3,000	600
400	0.3	10,400	(4,800)	5,600	1,680
500	0.4	13,000	(6,000)	7,000	2,800
600	0.1	15,600	(7,200)	8,400	840
	1.0			Expected value = 5,920	

Number of pages	Probability	Contribution $65 per page	Prob. × contribution
		$	$
24	0.2	1,560	312
32	0.4	2,080	832
40	0.3	2,600	780
48	0.1	3,120	312
	1.0	Expected value = 2,236	

Total contribution	$5,920 + $2,236	= $8,156
Less fixed costs	$2,000 + $700 + $2,800 + $800 + $200	= ($6,500)
Expected profit		$1,656

Objective Test Question 11: RS Group

(a)

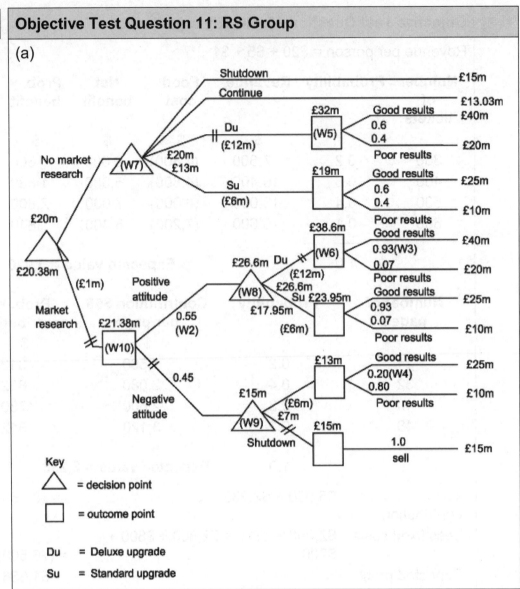

Key

△ = decision point

☐ = outcome point

Du = Deluxe upgrade

Su = Standard upgrade

Workings 2, 3 and 4

A probability tree is the best way of understanding the dependent probabilities given in the question.

The probability of the prediction depends upon whether the results are good or poor.

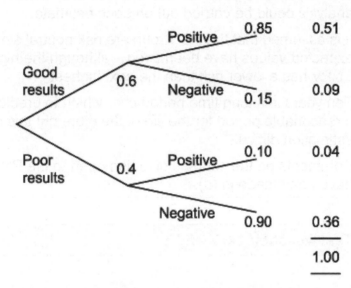

Joint probabilities

(W2) p(positive attitude) = 0.51 + .04 = 0.55

(W3) p(good results/positive attitude) =

$$\frac{\text{p(good results and positive attitude)}}{\text{p(positive attitude)}}$$

$$= \frac{0.09}{0.45} = 0.20$$

(W4) p(good results/negative attitude) = $\dfrac{\text{p(good results and negative attitude}}{\text{p(negative attitude)}}$

(W5) Expected profit = $40m × 0.6 + $20m × 0.4 = $32m

(W6) Expected profit = $40m × 0.93 + $20m × 0.07 = $38.6m

(W7) The deluxe upgrade provides an expected profit of ($32m – $12m) $20m

(W8) Deluxe upgrade profit = $38.6m – $12m = $26.6m

Standard upgrade profit = $23.95 – $6m = $17.95m

∴ Deluxe upgrade is recommended.

(W9) Standard upgrade profit = $7m

Shutdown and sell site = $15m

∴ Shutdown and sell is recommended

(W10) Expected profit = $26.6m × 0.55 + $15m × 0.45 = $21.38m

(b)   In order to maximise expected profit:

Undertake the market research.

   If the attitude is positive upgrade deluxe.

   If the attitude is negative shutdown and sell the site.

(c)   Comment

   (i)   This assumes that all estimates are correct; sensitivity analysis could be carried out on each estimate.

   (ii)   It is assumed that the RS Group are risk neutral since expected values have been used – although the highest ENPV has a lower risk than the next highest.

   (iii)   Ten years is a long time period over which to predict profits – a reasonable period for the life of the store but this makes estimation difficult.

   (iv)   Comments on the courses of action open to the RS Group have been made in (a).

Objective Test Question 12: X and Y

B

Without information, the expected profits are:

Product X: $20,000 × 0.2 + $15,000 × 0.5 + $6,000 × 0.3   = $13,300

Product Y: $17,000 × 0.2 + $16,000 × 0.5 + $7,000 × 0.3   = $13,500

So without information, product Y would be selected.

With perfect information, product X would be selected if the market was good, and product Y in the other two cases. The expected value would then be:

$20,000 × 0.2 + $16,000 × 0.5 + $7,000 × 0.3   = $14,100

The expected value of perfect information is therefore $14,100 – $13,500 = $600

Objective Test Question 13: Venus department store

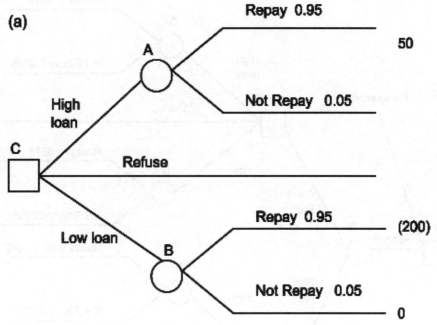

At points A and B calculate Expected Values

At A	EV = (0.95 × 50) + (0.05 × (200))	**= 37.5**
At B	EV = (0.95 × 20) + (0.05 × (30))	**= 17.5**
At C	compare the EVs of $37.5 and $17.5.	

Recommendation; if a customer requests a loan give him/her a high loan limit.

(b)

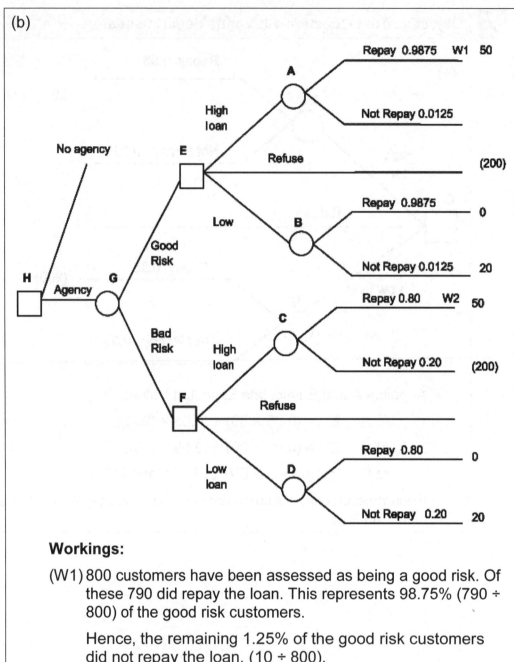

Workings:

(W1) 800 customers have been assessed as being a good risk. Of these 790 did repay the loan. This represents 98.75% (790 ÷ 800) of the good risk customers.

Hence, the remaining 1.25% of the good risk customers did not repay the loan. (10 ÷ 800).

(W2) In a similar way to (W1), 160 out of the 200 bad risk customers did repay the loan, i.e. 80%.

40 out of the 200 bad risk customers did not repay the loan, i.e. 20%.

Expected values

At A	$(0.9875 \times 50) + (0.0125 \times (200))$	=	$46.875
At B	$(0.9875 \times 20) + (0.0125 \times (30))$	=	$19.375
At C	$(0.8 \times 50) + (0.2 \times (200))$	=	0
At D	$(0.8 \times 20) + (0.2 \times (30))$	=	$10.00

Decisions

At E compare A and B. Choose A, i.e. give customers a high loan.

At F compare C and D. Choose D, i.e. give customers a low loan.

Expected values

At G $(0.8 \times 46.875) + (0.2 \times 10.00)$ = $39.5

Decision

At H compare "No agency" (return = $37.50) with the "agency" (return = $39.50).

The information from the agency is expected to increase profits by $2 per rating. This is the value of the information.

(c) Perfect information is a forecast that is 100% accurate. In the context of this problem it would be the credit rating agency providing an accurate forecast of the customer's ability to repay the loan.

If the new agency is approached

Forecast	Decision	Outcome	Profit	Probability	Expected value
Good risk	High loan	Repay	$50	0.95	47.50
Bad risk	Refuse loan	Nothing	$0	0.05	0
					$47.50

The expected return with perfect information	=	$47.50
The expected return with no information	=	($37.50)
Therefore the value of the information is	=	$10.00

Objective Test Question 14: Stress testing

The revised profit for the month would be $4,600

	Original	Adjustment	Revised
	$000		$
Sales	64	+ (30,800 – 28,000)/2	65,400
Material costs	(28)	× 110%	(30,800)
Labour costs	(12)		(12,000)
Overhead costs	(18)		(18,000)
Gross profit	6		4,600

Data Set Question: Two-stage process

The product can be manufactured in **four** mutually exclusive ways:

(i)   Through A1, then B1

(ii)   Through A1, then B2

(iii) Through A2, then B1

(iv)   Through A2, then B2

The probability of a perfect item being produced can be quickly solved with contingency tables. The first three columns are completed as illustrated previously, then the probabilities of producing a perfect item by each method are extracted and multiplied.

Contingency table	A1	A2	Total	Manufacturing method A1B1	A1B2	A2B1	A2B2
Defective (2%, 6%)	10	30	40				
Perfect	490	470	960	490/1,000	490/1,000	470/1,000	470/1,000
	500	500	1,000				
	B1	B2	Total				
Defective (2%, 6%)	20	10	30				
Perfect	480	490	970	480/1,000	490/1,000	480/1,000	490/1,000
	500	500	1,000				
Probability of a perfect item (e.g. 490/1,000 × 480/1,000)				0.2352	0.2401	0.2256	0.2303

Therefore, P (Perfect item) = P(A1 B1 or A1 B2 or A2B1 or A2B2) = P(A1 B1) + P(A1 B2) + P(A2B1) + P(A2B2)

= 0.2352 + 0.2401 + 0.2256 + 0.2303

= 0.9312

Since the total production is 10,000 items pa, the expected number of perfect items is 0.9312 × 10,000 = 9,312.

The profit on each of these is £80, therefore the expected profit on the perfect items is 9,312 × $80 = $744,960.

P(perfect item) = 0.9312, and so P(defective item) = 1 − 0.9312 = 0.0688.

Therefore, expected number of defects is 0.0688 × 10,000 = 688. The loss on each of these is $10, therefore the expected loss on the defective items is 688 × $10 = $6,880.

The expected net profit = $744,960 − $6,880 = **$738,080**.

This is the average profit that the company might expect to make per annum.

Case Study Style Question: Driverless buses

To: Sebastian Cohard   **From:** Financial Manager

Date: Today   **Subject:** Driverless bus investment

Use of expected values

The figures suggest that the majority investment into Robobus has the highest expected value, but expected value adopts a neutral position with regard to the evaluation of risk.

The problem with the assumption of risk neutrality is that the market will either be slow or strong in this one-off scenario. Presuming market predictions are correct then the resulting values are as follows:

In a slow market

Majority investment in Robobus: $6.5m −$7.2m = −$0.7m

Minority investment in Robobus: $2m − $1m = $1m

Joint venture with Newtech: $5.5m − $5.5m = $0

In a strong market

Majority investment in Robobus: $30m − $7.2m = $22.8m

Minority investment in Robobus: $10m − $1m = $9m

Joint venture with Newtech: $25m − $5.5m = $19.5m

This presents a slightly different viewpoint of the investment decision. If the market turns out to be slow for driverless buses, then the majority investment in Robobus is the only one that generates a loss.

In fact, the only one that gives a positive overall NPV is the minority investment, which was the least attractive on the basis of expected values.

The reason that the majority investment in Robobus has such a high expected value is that in a strong market, it outweighs the results of the other two choices.

With the figures given, it is four times more likely that the market will be slow rather than strong and therefore the minority investment would be a wiser choice than the majority one.

The safest choice overall would be to undertake the minority investment as it always gives a positive NPV. The most risky choice would be to undertake the majority investment as its spread of potential NPVs is the largest and in the most likely scenario it produces a negative NPV.

The board's attitude to risk will therefore play a large part in which option they choose to take.

As the decision is not clear cut, it would be worth conducting some sensitivity analyses to provide further information. For instance, it might be worth investigating at what market level the three different choices would break even. Further market research may provide more robust figures to work with.

The board could also potentially use this data to try and reduce the price that would be accepted by Robobus for the majority shareholding.

Financial Manager

Risk Management

Chapter learning objectives

Lead	Component
D2: Risk and Control	Analyse types of risk in the medium term
	(a) Analyse types of risk
	(b) Managing risk

1   Chapter summary

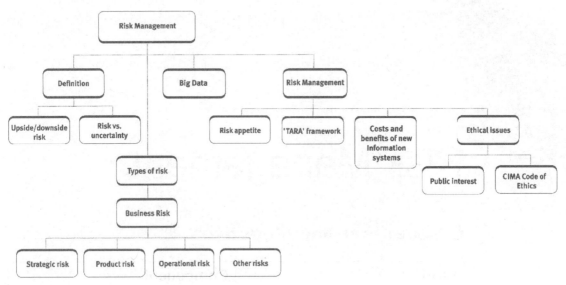

2   What is risk?

As we've seen in previous chapters, 'risk' in business is the chance that future events or results may not be as expected.

Risk is often thought of as purely bad (pure or 'downside' risk), but it must be considered that risk can also be good – the results may be better than expected as well as worse (speculative or 'upside' risk).

 Downside risk examples

The term 'risk' is often associated with the chance of something 'bad' happening, and that a future outcome will be adverse. This type of risk is called '**downside' risk** or **pure risk**, which is a risk involving the possibility of loss, with no chance of gain.

Examples of pure risk are the risk of disruption to business from a severe power cut, or the risk of losses from theft or fraud, the risk of damage to assets from a fire or accident, and risks to the health and safety of employees at work.

Not all risks are pure risks or down-side risks. In many cases, risk is two-way, and actual outcomes might be either better or worse than expected. **Two-way risk** is sometimes called speculative risk. For many business decisions, there is an element of **speculative risk** and management are aware that actual results could be better or worse than forecast.

For example, a new product launch might be more or less successful than planned, and the savings from an investment in labour-saving equipment might be higher or lower than anticipated.

Risk and uncertainty

All businesses face risk such as in the variability of future potential returns. Risk is inherent in a situation whenever an outcome is not inevitable. Risk can be managed: the term "risk" is used where it is possible to assign probabilities to the different possible outcomes.

In contrast, the term "uncertainty" is used where this is not possible. Uncertainty, in contrast to risk, arises from ignorance and a lack of information; uncertainty is uncontrollable. By definition, the future cannot be predicted under conditions of uncertainty because there is insufficient information about what the future outcomes might be or their probabilities of occurrence.

In business, uncertainty might be an element in decision-making. For example, there might be uncertainty about how consumers might respond to a new product or a new technology, or how shareholders might react to a cut in the annual dividend. Uncertainty is reduced by obtaining as much information as possible before making any decision.

 ## 3 Why incur risk?

Businesses must be able to identify the principal sources of risk if they are to be able to assess and measure the risks that the organisation faces.

Risks facing an organisation are those that affect the achievement of its overall objectives, which should be reflected in its strategic aims. Risk should be managed and there should be strategies for dealing with risk.

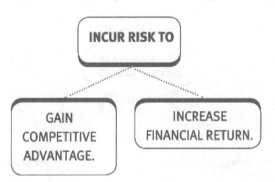

- To generate higher returns a business may have to take more risk in order to be competitive.

- Conversely, not accepting risk tends to make a business less dynamic, and implies a 'follow the leader' strategy.

- Incurring risk also implies that the returns from different activities will be higher – 'benefit' being the return for accepting risk.

- Benefits can be financial – decreased costs, or intangible – better quality information.

- In both cases, these will lead to the business being able to gain competitive advantage.

For some risks there is a market rate of return e.g. quoted equity – where a shareholder invests in a company with the expectation of a certain level of dividend and capital growth. However, for other risks there may not be a market rate of return e.g. technology risk – where a company invests in new software in the hope that it will make their invoice processing more efficient. The important distinction here is that the market compensates for the former type of risk, but might not for the latter.

4 CIMA's risk management cycle

Risk management should be a proactive process that is an integral part of strategic management.

This perspective is summarised in **CIMA's risk management cycle**, illustrated below:

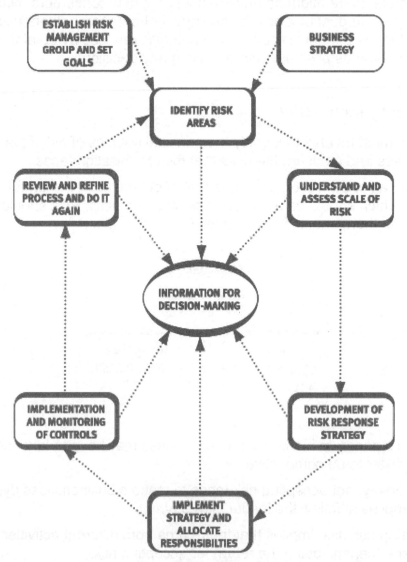

Source: Chartered Institute of Management Accountants (2002), Risk Management: A Guide to Good Practice, CIMA.

5   Identifying and categorising risks

Many organisations categorise risks into different types of risk. The use of risk categories can help with the process of risk identification and assessment.

There is no single system of risk categories. The risk categories used by companies and other organisations differ according to circumstances. Some of the more commonly-used risk categories are described below.

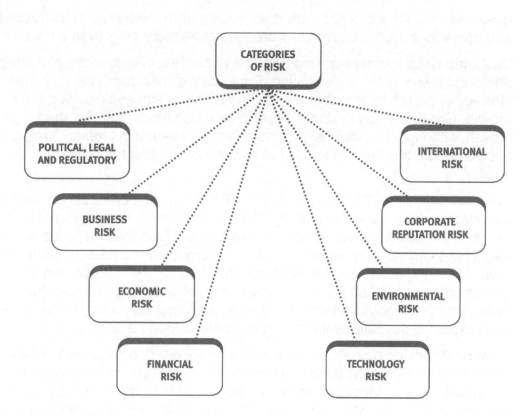

6   Business risk

Business risk is the risk businesses face due to the nature of their operations and products. Some businesses for instance are reliant on a single product or small range of products, or they could be reliant on a small key group of staff. The risks can be considered in different categories:

Strategic risk	Risk that business strategies (e.g. acquisitions/product launches) will fail.
Product risk	Risk of failure of new product launches/loss of interest in existing products.
Commodity price risk	Risk of a rise in commodity prices (e.g. oil).
Product reputation risk	Risk of change in product's reputation or image.
Operational risk	Risk that business operations may be inefficient or business processes may fail.

| Contractual inadequacy risk | Risk that the terms of a contract do not fully cover a business against all potential outcomes. |
| Fraud and malfeasance risk | Malfeasance means doing wrong or committing an offence. Organisations might be exposed to risks of fraud, or of actions by employees that result in an offence or crime. |

Business risks for a company are risks arising from the nature of its business and operations. Some businesses are inherently more risky than others.

Strategic risks are risks arising from the possible consequences of strategic decisions taken by the organisation. For example, one company might pursue a strategy of growth by acquisitions, whilst another might seek slower, organic growth. Growth by acquisition is likely to be much more high-risk than organic growth, although the potential returns might also be much higher. Strategic risks should be identified and assessed at senior management and board of director level.

Product risk is the risk that customers will not buy new products (or services) provided by the organisation, or that the sales demand for current products and services will decline unexpectedly. A new product launched on to the market might fail to achieve the expected volume of sales, or the take-up will be much slower than expected. For example, the demand for 'third generation' (3G) mobile communications services has been much slower to build up than expected by the mobile telephone service providers, due partly to the slower-than-expected development of suitable mobile phone handsets.

Commodity price risk. Businesses might be exposed to risks from unexpected increases (or falls) in the price of a key commodity. Businesses providing commodities, such as oil companies and commodity farmers, are directly affected by price changes. Equally, companies that rely on the use of commodities could be exposed to risks from price changes. For example, airlines are exposed to the risk of increases in fuel prices, particularly when market demand for flights is weak, and so increases in ticket prices for flights are not possible.

Product reputation risk. Some companies rely heavily on brand image and product reputation, and an adverse event could put its reputation (and so future sales) at risk. Risk to a product's reputation could arise from adverse public attitudes to a product or from adverse publicity: this has been evident in Europe with widespread hostility to genetically-modified (GM) foods. There could also be a risk from changes in customer perceptions about the quality of a product. For example, if a car manufacturer announces that it is recalling all new models of a car to rectify a design defect, the reputation of the product and future sales could be affected.

Operational risk refers to potential losses that might arise in business operations. It has been defined broadly as 'the risk of losses resulting from inadequate or failed internal processes, people and systems, or external events' (Basel Committee on Banking Supervision). Operational risks include risks of fraud or employee malfeasance, which are explained in more detail later. Organisations have internal control systems to manage operational risks.

Contractual inadequacy risk may arise where a business has negotiated contracts and other business transactions without adequate consideration of what may happen if things don't go according to plan. For example, a builder may have a fixed completion date to complete the construction of a house. If he does not complete on time, he may have to pay compensation to the house purchaser. Similarly, there is also a risk that the purchaser does not have the funds when payment is due. This risk may be mitigated by having terms in the contract as to what rights he will have in such circumstances. Clearly, if the builder does not consider either or both of these possibilities when agreeing to build the house, then there is an unidentified and unquantified risk of loss.

Fraud and employee malfeasance risk

Malfeasance means doing wrong, or committing an offence or fraud. This is the risk of actions by employees that result in fraud, an offence or crime.

Examples of employee malfeasance include deliberately making false representations about a product or service in order to win a customer order, exposing the organisation to the risk of compensation claims for mis-selling, committing a criminal offence by failing to comply with statutory requirements, such as taking proper measures for the safety and protection of employees or customers.

Risks from illegal activities by employees should be controlled by suitable internal controls, to ensure that employees comply with established policies and procedures.

 7   Risk management

Risk management is defined as **'the process of understanding and managing the risks that the organisation is inevitably subject to in attempting to achieve its corporate objectives'**

CIMA Official Terminology

The traditional view of risk management has been one of protecting the organisation from loss through conformance procedures and hedging techniques – this is about avoiding the **downside** risk.

The new approach to risk management is about taking advantage of the opportunities to increase overall returns within a business – benefiting from the **upside** risk.

The following diagram shows how risk management can reconcile the two perspectives of conformance and performance:

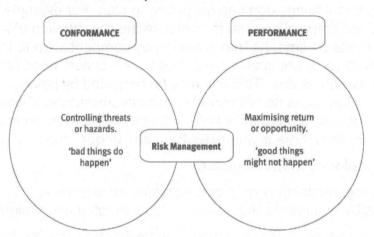

Source: IFAC, Enhancing Shareholder Wealth By Better Managing Risk

Risk management and shareholder value

Ernst and Young have developed a model of shareholder value in which

Shareholder value = Static NPV of existing business model + Value of future growth options

which more simply put is 'the sum of the value of what a company does now and the value of what they could possibly do in the future'.

Good risk management allows businesses to exploit opportunities for future growth while protecting the value already created. By aligning risk management activity to what the shareholders consider vital to the success of the business, the shareholders are assured that what they value is protected.

Ernst and Young identify four stages:

(a) Establish what shareholders value about the company – through talking with the investment community and linking value creation processes to key performance indicators.

(b) Identify the risks around the key shareholder value drivers – the investment community can identify those factors that will influence their valuation of the company. All other risks will also be considered, even if not known by investors.

(c) Determine the preferred treatment for the risks – the investment community can give their views on what actions they would like management to take in relation to the risks. The risk/reward trade-off can be quantified by estimating the change in a company's market valuation if a particular risk treatment was implemented.

(d) Communicate risk treatments to shareholders – shareholders need to be well informed, as a shared vision is important in relation to the inter-related concepts of risk management and shareholder value.

8 Risk management strategy

For many businesses the specific formulation of a risk strategy has been a recent development.

In the past a formal strategy for managing risks would not be made but rather it would be left to individual managers to make assessments of the risks the business faced and exercise judgement on what was a reasonable level of risk.

This has now changed: failure to properly identify and control risks has been identified as a major cause of business failure (take Barings Bank as an example).

A framework for board consideration of risk is shown below:

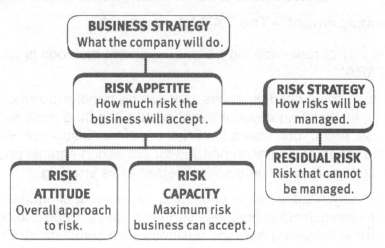

 Risk appetite can be defined as the amount of risk an organisation is willing to accept in pursuit of value. This may be explicit in strategies, policies and procedures, or it may be implicit. It is determined by:

- **risk capacity** – the amount of risk that the organisation can bear, and

- **risk attitude** – the overall approach to risk, in terms of the board being risk averse or risk seeking.

The way that the organisation documents and determines the specific parts of its risk strategy will have to link to the business strategy and objectives.

Overall the risk management strategy is concerned with trying to achieve the required business objectives with the lowest possible chance of failure. The tougher the business objectives, however, the more risks will have to be taken to achieve them.

Residual risk is the risk a business faces after its controls have been considered.

Example 1: Risk

Which of the following statements is true? Select ALL that apply.

- A small company will always have a higher risk appetite than a larger company.

- A company with a divisionalised structure will always seek out risky investments.

- A functional structure limits risk by limiting diversification.

- A large company is more risk averse than a small company.

9 Risk management – The TARA framework

An alternative way of remembering risk management methods is via the mnemonic **'TARA'**:

Transference. In some circumstances, risk can be transferred wholly or in part to a third party, so that if an adverse event occurs, the third party suffers all or most of the loss. A common example of risk transfer is insurance. Businesses arrange a wide range of insurance policies for protection against possible losses. This strategy is also sometimes referred to as **sharing**.

Avoidance. An organisation might choose to avoid a risk altogether. However, since risks are unavoidable in business ventures, they can be avoided only by not investing (or withdrawing from the business area completely). The same applies to not-for-profit organisations: risk is unavoidable in the activities they undertake.

Reduction/mitigation. A third strategy is to reduce the risk, either by limiting exposure in a particular area or attempting to decrease the adverse effects should that risk actually crystallise.

Acceptance. The final strategy is to simply accept that the risk may occur and decide to deal with the consequences in that particular situation. The strategy is appropriate normally where the adverse effect is minimal. For example, there is nearly always a risk of rain; unless the business activity cannot take place when it rains then the risk of rain occurring is not normally insured against.

Risk mapping

A common qualitative way of assessing the significance of risk is to produce a **'risk map'**.

- The map identifies whether a risk will have a significant impact on the organisation and links that into the likelihood of the risk occurring.

- The approach can provide a framework for prioritising risks in the business.

- Risks with a significant impact and a high likelihood of occurrence need more urgent attention than risks with a low impact and low likelihood of occurrence.

- Risks can be plotted on a diagram or map, as shown below; the map can provide a useful framework to determine an appropriate risk response:

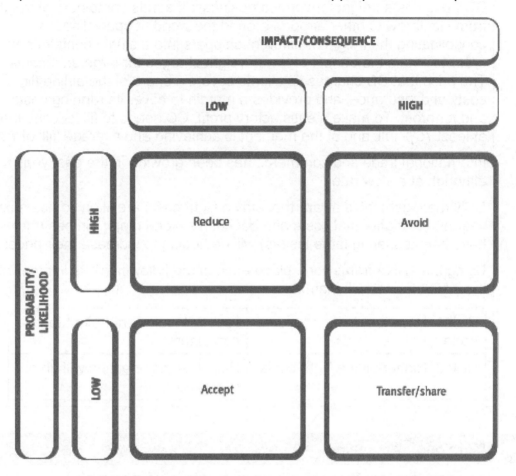

Example 2: Risk Treatment

State whether the following activities would result in a risk retention or risk avoidance strategy:

- An organisation sells a subsidiary in a politically unstable country.

- The Board of a company decides that they have a low risk appetite and therefore reject a potentially profitable contract.

- The organisers of an outdoor sporting event decide that the risk of rain is low, and take no further action regarding the probability of rain occurring.

Example 3: CC Freight

CC Freight is a freight forwarding business. It sends containers of freight from Heathrow to other airports around the world. It specialises in consolidating the freight of different shippers into a single container, in order to obtain the benefit of lower freight charges for large shipments. The price that CC charges its clients covers a share of the airline flight costs and insurance, and provides a margin to cover its running costs and for profit. To make a satisfactory profit, CC needs to fill its containers at least 75% full, and at the moment is achieving and average 'fill' of 78%.

International trade and commerce has been growing in the past year, although at a slow rate.

CC's management is aware that airline flight costs are likely to rise next year due to higher fuel costs and because several major airlines (that have been suffering large losses) will be hoping to increase their prices.

Using the TARA framework, place each of the following risks in a cell of the TARA framework matrix:

Risk 1: Downturn in international trade	Risk 2: Insufficient freight to fill containers
Risk 3: Higher airline flight costs	Risk 4: A major airline will go out of business

More on risk mapping

The potential loss from an adverse outcome is a function of:

- the probability or likelihood that the adverse outcome will occur, and

- the impact of the outcome if it does occur.

When an initial review is carried out to identify and assess risks, the assessment of both probabilities and impact might be based on judgement and experience rather than on a detailed statistical and numerical analysis.

- In an initial analysis, it might be sufficient to categorise the probability of an adverse outcome as 'high', 'medium' or 'low', or even more simply as 'high' or 'low'.

- Similarly, it might be sufficient for the purpose of an initial analysis to assess the consequences or impact of an adverse outcome as 'severe' or 'not severe'.

Each risk can then be plotted on a risk map. A risk map is simply a 2 × 2 table or chart, showing the probabilities for each risk and their potential impact.

Example

The following simple risk map might be prepared for a firm of auditors:

		Impact/consequences	
		Low	**High**
Probability/likelihood	**High**	New audit regulations for the profession	Loss of non-audit work from existing clients
	Low	Increases in salaries above the general rate of inflation	Loss of audit clients within the next two years

Using a risk map

A risk map immediately indicates which risks should be given the highest priority.

- High-probability, high-impact risks should be given the highest priority for management, whether by monitoring or by taking steps to mitigate the risk.

- Low-probability, low-impact risks can probably be accepted by the organisation as within the limits of acceptability.

- High-probability, low-impact risks and low-probability, high-impact risks might be analysed further with a view to deciding the most appropriate strategy for their management.

For each high-probability, high-impact risk, further analysis should be carried out, with a view to:

- estimating the probability of an adverse (or favourable) outcome more accurately, and

- assessing the impact on the organisation of an adverse outcome. This is an area in which the management accountant should be able to contribute by providing suitable and relevant financial information.

10 Ethical issues as sources of risk

A conceptual framework that requires a management accountant to identify, evaluate and address threats to compliance with the fundamental principles, rather than merely comply with a set of specific rules which may be arbitrary is in the **public interest**.

Failing to adhere to these fundamental principles poses a **reputation risk** to companies. Some companies rely heavily on brand image and product reputation, and an adverse event could put its reputation (and so future sales) at risk.

Risk to a product's reputation could arise from adverse public attitudes to a product or from adverse publicity. There could also be a risk from changes in customer perceptions about the quality of a product. A good reputation can be very quickly eroded if companies suffer adverse media comments or are perceived to be untrustworthy. This could arise from issues in environmental performance, social performance, health & safety performance.

CIMA's Code of Ethics has a 'threats and safeguards' approach. If identified threats are other than clearly significant, a management accountant should apply safeguards to eliminate the threats or reduce them to an acceptable level such that compliance with the fundamental principles is not compromised.

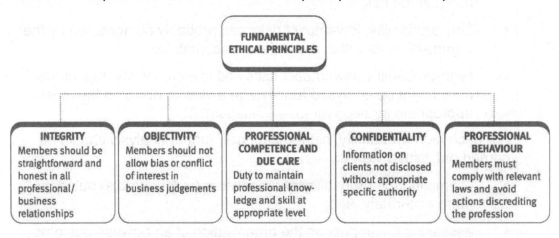

The CIMA Code of Ethics

As Chartered Management Accountants, students throughout the world have a duty to observe the highest standards of conduct and integrity, and to uphold the good standing and reputation of the profession. They must also refrain from any conduct which might discredit the profession. Members and registered students must have regard to these guidelines irrespective of their field of activity, of their contract of employment or of any other professional memberships they may hold.

The Institute promotes the highest ethical and business standards, and encourages its members to be good and responsible professionals. Good ethical behaviour may be above that required by the law. In a highly competitive, complex business world, it is essential that CIMA members sustain their integrity and remember the trust and confidence which is placed on them by whoever relies on their objectivity and professionalism. Members must avoid actions or situations which are inconsistent with their professional obligations. They should also be guided not merely by the terms but by the spirit of this Code.

CIMA members should conduct themselves with courtesy and consideration towards all with whom they have professional dealings and should not behave in a manner which could be considered offensive or discriminatory.

CIMA has adopted a code of ethics based on the IFAC (International Federation of Accountants) code of ethics which was developed with input from CIMA and the global accountancy profession.

The CIMA Code of Ethics is freely available on CIMA 's website – cimaglobal.com > Standards and ethics > Code of ethics.

If a member cannot resolve an ethical issue by following this code or by consulting the ethics support information on CIMA's website, he or she should seek legal advice as to both legal rights and any obligations (s)he may have.

The code of ethics is in three parts:

- Part A establishes the fundamental principles of professional ethics and provides a conceptual framework for applying those principles.

- Parts B and C illustrate how the conceptual framework is to be applied in specific situations:

    - Part B applies to professional accountants in business.

    - Part C applies to professional accountants in public practice.

11 Example threats and safeguards

Ethical threat	Safeguard
Conflict between requirements of the employer and the fundamental principles For example, acting contrary to laws or regulations or against professional or technical standards. (Intimidation threat)	• Obtaining advice from the employer, professional organisation or professional advisor. • The employer providing a formal dispute resolution process. • Legal advice.

Preparation and reporting on information	Accountants need to prepare/report on information fairly, objectively and honestly. However, the accountant may be pressurised to provide misleading information. (Intimidation threat)	• Consultation with superiors in the employing company. • Consultation with those charged with governance. • Consultation with the relevant professional body.
Having sufficient expertise Accountants need to be honest in stating their level of expertise – and not mislead employers by implying they have more expertise than they actually possess. Threats that may result in a lack of expertise include time pressure to carry out a duty, being provided with inadequate information or having insufficient experience.		• Obtaining additional advice/training. • Negotiating more time for duties. • Obtaining assistance from someone with relevant expertise.
Financial interests Situations where an accountant or close family member has financial interests in the employing company. Examples include the accountant being paid a bonus based on the financial statement results which he is preparing, or holding share options in the company. (Self-interest threat)		• Remuneration being determined by other members of management. • Disclosure of relevant interests to those charged with governance. • Consultation with superiors of relevant professional body.
Inducements – receiving offers Refers to incentives being offered to encourage unethical behaviour. Inducements may include gifts, hospitality, preferential treatment or inappropriate appeals to loyalty. Objectivity and/or confidentiality may be threatened by such inducements. (Self-interest threat)		• Do not accept the inducement! • Inform relevant third party such as a senior manager.

Inducements – giving offers	• Do not offer the inducement!
Refers to accountants being pressurised to provide inducements to junior members of staff to influence a decision or obtain confidential information. (Intimidation threat)	
Confidential information	• Disclose information in compliance with the relevant statutory requirements, e.g. money laundering regulations.
Accountants should keep information about their employing organisation confidential unless there is a right or obligation to disclose, or they have received authorisation from their client.	
However, the accountant may be under pressure to disclose this information as a result of legal processes such as anti-money laundering/terrorism – in this situation there is a conflict between confidentiality and the need for disclosure.	
Whistleblowing	• Follow the disclosure requirements of the employer, e.g. report to those responsible for governance. Otherwise disclosure should be based on the assessment of: legal obligations, whether members of the public will be adversely affected, gravity of the matter, likelihood of repetition, reliability of the information and reasons why employer does not want to disclose.
Situations where the accountant needs to consider disclosing information, where ethical rules have been broken.	

12   The public interest

The distinguishing mark of a profession is the acceptance of a responsibility to the public. The accountancy profession's public includes:

- Clients
- Credit providers
- Governments
- Employees
- Employers
- Investors.

The public interest can be defined as that which supports the good of society as a whole, as opposed to what serves the interests of individual members of society, or of specific sectional interest groups.

For an accountant, acting in the public interest is acting for the collective well-being of the community of people and institution that it serves.

The concept of public interest may affect the working of an organisation in a number of ways. The actions of the organisation itself may be harmful to society, for example from excessive pollution or poor treatment of the labour force. The government may then decide, in the public interest, to limit the actions of that organisation for the greater good of society as a whole.

13 Organisations as 'shapers of society'

Businesses can manage their reputational risk either by applying their own positional power, or in more specific terms by changing society for the better in terms of the 'public interest.'

For example, organisations can amend or shape society by the products that are made available. It can be argued that McDonald's has assisted poor eating habits in society overall, by making available cheap 'fast food'.

To be a shaper of society in the public interest, organisations must 'improve' society, however that term is defined. For example, it can be argued that Toyota's research into solar powered cars is seen as an obligation to society of providing pollution free transport rather than continuing to manufacture petrol-burning cars. The act of investment in solar power not only shows the company's commitment to this area, but shapes society by raising the issue of environmental concern.

14 Costs and benefits of information systems

New information systems may be implemented as part of a business' risk strategy. When an organisation sees a possibility for introducing a new information system, an evaluation of the new system should be made to decide whether the potential benefits are sufficient to justify the costs.

The value of information

- Collecting and processing information for use by managers has a cost.

- The value of the information to the business must be greater than the cost. In other words, the benefits of the new IS should be greater than its cost. If this is the case, the new IS is worth implementing.

 Cost-benefit analysis (CBA) can be used to assess the expected costs and benefits of the IS.

The benefit of management information must exceed the cost (**benefit > cost**) of obtaining the information.

The design of management information systems should involve a cost/benefit analysis. A very refined system offers many benefits, but at a cost. The advent of modern IT systems has reduced that cost significantly. However, skilled staff have to be involved in the operation of information systems, and they can be very expensive to hire.

Illustration 1

Production costs in a factory can be reported with varying levels of frequency ranging from daily (365 times per year) to annually (1 time per year). Costs and benefits of reporting tend to move as follows, in response to increasing frequency of reporting.

- **Costs:** Information has to be gathered, collated and reported in proportion to frequency and costs will move in line with this. Experience suggests that some element of diseconomy of scale may set in at high levels of frequency.

- **Benefits:** initially, benefits increase sharply, but this increase starts to tail off. A point may come where 'information overload' sets in, and benefits actually start to decline and even become negative. If managers are overwhelmed with information, then this actually starts to get in the way of the job.

The position may be represented graphically as follows:

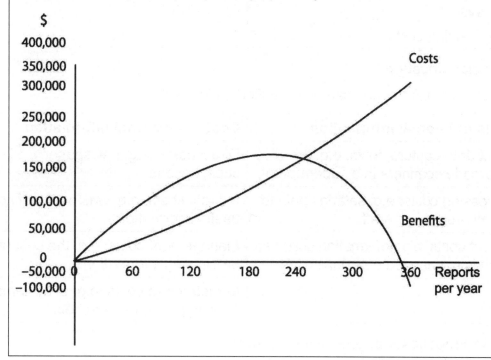

An information system is just like any part of a business operation. It incurs costs and it offers benefits. In designing an information system, the accountant has to find some means of comparing the two for different options and determining which option is optimal. In this sense, system design follows the same practices for investment appraisal and decision making. In the above case it can be seen that net benefits (benefits less costs) are maximised at around 120 reports per year – suggesting an optimal information cycle of about 3 days. The system should be designed to gather, collate and report information at three-day intervals. This is an over-simplified example but it serves to illustrate a general logic which can be applied to all aspects of information system design.

The costs of a new system

Initial costs	Running costs
• Costs to design and develop system if software is bespoke. • Purchase price of software if it is not bespoke. • Purchase cost of new hardware. • Cost of testing and implementation of the new system. • Training costs.	• Cost of labour time to run the system. • Cost of materials, e.g. replacement parts. • Cost of service support, e.g. IT helpdesk.

Cost classification

The costs of information can be classified as follows:

Costs of internal information	Costs of external information
Direct data capture costs, e.g. the cost of barcode scanners in a supermarket.	Direct costs, e.g. newspaper subscriptions.
Processing costs, e.g. salaries paid to payroll processing staff.	Indirect costs, e.g. wasted time finding useful information.
Indirect costs, e.g. information collected which is not needed or is duplicated.	Management costs, e.g. the cost of processing information.
	Infrastructure costs, e.g. of systems enabling internet searches.

The indirect costs of producing information

The most expensive cost of producing information is probably the cost of labour. People are needed to collect data, input data into the system, process the data and then output the resulting information. Throughout this process, the company needs to pay their wages and thus labour becomes part of the cost of producing information. When **new people are hired, a process is changed** or **software** is **upgraded**, then staff will require training.

Training, or re-training, is expensive in terms of:

1   Paying for the trainer

2   Paying wages for people being trained

3   Paying the wages for someone to do the normal work for the person being trained

4   Paying for the costs of the training venue

5   Lost productivity whilst people are being trained

6   Slower productivity whilst people 'learn on the job'.

Other indirect costs of providing information are those that are impossible to predict and quantify, and they may include:

- Loss of staff morale

- Delays caused in other projects of the business

- General dislocation caused by system change

- Upsetting customers from system change

- Incompatibility with other systems

- Unexpected costs of software amendments, tailoring and maintenance

- Cost of failure due to inappropriate systems or faulty implementation.

Further, more 'intangible' indirect costs of producing information include:

- Reduced quality of information, due to information overload

- Poor decision making, due to information overload

- Too many areas to focus on – so issues are not followed up

- Focus on the wrong things – i.e. only on those business areas and targets that are easy to measure and report on.

Benefits of a new Information System

These benefits could include:

- Enhanced efficiency and capacity – e.g. resulting in labour savings.

- Better quality of information – information may be more accurate, complete, understandable and timely.

- Better access to information – e.g. by means of an Intranet.

- Improved sharing of information – e.g. through the creation of a database.

- Improved communication – e.g. through the introduction of an email system.

- Better decision making and customer service.

Although it is sometimes difficult to do so, these benefits should be quantified in monetary terms.

Cost-benefit analysis

A sales director is deciding whether to implement a new computer-based sales system. His department has only a few computers, and his sales people are not computer literate. He is aware that computerised sales forces are able to contact more customers and give a higher quality of service to those customers. They are more able to meet commitments, and can work more efficiently with production and delivery staff.

His financial cost/benefit analysis is shown below:

Costs

New computer equipment:

- 10 network-ready PCs with supporting software @ $2,000 each
- 1 server @ $3,000
- 3 printers @ $1,000 each
- Cabling & Installation @ $4,000
- Sales Support Software @ $10,000

Training costs:

- Computer introduction – 8 people @ $300 each
- Keyboard skills – 8 people @ $300 each
- Sales Support System – 12 people @ $500 each

Other costs:

- Lost time: 40 man days @ $150/day
- Lost sales through disruption: estimate: $10,000
- Lost sales through inefficiency during first months: estimate: $10,000

Total cost: $76,800

Benefits

- Tripling of mail shot capacity: estimate: $30,000/year
- Ability to sustain telesales campaigns: estimate: $15,000/year
- Improved efficiency and reliability of follow-up: estimate: $30,000/year
- Improved customer service and retention: estimate: $20,000/year
- Improved accuracy of customer information: estimate: $5,000/year
- More ability to manage sales effort: $20,000/year

Total Benefit: $120,000/year

15 Risks

Computer systems have unique risk and control issues that need to be addressed by the business. As with any risk factor the company needs to make an assessment of the risks and decide on the appropriate level of control to reduce the risks to an acceptable level.

A risk to a computer system could be anything that prevents the managers getting the information they need from the system at the time that they need it.

 Risks to information processing facilities may arise from:

- Dissatisfied employees might deliberately modify or destroy information in the system.

- A hacker or industrial spy might break into the system.

- Viruses or malicious software could be introduced.

- Accidental mistakes could be made on input to the system.

- Inadequate security of the hardware or data.

- Faults in the hardware system.

Such risks result in the loss of information (or the loss of its integrity or confidentiality), business disruption and a loss of time and money. Costs may be incurred.

 Further detail on risks

Risks to information security can be categorised as follows:

Risks	Description
Risk of hardware theft	This risk might seem fairly obvious, but the theft of computer hardware is common.
Physical damage to hardware and computer media (disks, etc)	Physical damage can be caused by: • malicious damage • poor operating conditions causing damage to equipment and magnetic files • natural disasters, such as fire and flooding.
Damage to data	Data can be damaged by hackers into the system, viruses, program faults in the software and faults in the hardware or data storage media. Software, particularly purpose-written software, can become corrupted. Programs might be altered by a hacker or computer fraudster. Alternatively, a new version of a program might be written and introduced, but contain a serious error that results in the corruption or loss of data on file.

Operational mistakes	Unintentional mistakes can cause damage to data or loss of data; for example, using the wrong version of computer program, or the wrong version of a data file, or deleting data that is still of value.
Fraud and industrial espionage	This can lead to the loss of confidentiality of sensitive information, or the criminal creation of false data and false transactions, or the manipulation of data for personal gain.

Data protection legislation

Some countries give individuals the right to seek compensation against an organisation that holds personal data about them, if they suffer loss through the improper use of that data. In the UK, for example, rights are given to 'data subjects' by General Data Protection Regulation (GDPR). There could be a risk that an organisation will improperly use or communicate personal data about individuals, in breach of the legislation.

Erroneous input

Many information systems, especially those based on transaction processing systems and with large volumes of input transactions, are vulnerable to mistakes in the input data.

- Some input items might be overlooked and omitted. Other transactions might be entered twice.

- There might be errors in the input data, particularly where the data is input by humans rather than by electronic data transfer. For example, in a system relying on input via keyboard and mouse, data accuracy depends on the ability of the operator to input the data without making a mistake.

Where input errors are high, the integrity of the data and information becomes doubtful.

Hacking

Hacking is the gaining of unauthorised access to a computer system. It might be a deliberate attempt to gain access to an organisation's systems and files, to obtain information or to alter data (perhaps fraudulently).

Once hackers have gained access to the system, there are several damaging options available to them. For example, they may:

- gain access to the file that holds all the user ID codes, passwords and authorisations

- discover the method used for generating/authorising passwords

- interfere with the access control system, to provide the hacker with open access to the system

- obtain information which is of potential use to a competitor organisation

- obtain, enter or alter data for a fraudulent purpose

- cause data corruption by the introduction of unauthorised computer programs and processing on to the system (computer viruses)

- alter or delete files.

Viruses

A virus is a piece of software that seeks to infest a computer system, hiding and automatically spreading to other systems if given the opportunity. Most computer viruses have three functions – avoiding detection, reproducing themselves and causing damage. Viruses might be introduced into a computer system directly, or by disk or e-mail attachment.

Viruses include:

- trojans – whilst carrying on one program, secretly carry on another

- worms – these replicate themselves within the systems

- trap doors – undocumented entry points to systems allowing normal controls to be by-passed

- logic bombs – triggered on the occurrence of a certain event

- time bombs – which are triggered on a certain date.

 Risks and benefits of internet and intranet use

Many organisations have intranet systems or use the Internet directly. Using an intranet or the Internet has obvious advantages, but also creates substantial risks.

The advantages of intranets and the Internet

- Employees have ready access to vast sources of external data that would not otherwise be available. Using external information can help to improve the quality of decision making.

- Organisations can advertise their goods and services on a website, and provide other information that helps to promote their image.

- Organisations can use the Internet to purchase goods or supplies, saving time and money. For example, the Internet is used regularly by businesses to purchase standard items such as stationery, and to reserve hotel rooms and purchase travel tickets.

- The Internet/intranet provides a means of operating an e-mail system. Communication by e-mail is fast and should remove the requirement for excessive quantities of paper. Using e-mails might also reduce the non-productive time spent by employees on the telephone.

- Intranets create the opportunity for more flexible organisation of work. For example, employees who are away from the office can access the organisation's IT systems and files through the Internet. Similarly, employees can work from their home but have full access to the organisation's systems.

The disadvantages of intranets and the internet

There are disadvantages with using intranets and the Internet.

- E-mail systems can become inefficient if too many messages are sent and users have to look through large amounts of 'junk mail' to find messages of value.

- E-mails can be disruptive, especially if a prompt appears on an individual's computer screen whenever a new message is received.

- Senders of e-mails often expect an immediate reply to their messages, and a delay in responding can create bad feelings and ill-will.

- Employees might waste too much time looking for information on the Internet, when the value of the information is not worth the time spent looking for it.

- Without suitable controls, employees might spend large amounts of time on the Internet or exchanging e-mails for their personal benefit, rather than in carrying out their work responsibilities.

The greatest problem with using intranets and the Internet, however, is the vulnerability of the organisation's IT systems to:

- unauthorised access by hackers, including industrial spies

- the import of viruses in attachments to e-mail messages and other malicious software.

16 Big Data

There are several definitions of Big Data, the most commonly used referring to large volumes of data beyond the normal processing, storage and analysis capacity of typical database application tools.

Although Big Data does not refer to any specific quantity, the term is often used when speaking about 'petabytes' and 'exabytes' of data.

The definition can be extended to incorporate the types of data involved. Big Data will often include much more than simply financial information. Examples of data which may input into Big Data systems include:

- social network traffic
- web server logs
- traffic flow monitoring
- satellite imagery
- streamed audio content
- banking transactions
- audio downloads
- web pages content
- government documentation
- GPS tracking
- telemetry from consumer and commercially operated vehicles
- financial market data.

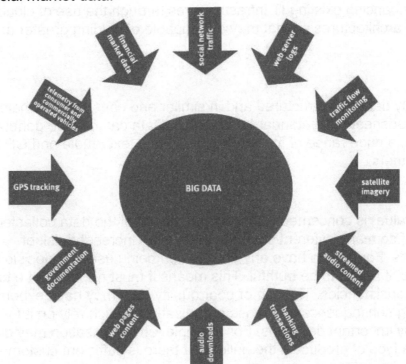

One of the key challenges of dealing with Big Data is to identify repeatable business patterns in this unstructured data, significant quantities of which is in text format. Managing such data can lead to significant business benefits such as greater competitive advantage, improved productivity and increasing levels of innovation.

17 The four V's

The four V's represent the defining characteristics of Big Data:

Velocity

Data is now streaming from sources such as social media sites at a virtually constant rate and current processing servers are unable to cope with this flow and generate meaningful real-time analysis.

Volume

The vast quantities of data generated are a key feature of 'Big Data': more sources of data, and an increase in data generation in the digital age means that the volume of data has increased to a potentially unmanageable level. Data analytics software have enabled very large data sets to be processed; data analytics enable a deeper understanding of customer requirements. For example, organisations can collect large amounts of external data about their customers from customers' use of the internet and social media.

When this data combines with internally generated data (from customer loyalty cards or transactions recorded at shop tills, for example) a more detailed profile of the customer can be established. Within the business, these advances have involved enhancing existing IT infrastructures through the use of cloud computing architectures so that they are capable of holding greater amounts of data.

Variety

Traditionally data was structured and in similar and consistent formats such as Excel spreadsheets and standard databases. Data can now be generated and collected in a huge range of formats including rich text, audio and GPS data amongst others.

Veracity

Veracity (value) is concerned with the truthfulness of the data collected. Because of so many different sources, there is an increased risk of inaccuracies. For data to have any value when being used for decision-making in business, it needs to be truthful. This means it must not present a bias, or contain inconsistencies. The use of poor quality data may have expensive and far reaching consequences for those organisations which rely on it for making strategically important decisions. For example, an organisation may decide to introduce a type of product in the belief that there is sufficient customer demand for it, which in reality may not be the case.

Example 4: Monterey Ltd

The Managing Director of Monterey Ltd has recently started looking at ways of gathering Big Data for her business. She is concerned that some of the sources of data she has chosen are unreliable, and may therefore lead her to inaccurate conclusions.

Which features may be missing for Monterey's Big Data?

A   Variety

B   Volume

C   Veracity

D   Velocity

How is Big Data is used

Consumer facing organisations monitor social media activity to gain insight into customer behaviour and preferences. This source can also be used to identify and engage brand advocates and detractors and assess responsiveness to advertising campaigns and promotions.

Sports teams can use data of past fixtures to tracking tactics, player formations, injuries and results to inform future team strategies.

Manufacturing companies can monitor data from their equipment to determine usage and wear. This allows them to predict the optimal replacement cycle.

Financial Services organisations can use data on customer activity to carefully segment their customer base and therefore accurately target individuals with relevant offers.

Health organisations can monitor patient records and admissions to identify risk of recurring problems and intervene to avoid further hospital involvement.

18   Big Data Management and analytics

Big Data management is the storage, administration and control of vast quantities of both structured and unstructured data.

The main aim of Big Data management is to ensure the data stored is high quality and accessible. Effective Big Data management can leverage large sets of data from a variety of relatively new sources such as social media sites.

New technologies combine traditional data warehouses with Big Data systems in a logical data warehousing architecture.

Big Data analytics is the process of scrutinising Big Data to identify patterns, correlations, relationships and other insights. This information can have a wide reaching effect on the organisation's competitive strategy and marketing campaigns and can therefore have a direct impact on future profitability.

Big Data sources may not fit into currently available data warehouses and Big Data analytics may require more advanced software tools than those commonly used in traditional data mining. Open source technologies such as Hadoop are increasingly utilised to manage the constantly evolving data processing requirements of Big Data.

Hadoop is an open source programming framework which enables the processing of large data sets by utilising multiple servers simultaneously.

19 Big Data: Benefits and risks

Several major business benefits arise from the ability to manage Big Data successfully:

1   Driving innovation by reducing time taken to answer key business questions and therefore make decisions

2   Gaining competitive advantage

3   Improving productivity.

Big Data Benefits: UPS
Delivery company UPS equips its delivery vehicles with sensors which monitor data on speed, direction, braking performance and other mechanical aspects of the vehicle.
Using this data to optimise performance and routes has led to significant improvements, including:
(i)   Over 15 million minutes of idling time were eliminated in one year, saving 103,000 gallons of fuel.
(ii)   1.7 million miles of driving were also eliminated in the same year, saving a further 183,000 gallons of fuel.

However, there are risks associated with Big Data:

1   **Availability of skills** to use Big Data systems, which is compounded by the fact that many of the systems are rapidly developing and support is not always easily and readily available. There is also an increasing need to combine data analysis skills with deep understanding of industry being analysed and this need is not always recognised.

2   **Security of data** is a major concern in the majority of organisations and if the organisation lacks the resource to manage data then there is likely to be a greater risk of leaks and losses.

3   **Data Protection** (GDPR) issues as organisations collect a greater range of data from increasingly personal sources (e.g. Facebook).

It is important to recognise that just because something CAN be measured, this does not necessarily mean it should be. There is a risk that valuable time is spent measuring relationships that have no organisational value.

Big Data Risks: Walmart

It is widely reported that Walmart tracks data on over 60% of adults in the US, including online and in-store purchasing patterns, Twitter interaction and trends, weather reports and major events. The company argues that this gives them the ability to provide a highly personalised customer experience.

Walmart detractors criticise the company's data collection as a breach of human rights and believe the company uses the data to make judgements on personal information such as political view, sexual orientation and even intelligence levels.

20 Practice questions

Objective Test Question 1: Benefit of an information system

Access to a larger market, targeted marketing, reduced costs and the elimination of intermediaries are just some of the benefits that could result from the implementation of:

A   knowledge management systems

B   e-commerce

C   web 2.0 tools

D   enterprise-wide systems

Objective Test Question 2: Intangible Costs of an information system

Which of the following is NOT an intangible cost of a new information system?

A   The opportunity cost of other projects foregone

B   Day to day running costs such as heating and insurance

C   Staff disruption during the implementation phase

D   The cost of dysfunctional behaviour due to resistance to change

Objective Test Question 3: TARA framework

Chen Products produces four manufactured products: Products 1, 2, 3 and 4. The company's risk committee recently met to discuss how the company might respond to a number of problems that have arisen with Product 2.

After a number of incidents in which Product 2 had failed whilst being used by customers, Chen Products had been presented with compensation claims from customers injured and inconvenienced by the product failure. It was decided that the risk committee should meet to discuss the options.

When the discussion of Product 2 began, committee chairman Anne Ricardo reminded her colleagues that, apart from the compensation claims, Product 2 was a highly profitable product.

Chen's risk management committee comprised four non-executive directors who each had different backgrounds and areas of expertise. None of them had direct experience of Chen's industry or products. It was noted that it was common for them to disagree among themselves as to how risks should be managed and that in some situations, each member proposed a quite different strategy to manage a given risk. This was the case when they discussed which risk management strategy to adopt with regard to Product 2.

Using the TARA framework, place each of the following strategies in a grey cell, against the 'TARA' element to which it is most likely to relate:

Transfer	
Avoid	
Reduce	
Accept	

Strategy 1: this would involve discontinuing the activity that is exposing the company to risk. In the case of Chen, this would involve ceasing production of Product 2. This would be pursued if the impact (hazard) and probability of incurring an acceptable level of liability were both considered to be unacceptably high and there were no options for transference or reduction.	Strategy 2: this would involve the company accepting only a portion of the risk. Although an unlikely possibility given the state of existing claims, insurance against future claims would serve to limit Chen's potential losses and place a limit on its losses. Outsourcing manufacture may be a way of transferring risk if the outsourcee can be persuaded to accept some of the product liability.
Strategy 3: This would involve seeking to retain a component of the risk (in order to enjoy the return assumed to be associated with that risk) but to reduce it and thereby limit its ability to create liability. Chen produces four products and it could reconfigure its production capacity to produce proportionately more of Products 1, 3 and 4 and proportionately less of Product 2. This would reduce Product 2 in the overall portfolio and therefore Chen's exposure to its risks. This would need to be associated with instructions to other departments (e.g. sales and marketing) to similarly reconfigure activities to sell more of the other products and less of Product 2.	Strategy 4: This would involve taking limited or no action to reduce the exposure to risk and would be taken if the returns expected from bearing the risk were expected to be greater than the potential liabilities. The case mentions that Product 2 is highly profitable and it may be that the returns attainable by maintaining and even increasing Product 2's sales are worth the liabilities incurred by compensation claims.

Objective Test Question 4: Risk appetite

Use the words and phrases in the table provided below to complete the following paragraphs:

high risk	reduction	risky
avoidance	low risk	TARA
transference	more	appetite

An organisation is likely to have a portfolio of projects, some incurring more risk than others, so that the overall risk _____ is met from that portfolio.

A _____ appetite will indicate that the organisation will normally seek a higher number of higher-risk/return activities as the organisation is willing to accept _____ risk and its risk capacity has not been reached. However, a _____ appetite indicates that a higher number of low-risk/lower-return activities will be preferred.

The way that an organisation manages risk will also affect its risk strategy. Using _____ as an example of risk management, the overall risk strategy of an organisation can be explained as follows:

- A strategy of primarily self-insurance may limit the organisation's strategy regarding undertaking _____ projects. Self-insurance implies risk minimisation as an overall strategy.

- A risk strategy of risk _____ may imply an overall strategy that incorporates a higher level of risk. However, risk will then be limited by the amount of insurance premiums. Where premiums become too high, the risk strategy determines that, overall, the organisation will seek less risky projects.

- A strategy of _____ implies that the organisation wants to limit the total amount of risk.

- Finally, a strategy of risk _____ may imply that the risk capacity of the firm is being reached and while additional risk can be accepted, the amount of risk that can be taken on is limited.

Risk capacity is also important when determining the desired method of expansion within an organisation. Where the organisation has a high risk capacity the overall risk strategy is likely to be directed to taking on higher risk projects. However, where the organisation's total risk capacity is being reached, then projects with a lower amount of risk will be expected.

Case Study Style Question: The ZXC Company

The ZXC company manufactures aircraft. The company is based in Europe and currently produces a range of four different aircraft. ZXC's aircraft are reliable with low maintenance costs, giving ZXC a good reputation, both to airlines who purchase from ZXC and to airlines' customers who fly in the aircraft.

ZXC is currently developing the 'next generation' of passenger aircraft, with the selling name of the ZXLiner. New developments in ZXLiner include the following.

- Two decks along the entire aircraft (not just part as in the Boeing 747 series) enabling faster loading and unloading of passengers from both decks at the same time. However, this will mean that airport gates must be improved to facilitate dual loading at considerable expense.

- 20% decrease in fuel requirements and falls in noise and pollution levels.

- Use of new alloys to decrease maintenance costs, increase safety and specifically the use of Zitnim (a new lightweight conducting alloy) rather than standard wiring to enable the 'fly-by-wire' features of the aircraft. Zitnim only has one supplier worldwide.

Many component suppliers are based in Europe although ZXC does obtain about 25% of the sub-contracted components from companies in the USA. ZXC also maintains a significant R&D department working on the ZXLiner and other new products such as alternative environmentally friendly fuel for aircraft.

Although the ZXLiner is yet to fly or be granted airworthiness certificates, ZXC does have orders for 25 aircraft from the HTS company. However, on current testing schedules the ZXLiner will be delivered late.

ZXC currently has about €4 billion of loans from various banks and last year made a loss of €2.3 billion. ZXC's chief executive has also just resigned taking a leaving bonus of around two years' salary.

You have received the following email from the newly appointed Acting Chief Executive:

> **From:** Jack Van Gus, Acting Chief Executive
> **To:** A.N Accountant
> **Date:** 15 June 2014
>
> **Subject:** Risks
>
> Hi A.N.
> Unlike my predecessor, I am keen to proactively manage risks in this business—please could you Identify and explain the sources of business risk that could affect ZXC? I intend to use your report as a basis for a presentation to the Board
>
> Many thanks in advance
> Jack

Case Study Style Question: ZZ

ZZ is a music streaming company specialising in classical tracks and opera. It has a growing loyal customer base, which has largely been created through word of mouth and magazine adverts and editorials.

You have received the following email from the new Chief Executive:

> **From:** Donald Picton
> **To:** A.N. Accountant
> **Date:** 25.06.2014
> **Subject:** Big Data
>
> Good morning to you!
>
> As you know, ZZ does not use social media as I believe our customer base is largely comprised of an age bracket that wouldn't be likely to engage in such channels. However, I have just discovered that recently, a Twitter account has been created by an enthusiastic customer entitled @iloveZZ. It has several thousand followers already!
>
> This is all about 'Big Data', isn't it. Can you prepare me a report about it? I would like to understand the general risks and benefits of Big Data to ZZ.
>
> With many thanks and regards,
> D

Answers to examples and objective test questions

Example 1: Risk

None of the statements are true. There is no clear established link between corporate size, structure and development and the risk accepted by an organisation.

Example 2: Risk Treatment

- An organisation sells a subsidiary in a politically unstable country. **RISK AVOIDANCE**

- The Board of a company decides that they have a low risk appetite and therefore reject a potentially profitable contract. **RISK AVOIDANCE**

- The organisers of an outdoor sporting event decide that the risk of rain is low, and take no further action regarding the probability of rain occurring. **RISK ACCEPTANCE**

Example 3: CC Freight

Likelihood	High	Higher airline flight costs	Insufficient freight to fill containers
	Low	A major airline will go out of business	Downturn in international trade
		Low	High

Impact/consequences

- **High probability, high impact risk:** the business will be affected if the average 'fill' from containers falls from its current level of 78%. Profits will be unsatisfactory if the 'fill' is less than 75%, suggesting that there could be a high risk of falling and inadequate profitability due to a failure to win enough business.

- **Low probability, high impact risk:** a downturn in international trade will affect the volume of freight, and so would reduce CC's income. Since international trade has been growing, the likelihood of a downturn would seem to be low.

- **High probability, low impact risk:** it seems inevitable that airlines will charge higher prices, but CC can pass on these costs to its own customers, therefore the impact of this risk is low.

- **Low probability, low impact risk:** the collapse of a major airline is possible due to high losses, but is perhaps unlikely. If an airline did go out of business, international freight should not be affected, because business would switch to other airlines.

Example 4: Monterey Ltd

Answer C

Veracity refers to the accuracy and truthfulness of the data. If this is missing, it can lead to inaccurate conclusions being drawn.

Objective Test Question 1: Benefit of an information system

Answer B

E-commerce refers to the conducting of business electronically via some sort of communications link and may result in access to larger markets, targeted marketing, reduced costs and elimination of intermediaries.

Objective Test Question 2: Intangible Costs of an information system

Answer B

Day to day running costs, such as heating and insurance, should be tangible costs. Answers A, C and D all describe intangible costs.

Objective Test Question 3: TARA framework

Transfer	Strategy 2
Avoid	Strategy 1
Reduce	Strategy 3
Accept	Strategy 4

Objective Test Question 4: Risk appetite

An organisation is likely to have a portfolio of projects, some incurring more risk than others, so that the overall risk **appetite** is met from that portfolio.

A **high-risk** appetite will indicate that the organisation will normally seek a higher number of higher-risk/return activities as the organisation is willing to accept **more** risk and its risk capacity has not been reached. However, a **low-risk** appetite indicates that a higher number of low risk/lower-return activities will be preferred.

The way that an organisation manages risk will also affect its risk strategy. Using **TARA** as an example of risk management, the overall risk strategy of an organisation can be explained as follows:

- A strategy of primarily self-insurance may limit the organisation's strategy regarding undertaking **risky** projects. Self-insurance implies risk minimisation as an overall strategy.

- A risk strategy of risk **transference** may imply an overall strategy that incorporates a higher level of risk. However, risk will then be limited by the amount of insurance premiums. Where premiums become too high, the risk strategy determines that, overall, the organisation will seek less risky projects.

- A strategy of **avoidance** implies that the organisation wants to limit the total amount of risk.

- Finally, a strategy of risk **reduction** may imply that the risk capacity of the firm is being reached and while additional risk can be accepted, the amount of risk that can be taken on is limited.

Risk capacity is also important when determining the desired method of expansion within an organisation. Where the organisation has a high risk capacity the overall risk strategy is likely to be directed to taking on higher risk projects. However, where the organisation's total risk capacity is being reached, then projects with a lower amount of risk will be expected.

Case Study Style Question: The ZXC Company

EMAIL

To: Jack Van Gus

From: AN Accountant

Subject: ZXC – Sources of business risk

Date: 19 June

Hi Jack,

In response to your email, please find below some notes about the potential sources of business risks that may affect our business in the coming months.

Product/market risk

This is the risk that customers will not buy our new products (or services), or that the sales demand for current products and services will decline unexpectedly. For ZXC, there is the risk that demand for the new aircraft will be less than expected, either due to customers purchasing the rival airplane or because airports will not be adapted to take the new ZXLiner.

Commodity price risk

Businesses might be exposed to risks from unexpected increases (or falls) in the price of a key commodity.

Part of the control systems of the ZXLiner rely on the availability of the new lightweight conducting alloy Zitnim. As there is only one supplier of this alloy, then there is the danger of the monopolist increasing the price or even denying supply. Increase in price would increase the overall cost of the (already expensive) ZXLiner, while denial of supply would further delay delivery of the aircraft. ZXC needs to maintain good relations with their key suppliers to mitigate this risk.

Product reputation risk

Some companies rely heavily on brand image and product reputation, and an adverse event could put its reputation (and so future sales) at risk. While the reputation of ZXC appears good at present, reputation will suffer if the ZXLiner is delayed significantly or it does not perform well in test flights (which have still to be arranged). Airline customers, and also their customers (travellers) are unlikely to feel comfortable flying in an aircraft that is inherently unstable. ZXC must continue to invest in R&D and good quality control systems to mitigate the effects of this risk.

Credit risk

Credit risk is the possibility of losses due to non-payment by debtors or the company not being able to pay its creditors, which will adversely affect the company's credit rating.

Given that the ZXLiner has not been sold at present, there are no debtors. However, ZXC is heavily dependent on bank finance – any denial of funds will adversely affect ZXC's ability to continue to trade. Credit risk is therefore significant at present.

Currency risk

Currency risk, or foreign exchange risk, arises from the possibility of movements in foreign exchange rates, and the value of one currency in relation to another. ZXC is currently based in Europe although it obtains a significant number of parts from the USA. If the €/$ exchange rate became worse, then the cost of imported goods for ZXC (and all other companies) would increase. At present, the relatively weak US$ is in ZXC's favour and so this risk is currently negligible.

Interest rate risk

Interest rate risk is the risk of unexpected gains or losses arising as a consequence of a rise or fall in interest rates. Exposures to interest rate risk arise from borrowing and investing. As ZXC do have significant bank loans, then the company is very exposed to this risk. As interest rates are expected to rise in the future then ZXC would be advised to consider methods of hedging against this risk.

Gearing risk

Gearing risk for non-bank companies is the risk arising from exposures to high financial gearing and large amounts of borrowing. Again, ZXC has significant amounts of bank loans. This increases the amount of interest that must be repaid each year. In the short term ZXC cannot affect this risk as the bank loans are a necessary part of its operations.

Legal risk or litigation risk

The risk arises from the possibility of legal action being taken against an organisation. At present this risk does not appear to be a threat for ZXC. However, if the ZXLiner is delayed any further there is a risk for breach of contract for late delivery to the HTS company. There is little ZXC can do to guard against this risk, apart from keep HTS appraised of the delays involved with the ZXLiner.

Regulatory risk

This is the possibility that regulations will affect the way an organisation has to operate. In terms of aircraft, regulation generally affects noise and pollution levels. As the ZXLiner is designed to have lower noise and pollution levels than existing aircraft then this risk does not appear to be a threat to ZXC.

Technology risk

Technology risk arises from the possibility that technological change will occur or that new technology will not work. Given that ZXC is effectively producing a new product (the ZXLiner) that has not actually been tested yet, there is some technology risk. At worse, the ZXLiner may not fly at all or not obtain the necessary flying certificates. ZXC appear to be guarding against this risk by not decreasing its investment in product development.

Economic risk

This risk refers to the risks facing organisations from changes in economic conditions, such as economic growth or recession, government spending policy and taxation policy, unemployment levels and international trading conditions.

Demand for air travel is forecast to increase for the foreseeable future, so in that sense there is a demand for aircraft which ZXC will benefit from. The risk of product failure is more significant than economic risk.

Environmental risk

This risk arises from changes to the environment over which an organisation has no direct control, such as global warming, to those for which the organisation might be responsible, such as oil spillages and other pollution.

ZXC is subject to this risk – and there is significant debate concerning the impact of air travel on global warming. At the extreme, there is a threat that air travel could be banned, or made very expensive by international taxation agreements, although this appears unlikely at present. ZXC need to continue to monitor this risk, and continue research into alternative fuels etc. in an attempt to mitigate the risk.

With regards

AN Accountant

Case Study Style Question: ZZ

EMAIL

To: D. Picton

From: AN Accountant

Date: 19 June 2014

Subject: Big Data

Good Morning Donald,

In response to your email, please find some notes about Big Data.

Big Data management involves using sophisticated systems to gather, store and analyse large volumes of data in a variety of structured and unstructured formats. Companies are collecting increasing volumes of data through everyday transactions and marketing activity. If managed effectively, this can lead to many business benefits, although there are risks involved.

Benefits

As ZZ is a web-based business it is likely that all of its sales transactions take place over the internet. This is likely to result in a greater volume of data being collected for each transaction, which ZZ can use to better understand its customer preferences and buying patterns. This can help to ensure that the right type of track is available to customers and can also drive more targeted and effective marketing campaigns.

One ever-growing source of largely unstructured data is the wide range of social media channels now available. ZZ have chosen not to develop social media networks in the belief that customers will not want to engage in this way. The @iloveZZ Twitter feed, along with its followers, suggests that this may no longer be the case and so ZZ have an opportunity to gather data from this source in order to obtain a greater insight into customer interests.

As ZZ has a loyal customer base, they can also harness the data collected through transactions and social media networks to maximise this loyalty. Certain customers may be defined as key advocates of the company's product and this can be used effectively in marketing campaigns to show the positive customer feedback ZZ receives.

Risks

ZZ is currently not using social media and therefore not collecting data in this way. There is a risk that the company falls behind its competitors who may well be harnessing the powerful data available from this source. Although ZZ currently has a loyal customer base, these customers may be tempted to switch to other streaming services if they are engaged through Twitter and Facebook based marketing.

Even if ZZ decides that they should develop a social media strategy there is a danger that significant volumes of data are collected and stored but not used properly. Not only will this be a waste of potentially useful information, but it will also cost money and use up storage space on the company's systems.

Index